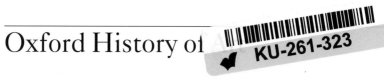
After Modern Art 1945–2017

SECOND EDITION

David Hopkins

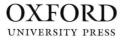

OXFORD
UNIVERSITY PRESS

OXFORD
UNIVERSITY PRESS

Great Clarendon Street, Oxford, OX2 6DP,
United Kingdom

Oxford University Press is a department of the University of Oxford.
It furthers the University's objective of excellence in research, scholarship,
and education by publishing worldwide. Oxford is a registered trade mark of
Oxford University Press in the UK and in certain other countries

First published 2000 by Oxford University Press
Second edition published 2018

Published in the United States of America by Oxford University Press
198 Madison Avenue, New York, NY 10016, United States of America

British Library Cataloguing in Publication Data
Data available

Library of Congress Control Number: 2018932147

ISBN 978–0–19–921845–5

Printed in Great Britain by
Bell & Bain Ltd., Glasgow

Contents

	Introduction	I
Chapter 1	**The Politics of Modernism** Abstract Expressionism and the European *Informel*	5
Chapter 2	**Duchamp's Legacy** The Rauschenberg–Johns Axis	35
Chapter 3	**The Artist in Crisis** From Bacon to Beuys	63
Chapter 4	**Blurring Boundaries** Pop Art, Fluxus, and their Effects	89
Chapter 5	**Modernism in Retreat** Minimalist Aesthetics and Beyond	121
Chapter 6	**The Death of the Object** The Move to Conceptualism	149
Chapter 7	**Postmodernism** Theory and Practice in the 1980s	183
Chapter 8	**The 1990s** A New *Fin de Siècle*?	217
Chapter 9	**Art and the New Millennium**	241

Notes   275

Further Reading   285

Timeline   296

Galleries/Museums   309

Picture Credits   311

Index   319

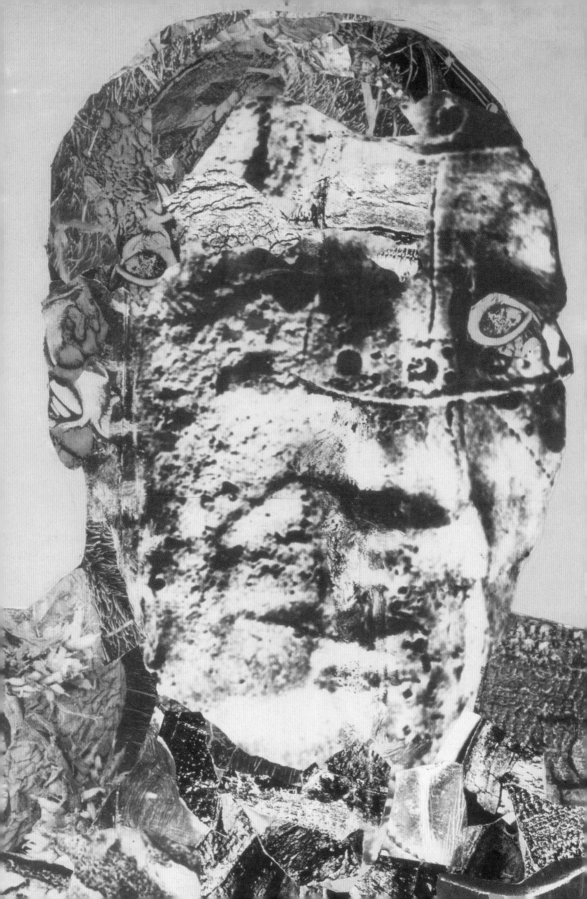

Introduction

On 9 August 1945 an atom bomb fell on Nagasaki in Japan, bringing the Second World War to a close. During the six years of the conflict an incalculable number of people had lost their lives. Soon the West would become aware of the horrors of the Holocaust visited on Germany's Jewish population. Stalin's atrocities in Russia would also become apparent. Before long a new ideological Cold War between Eastern Europe and America would structure international relations in the West. These are the stark realities from which this history of post-war Western art stems. The German marxist Theodor Adorno once asserted that it would be barbaric to write lyric poetry after Auschwitz.[1] How, he implied, could art measure up to the immensities of technological warfare and the extermination of whole populations? Art in the age of the mass media would, in his view, have to take on a resistant character if it were not to become ineffectual and compromised. Much of this book examines the continuation of an 'avant-garde' artistic project after 1945, although not necessarily in Adorno's terms. The art it discusses is therefore frequently challenging, provocative, and 'difficult'. One of my main aims has been to retain a sense of its inner dynamic by emphasizing the critical and theoretical debates that nourished it, informed its contexts, and continue to make it meaningful.

This book's framework is broadly chronological, with much of the established artistic canon in place, although a number of non-standard names and lesser-known works have been included. One of the aspirations of recent art history has been the abandonment of an artist-led conception of the subject in favour of examining how representations of various kinds are culturally produced. Whilst this book deals extensively with issues of cultural politics, gender identity, and the institutional support structures for art (the market, critics, education, and galleries), I have felt it necessary to preserve a strong sense of the historical agency of individual artists. In many ways this is appropriate to the period. Despite an ideologically motivated call for the 'death of the author', the fact remains that in real terms the prestige of individual artists has continued to be paramount. An archaeology of art's societal position is also more difficult to achieve for an era that is so close to us. The most pressing task still seems to be one of structuring the period as a historical entity, and making it coherent. As yet, few books have attempted to encompass the whole period from 1945 to the early 2000s. Those that have done so have often ended up looking self-defeatingly encyclopaedic or self-protectively partisan.

Detail of 48

1

The latter point notwithstanding, I should acknowledge that my interpretation has its biases. Although I have attempted to balance a range of contrasting opinions, this book would lack urgency if it lacked a viewpoint. Broadly speaking, I argue that the Duchampian attack on traditional aesthetic categories has been the engine behind the distinctive shifts in post-war art. As a consequence, photography, performance, conceptual proposals, installation art, film, video, and appropriations from mass culture play an equal part in this book alongside painting and sculpture. I have also avoided an overly narrow schematization of the period in terms of art movements. Whilst subsections deal with the various artistic formations, my chapters are largely thematic in orientation. They deal with Modernism and cultural politics, the establishment of the Duchampian model, the artist's persona, art and commodity culture, aesthetic debates, the questioning of the art object, the shift to a postmodern cultural situation, and the effects wrought by processes of globalization. These themes are related to the gradual demise of Modernism, which in turn involves an ongoing examination of the dynamic interplay between European and American art. In the past, general histories of the period tended to be heavily slanted towards America. It would be a distortion to deny American art's central importance, but I have tried throughout the book to deal with how this was negotiated and often opposed in Europe. The last chapter, on recent art, contains comparatively little emphasis on the USA.

The book's historical trajectory largely follows from the above. The narrative begins with the immediate post-war situation, dwells on the period up to the end of the Cold War in 1989, and ends with two chapters about the art of the 1990s and early 2000s up to 2017. Writing a book of this scope imposes an enormous commitment of time and energy. Various people have helped along the way. I am particularly grateful to Kate Tregaskis for reading early drafts and to my former colleague Simon Dell, who commented on the first version of the manuscript. My colleague at Glasgow University, Dominic Paterson, was very helpful in discussing the ideas for the final chapter in this revised version of the book. A note of thanks also goes to Leila Riszko, Cassils, and Merlin James. Last, but far from least, my wife Claudia provided much-needed support and assistance. Beyond this, my many intellectual debts are acknowledged in the text itself.

Katharine Reeve's comments on the original text were deeply appreciated, whilst Simon Mason, my commissioning editor, was wonderfully enthusiastic. This expanded edition is largely due to the urgings of Matthew Cotton and Luciana O'Flaherty. Rosanna van den Bogaerde's efforts in obtaining illustrations are also gratefully acknowledged, as is Neil Morris's editorial help with the new manuscript. This book largely derives from my teaching over a thirty-year period. My students at Edinburgh College of Art and at the Universities of Edinburgh and St Andrews often shared unknowingly in formulating the arguments of its early chapters. Since 2006 my students on the MLitt degree course in *Art; Politics; Transgression: Twentieth Century Avant-Gardes* at the University of Glasgow have been respondents to my thoughts on its final chapters. My sincere thanks to them.

David Hopkins

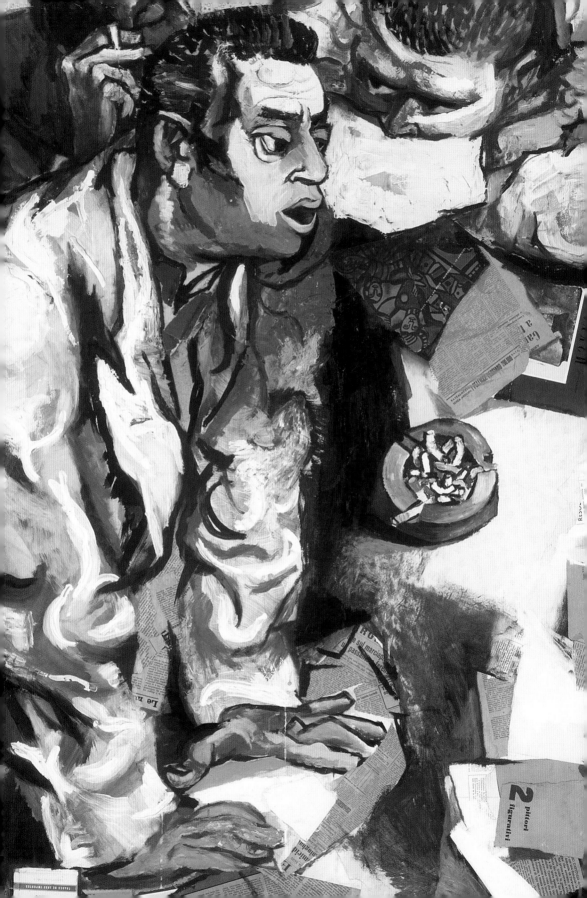

The Politics of Modernism

Abstract Expressionism and the European *Informel*

1

Look closely at the image on page 6 of this book [1]. It appears to be an icon of post-war experimental art—an early 1950s abstraction by the American painter Jackson Pollock. However, read the caption and it is revealed to be a pastiche by Art & Language, a group of post-1960s Conceptual artists. In many ways it encapsulates the politics underpinning the subject of this chapter, the rise of Modernism after the Second World War. But how exactly?

Give the image a couple of seconds, and something reveals itself among the abstract brushstrokes: Lenin's leftward-inclined profile, with familiar pointed beard. This peculiar marriage of styles is clearly bound up with two divergent artistic principles; realism and abstraction. In the immediate post-war years these were the dominant aesthetic orientations linked to the cultural climates of the world's most powerful political rivals. Communist Russia favoured legible Socialist Realism for a collective audience, whilst capitalist America and Western Europe in general attached considerable cultural kudos to the notion of a difficult or avant-garde art. Like Art & Language's hidden image of Lenin, the art of post-war Russia and Eastern Europe is 'invisible' in the pages that follow. But the aesthetic and ideological alternatives it represented continued to be strangely active, usually at a submerged level. The direction of American and European art in the early Cold War years was haunted by discarded options.

Lost politics: Abstract Expressionism

A logical place to start is in America just before the Second World War. The spectacle of the 1930s Depression had encouraged many young artists to adopt left-wing principles. Established as part of President Roosevelt's New Deal, the Federal Art Project provided work for large numbers of them, actively encouraging the production of public murals in styles related to Soviet Socialist Realism. Certain areas of the Project also allowed artists room to experiment. Several painters who were to emerge as important avant-garde figures after the war, such as Jackson Pollock, Mark Rothko, and Arshile Gorky, benefited from the liberal atmosphere of the Project's New York-based 'easel section'.

Pollock and Rothko had strong Marxist sympathies (hence the aptness of [1] as a reminder of Pollock's residual concerns). They supported the

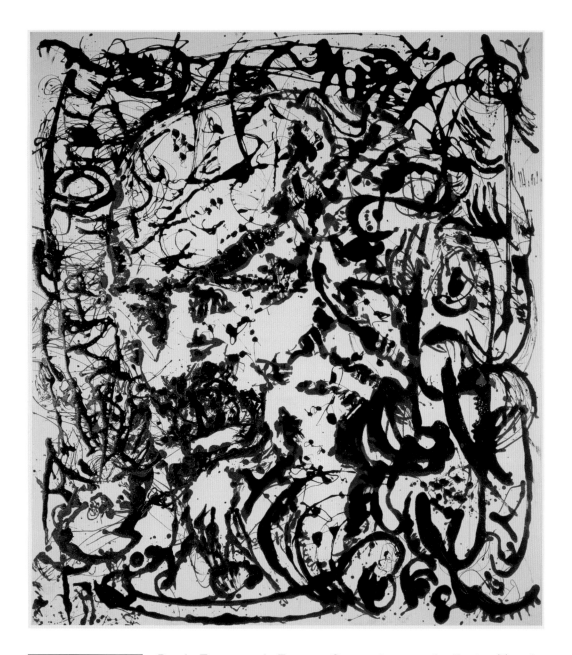

1 Art & Language

Portrait of V. I. Lenin by V. Charangovich (1970) in the Style of Jackson Pollock II,1980

Popular Front set up by European Communists to combat Fascism. They also sympathized with the way that pre-war European avant-garde formations such as French Surrealism or Dutch *de Stijl* had combined commitments to artistic innovation with radical social or political visions. All in all, the outlooks of Pollock and Rothko were internationalist. In this they departed from the isolationist ideology of the Federal Art Project. For all its tolerance, the Project's basic concern was to promote socially accessible American vernacular imagery. For Pollock and Rothko such concerns were far too narrow.

From the mid-1930s both artists belonged to the Artists' Union, an organization dedicated to improving the conditions of working artists. It is significant, however, that Rothko, along with other artists and intellectuals, severely modified his political activities in the late 1930s when the American Artists' Congress, a body allied with the Popular Front, supported a series of controversial Soviet manoeuvres including Stalin's show trials, the Ribbentrop Pact of 1939, and the invasion of Finland. This dispute heralded an increasing disillusionment with political engagement on the part of many avant-garde artists in New York. In 1938 the French surrealist leader André Breton had joined the Mexican muralist Diego Rivera and the exiled communist Leon Trotsky to compose an important manifesto entitled *Towards a Free Revolutionary Art*, which asserted that artistic and socialist radicalism should go hand in hand.[1] The New Yorkers welcomed its refutation of Soviet aesthetic dogma but they gradually became wary of its affirmation of (socialist) revolutionary politics.

A contributing factor to their political pessimism was America's entry into the Second World War in 1942. The irrational basis for mankind's actions seemed to them irrefutable. In this atmosphere the arrival in the United States of various émigrés associated with pre-war Surrealism (including André Breton, Max Ernst, and André Masson between 1939 and 1941) was remarkably well timed. It had seemed previously that two main aesthetic options were on offer: on the one hand realist modes, which although signalling social purpose seemed pictorially limited; and on the other post-cubist European abstraction, which could look emotionally arid. The New Yorkers now found that Surrealism's commitment to the unconscious and myth allowed them to instil loaded content into their increasingly abstract pictures without directly addressing politics. In a famous letter to *The New York Times* in 1943 the painters Rothko and Adolph Gottlieb defended their recent work against critical incomprehension by asserting the profundity of its content: 'There is no such thing as good painting about nothing. We assert that only that subject matter is valid which is tragic and timeless.'[2]

Such concerns united an expanding group of artists, including figures such as Pollock, Rothko, Arshile Gorky, Willem de Kooning, Barnett Newman, Robert Motherwell, Clyfford Still, and Adolph Gottlieb. Although they were soon to be labelled 'Abstract Expressionists' (a term coined in 1946 by Robert Coates in an exhibition review), they never organized themselves into a coherent avant-garde formation. They were, however, unified to some extent by the patronage of Peggy Guggenheim. This wealthy heiress was beginning to shift the emphasis away from Surrealism at her newly established Art of This Century Gallery, and she gave several Abstract Expressionists early exhibitions, notably Pollock. Critics such as James Johnson Sweeney and, most significantly, Clement Greenberg started to support the new tendencies from 1943, whilst exhibitions such as Howard Putzel's *A Problem for Critics* (1945) overtly fished for ways of characterizing the new aesthetic momentum. Personal friendships aside, the artists themselves prized their individuality. Attempts at group definition tended to be short-lived. These included the formation of the Subjects of the Artist school in 1948–9 and the Studio 35 discussions held in 1950.

What was distinctive about the work produced by this loosely defined group? Jackson Pollock's *The Guardians of the Secret* [2] demonstrates how stylistic borrowings from cubist-derived abstraction, Expressionism, and

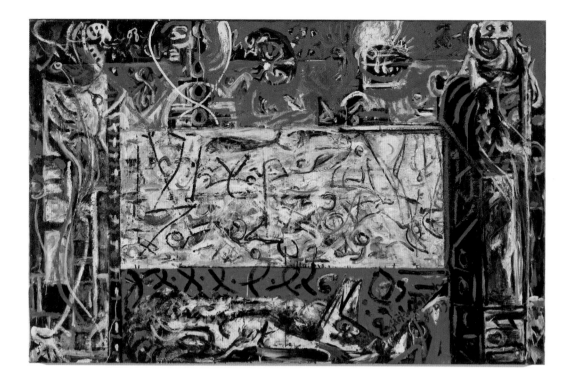

2 Jackson Pollock

The Guardians of the Secret, 1943

Pollock's art was far from simply 'therapeutic', but this painting deals powerfully with the way in which the entry into psychic space requires mythic/symbolic mediators. Pollock was interested in Jungian psychoanalysis, and the fact that interpreters have seen an allusion to the 'Egyptian Book of the Dead' here, with the dog at the bottom actually representing Anubis—the jackal-headed guardian of the Egyptian underworld— further suggests a descent into nether regions.

Surrealism tended to be fused with a growing interest in myth and primitivism (although key figures such as Robert Motherwell and Willem de Kooning were less taken with the latter). The loose, frenetic handling of paints conveys expressive urgency, particularly in the central section where a form reminiscent of a scroll or tablet bearing calligraphy is pointedly untranslatable. Presumably this represents the 'secret' of the title. The figures at left and right—which amalgamate influences from Picasso (a key exemplar for Pollock) and American Indian totems—are possibly archaic guardian sentinels. The picture has been interpreted as an analogue for the perils of Pollock's practice. His troubled personal background, which led to alcoholism and the decision to enter Jungian analysis at the end of the 1930s, predisposed him to see surrealist procedures such as automatism (a kind of elevated doodling deriving from unconscious impulses) as a means towards self-realization.

This picture also foreshadows later developments in Pollock's work. Put rather crudely, the calligraphic 'secret' eventually swamped the entire surfaces of Pollock's massive 'drip paintings' of 1947–51 [**3**]. These uncompromisingly abstract works were produced in a dramatically different fashion from his earlier paintings. Using sticks rather than brushes, Pollock rhythmically hurled and spattered industrial paints onto huge expanses of unstretched canvas placed on his studio floor. In formal terms, a daring step beyond Cubism and pre-war abstraction was achieved. A continuous visual 'field' was created which was accented by the fluid syntax, and associated punctuational concentrations of line and colour, rather than distinct compositional foci.

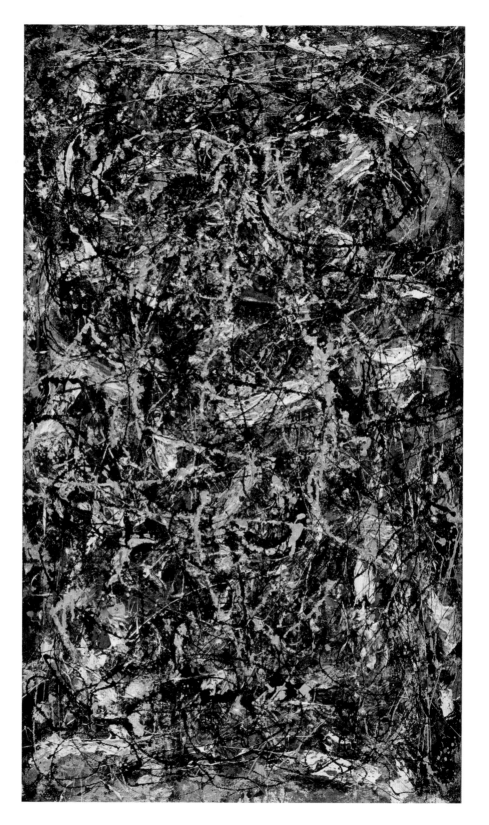

3 Jackson Pollock

Full Fathom Five, 1947

This comparatively small canvas was one of the first in which Pollock used his 'drip painting' technique. Given that the canvas was placed horizontally, the title, an allusion to Shakespeare's *The Tempest* ('Full fathom five thy father lies...'), conveys a sense of the image containing hidden depths, as does the incorporation of enigmatic foreign bodies (keys etc.) among the skeins of paint.

At the same time, Pollock's manner of working suggested a radical rethinking of picture-making's orientation from a vertical register (the wall or easel) to the horizontal. The figurative mediators from earlier works were submerged in an automatist tracery directly indexed to Pollock's bodily actions and impulses. In certain instances, such as the enormous *One (Number 31)* of 1950, it seemed as though Pollock had completely dispensed with elements of figuration. However, photographs of him at work on another significant work of that year, *Autumn Rhythm*, suggest that initial indications of animals or figures were later assimilated into broader visual patterns. The fact that Pollock, as he told his wife, the painter Lee Krasner, chose to 'veil' what may have been uncomfortably personal (and formally expendable) imagery returns us at this point to Art & Language's ironic opening image. Psychological remnants notwithstanding, this reminds us of a lost political dimension to Pollock's practice.

Cold War aesthetics

Politics returns more obliquely here in relation to the wider cultural ambience of late 1940s America. The art historian Michael Leja has shown that, as much as Abstract Expressionists like Pollock and Rothko dabbled in psychoanalysis and classical myth (and it should be noted that Pollock apparently read little), they were also directly affected by the topical theme of 'Modern Man'. Whether embodied in magazine articles, films, or socio-philosophical treatises (by the likes of Lewis Mumford and Archibald MacLeish), this line of thought held man to be fundamentally irrational, driven by unknowable forces from within and without. Hence the typical film noir plot in which the haunted hero-figure becomes enmeshed in crime or violence for reasons beyond his control.[3] It is not difficult to imagine Pollock mythologizing himself in such terms, but the larger point is that, however much Abstract Expressionist bohemianism, which involved infamous brawls at New York's Cedar Tavern, continued a venerable anti-bourgeois tradition, it was inevitably part and parcel of this wider discourse. And in certain ways this was the ideology of a newly emerging class of business liberals.

Basically, the interests of this emergent class were expansionist in global terms, in opposition to the isolationist policies of the older conservative political establishment. Thus Modern Man discourse, as articulated by the liberal ideologue Arthur Schlesinger in his influential *The Vital Center* (1949), paradoxically saw alienation and insecurity as the necessary accompaniments of the West's freedoms: 'Against totalitarian certitude, free society can only offer modern man devoured by alienation and fallibility.'[4] Psychoanalysis, which was as popular with the new liberal intelligentsia as with artists like Pollock, thus served to explain man's alienation in a frightening but free world and to expose the irrational basis of extreme political options such as Fascism and Communism. Critics occasionally hinted at parallels between Pollock's psychic outpourings and the forces unleashed at Hiroshima and Nagasaki. There is a sense, then, in which Pollock ironically spoke to bourgeois needs, positing irrationality not only as man's lot but also as something controllable, just as America's governing elite saw the advances of psychoanalysis and nuclear technology as means of harnessing anarchic forces. His ability to express such contradictory concerns possibly helps explain his appeal to a liberal middle-class audience.[5] By 1948 his apparently unassimilable images had acquired appreciable market success, signalling Abstract Expressionism's cultural breakthrough.[6] However, the role played by Clement Greenberg's criticism of his work, to be discussed later in this chapter, should not be underestimated.

The upshot of the above, in the words of the art historian T. J. Clark, is that 'capitalism at a certain stage... *needs* a more convincing account of the bodily, the sensual, the "free"... in order to extend its colonization of every-day life'.[7] In terms of economics, Serge Guilbaut has noted that such a process of colonization was originally extended to American art via the needs of a wealthy art-buying class starved of imports from France's prestigious art market during the war.[8] By the early 1950s this social sector, which incorporated the liberal intellectuals described above, was backing President Truman's increasingly imperialist foreign policy and his stepping-up of a Cold War against Communism (as initially symbolized by America's intervention in the Greek crisis of 1947).

Despite the best efforts of conservative anti-modernists such as the Senator for Michigan, George Dondero, the 'freedom' which liberals read into the paintings of Pollock and his contemporaries came to signify America's democratic values as opposed to the conformism of official communist culture. Just as the Marshall Plan (initiated in 1947) sought to extend America's influence in Europe through much-needed economic aid, so America's new radical avant-garde art was eventually exported in the late 1950s under the auspices of New York's Museum of Modern Art (MoMA). American art now appeared to epitomize Western cultural values. However, this had been implied as early as 1948 by the critic Clement Greenberg. Bordering on chauvinism, he asserted: 'The main premises of Western painting have at last migrated to the United States, along with the center of gravity of industrial production and political power.'[9]

Art historians such as Guilbaut have argued that in the later 1950s the American government's promotion of Abstract Expressionism abroad amounted to cultural imperialism. As stated, New York's MoMA organized the touring exhibitions in question. Founded in 1929 as the first museum solely dedicated to modern art in the West, MoMA was well placed to position the American painting of the 1940s as the crowning culmination of a history of modern art from Impressionism onwards. Under its International Program (organized by Porter McCray), exhibitions underwritten by this logic regularly toured Europe in the late 1950s, most notably *The New American Painting* of 1958–9, curated by Alfred J. Barr and seen in eight countries. Something of America's success in imposing its artistic authority on Europe can be gauged from the fact that when, in 1959, the Abstract Expressionists were shown en masse at the second *Documenta* exhibition in Kassel (America's contribution representing about one-sixth of the total works on display), McCray was allowed to choose works himself since the German selectors felt unequal to the task.

At this point Art & Language's opening image [1] can clearly be seen as a demonstration, in line with the thought of historians such as Guilbaut and Leja, that Abstract Expressionism was unwittingly infused with the politics of the Cold War. It is important, however, to stress that this is a selective and inevitably partial interpretation of history. Its value lies in accounting for the extent to which US-based Modernism quickly commanded authority in the West. In fact the impetus behind official American backing for Abstract Expressionism and its offshoots came as much from local European antagonisms as from the imagined evils of Russian Communism.

Art and social function

In France and Italy after the war, the emergence of strong communist parties (initially invited to join coalition governments due to their roles in wartime resistance to Fascism) led to debates among artists concerning the competing claims of a socially oriented realism and those of self-expressive experimentalism. Ironically, these arguments revive the aesthetic choices open to American artists at the end of the 1930s.

Post-war Italy was politically volatile, with frequent changes of government. The eventual triumph of the Christian Democrats was resented by increasingly marginalized socialist and communist groups, and artistic positions reflected passionate political convictions. Realist critics, working in the wake of an important movement in film exemplified by Roberto Rossellini's Resistance story, *Rome, Open City* of 1945, regularly clashed with abstractionists. There were lively exchanges between groups linked to the PCI (Partito Communista Italiano) such as the Fronte Nuovo delle Arti (founded in 1946) and pro-abstraction groups such as Forma (launched in 1947). The painter Renato Guttuso was attached to the former group until 1948 when it dissolved due to particularly inflexible policies on Realism on the part of the PCI. As an artist he combined elements of Picasso's post-cubist vocabulary with stylistic and iconographic allusions to Italy's pictorial traditions in large-scale 'history paintings' addressed to matters of public concern. In 1942 his attempt at a modern religious painting, *Crucifixion,* provoked the indignation of catholics due to the inclusion of a naked Magdalene. His commitment to a practice of painting embodying public or moral discourse is perhaps most directly expressed in the later work *The Discussion* of 1959–60 [4].

In France, communist-affiliated Realists proved stubborn opponents of America's cultural and political aspirations for Europe. The country which had held unquestioned art-world dominance before 1939 was now severely demoralized after years of occupation. Rather than prestigious artistic formations there now existed a complex cluster of factions. Among these, Socialist Realists attached to the PCF (French Communist Party) were again engaged in heated debates with abstractionists. After the expulsion of communists from the government in 1947, they adopted an extreme opposition to American influence in France (millions of dollars were being poured into the country as part of the Marshall Plan, with the hidden agenda of securing a stable, centrist position between the communists and the right-wing Gaullists).[10] This was accompanied by hard-line support for an art addressed to themes reflecting the workers' historical heritage in accordance with the policies of the Soviet cultural ideologue Andrei Zhdanov. Artists such as Boris Taslitzsky and André Fougeron produced large paintings on themes such as Resistance heroism or industrial unrest.

4 Renato Guttuso

The Discussion, 1959–60

According to the artist this painting depicted an 'ideological discussion'. As such it evokes the stormy realist–abstraction debates, and related political differences, among artists in Italy after the Second World War. Stylistically, the work skilfully weds the rhythms of Italian baroque art to the pre-war modernist idioms of Picasso and Cubism.

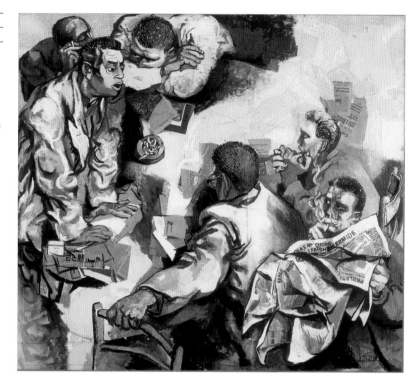

France had a strong tradition of large-scale paintings of public import. The examples of the nineteenth-century painters David, Géricault, and Courbet were particularly vivid, and young French artists now looked to the example of senior figures such as Fernand Léger and Pablo Picasso, both of whom were attached to the PCF. In 1951 Picasso was to produce the *Massacre in Korea*, which implicitly criticized American intervention in the Korean conflict. However, Picasso's eclectic use of modernist idioms conflicted with the uncompromising realism of painters such as Fougeron. Even Fougeron was criticized by the ex-surrealist, communist critic Louis Aragon for straying onto Trotskyist aesthetic territory with the anti-realist dislocations of scale of his *Civilisation Atlantique* of 1953 [**5**]. (As already noted, Trotsky and Breton had argued that art should be revolutionary in its form as well as its politics.) The imagery in *Civilisation Atlantique* amounted to a denunciation of the stepping-up of American Cold War policy in the early 1950s. Conceived very much as a 'history painting' addressing a broad public, it juxtaposed photographically derived images in a wilfully illustrational and populist manner. This was the antithesis of Abstract Expressionism, the embodiment of America's aesthetic latitude.

However, although Abstract Expressionist individualism was promoted by the American establishment to counter the collectivist ideals of Socialist Realism, the works by the Abstract Expressionists themselves were actually predicated on the notion of public address. As well as recalling his Federal Art Project background, Pollock's experiments in pictorial scale partly derived from his enthusiasm for murals by socially committed Mexican painters of the 1930s and 1940s such as José Clemente Orozco, David

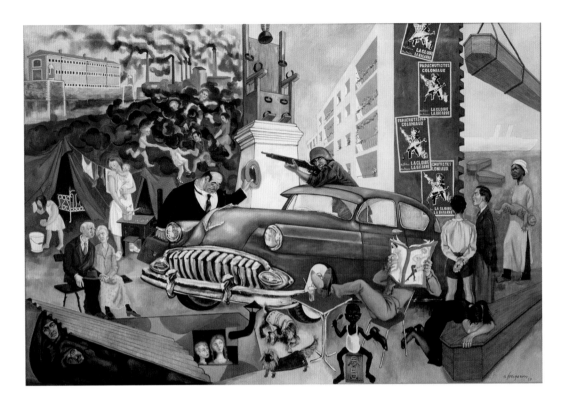

5 André Fougeron

Civilisation Atlantique,
1953

This enormous, collage-like
painting is crammed with
anti-American allusions.
An electric chair sits on
the plinth at the top centre
(the Rosenbergs were
electrocuted as Russian
spies in 1953). A GI
nonchalantly reads a
pornographic magazine.
The car behind him is
surrounded by images
redolent of capitalist
decadence and imperialist
aggression.

Siqueiros, and Diego Rivera. In this sense his paintings carried residues of a
public function. Barnett Newman, who alongside Rothko represented a
tendency in Abstract Expressionism away from Pollock's linear gesturalism
in favour of expanses of colour, exemplifies the contradictions involved here.
His *Vir Heroicus Sublimis* of 1950–1 [6] presents the complete antithesis to
Fougeron's *Civilisation Atlantique* in visual terms. Abandoning what he
once described as the 'props and crutches' of conventional figurative subject
matter, Newman presents an uncompromising 15-foot- (4.6-metre-) wide
field of solid red broken only by 'zips' of colour. In its resolute elimination of
traditional composition this has direct affinities with Pollock's drip paintings of the previous years [3]. But Newman's work, like Fougeron's, implicitly
assumes it has a public to address, if only by virtue of its scale. The question is,
who constitutes this public? Recalling the early political sympathies of the
Abstract Expressionists, Newman stated grandly in the late 1940s that,
read properly, his works would signify 'the end of all state capitalism and
totalitarianism'.[11] Ironically, of course, those able to buy and interpret them
tended to be upholders of state power.

Shrewdly noting the Abstract Expressionists' moves away from what he
termed the 'cabinet picture', the critic Clement Greenberg wrote: 'While
the painter's relation to his art has become more private . . . the architectural
and presumably social location for which he destines his produce has
become, in inverse ratio, more public. This is the paradox, the contradiction,
in the master-current of painting.'[12] Greenberg was correct in pinpointing
the paradox. But whereas he was to number scale amongst the purely formal
innovations of the new 'master-current' and eventually to denigrate the 'private'

6 Barnett Newman

Vir Heroicus Sublimis,
1950–1

The assertive flatness of the implacable field of red is emphasized by the linear vertical 'zips'. Rather than functioning as drawing within space, these reinforce and delimit the space as a whole. White zips in Newman's works also evoke primal beginnings: the separation of light from darkness, the uprightness of man in the void.

concerns of the artists, he appears to have lost track of the politics latent in their practice. So, to a degree, did the Abstract Expressionists. Or rather, political engagement for them gave way to a sense of awe in the face of historical forces. Whilst artists such as Newman and Robert Motherwell developed anarchist sympathies and saw their works as implicitly negating the values of American culture, the public statements of Rothko and Newman in the late 1940s were full of invocations of tragedy and sublimity. 'We are re-asserting man's natural desire for the exalted...instead of making *cathedrals* out of Christ, man, or "life", we are making them out of ourselves, out of our feelings', wrote Newman.[13] Leaving aside the complex dialogue between aesthetic integrity and political commitment outlined above, this concern with metaphysics suggests a new line of comparison with the French painting of the period.

The bodily and the transcendent: France and America

After the war France was obsessed with *épuration* (purging or cleansing). This desire to expunge memories of the Nazi occupation of the country manifested itself in the ruthless hounding out of Nazi collaborators. This climate also bred existential philosophies emphasizing moral probity and the dilemma of personal freedom, as developed by the likes of Jean-Paul Sartre and Maurice Merleau-Ponty. Its artistic spin-off was a trend established in a series of exhibitions at René Drouin's gallery from 1943 onwards. (Drouin had originally set up in partnership with the Italian-born Leo Castelli, but the latter left for America in 1941 and would later open a New York gallery, as will be seen.)

The painter Jean Fautrier's *Otages* ('Hostages') exhibition at Drouin's in October 1945 was one of the first signs of this new artistic direction. Fautrier had been held briefly by the Gestapo in 1943 on suspicion of Resistance activities, and, while in hiding at a sanatorium at Châtenay-Malabry on the outskirts of Paris, had produced a series of heads and torsos morbidly inspired by sounds from the surrounding woods where the occupying forces regularly tortured and executed prisoners [7]. The disturbing pulverization

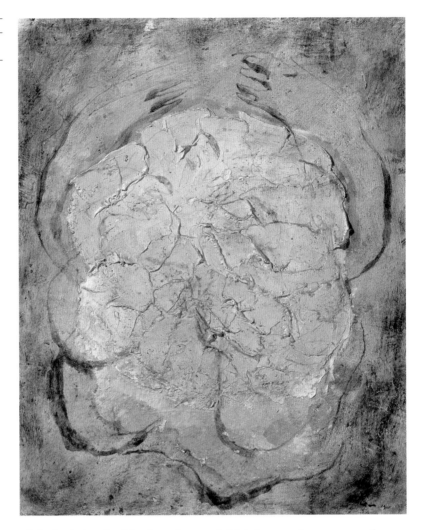

7 Jean Fautrier

La Toute Jeune Fille (Very Young Girl), 1942

Such barely recognizable human images were the outcome of a dialogue with materials. Layers of thick paste were applied to an absorbent sheet of rag paper laid on a canvas, with a layer of coloured paste and varnish finally added to the confection.

of the body involved in these images (which in some instances produces a perversely erotic effect due to the powdery surfaces) marks a move towards the *informel*—an aesthetic of brute materiality and formlessness. This was to be consecrated in critical terms by the writer Michel Tapié, in relation to artists such as the German-born Wols (short for Alfred Otto Wolfgang Schulze) and Jean Dubuffet.

The collapse of structural cohesion in this kind of work can be seen as a deliberate negation of the utopian pre-war geometric abstraction epitomized by the Dutch modernist Piet Mondrian. Whilst much of it retains links to organic or bodily subject matter, the work of Wols in particular posits a new gestural, abstract language in which the worrying of the picture surface by the artist's scratchings and spillages [8] has some affinities with Pollock. However, Wols was very much an easel-painter. Furthermore, large areas of his output have a distinctly precious quality. His early drawings and watercolours, many of which recall the spidery graphics of the Swiss-born modernist Paul Klee, were displayed at Drouin's in December 1945 in small illuminated boxes. Like the Abstract Expressionists, Wols internalized the

8 Wols (Alfred Otto Wolfgang Schulze)

Manhattan, 1948–9

Wols's painted surfaces register a variety of different activities. Paint was stencilled, smeared, trickled, or thrown onto his canvases. Markings were incised using the artist's fingers or sticks. In essence, though, these images were more traditional in conception than the 'drip paintings' being produced in New York by Pollock at the same time. Ironically, as is apparent from the overall shape of the dominant configuration, this painting is actually based on a map of Manhattan Island.

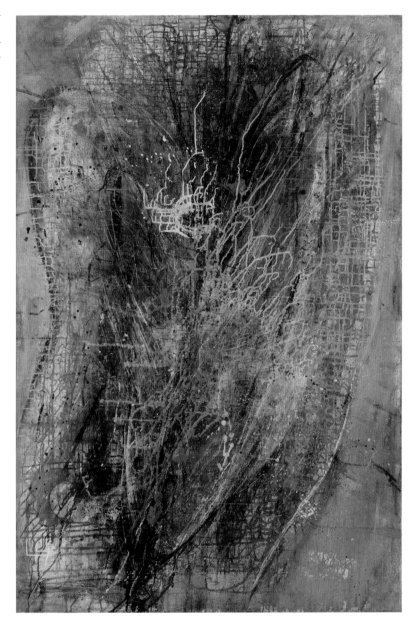

tragic nature of his times. His art was suffused with romantic self-pity, primordial longings, inchoate gestures. As with the Americans, such pre-occupations were echoes of surrealist interests in myth and primitivism, but they could border on the maudlin.

With the most influential *informel* artist, Jean Dubuffet, introspective outpourings were combined with a more robust revival of other surrealist obsessions: the art of children, the untrained, and the insane. Dubuffet explored imagery related to these sources in his *hautes pâtes* (raised pastes) which, although they preceded those of Fautrier, were not exhibited until his important *Mirobolus, Macadam et Cie* exhibition of January 1946. He also

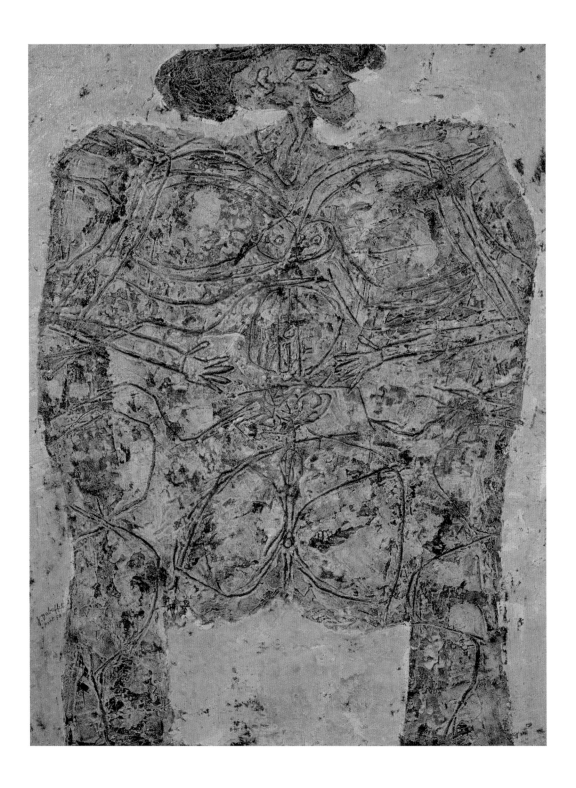

explored processes of engraving and gouging into resistant surfaces such as tarmacadam or oil mixed with gravel [**9**]. Such images had distinct associations with the wall graffiti and indentations redolent of the sufferings of occupied Paris, which Brassaï photographed [**10**]. For Dubuffet, a kind of communality was evoked by these markings. His talk of 'instinctive traces' and the ancestral basis for spontaneous sign-production (again comparable with the Abstract Expressionists' understanding of myth) was furthermore bound up with a revulsion at received notions of the beautiful. He was thus more essentially disdainful of art as an institution than the Abstract Expressionists.

Ideas of a counter-aesthetic sphere came to be consolidated in France by the critic Michel Tapié, who developed the notion of *un art autre* whilst Dubuffet himself formed a collection of *Art Brut* (raw art, largely produced by social outsiders and the insane) which was shown at Drouin's gallery between 1947 and 1950.[14] Anti-aesthetic principles inform Dubuffet's *Corps de Dames* series of 1950 [**9**]. Turning to the female nude because of its

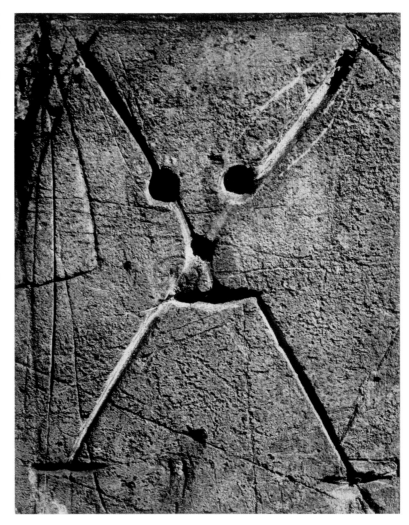

links with 'a very specious notion of beauty (inherited from the Greeks and cultivated by the magazine covers)',[15] Dubuffet saw the celebration of a massively ravaged and distorted body image, splayed out like a map to the picture's limits, as part of an 'enterprise for the rehabilitation of scorned values'.[16] However, his obsessive investigation of the innards of his subjects also has a charged psychological atmosphere, evoking children's fantasies of bodily investigation and possibly infantile urges towards the destruction of the insides of the maternal body, as discussed by the British psychoanalyst Melanie Klein in the 1930s.[17]

This concentration on abject bodily imagery in *informel* art has led to a suggestion that it may have connections with the thought of the French writer Georges Bataille. In the 1930s Bataille had developed influential notions of formlessness and 'base seduction', involving a materialist embrace of the repellent, the excessive, and the bodily, in order to undercut the idealist aesthetics he associated with Surrealism. Bataille in fact collaborated with Fautrier on certain projects, but the writer's savage anti-humanism was simply one position among several on offer from literary figures of the calibre of Jean Paulhan, Francis Ponge, and Sartre.[18] Given, however, that a Bataillean aura of 'base seduction' emanates from Fautrier's or Dubuffet's depictions of bodies, it helps set up a pointed contrast with the fate of the figure in one of their American counterparts, the Abstract Expressionist Mark Rothko.

In the 1940s Rothko's paintings had moved from a concern with semi-figurative allusions to mythic and primitivist deities to a more abstract post-cubist idiom in which residues of figuration lingered in soft-edged interacting patches of colour (pre-eminently in the *Multiforms* of 1948–9). Whilst Rothko believed that the most significant artistic subject of the past had been the single figure 'alone in a moment of utter immobility',[19] he had gradually eliminated literal evocations of living presences from his work, feeling that the image of the figure could no longer possess spiritual gravitas. (A Russian immigrant, Rothko had been raised as a Jew, a religious background he shared with Barnett Newman. This partly predisposed him towards the elimination of identifiably hieratic imagery.) For related reasons he was opposed to the kind of figural distortion practised by Dubuffet.

By the turn of the 1950s Rothko had arrived at the pictorial format which was to serve him for the rest of his career: horizontal lozenges of soft-edged colour hovering in a large vertically oriented field [**11**]. These clouds of colour were seen by him as abstract 'performers' possessing tragic or ethereal demeanours. In a sense, then, they became stand-ins for the body, although landscape associations were also present. Subject matter therefore continued to be central to his abstractions but, as with Pollock, a radical 'veiling' of the personal was enacted in favour of primal or transcendent invocations. It should be added that, at exactly the time Rothko started bodying forth such impalpable presences, his Abstract Expressionist colleague Willem de Kooning—a painter who never went so far as Pollock, Rothko, or Newman in the direction of abstraction—was embarking on painting a series of insistently physical images of women [**23**]. Comparable with Dubuffet's *Corps de Dames,* these represent counter-propositions to Rothko.

Rothko's transcendentalism clearly diverges from the concerns of Fautrier or Dubuffet. The Bataillean tenor of their *informel* aesthetic can further be

11 Mark Rothko

Green & Maroon, 1951

In Rothko's abstractions the bounds of physical contingency were evacuated in favour of a glimpse of impersonal, cosmic imperatives. The scale of the works was calculated so that spectators could measure their physical size against the coloured masses. This could lead to the feeling of being enveloped or transported out of the body.

contrasted with the mainstream Breton-derived surrealist position which broadly informed Abstract Expressionism. In the case of an artist such as the Armenian-born Arshile Gorky, whom Breton particularly praised, this bred a highly aestheticized iconography of sexuality. Constructed from inter-actions between elegant skating lines and languorous smudges of colour, Gorky's semi-abstractions seemed to evoke sultry or neurotic reveries centring on the body. But they also spoke of the over-refined European sensibility that *informel* artists like Dubuffet, with their embrace of matter, were trying to bypass.

The Abstract Expressionists' hankerings after (pre-war) European sophis-tication often sat uneasily alongside their desire to assert their Americanness. Robert Motherwell is significant in this respect. He was the most intensively educated participant in the group (he studied at Harvard and Columbia University), and in the early 1940s had been close to the émigré surrealists. Later in that decade he became affected by the poetry bound up with Surrealism's artistic predecessor, Symbolism, in particular that of Baudelaire and Mallarmé. This esoteric climate lies behind the literary allusions packed into his large series of *Elegies to the Spanish Republic* initiated by *At Five in the Afternoon* of 1949, a work rooted in Motherwell's imaginary identification with the Spanish struggle against Fascism [**12**]. By identifying with Europe's recent past Motherwell could be seen as commenting ironically on the draining of political purpose from Abstract Expressionist art. (He must have been aware that at this time, the late 1940s, America was solidifying its Cold War stance.) However, on other occasions Motherwell sacrificed his European credentials to argue for America's new-found aesthetic superiority. In a discussion among artists and critics on the subject of pictorial finish, held in 1950, he argued that the work of contemporary French painters was too reliant on 'traditional cri-teria', such as the notion of the 'beautifully made object', whereas American art tended to forgo the niceties of finish in favour of process.[20]

12 Robert Motherwell

At Five in the Afternoon, 1949

This painting deliberately combines a host of allusions to Spanish culture, such as the stark black/white contrasts of Goya, Velasquez, and Picasso, the Spanish poet Lorca's lament to a dead bullfighter, *Llanto por Ignacio Sánchez Mejías*, and the (related) enlarged images of a bull's genitalia (a powerful metaphor for the virility of Abstract Expressionism, to be discussed early in Chapter 2). The Spanish Civil War was also at issue here, and the rounded forms pressing against dark 'bars' generate weighty metaphorical contrasts between freedom and constraint, life and death.

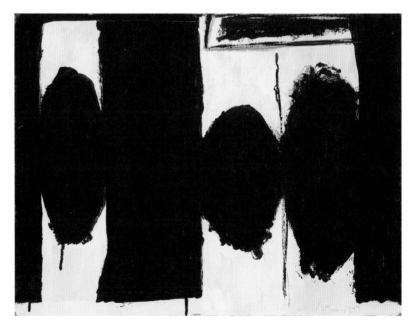

Motherwell came close here to the critic Clement Greenberg, who had played off French and American art, in the figures of Dubuffet and Pollock, in an interesting double review of February 1947. At one point Greenberg asserted that Dubuffet 'means matter, material, sensation, the all too empirical world' as opposed to the 'mysticism' of the Americans. Here he seems to be endorsing much that has been suggested above. Later, however, he reversed his terms in favour of Pollock, who was described as 'American and rougher and more brutal…less of an easel-painter in the traditional sense than Dubuffet'.[21] It is telling that gender metaphors now appear to be in play. Greenberg's shift in emphasis allows American art to end up 'rougher' than French art while ensuring that it remains elevated above 'matter'. Implicitly it is more 'masculine'. Issues of gender will emerge again later, but it should be noted that Greenberg's desire to assert American superiority was also linked to the Cold War politicking discussed earlier in this chapter. Both he and Motherwell were correct to argue that Pollock and his contemporaries had moved beyond the aesthetics of easel-painting, which in turn allowed for a freer engagement with materials, but it is evident that their critical terminologies subtly opposed a model of a thrusting American art to a European model now conveniently implied to be effete. Greenberg was subsequently to become massively influential in setting the critical pace of the post-war period. It is appropriate, then, to examine his ideas in detail.

Modernism

Given much that has been said, it may appear surprising that Clement Greenberg's early art criticism of 1939–40, produced mainly for the left-oriented journals *Partisan Review* and *The Nation*, was heavily influenced by (Trotskyist) Marxism. In important texts such as *Avant Garde and Kitsch* and *Towards a New Laocoon*,[22] Greenberg asserted that the current position of avant-garde art should be understood in the light of its historical relations to capitalism. He argued that, after 1848, the increasing alienation of artists from their own class (the bourgeoisie with its debased cultural values) led to a paradoxical situation in which, unable to communicate with their audience, avant-gardists took it upon themselves to maintain an ongoing self-critical purification of art's means, while ambivalently retaining economic links to the ruling class. Like the Frankfurt School marxist Theodor Adorno, Greenberg felt that art's autonomy had to be preserved against the incursions of mass culture, as a kind of mute repudiation of capitalism's values. At the same time, he argued that each art had to avoid confusion with its fellow arts—a situation which could only lead to the weakening of the criteria for self-definition (and critical evaluation) within the various art forms. Academic painting of the nineteenth century had, for instance, been too reliant on 'literary' effects; the arts should now follow the example of music's essential abstractness.

This amounted to a formalist prescription for the abstract painting Greenberg was later to support as a critic. But it also became the basis on which a model of the unfolding of the avant-garde's destiny was constructed such that any painting hoping to qualify as art had, necessarily, to address a set of problems intrinsic to the nature of painting posed by previous avant-gardes. One painterly value that Greenberg notoriously stressed was that of

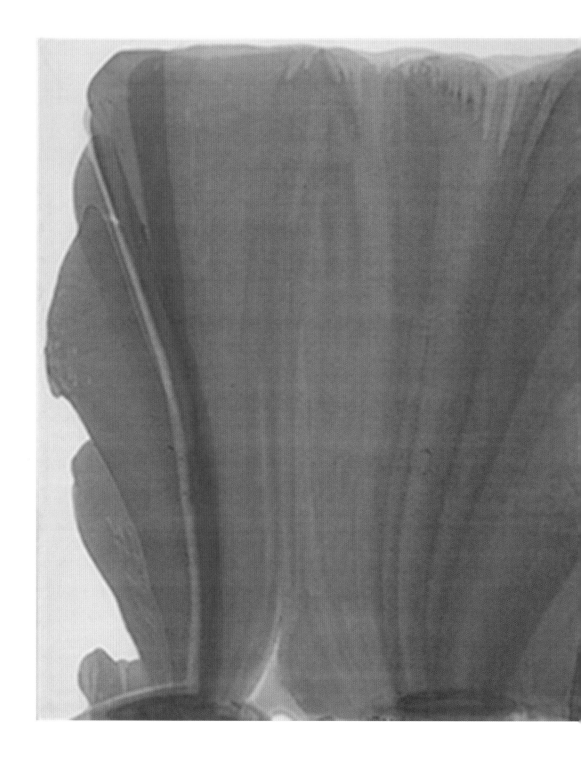

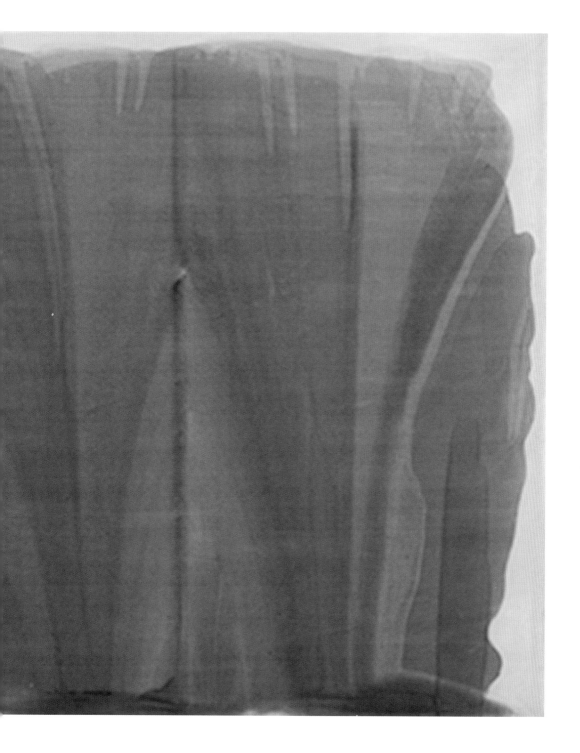

13 Morris Louis

Blue Veil, 1958–9

In Louis's enormous 'veils'
of the 1950s the physical
operations of pouring paint
or tilting a canvas so that the
paint floods down it are
powerfully implied.

'flatness'. By the late 1940s and early 1950s he was to argue that certain instances of Abstract Expressionist painting had managed to answer the pictorial challenges raised by European artistic precedents such as Post-Impressionism, Analytic and Synthetic Cubism, and various forms of abstraction. This had been a twofold operation. First, painters had worked to establish a convincing pictorial balance between emphatic surface flatness and implied depth. Second, since that involved eliminating conventional compositional structure, an 'all-over' conception of the picture had had to be developed such that, rather than being staged as a system of internal relations, it consisted of a 'largely undifferentiated system of uniform motifs that look[s] as though it could be continued indefinitely beyond the frame'.[23] This formal breakthrough to a specifically 'American' mode of avant-garde painting was largely credited to Pollock [3], although Greenberg had to concede that a West Coast painter, Mark Tobey, had beaten Pollock to it with his 'white writing' pictures of 1944, works which were nevertheless rejected as 'limited cabinet art'.[24]

What is particularly striking here is the way in which Greenberg's reading of Pollock edits out his Jungianism and the drama of 'veiling' discussed earlier. Questions of subject matter, which had been crucial to painters such as Pollock, Rothko, and Newman, were simply deemed extraneous; indeed, in a 1947 overview of American art Greenberg had voiced some discomfort with Pollock's 'Gothicism'; his art's 'paranoia and resentment', which were said to 'narrow it'.[25] In the same review Greenberg made his own aesthetic interests clear. He advocated a 'bland, balanced, Apollonian art ... [which] takes off from where the most advanced theory stops and in which an intense detachment informs all'. This classical formulation clearly foreshadows his later espousal of Post-Painterly Abstraction [13], but it represents the very antithesis of Pollock—the Pollock who once famously talked of being 'in' his paintings. Significantly, though, this impersonal formalism went hand in hand with changes in Greenberg's politics at the end of the 1940s. As John O'Brian notes, Greenberg's resignation from *The Nation* in 1949 was partly motivated by antipathy towards its Soviet sympathies, and in the early 1950s he became strongly anti-communist, in line with McCarthyism, to the extent of helping to found the American Committee of Cultural Freedom (ACCF), later discovered to be funded by the CIA through a system of dummy foundations.[26]

With an almost utopian belief that capitalism could extend America's newly created middle-brow culture to the masses, Greenberg gradually modified his earlier sense of the avant-garde's oppositional stance in relation to bourgeois culture. This critical turnabout obviously paralleled the ways in which Abstract Expressionism was manoeuvred to fit the class interests underpinning America's Cold War ideology. Yet what is particularly telling here is the way that, by the time of his seminal essay on 'Modernist Painting' of 1961, Greenberg had seen fit to drop his earlier reliance on the idea of an artistic avant-garde in favour of a key monolithic concept of Modernism (with a capital M).

Greenberg's conception of Modernism as synonymous with formal completion or inviolability (which could be seen as keyed to America's post-war imagining of its world position) was to fuel a mutually self-aggrandizing tradition of painting and art criticism in the 1950s and 1960s. Three of the principal painters concerned, Helen Frankenthaler, Morris Louis, and Kenneth Noland, were introduced by Greenberg in April 1953 when the two Washington-based male artists were taken by the critic to Frankenthaler's studio in New York. Her near-legendary painting *Mountains and Sea* (1952: National Gallery of Art, Washington) particularly impressed Louis in terms of its abandonment of the traditional build-up of brushmarks in favour of a process of 'staining' such that acrylic pigments were allowed to soak into large areas of unprimed canvas (a technique with which Pollock had briefly experimented in 1951–2). Given that colour here was literally at one with the weave of the canvas, rather than lying on top of it, the technique tied in with the Modernist imperative towards flatness. Indeed, it achieved what Greenberg and his disciple Michael Fried were to describe as a supreme 'opticality' in so far as the colour—literally poured or spilled in plumes and rivulets onto the canvas in the case of Louis's aptly titled *Veils* of the mid-1950s [13]—not only formed an evenly textured field but also gave an effect of luminosity.

In terms of the rigorous hair's-breadth distinctions of Greenberg's criticism, this represented a step beyond the all-over abstractions of Pollock and Newman. However, this dour masculinist discourse of aesthetic one-upmanship obscures the fact that Louis's 'veils' may have 'feminine' connotations (a point worth contrasting with Pollock's very different understanding of 'veiling', as mentioned earlier). Feminist writers have persuasively argued that Frankenthaler's stained canvases have, in the past, suffered from being designated 'feminine' (and hence closer to the natural, the merely decorative, or the intuitive as opposed to the cultural), but interpreting Louis's work in this way suggests that social stereotypes regarding gender might equally be overturned within works by male artists.[27]

Definitions of Modernism

In terms of its historical/critical usage, 'modernism' (with a small m) normally covers two impulses. The first of these involves the demand (first voiced self-consciously in the nineteenth-century French poet Baudelaire's critical writings) that the visual arts should reflect or exemplify broad processes of modernization and their societal effects. The second is bound up with the evaluation of the *quality* of works of art. Here works of art have to measure up to criteria of aesthetic innovation while being distinguishable from a set of indicators of 'non-art' status (the terms 'academic' or 'kitsch' being two such pejorative terms).

Greenberg's capitalization of the word 'Modernism' implies a formalization of the second of these definitions, whilst its subsequent elaboration as a theory implicitly downplays the consequences of the first definition, with which the notion of a socially disaffirmative avant-garde is bound up. As explained by Greenberg in his key 'Modernist Painting' essay of 1961, 'The essence of Modernism lies ... in the use of the characteristic methods of a discipline to criticize the discipline itself, not in order to subvert it but to entrench it more firmly in its area of competence.' The warning against the subversion of the discipline is included to rule out socially generated anti-art impulses, such as Dada and much of Surrealism, from the Modernist master plan; Greenberg was notoriously opposed to the French proto-dadaist, Marcel Duchamp.

The fallout from Modernism: critiques of Greenberg

The critical parameters set up by Greenberg and Fried to legitimate Post-Painterly Abstraction had the effect of marginalizing other practices of abstraction, deriving from different conditions, in Europe. In Britain, the post-war atmosphere of austerity in London, presided over by a new, guardedly optimistic, Labour government, created the conditions for the emergence of an existentially tinged figuration (see the discussion of Bacon in Chapter 3). However, away from the metropolis, a group of its former residents—Ben Nicholson, Barbara Hepworth, and the Russian émigré Naum Gabo—had weathered the war years in and around St Ives in Cornwall, already a well-established artists' centre. Their geometric abstraction, which had won international recognition in the 1930s, had a decisive effect after the war on the painter Peter Lanyon. He began to reformulate his basic commitment to the Cornish landscape in terms of the post-cubist space and interpenetration of interior and exterior volumes derived from their painting and sculpture respectively.

By the early 1950s Lanyon's work managed to reconcile the rural nostalgia typical of Neo-Romanticism (an important phenomenon of the war years encompassing painters such as Graham Sutherland and John Piper) with an expressionist handling and acknowledgement of the picture plane in line with Abstract Expressionism [14]. It was not, however, until the late 1950s that Lanyon and other St Ives-based abstractionists such as Patrick Heron and Roger Hilton fully absorbed the implications of recent American art. (A notable exception here is Alan Davie, a Scottish-born painter connected with the Cornish group, who had seen Pollock's works in Venice as early as 1948 and subsequently fused his gesturalism with primitivist and ritual allusions in a series of uncompromising abstracts of the early 1950s.) For the other painters, the Tate Gallery's *Modern Art in the United States* exhibition of 1956 was something of a revelation, while the *New American Painting*, backed, as noted earlier, by the International Program of MoMA, consolidated America's Modernist supremacy in 1959.

14 Peter Lanyon

Bojewyan Farms, 1951–2

Bojewyan is a small village near St Just in Cornwall, England. At the time of the painting local farmsteads were falling empty because they were uneconomic. Lanyon saw this as a serious threat to the region. His painting contains hints of a symbolic revival of fortunes. Several animal images and womb-like shapes are incorporated into the design. The Cornish landscape is suggested through rugged interlocking forms. (At the top left the curve of the coastline is legible.)

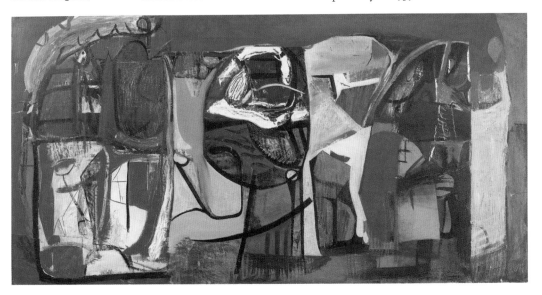

Lanyon, who had already forged a style of his own, was to gain some degree of commercial success in America in the late 1950s and to develop personal links with Rothko in particular. His colleagues, however, were generally deemed derivative by the American critical establishment, and further British responses to Post-Painterly Abstraction by painters such as Robyn Denny and Richard Smith, which culminated in two highly original environmentally conceived exhibitions of 1959 and 1960 (*Place* at the ICA and *Situation* at the RBA Gallery in London), seem hardly to have registered with Greenberg and Fried. In 1965 the latter opened his important essay in *Three American Painters,* the catalogue to an exhibition of Kenneth Noland, Jules Olitski, and Frank Stella at the Fogg Art Museum, Harvard, with the declaration: 'For twenty years or more almost all the best new painting and sculpture has been done in America.'

The painter and critic Patrick Heron leapt to the defence of British art, detecting a degree of cultural imperialism on the part of America's art cognoscenti. Aggrieved that the Modernist critics had failed to acknowledge that the 'first invaluable bridgehead of approval' for Abstract Expressionism had been formed in Britain, he astutely recognized that the increasing tendency in (Post-Painterly) abstraction towards flatness, symmetry, and a 'centre-dominated format' was fundamentally at odds with 'European resources of sensibility'.[28] According to Heron, European abstraction tended towards a 're-complication' of the pictorial field, favouring a resolution of 'asymmetric, unequal, disparate formal ingredients' in terms of an overall 'architectonic harmony'.[29] (See, in this respect, the discussion of 'relational' and 'non-relational' art in Chapter 5.) Possibly Heron misconceived Greenberg's and Fried's view of Modernism as intrinsically progressive, preprogrammed to fulfil a historical logic. He demonstrates, however, that there were whole areas of European abstract art that fell outside the terms of the American critics. Histories of post-war art have, possibly correctly, disparaged much French abstraction, such as that of the *tachiste* Georges Mathieu, or Nicolas de Staël, for appearing fussy or 'tasteful' alongside, say, Pollock or Rothko. However, a figure such as the painter/poet Henri Michaux [15] can hardly be thought answerable to Modernist criteria, although his works have superficial visual links with Pollock's.

Its formal rigours aside, Greenbergian Modernism was primarily urban in tenor, an art of large metropolitan cultures. In this respect, Pollock, for all his Gothicism, excited Greenberg because he attempted 'to cope with urban life' and with a related 'lonely jungle of immediate sensations, impulses and notions'.[30] In these terms, British abstractionists such as Lanyon, working from landscape motifs in a tradition rooted in the eighteenth century, would have seemed anachronistic. (Something similar might be said of the American West Coast painter, Richard Diebenkorn, who produced powerful series of Albuquerque and Berkeley landscapes in the early 1950s.) Despite the fact that he had a strong stylistic influence on both Lanyon and Diebenkorn, and himself produced a sequence of paintings derived from landscape at the end of the 1950s, it was the Dutch-born Willem de Kooning, rather than Pollock, who produced the most distinctively urban-rooted Abstract Expressionist canvases. De Kooning had had a rigorous academic art training at the Rotterdam Academy. Consequently, for most

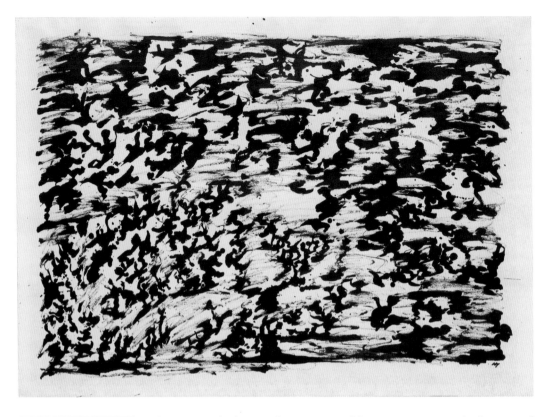

of his career the human figure remained his starting point, whether tugged apart and assimilated to the infrastructure of Synthetic Cubism, as in the early 1940s, or bodied forth in expressionist slashes and swipes of oil paint, as in the *Women* of the early 1950s [**23**].

De Kooning came closest to abstraction in the sequence of black-and-white canvases of 1947–9 [**16**], where pictorial planes lock together to produce an all-over pictorial field analogous to Pollock's contemporary productions. However, references to body parts, buildings, and landscape, claustrophobically compacted together in a fierce collision of energies, can still be discerned. De Kooning's friend Edwin Denby recalled late-night walks with the painter during the Depression, with the latter 'pointing out to me on the pavement the dispersed composition—spots and cracks and bits of wrappers and reflections of neon light'.[31] However much de Kooning's canvases insist on their post-cubist formal austerity, they distil a film-noir poetics which powerfully links them with the ideological reverberations of this genre noted in earlier discussions of the Modern Man theme. In this sense, they resonate with the work of contemporary photographers such as Weegee [**58**].

It is perhaps not surprising that, in the final analysis, Greenberg found what he described as de Kooning's Picassoesque *terribilità* as disquieting as Pollock's Gothicism. He had little stomach for those 'practices of negation' which the art historian T. J. Clark pinpoints as lying at the heart of modernism.[32] Though he may well have understood Pollock, de Kooning, and the other Abstract Expressionists comprehensively, Greenberg represented them

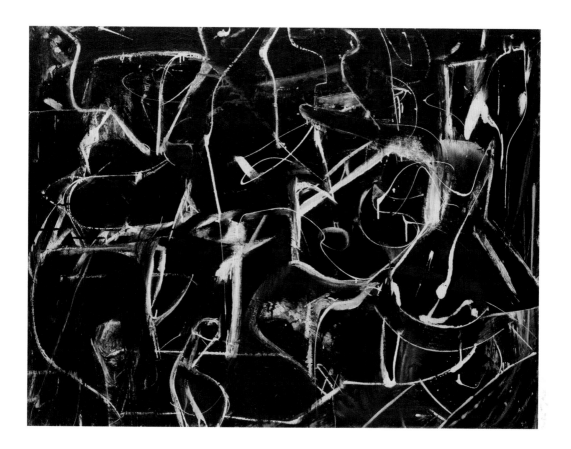

16 Willem de Kooning

Untitled, 1948–9

In de Kooning's black canvases the elimination of colour was conditioned as much by financial constraints as by the need to simplify pictorial problems in the spirit of Analytic Cubism. The deliberately artless use of shiny enamel house paints (a strategy also adopted by Pollock at this time) evokes the wet night-time sidewalks of New York City, whilst disembodied lines, evocative of graffiti and other forms of signage, skid, loop, and zigzag across the canvas like reckless city drivers.

only partially and selectively. His critical legacy, based on the view, as reformulated by Clark, that 'art can substitute *itself* for the values capitalism has made useless',[33] had an undeniable grip on art up until the late 1960s. But other critical options were also on offer in the early 1950s. The critic Harold Rosenberg, whose reputation was largely overshadowed by that of Greenberg, produced a very different account of certain of the Abstract Expressionists. He wrote: 'At a certain moment the canvas began to appear to one American painter after another as an arena in which to act—rather than as a space in which to reproduce, re-design or "express" an object…What was to go on the canvas was not a picture but an event.'[34] This conception of a risk-laden encounter between artist and work, although the starting point for later caricatures of Pollock as paint-flinging existential hero, has been shown by the art historian Fred Orton to constitute a refusal to submit to that silencing of the American left in the later 1940s with which Greenberg's Modernist aesthetics seems to have been bound up. In Orton's analysis, Rosenberg's past marxist affiliations meant that, for him, 'Action [was] the prerequisite of class identity', since 'all the relations of capitalist society forbid the working class to act except as a tool'.[35] On this analysis, a politics *was* still embedded in certain fundamental tenets of Abstract Expressionism, despite Greenberg's clean-up campaign.

The other implication of Rosenberg's essay was that, rather than being bound up with the contemplative processes of aesthetic decision-making and judgement, Abstract Expressionist painting was fundamentally 'performative'. Whilst this only fully applied to Pollock's drip paintings, it found an echo in a text of 1958 responding to the needs of a later, significantly different, aesthetic climate. Here the American organizer of Happenings, Allan Kaprow, saw Pollock as opening up two avenues within post-war art. One involved continuing in a Modernist vein. The other offered a radical option to artists: 'To give up the making of paintings entirely—I mean the single flat rectangle or oval as we know it...Pollock, as I see him, left us at the point where we must become preoccupied with and even dazzled by the space and objects of our everyday life.'[36] It remains to be seen, in the chapters that follow, which direction prevailed.

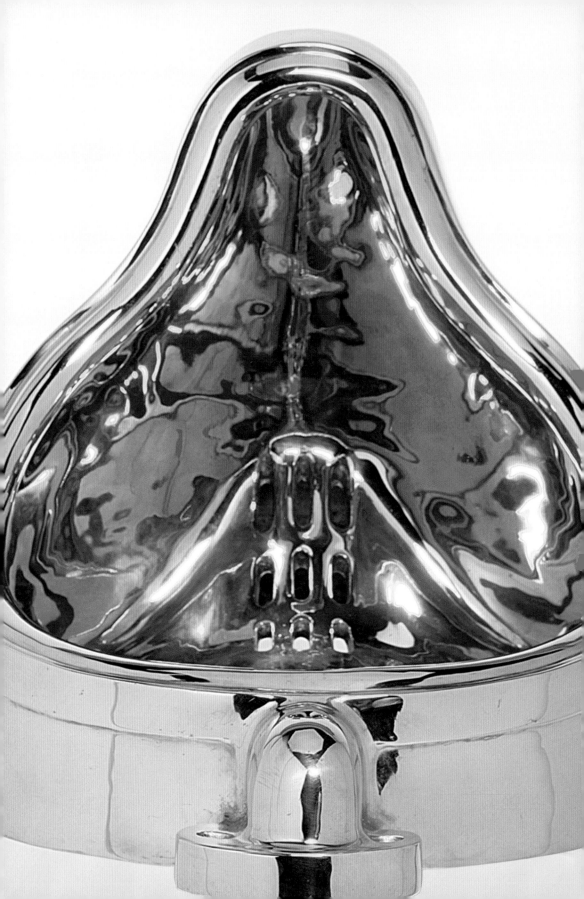

Duchamp's Legacy

The Rauschenberg–Johns Axis

The shift in art-world domination from Paris to New York in the post-war period is summed up by Marcel Duchamp's *Boîte-en-valise* [**17**]. The work comprises a collection of miniatures and samples of the French-born artist's pre-1935 output. Included, for example, is a tiny version of *Fountain*, the retitled men's urinal which emblematizes Duchamp's one-time involvement with the iconoclasm of Dada. Ever since the demise of the Dada movement in the early 1920s Duchamp had moved between Paris and New York. Based in France when a new European war seemed imminent, he had sensibly decided to 'pack his bags'.

The objects presented in the *Boîte* attested to cultural mutations. Early oil paintings by the artist were represented via reproductions. Objects which had once been 'readymades' (the term Duchamp applied to the mass-produced objects he had accorded art status) now had a paradoxically crafted quality (the urinal is a case in point). The *Boîte* also spoke of commodification. Part of an edition (initially a deluxe one of twenty-four), it represented, in Duchamp's words, 'mass production on a modest scale'. Overall it had a dual function. It was a portable museum, regrouping the oeuvre of an iconoclast. But it was also a travelling salesman's display case.

The *Boîte* exemplifies the transition between two worlds: the old Europe of the museum and the connoisseur, and the young America of the commercial gallery and the artistic commodity. Duchamp's acceptance that art should incorporate the dominant modes of social production was a radical alternative to Greenberg's Modernism, as discussed in Chapter 1. Greenberg had demanded that art remain true to its medium, purifying its means, maintaining aesthetic (and social) distance. For Duchamp, and those following in his wake, art's very identity was in question.

Marcel Duchamp

In the early 1940s Duchamp was installed again in New York, the location of his Dada activities between 1915 and 1923. Although his works of that period, the readymades and the enigmatic *Large Glass*, were legendary among a small community, Duchamp maintained a deliberately underground profile. His *Boîte*, which was shown at Peggy Guggenheim's gallery in late 1942, poignantly spoke of the sense of cultural transplantation felt by many émigré artists from Europe. However, unlike the French surrealists with whom he was friendly, Duchamp had little obvious appeal for the rising generation

Detail of 30

35

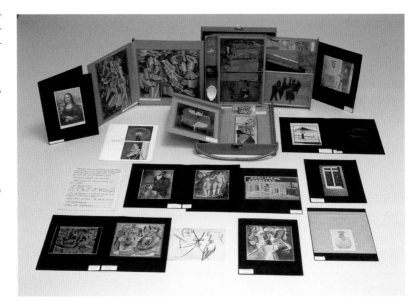

17 Marcel Duchamp

Boîte-en-valise, 1935–41

Duchamp's *Boîte* unpacked in such a way that certain sections slid out to become free-standing display boards, whilst a sheaf of folders and black mounts bore other reproductions of works from his output. In all, it contained sixty-nine items. These included a miniature version of the *Large Glass* [**18**] on celluloid and, next to it, three tiny versions of earlier readymades. These were, at the top, *Paris Air* of 1919 (a chemist's ampoule, emptied of its contents and then resealed by Duchamp); in the middle, *Traveller's Folding Item* of 1916 (a typewriter cover); and, at the bottom, *Fountain* (1917), the men's urinal which had originally been rotated 90 degrees to sit on a plinth but was here ironically restored to a functional position.

of Abstract Expressionist artists. He had renounced art which appealed solely to the eye, or, in his terms, 'retinal' art, as early as 1912. Two alternative paths had opened up for Duchamp. One was embodied in the conceptual challenge posed by the readymades. The other involved the creation of a machine-age iconography, rendered in a dry, ironic, linear style. In the case of the *Large Glass*, he created a set of sci-fi mechanomorphs snagged in a complex machinery of human aspirations ranging from romantic love to scientific certainty [**18**].

Duchamp's likely attitude to Abstract Expressionism can be gauged from a small work of 1946, entitled *Wayward Landscape*, which was incorporated as an original item in one example from the first, exclusive, edition of *Boîtes*. At first glance it appears to be an abstract painting. In fact it is a large semen stain on funereal black satin. Although it was essentially private, an unconventional parting gift for his lover Maria Martins, succinctly evoking the embalming of desire, it stands as one of the first examples of what, in the 1960s, became known as Body Art; that is, art directly linked to the body and to bodily identity. Beyond this, some knowledge of the rich iconography of Duchamp's *Large Glass*, properly titled *The Bride Stripped Bare by her Bachelors, Even*, yields another reading. It should be emphasized that this is indeed a reading since it is largely based on Duchamp's notes, chiefly those from the so-called *Green Box*. These were seen by him as integral to the work. (Once again, Duchamp emerges as a pioneer of a new expressive form, this time the text-related art of the 1960s.)

Turning to the *Glass* [**18**], at the left of their lower 'Domain', a huddle of diagrammatized Bachelors attempt to excite the Bride, with her orgasmic 'blossoming', in the upper Domain. Apart from triggering her 'stripping', the Bachelors' communal arousal produces 'love gasoline' which, once refined in the receptacles to which they are hooked up, is 'dazzled' into the Bride's orbit via a set of optical devices (the 'Oculist Witnesses' in the lower right of the *Glass*). Most of the droplets of love gasoline fall sadly short of their target in an area

The Bride Stripped Bare by her Bachelors, Even (The Large Glass), 1915–23

This work's technical inventiveness matches its iconographic density. It consists of two panes of glass set one above the other (the work shattered in transit in 1927 and was patiently reconstructed by Duchamp). The 'Oculist Witnesses' (lower right) were produced by meticulously scraping away a section of 'silvering' applied to that area of the Glass. Elsewhere, random procedures were utilized. The positions of the nine holes representing the Bachelors' 'shots' (upper right) were determined by firing paint-dipped matchsticks at the work from a toy cannon.

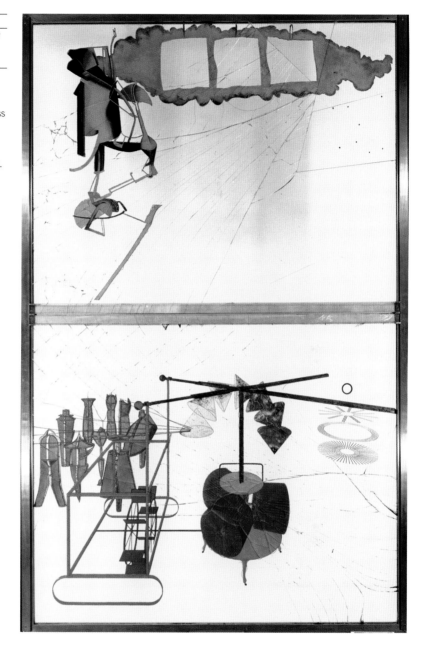

designated as that of the 'Shots'. This short description evokes something of the *Glass*'s bleak hilarity as a satire on sexual relations, but from it the significance of *Wayward Landscape* can be appreciated; it is one of the Bachelors'/Duchamp's 'shots'. As a comment on male expressive/sexual urgency the gesture ironizes the new vogue for painterly bravado in American art linked to assertively male artists such as Pollock, shortly to embark on his drip paintings.

The reduction of the grand rhetoric of Abstract Expressionism to these terms is typical of Duchamp's deflationary anti-aesthetic impulse and yet again prefigures an entire post-war attitude. It is also typical of Duchamp that, in the later 1940s, he made no overt display of his distaste for contemporary trends. In 1945 members of the American avant-garde, along with several surrealist émigrés, published a special edition of their art journal *View* containing a comprehensive range of accounts of Duchamp's activities, including André Breton's essay decoding the *Large Glass*. This ensured a gradual dissemination of his concepts. Meanwhile Duchamp himself had begun planning a new project. This, his final full-scale work—its short title being *Etant Donnés* ('Given…'), a title deriving from a cryptic note for the *Large Glass*—was begun in secret around 1946 and not revealed publicly until 1969, months after his death in 1968. Its full effects were thus programmatically postponed as if Duchamp, who was obsessed with chess, calculated his game with posterity in advance.

Etant Donnés is permanently installed in the Philadelphia Museum of Art. As such it is one of the first examples of the installation genre which would flourish later. (The German Dadaist Kurt Schwitters's environmentally conceived *Hanover Merzbau* of 1923 was another important early installation.) *Etant Donnés* consists of a battered door through which the spectator peers via eyeholes at a floodlit tableau. This consists of a mannequin, representing a naked female, lying open-legged in a patently artificial landscape. She holds aloft a lamp, confounding an initial sense that she has been violated.

In a sense the work amounts to a hyperreal translation of the schematic ideograms of the *Large Glass* into grossly embodied form. It is as though the Bride who, for Duchamp, possessed unknowable, fourth-dimensional characteristics, has fallen to earth in our measurable world. The door acts as a barrier between profane and spiritual domains, so that the spectators of the work become the Bachelors who, in the *Glass*, were constrained by perspectival and gravitational laws. The (male) spectator's enforced viewpoint ensures that the shocking split-second view through the holes effectively brings about the Bride's 'blossoming'. The installation therefore endows sight with the power of an invisible erotic transmission, as though investing Duchamp's bugbear, the sphere of the retinal, with a power untapped by conventional painting.

In 1957 Duchamp delivered an important lecture, 'The Creative Act', in which he argued that 'the work of art is not performed by the artist alone' and that the spectator's point of view effects the all-important 'transubstantiation' of inert matter into art.[1] The ritualistic, Catholic overtones here relate interestingly to *Etant Donnés*, but most important is the strategic belittling of the Modernist conception of the art object's internal self-sufficiency in favour of a sense of its dependence on contingent, external factors such as audience participation. Indeed, Duchamp's concern with the *spectator*'s share, to say nothing of his interest in the gendering of the relationship between spectator and artwork, would hover as a conceptual aura around much of the ambitious anti-Modernist art produced elsewhere in his lifetime.

The spectator's share: Cage, Rauschenberg, and assemblage

The prime mover in disseminating Duchamp's ideas in America was not the man himself, but John Cage. Having trained as a musician with Schoenberg, the Californian-born Cage was gradually establishing his avant-garde credentials with his 'prepared piano' when, in 1942, he first met Duchamp. His later interest in the Zen Buddhist philosophy of D. T. Suzuki, with whom he studied in 1945, led him to harness Duchamp's love of paradox and gratuitous humour to a more evangelical conception of the need to abolish watertight distinctions between art and life. In line with Zen doctrines of passivity, Cage saw the imposition of mind or human will as the enemy of creation; art consisted in 'purposeless play', charged with the imperative of 'waking us up to the very life we're living'.[2] The main Duchampian model here was undoubtedly that of the readymade which, in the case of *Fountain*, miniaturized in the main section of the *Boîte* [**17**], had challenged the spectator to 'find a new thought for that object' through the elimination of authorial intervention.[3]

In the early 1950s Cage's utilization of chance in his own musical compositions, reinforced by the publication, in 1951, of Robert Motherwell's pioneering Dada anthology *The Dada Painters and Poets*, strongly appealed to visual artists oppressed by the relentless interiority of Abstract Expressionism. The fulcrum for this shift of emphasis was Black Mountain College in North Carolina, where Cage occasionally taught.

Among Black Mountain's students, a pre-eminent figure was the Texan-born painter Robert Rauschenberg, whose first solo exhibition Cage had admired in New York in 1952. Rauschenberg's intuitive appreciation of Cage's Dada-derived ideas led to a spontaneous interdisciplinary 'happening', to which several faculty members contributed, in the summer of 1952. Looking back to the Dada provocations recounted in Motherwell's book, but also anticipating the performance genre that developed in the 1960s (see Chapter 6), the event involved the participants carrying out simultaneous actions. John Cage read texts such as the American Bill of Rights from a stepladder; Rauschenberg played scratchy Edith Piaf records; and the dancer Merce Cunningham danced in and around the audience, who were strategically decentred by being seated in a sequence of square or circular formations. However, aside from the 'purposeless play' of the performers' actions, the surest indications of the importation of Cage's Zen aesthetics into a visual/performing-arts context were Rauschenberg's *White Paintings* of 1951, which hung in cross-formations from the ceiling as part of the environment. These pictures, usually consisting of several modular white-painted panels abutted together, reflected a pronounced discomfort with Abstract Expressionist bombast; they were passive receptors, awaiting events rather than prescribing sensations. As markers of an artistic *tabula rasa* they were not completely unprecedented. The Russian artist Malevich had produced his *White on White* paintings in 1918 as an outcome of different metaphysical preoccupations. However, Rauschenberg's pictures broke decisively with Modernist assumptions of aesthetic self-containment. They questioned whether art experiences should actually be sought from *within* objects. Cage responded in appropriate Zen style. His notorious *4'33"* of late 1952 involved a concert audience being enjoined to 'listen' to a piano piece consisting of three sections. Each section consisted of silence.

The precedent of Duchamp hovered behind much of this but the Cagean emphasis on Eastern philosophy arguably repressed the French artist's bodily preoccupations. These eventually resurfaced in Rauschenberg's work, but it is

Black Mountain College was a small but progressive art school with a strong community ethos, the opening of which, in 1933, had signalled a trend towards greater humanities and arts provision in American higher education. In that year a victim of the Nazis' dissolution of the Dessau-based Bauhaus, the abstract painter Josef Albers, was invited to join the college staff, subsequently becoming head. Albers's analytic attitudes towards colour interaction, along with other principles linked to Bauhaus teaching, thus became incorporated into US art education. His avowedly apolitical position and tendency to downplay European tradition made him a suitably liberal and diplomatic figurehead during a period of international tensions. Various influential practitioners taught summer schools at the institution in the late 1940s and early 1950s including John Cage and his collaborator, the choreographer Merce Cunningham, and the poet Charles Olson, who was to succeed Albers as director in 1952.

necessary first to chart his early career in some detail. For a time Rauschenberg oscillated in mercurial fashion between dadaist/Duchampian and Abstract Expressionist principles. The *White Paintings* were succeeded, dialectically, by all-black ones, in which matt or gloss paint was applied to bases covered with fabric or crumpled paper. Whereas their all-overness followed the new pictorial orthodoxies of Newman and Rothko, their blank, crackling resistance to optical pleasures parodied Greenbergian injunctions. Constantly alert to metaphor, Rauschenberg gradually introduced extra-artistic materials into his painting. The cubists had pioneered the use of collage fragments within pictorial constructs earlier in the century, and the dadaist Kurt Schwitters had taken the non-hierarchical implications of this further by incorporating rubbish into his *Merz* assemblages in the 1920s and 1930s. Partly in the spirit of Schwitters, Rauschenberg incorporated newspapers into the bases for his work. In 1952 he produced *Asheville Citizen*, a two-part painting in which a whole sheet of newspaper, lightly brushed with brown-black paint evoking scatological associations, was very much the picture's subject.

The consequences of this were far-reaching. As the critic Leo Steinberg later wrote in his important essay *Other Criteria*, Rauschenberg appeared to be implying that 'any flat documentary surface that tabulates information is a relevant analogue of his picture plane', with the implication that his work 'stood for the mind itself...ingesting incoming unprocessed data to be mapped in an overcharged field'.[4] In subsequent works Rauschenberg assimilated the gridded variegation of text and photography in newspaper layout to a new conception of the pictorial ground as, in Steinberg's terms, a 'flatbed' or work surface on which to pin heterogeneous images. An early example of such a practice was *Rebus* of 1955, in which fragments from different worlds—a printed reproduction of a flying insect, photographs of runners, a reproduction of Botticelli's *Birth of Venus*, a page of comic-strip imagery—were laid out in a line, punctuated by daubs of paint, as though constituting some indecipherable message.

By the early 1960s Rauschenberg had developed the technique to the extent of stacking up a whole array of divergent forms of information [**60**], reflecting the fact that throughout the 1950s America had seen a dizzying expansion in consumerism and the mass media. For instance, as a sign of things to come, receipts for television sales on Madison Avenue in New York escalated from 12.3 to 128 million dollars between 1949 and 1951.[5] According to the critic Brian O'Doherty, the perceptual adjustments involved in responding to this proliferating image culture led Rauschenberg to develop an aesthetic of the 'vernacular glance'.[6]

Rauschenberg's inventiveness took a further turn in his so-called *Combines*. Here the full repertoire of Duchamp's readymades (which, as well as unitary objects, had included poetic or unexpected combinations of objects, as in the assisted readymade, *Bicycle Wheel*, of 1913) were brought into a realignment with fine-art practices in constructions fusing everyday objects, painting, and sculpture. In the case of one of these Combines, the notorious *Bed* of 1955 [**19**], the move from a horizontal to vertical orientation in the object's upright placement sets up an anthropomorphic counterpoint to Pollock's floor-based action paintings. In being placed in the 'vertical posture of "art"',[7] the object sheds its normal links with our sleeping and dreaming, and thus with the notion of psychic revelation synonymous with Pollock's practice.

These bodily associations go deeper, however; from the outside to the inside, so to speak. As with a short flurry of red canvases of 1953–5, *Bed* appears to equate paint with bodily fluids, as though making palpable the violence that Willem de Kooning acted out on the bodies of his contemporaneously produced *Women* [**23**]. Violent associations aside, stained bed sheets inevitably have sexual connotations and, given that Rauschenberg had described his *White Paintings* to one of his first curators as being 'presented with the innocence of a virgin',[8] it is tempting to think that he might have seen *Bed* as a counter-proposition to these in the spirit of the dadaist Francis Picabia, who, in 1920, had blasphemously titled an ink splash *Sainte Vierge*. Picabia had been a close friend of Duchamp, and it becomes clear that with *Bed* Rauschenberg came close to recapitulating their scurrilous bodily repartee.[9]

Whatever the precise bodily associations of *Bed*, and a polymorphously perverse co-mingling of blood, semen, and faeces may certainly be involved,[10] the way in which such flows are brought into counterpoint with the geometrical symmetry of the quilt produces an overarching gendered dialogue. Paint, which ultimately connotes the fine-art tradition, is anarchically set against a product of the handicrafts or applied arts. The male sphere of cultural production intrudes into the female sphere of domestic labour. This transgression of categories also mobilizes deep-seated notions of purity and defilement, and encourages speculation about the way societies make use of taboos regarding bodily 'pollution' for purposes of social containment, a topic later studied by the anthropologist Mary Douglas.[11] Earlier, in 1953, Rauschenberg had symbolically equated materials with incompatible cultural value in his concurrently produced *Dirt Paintings* and *Gold Paintings*, the former consisting of compacted earth in shallow boxes, the latter of gold leaf overlaid on collage bases.

There are implicit democratizing impulses at work here, but the sociopolitical resonances of Rauschenberg's practice would not fully emerge until later. In 1958–9 critics began to codify the evident Duchampian disrespect for aesthetic boundaries, in both Rauschenberg's work and that of a growing body of fellow practitioners including Rauschenberg's ally Jasper Johns, in

19 Robert Rauschenberg

Bed, 1955

Critics at the time darkly
remarked that *Bed* looked
as if an axe murder had
been committed in it.
Rauschenberg saw it
differently. His greatest
fear, he once confided,
was that somebody might
try to crawl into it.

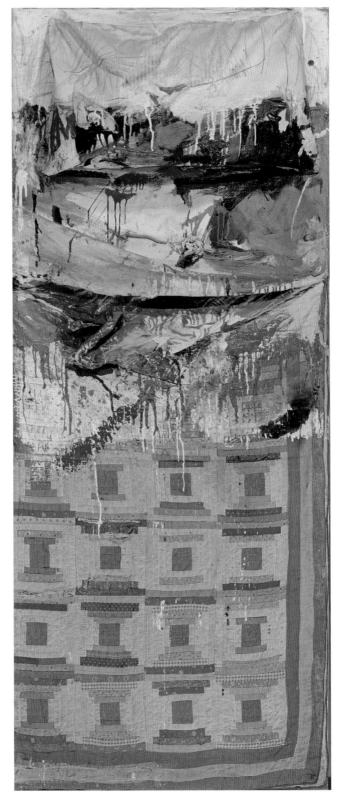

terms of a notion of 'Neo-Dada'.[12] But if such work embraced provisional structures and hybrid juxtapositions, it was hardly openly nihilistic, as was often the case with Dada. Consequently the term 'assemblage' quickly came to replace it. This genre reached its apotheosis in William Seitz's exhibition *The Art of Assemblage*, held at MoMA, New York, in 1961.

Seitz's curatorial recognition of what was dubbed a newly aestheticized 'urban collage environment' led to several artistic rehabilitations in his catalogue for the show. A late Picasso sculpture, *Baboon and Young*, of 1951, in which a toy car's body brilliantly doubles for the ape's features, now stood as a precursor of current preoccupations. In the exhibition itself, though, Picasso was downplayed in favour of Duchamp. Particularly significant was the inclusion of the reclusive Joseph Cornell, one of the few Americans to have responded inventively to Surrealism before the war. Over the years, Cornell had patiently constructed boxed miniaturized environments [20]. Their claustrophobic interiors, brimming with allusions, from French Symbolist poetry to Hollywood film, echoed his lifestyle in the New York suburbs caring for a demanding mother and a crippled brother. Cornell's boxes represented a new artistic genre and were spiritualized counterweights to Duchamp's more materially oriented *Boite-en-valise*. However, Cornell was not as other-worldly as is sometimes suggested. By 1949 he had insinuated himself into Charles Egan's gallery in New York, where the young Rauschenberg, soon to show there, quickly absorbed his poetics of confinement, as did Jasper Johns somewhat later.

In stark contrast to Cornell's late Romantic sensibility, Seitz's catalogue also alluded briefly to West Coast American tendencies in the constructions of Ed Kienholz and Bruce Conner. These artists mobilized vernacular idioms and outright ugliness to mock social hypocrisies (see Chapter 4). Such developments led Seitz at one point to define assemblage as a 'language for impatient, hyper-critical and anarchic young artists'.[13] This instancing of youth culture affiliations is significant. In the 1950s America had witnessed the emergence of Beat culture, as exemplified by writers such as Jack Kerouac and the poet Allen Ginsberg. The latter produced nightmarish urban visions of 'angelheaded hipsters burning for the ancient heavenly connection to the starry dynamo in the machinery of the night'.[14] His image-saturated, open-form incantations, partly deriving from ideas of 'Projective verse' developed by the Black Mountain professor Charles Olson, have broad analogies with Rauschenberg's collaged surfaces. But, technicalities aside, Ginsberg was articulating the disaffection of a generation born under the signs of Hiroshima and Nagasaki. (John Cage's promotion of Japanese philosophy has a socially critical inflection in this context.) There was much in American culture at large for the ethically sensitive to feel uneasy about.

McCarthyism and masculinity

In the early 1950s the Cold War was at its height. The Korean conflict, entered by America to combat an imagined global expansion of Communism, had ended inconclusively in 1953. At home President Truman's 'Loyalty Order' of 1947, whereby government workers had been investigated for Soviet sympathies, had led to the Alger Hiss trial in 1950 in which dubious

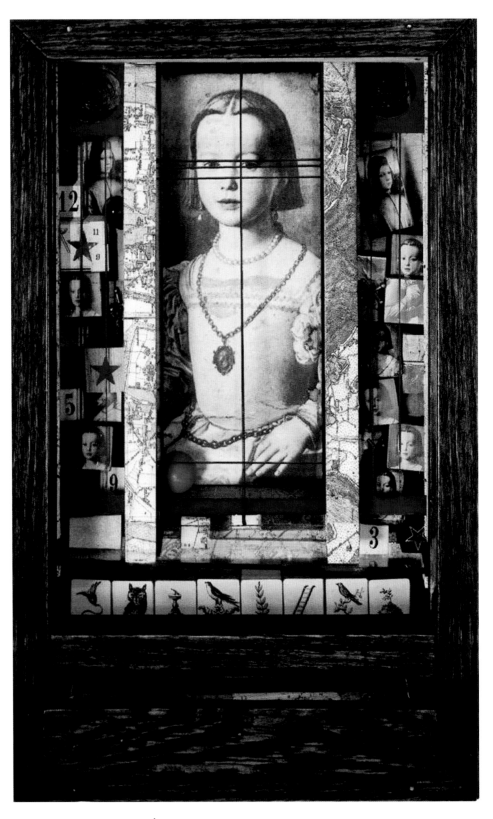

secret documents eventually secured the former State Department official's conviction for spying. The years 1950–4 saw the inexorable rise of Senator Joseph McCarthy, backed by the return of a Republican government in 1952 headed by President Eisenhower. McCarthy's reign of terror, which involved all manner of spurious accusations being levelled at suspected communists, eventually ended in November 1957 when he was officially censured.

In such an atmosphere, artists with leftist instincts understandably felt vulnerable. To what extent did Rauschenberg reflect the Beat writers' distaste for American chauvinism? In late 1952 and early 1953 he had travelled extensively in Europe with a close friend of the period, the painter Cy Twombly. Their desire to absorb European culture had symbolic weight at a time when American painting was relatively inward-looking. Italy, and Rome in particular, proved revelatory, and Rauschenberg twice visited the studio of the Rome-based painter Alberto Burri, whose *Sacchi* [21] of the early 1950s, consisting of patched and stitched burlap bags mounted on stretchers, were part of an *informel* movement paralleling that in France.

Italian *informel* had its own distinctive character, particularly in the paintings of Lucio Fontana, who powerfully rearticulated the spatial dynamism of early twentieth-century Italian futurist art by opening up his picture planes via punctures and slashes. But Burri's work, like that of his French contemporaries, had sadistic bodily associations. Tears and bursts in the sacking of certain works appeared to be linked metaphorically to their blood-red colouration [21]. These must surely have affected Rauschenberg's contemporaneous red paintings, to say nothing of *Bed*. Burri's achievements have tended to drop out of general accounts of post-war art, but he was

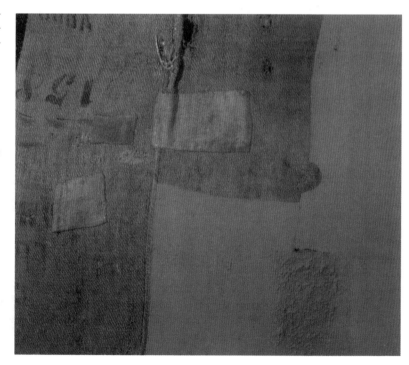

clearly influential internationally. He had several exhibitions in New York in 1953–5 and was accorded a role in Seitz's 1961 assemblage exhibition.

Rauschenberg's travelling companion Twombly also took elements from *informel* art, this time Dubuffet's graffiti vocabulary. Eventually he was to produce paintings marrying the gesturalism of Pollock and de Kooning to inchoate scribbles evoking the splotches, revisions, and erasures of childish script. His commitment to the sensuality of Mediterranean culture, which would lead to his settling permanently in Rome in the early 1960s, is conveyed by an ambivalent tribute to Raphael's Vatican fresco of the *School of Athens* [**22**].

In their embrace of Burri and Dubuffet, Rauschenberg and Twombly were staking out new territory, considering that American critics such as Greenberg, whilst extolling Dubuffet's achievements, nevertheless stressed

the superior virility of American art. In this sense the artists might be seen as strategically importing the private or the visceral into a more stoical or 'manly' avant-garde climate. By 1964 Rauschenberg had been taken up by the American critical establishment, to the extent that its political manoeuvring may have contributed to his winning the prestigious Grand Prize at the Venice Biennale, whilst Twombly was virtually written off by American critics for appearing too 'European'.[15] However, in the early 1950s they both implicitly aligned themselves with the bodily indulgences of *informel* aesthetics. The chauvinism of McCarthy's politics would have been reflected for them in the assertively macho challenge presented by their artistic elders, the Abstract Expressionists.

In 1953–4 it was de Kooning more than anybody else who epitomized the male-centredness of Abstract Expressionism. He was now producing semi-figurative images of women [23] which responded, possibly ironically, to Dubuffet. Whatever his personal attitude may have been—and he talked of savouring the 'fleshy part of art' encapsulated in the tradition of the European nude but of simultaneously wishing to get beyond it to the 'idea of the idol'—such aggressive images could hardly avoid upholding macho stereotypes.[16] This was reinforced by the well-known predilection of certain Abstract Expressionists for hard drinking and domestic violence.

For younger artists who felt ill at ease with such overbearing masculinism, defiance could take forms that were already sanctioned in structures of male avant-garde succession. This is encapsulated in a Duchampian gesture Rauschenberg carried out after his return to America in 1953 implicating de Kooning in an Oedipal scenario. Rauschenberg persuaded the older artist to donate a drawing to him for the purpose of erasure. Whilst de Kooning

Women and the male art world: Lee Krasner

The masculine exclusivity of Abstract Expressionism is made especially clear when considering the effects it had on female artists attempting to work within it. The case of Jackson Pollock's wife, Lee Krasner, is particularly interesting here. The art historian Anne Wagner has shown that, during the height of Pollock's fame in the late 1940s, Krasner's response to his work, the so-called *Little Images* of 1946–9, involved a deliberate muting of his painterly heroics, a kind of self-abnegation necessitated paradoxically by the need to *preserve* her sense of self. (At the time she apparently worked in the cramped conditions of a converted bedroom, whilst Pollock occupied the main studio in their home.)

In the year before Pollock's premature death, Krasner made powerful collages, possibly drawing on the huge semi-abstract paper-cuts that the veteran French Modernist Henri Matisse was producing around this time. In one of these collages she made use of offcuts from her husband's canvases, as if rehearsing the problematics of retaining a separable identity [24]. Later on, at the end of the 1950s, she ironically allowed herself to develop the kind of expansive Abstract Expressionist style she had earlier needed to suppress. The upshot of this account is to show that, as in earlier instances in twentieth-century art, the structural position of female artists, as underwritten by socially and culturally determined frameworks of male–female relations, frequently placed female practitioners in a position of compromise with regard to career interests. This situation was naturally exacerbated, and made acutely vivid, when, like Krasner and Pollock, the artists were married.

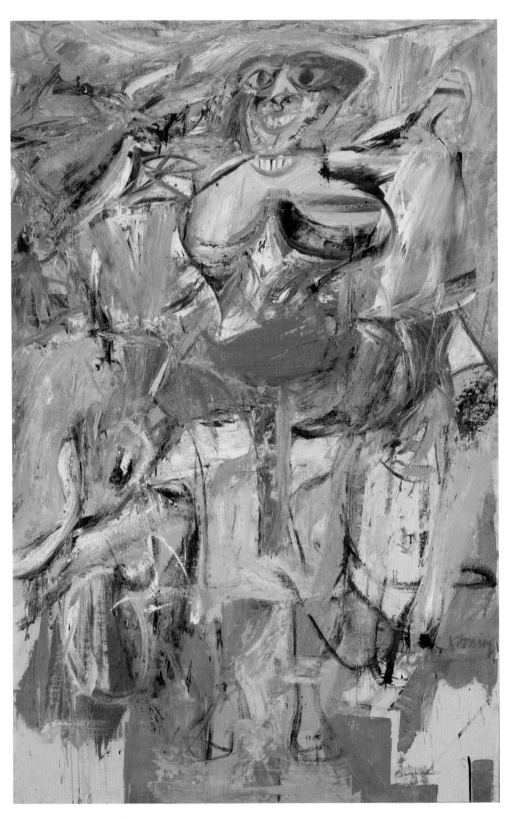

retained some authority by ensuring that the drawing he supplied was stubbornly greasy, the eventual ghostly trace was designated *Erased de Kooning* and signed 'Robert Rauschenberg'. This added a twist to the denial of authorial presence in his earlier *White Paintings*.

However, this gesture symbolically effaced not just the paternal signature but also something of the heterosexual masculinity attaching to it. Although briefly married at the start of the 1950s, Rauschenberg had come to recognize that his sexual orientation was bisexual. The social climate was hardly conducive to this. McCarthyism explicitly correlated homosexuality with Communism to the extent that, during its purges, more homosexuals than communists ended up losing their jobs in the Federal government. In 1954 the young painter Jasper Johns replaced Twombly as Rauschenberg's artistic ally. This was simultaneously the beginning of a romantic relationship between them which, given the sexual mores of the period, quite apart from Abstract Expressionism's obligatory masculinism, would only be expressed through a highly coded pictorial syntax. Duchamp's use of oblique bodily metaphor and authorial indeterminacy again provided a model here. But it was to be Jasper Johns who followed it most closely.

Metaphors of sexual identity: Jasper Johns

Johns's earliest works, which are veritable icons of post-war art, appeared *sui generis*, the artist having destroyed much of his preceding output. He acquired critical success when the art dealer Leo Castelli, invited by Rauschenberg to their shared studio, bought up his entire production, exhibiting it, before Rauschenberg's, in early 1958. Looking at images such as *Target with Plaster Casts* and *Flag* of 1954–5 [**26**, **28**], it is apparent that, quite apart from inheriting Rauschenberg's dissolution of painting/object distinctions via the use of readymade subject matter, Johns's use of compartments in the former owes something to Cornell. His use of public emblems has a more esoteric source in earlier American artists such as Marsden Hartley and Charles Demuth. The latter's painting *I Saw the Number 5 in Gold* of 1928 was essayed in Johns's *Number 5* (1955) and later numbers pictures [**29**].

Hartley and Demuth were both homosexuals, and the latter had been an associate of Duchamp in the New York Dada days. From this Johns's identification with a specific artistic lineage becomes clear. Among Duchamp's strangest gestures had been the creation of a female alter ego, Rrose Sélavy (a verbal pun on 'Eros, c'est la vie'). This figure, whose visual manifestations consisted of photographs by the American artist Man Ray of Duchamp in drag, appeared on the label of the perfume bottle *Belle Haleine/Eau de Voilette* [**25**]. A Dada skit on the cosmetics/hygiene industry, this was simultaneously a succinct formulation of Duchamp's understanding of art as (feminized) consumption as opposed to (masculinized) production, as later exemplified by the *Boîte-en-valise*. Duchamp's sexuality, whilst ostensibly heterosexual, was obviously put into question by this gesture. At the same time his dandyish persona, involving an aristocratic disdain for what he variously deemed the 'splashy' or 'olfactory' side of painting, to say nothing of its retinal associations, won him many gay sympathizers.

In *Target with Plaster Casts* [**26**] Johns seems subtly to have invoked Duchamp. This painting/sculpture sets up a perceptual/conceptual interplay

24 Lee Krasner

Bald Eagle, 1955

Lee Krasner was a central figure of Abstract Expressionism. She trained in the late 1930s with Hans Hofmann, the German painter whose teaching transmitted many of the principles of Modernist abstraction to the New York painters. She was employed on the Federal Art Project and in 1936 met Jackson Pollock, whom she was to marry in 1945. Early accounts of her career emphasized the extent to which she was overshadowed by Pollock. Her work is now beginning to be examined in its own terms.

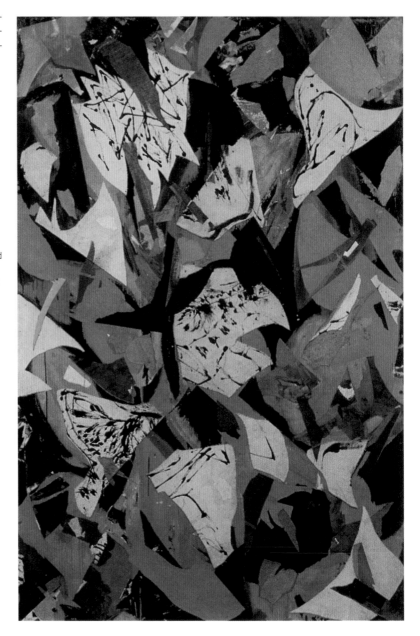

between an exposed (but numberless) target below and a set of closable boxes above containing casts of body parts, which, in certain cases, such as that of the green-painted penis third from right, blatantly signify as 'male'. The allusion seems to be to the Bachelors firing their shots at the Bride in the *Large Glass* [**55**]. More broadly the imagery may dramatize the insecurites of gay identity at a time when homosexuality was virulently proscribed, mobilizing metaphors of sexual 'outing' and 'closeting' or invoking social targeting, as symbolized by the fragmented body parts. In spite of its reticence, it appears to speak volumes about a society obsessed with fantasmatic inner demons and their expulsion. This relates it to Rauschenberg's *Bed* [**19**],

25 Marcel Duchamp and Man Ray

Belle Haleine, Eau de Voilette, 1921

The text on the label punningly translates as 'beautiful breath/veil water'. Duchamp's female alter ego, Rrose Sélavy, peers out from above it.

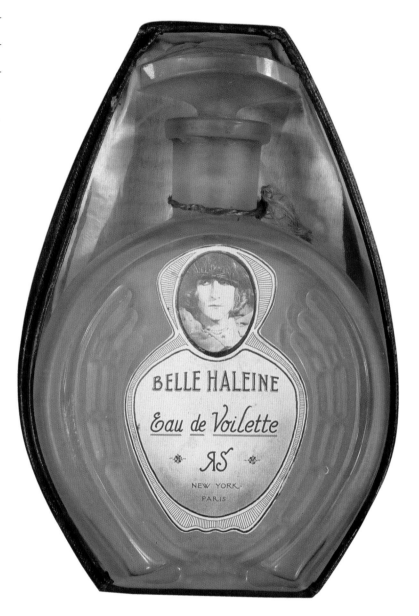

as discussed earlier, and reprises the apocalyptic urgency of the Beat writers, several of whom were gay.

A more intriguing Duchampian parallel is with *Etant Donnés* which, as explained, involved directing the spectator's vision not at a male but at a female sexual organ. Johns must have been aware that, late in 1953, Duchamp had exhibited an enigmatic cast of a body part in New York entitled *Female Fig Leaf*, a positive cast obtained from the pudendum of the 'nude' in *Etant Donnés*. It is unlikely that he knew of Duchamp's secret work on the installation, although John Cage, who was close to both Rauschenberg and Johns, may have known something of it. However, Johns appears to have tracked Duchamp's thought like a detective. Although he did not meet his spiritual mentor until 1959 (the

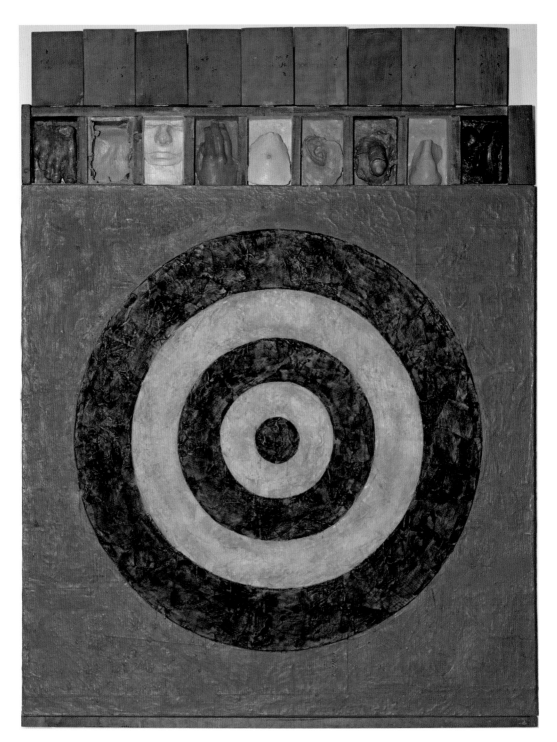

26 Jasper Johns

Target with Plaster Casts,
1955

year, incidentally, when the first book on Duchamp, by Robert Lebel, was published), he could have divined a great deal from the 1945 edition of *View* mentioned earlier. In 1954 much of Duchamp's output, assembled by the collector Walter Arensberg, went on show at the Philadelphia Museum of Art.

I-Box, 1962

Here Morris presented a
small rectangular structure
with a door shaped as a
letter 'I'. When opened,
the door gave on to a
photograph of the artist, his
phallus rhyming with the
'I' connotative both of the
viewer's looking (eye) and
the artist's identity.

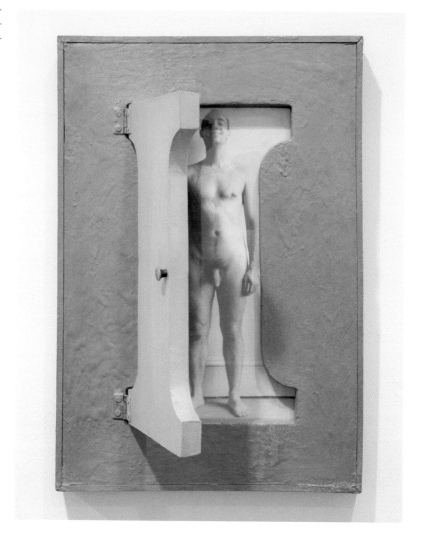

If *Target with Plaster Casts* does indeed transpose the dynamics of
gendered looking from the *Large Glass* and *Etant Donnés* into homoerotic
terms, a coda to this dialogue is provided by a slightly later work of art. The
American sculptor Robert Morris's *I-Box* of 1962 [**27**] was produced at a
yet further stage in the iconographic reception of Duchamp. The latter's
notes for his *Large Glass* were now available in English (the translation
came out in 1960), whilst Johns's *Target*, an echo of a work as yet invisible
to the art community, could be construed as virtually predicting the trajectory of Duchamp's activities. In his voyeuristic *I-Box* Morris surely had
the boxes at the top of Johns's *Target* in mind, but their fragmented contents were seemingly reconstituted in the image of a self-confident and
possibly heterosexual male. The latter point is made tentatively since much
depends on the sexual orientations Morris imagined himself addressing.
And, whilst *I-Box* appears to reverse the terms of *Etant Donnés*, to what
extent may the latter, materializing slowly elsewhere, have responded to

Morris or Johns? There is no clear historical resolution to any of this. What is clear, though, is the sheer elasticity of the gender metaphors Duchamp put into play.

The aesthetics of indifference

The Duchampian model also appealed to Johns, as it did to Rauschenberg, for its anti-Modernist potential. Once again, de Kooning becomes pivotal here. His return to the figure in the early 1950s [23], a return paralleled in the work of numerous contemporaries dubious about the faith Newman or Rothko placed in abstraction's ability to embody content, was seen by Modernist critics, notably Greenberg, as a failure of aesthetic nerve. Greenberg eventually coined the poetic phrase 'homeless representation' to describe de Kooning's adaptation of 'descriptive painterliness...to abstract ends'.[17]

Looking at Johns's *Flag* [28], in which the American flag is taken as the subject for a painting/collage, one sees his response to the discontents brewing in the Greenberg camp. Quite simply, it is impossible here to separate out the representational content of the image from its insistence on functioning as a flatly abstract Modernist painting. The paradox is set up by Johns's use of a pre-designed, two-dimensional sign as his subject. He would subsequently move on to making use of letters and numbers, generically described by him as 'things the mind already knows'. Such entities might be thought to have some substantial existence, but in fact hover somewhere between physical and conceptual states. They are, in this sense, *homeless*. Johns therefore established that it *was* possible to make 'homeless' representations, subtly pre-empting

28 Jasper Johns
Flag, 1954–5

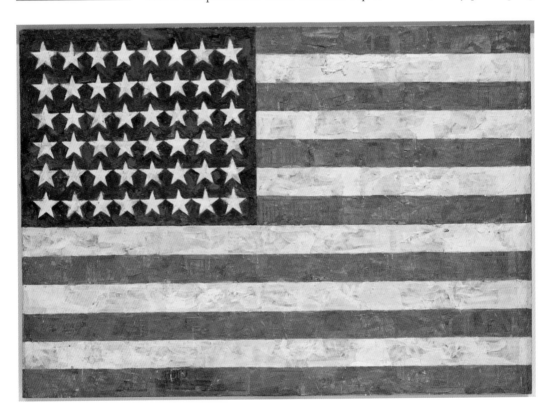

Greenberg's difficulty with late Abstract Expressionism, although hardly, in terms of his banal subject matter, endorsing de Kooning.

If *Flag* reintroduced a kind of phantom-like conceptual subject matter into the Modernist painterly field, while simultaneously preserving the all-over integrity of it, Johns further ironized matters by supplying the image with an encaustic 'skin'. As with other paintings by Johns of this period, *Flag* utilized an unusual technique in which encaustic (pigment mixed with hot wax) was laid over a base of torn newspaper fragments. The use of a painterly medium which quickly solidified as the wax cooled ensured that the autographic mark was effectively frozen before it could achieve its full expansiveness.

Johns would have been aware that chance was one of Duchamp's principal means of short-circuiting his aesthetic habits, or introducing curbs on his expressivity. Duchamp had, for instance, permitted dust to build up on the lower section of his *Large Glass* [**18**] to determine part of its colouration (indeed, the *Glass* in its entirety became for Duchamp a 'delay in glass' rather than a consolidated art object). It seems, then, that Johns also used a principle of delay to interrogate the spontaneity of the Abstract Expressionist mark. In a painted construction of 1960 entitled *Painting with Two Balls*, this critique was allied to a scornful disdain for Abstract Expressionism's masculinism. Two small wooden balls were inserted into a gap manfully prising apart a canvas filled with embalmed painterly gestures. Johns thereby communicated an anxiety that, at any minute, the Modernist field might snap shut.

A further point occurs in relation to *Flag*: this is the evident sense of concealment arising from the use of a newspaper base. Here and there suggestive bits of newspaper show through the encaustic as though contemporary events are metaphorically being screened out.[18] Given that 1950s America was obsessed with concealment and exposure, Johns's procedures seem entirely apt. It is revealing, though, that Johns replicated the social evasions of the period when, in later interviews, he accounted for the genesis of *Flag*. He said that the idea for it came to him 'in a dream', as though downplaying his volition and relegating its origins to the unconscious, the province of Surrealism. This might seem disingenuous. The American flag could hardly have been more charged with political significance than it was at the height of the Cold War, and Johns's work appears to encode a mute ambivalence towards its authority. However, the flag was surely an active symbol in the collective or national unconscious. This generates precisely the kind of ambiguity regarding his artistic intentions that Johns relished.

Johns's indeterminate position with respect to the imposition of aesthetic or social readings from the outside has been shown by the art historian Moira Roth to arise from an 'aesthetics of indifference' uniting Johns, Rauschenberg, and John Cage. Unlike Abstract Expressionists such as Newman or Motherwell, these artists' fascination with Duchamp's dandyism predisposed them to avoid overt political alignments.[19] The sheer ambiguity cultivated by Johns in this respect is exemplified by a series of works from the late 1950s onward in which innocuous sequences of numbers were put through a series of painted and drawn variations [**29**]. The sequences were stepped such that they read horizontally, diagonally, and often vertically.

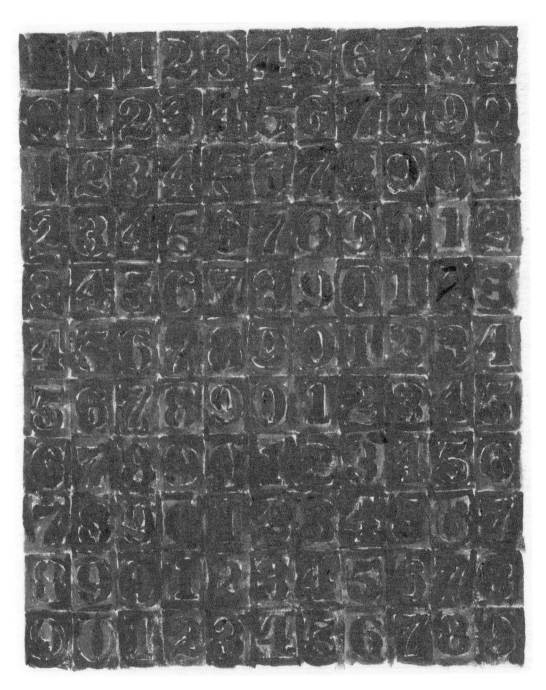

They thus replaced the arbitrary subjectivity embodied in the Abstract Expressionist painted surface with a self-evidently logical means of getting from one side of the pictorial field to the other. With such a system in place, Johns paradoxically freed himself to work around the numbers, courting the picture surface as devotedly as de Kooning. Roth emphasizes, however, that one could easily see the numbers as obliquely keyed to McCarthyism. Numerical sequences often acquired occult significance in the trials for spying, where 'codes were constantly on the verge of being cracked'.[20] It becomes clear that the numbers resist being counted, so to speak, on either interpretative side. They work, as Fred Orton has said of *Flag*, precisely 'in the space of difference', failing to confirm either one reading or another.[21]

There were, however, flickers of overt political comment in the larger artistic environment in New York. It tends to be overlooked that in 1953 another painter concerned with realigning subject matter with abstraction, Larry Rivers, produced a small critical storm with his *Washington Crossing the Delaware*. Painted in an irresolute, sketch-like manner, it loosely referred to a kitsch, academic icon of patriotism with the same title produced by Emanuel Leutze in 1851. This episode demonstrates that not all avant-garde practice in this period projected a paralysis of political will. Although figurative and more conservative formally than Johns's work, Rivers's image conveyed a polemical disrespect for a picture that was ubiquitous in America's schoolrooms.

It also gets overlooked that Duchamp, however aloof from worldly affairs he appeared, had similarly produced a work on the subject of George Washington. This was a collage entitled *Allégorie de genre* which *Vogue* magazine solicited for a competition to produce a cover portrait of George Washington for their 'Americana' edition of February 1943. Duchamp's solution conjured the images of Washington's profile and a map of America from a section of shrivelled bandage gauze. This had been stained with iodine, to evoke dual connotations of wounds and the stripes of the American flag, and studded with a scattering of disconsolate fake stars. Given that the gesture appeared to reflect on America's entry into the Second World War, it was, unsurprisingly, rejected. Duchamp, it seems, had come too uncomfortably close to anti-patriotism for the America that was eventually to adopt him as its own (he took up citizenship in 1947). Johns may easily have seen Duchamp's collage since it was reproduced in *VVV*, an American surrealist magazine, in 1944. Perhaps Johns forgot it. Twelve years later his *Flag* painting embalmed criticism of the state in ambiguities.

Readymades and replications

In 1960, as part of a then ongoing sequence of small-scaled sculptures, Johns produced *Painted Bronze (Ale Cans)*, in which casts taken from two beer cans appear on a plinth. This represented a new phase in Johns's reception of Duchamp, which now centred more squarely on the implications of the readymades. Rauschenberg and, to a lesser degree, Larry Rivers had long ago ushered commodified imagery into art, reflecting America's post-war consumer boom, but Johns's beer cans were more essentially esoteric. By succinctly turning the readymade or mass-produced back into art, as symbolized both by the pedestal on which the objects stood and by the utilization of the time-honoured sculptural process of bronze casting, Johns raised conceptual conundrums about the relationship between uniqueness and sameness. This is further dramatized by the way that the labels of the twinned objects were hand-painted to emphasize differences between them. In addition, one of the cast cans was 'opened' whilst the other remained 'sealed'.

Such gestures were seemingly reciprocated by Duchamp's own attention to issues surrounding readymades and replication in the 1960s. Showing some annoyance with the recent cult for Neo-Dada, he wrote, in 1962, to an old Dada ally, Hans Richter, complaining about the aestheticizing of his readymades. They had, he asserted, been thrown into the public's face in a spirit of defiance. However much interpreters felt he had elevated everyday objects to the status of art, he now declared that the readymades had been selected in a spirit of absolute indifference. Their whole anti-aesthetic rationale turned on the fact that they lacked uniqueness.[22] He may well have been reformulating past attitudes here to keep ahead of developments around him. However, questions relating to the paradoxical originality and reproducibility of the readymades had preoccupied him earlier. In a series of notes of the 1930s on a pseudoscientific category called 'infra-thin' he had speculated, in almost metaphysical fashion, on infinitesimal differences or thresholds between physical states. One example reads: 'The difference / (dimensional) between / 2 mass produced objects / [from the same mould] is an "infra thin".'[23] Without knowledge of this note, Johns paralleled it with his cans.

Duchamp pushed the consequences of reproducibility to a perverse conclusion when, in 1964, he authorized the Galleria Schwarz in Milan to produce limited editions (of eight signed and numbered copies) of fourteen readymades, each an 'original' from the same mould. There was probably a connection in Duchamp's mind here between the ironic individuality of mass-produced items and other examples of the infra-thin interface between moulds and casts such as the strange positive cast, taken from the pudendum

30 Sherrie Levine

Fountain (After Marchel Duchamp), 1991

Levine had pursued her dialogue with Duchamp in another direction in an installation of 1989 at Mary Boone's New York gallery entitled *The Bachelors (After Marcel Duchamp)*. Small frosted-glass versions of the Bachelors from Duchamp's *Large Glass* [**18**] were placed in a series of vitrines. Duchamp had conceived of his Bachelors as 'moulds' waiting to be filled. By transposing his diagrammatic prototypes into three-dimensional terms, Levine poignantly emphasized their emptiness and isolation.

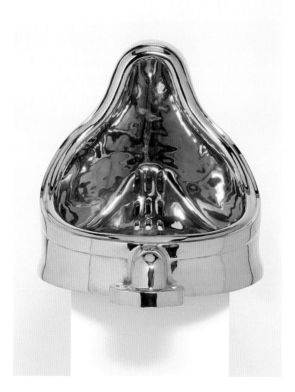

of the *Etant Donnés* mannequin, mentioned earlier. (Johns in fact acquired a version of this cast.) Quite apart from examples in Johns's work, the 1960s was to see many artists taking up body casting, exploiting all the poignant indexical traces or imprints of life created by such processes. These included the American sculptor George Segal and the French artist Yves Klein, who will be discussed in Chapter 3.

It was not until the 1980s, however, that artists registered the full consequences of the Duchampian concern with replication. The American Sherrie Levine, who specialized in appropriating pre-existing works of art by male Masters, made subtly ironic comments on the in-house masculinism of the Duchampian tradition by feminizing its imagery. In 1991 she produced a whole series of urinals with polished bronze surfaces, wittily re-enacting Johns's translation of the readymade principle back into art in his *Painted Bronze (Ale Cans)*. At the same time she made sophisticated allusions to the polished modernist sculptures of Constantin Brancusi, whose work Duchamp had helped sell, thereby projecting a combined aura of sex and commercial gloss onto what now seemed a rather dour original urinal [**30**]. Another 1980s artist, Robert Gober, produced a sculpture of two urinals side by side [**31**]. The fact that Gober's imagery often alluded to homosexuality had the effect of reclaiming Duchamp for masculinity, but a masculinity, of course, closer to that of artists such as Duchamp's arch-mediator, Jasper Johns, whose twinned ale cans Gober also echoed.

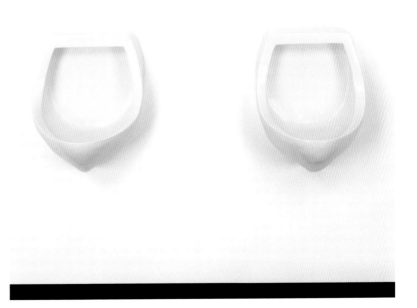

31 Robert Gober

Two Urinals, 1986

These highly stylized, non-utilitarian versions of plumbing fixtures evoke complex psychosexual concerns surrounding issues of hygiene and male bonding. At the same time, they participate in a witty dialogue with Jasper Johns's famous bronze cast of two ale cans, *Painted Bronze*, of 1960. Johns's cans themselves referred both to Duchamp and to the macho drinking culture of Abstract Expressionism. Gober thus brings an entire dialogue concerning male social/artistic camaraderie full circle.

Such metaphorical fine-tunings to the tradition of the readymade have turned into a rather monotonous endgame. Perhaps, more sympathetically, the process could be linked to the notion of genre. In Holland over the course of the seventeenth century, still life came to be constituted as a genre, a category of subject matter which painters could knowingly manipulate. The tradition of the readymade may have analogies. But the larger agendas set for post-war art by Duchamp, such as the concern with the gendered relation between the object and the spectator or the probing of the relationship between the original and the replica, hardly constitute genres in certain fundamental respects. They are not attached to specific kinds of objects, subjects, or techniques. Instead they rely on the dynamics of conceptual innovation. It is in this elusive area, resistant to conventional aesthetic criteria, that Duchamp had the greatest historical impact.

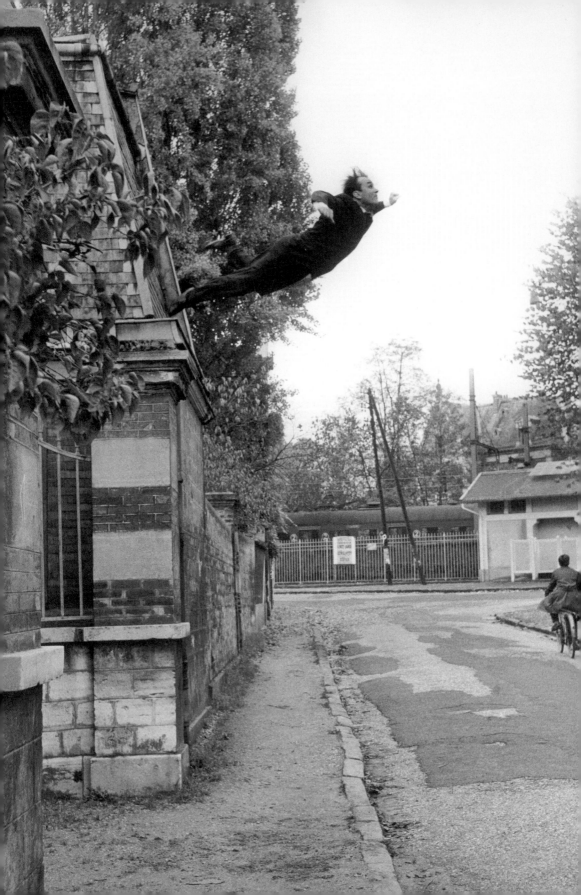

The Artist
in Crisis

From Bacon to Beuys

3

The image of the artist bequeathed to the post-war avant-gardes was a fundamentally heroic one. Whether Picasso's mercurial shifts of style, Duchamp's cerebral dandyism, or Mondrian's universalizing abstract vision were taken as benchmarks, the modernist artist was broadly understood to possess a superior sensibility. This model largely persisted after 1945. Photographs of Jackson Pollock by Hans Namuth depict him as haunted and brooding, a prototypical nonconformist. But societal changes slowly modulated the sense of the artist's special status. The cultural value attaching to the concept of uniqueness, for instance, was insidiously eroded by commodity production and the rise of reproductive technologies. How did artists register such changes? This chapter aims to provide some answers.

Bound up with artists' sense of self was their sense of what it is to be human. The previous chapters have largely concentrated on how American avant-gardists navigated between the competing aesthetic positions of Greenberg and Duchamp. In the process overtly human themes, alongside politics, often dropped out of their art. In general, it tended to be artists in European countries who reinvented humanist iconographies.

Humanism and individualism: British and French figuration in the 1950s

In Britain at mid-century the work of the sculptors Barbara Hepworth and Henry Moore had secured the country an international art profile it had lacked since the nineteenth century. Moore's figurative sculptures in particular managed to combine a universalizing rhetoric with a deep-rooted English inwardness and insularity. The best of his work, exemplified by the *Working Model for Reclining Figure* of 1951 [**32**], looked outward to the lessons of previous European avant-gardes and their primitivist models, although the formal risks of late constructivist sculpture, or Picasso's barbaric bodily distortions, were softened by a classically derived vision of bodily equilibrium. By contrast, it looked inward to the reassertion of 'timeless' national values—particularly those supposedly embodied in the English countryside—required by a country both victorious and depleted after the war. In tune with much Neo-Romantic imagery in British culture of this period, Moore evoked the archetypes of an island-bound race: rocks eroded by the tides, crustaceans emerging inquisitively from their shells. But if he spoke metaphorically of resilience and native caution, he was capable, at his

Detail of 39

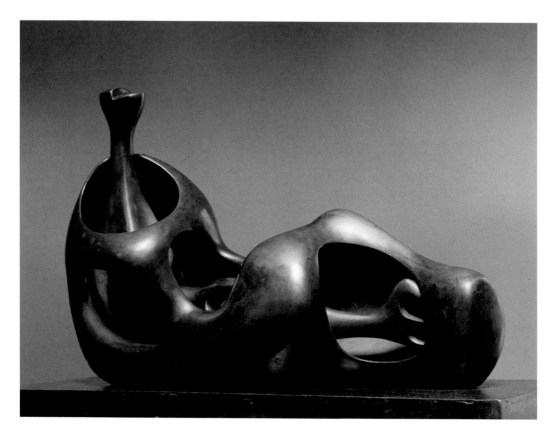

worst, of blandness. The outdoor *King and Queen* sculpture at Glenkiln in Scotland is perhaps a case in point.

Moore became the acceptable face of modernism for the post-war British establishment, whilst his commercial success was consolidated in New York with a retrospective at the Museum of Modern Art in 1946. His public sculptures—large, chunky semi-abstractions, cast in bronze, raised on plinths—ironically connoted 'tradition' located in front of Bauhaus-style buildings. However, his liberalism and sense of public duty, which probably compromised the quality of later productions, might be seen as reflective of the egalitarian ethos of the Labour government of the immediate post-war years. On the basis of the Beveridge Report of 1942, this administration laid the foundations for the welfare state with the National Health Service as its centrepiece. The Arts Council of Great Britain was formed in 1946. Moore's civic humanism, his capitulation, as a modernist, to the cultural liberalism of centralized state socialism, can be contrasted starkly with the intense introspection of the painter Francis Bacon. In 1946 Bacon's *Three Studies for Figures at the Base of a Crucifixion* received its public debut at the Lefevre Gallery, London. Depicting three Picassoesque hybrids united, in the critic John Russell's words, by a 'mindless voracity...a ravening undifferentiated capacity for hatred',[1] it represented the antithesis to Moore's magnanimity.

Unlike Moore, Bacon extracted a violent, anti-humanist message from Surrealism, mainly by turning, like certain *informel* painters in France, to the example of one of its dissident figures, Georges Bataille. In texts published

In formal terms, this sculpture manages to harmonize the claims of an aspiring, organic element within and the protective, enveloping characteristics of an outer casing. This is achieved via Moore's signature 'holes'. Moore's ability to reconcile humanist iconography with the stringent formal demands of modernism was almost unprecedented in post-war British sculpture, but, in the mid-1980s, his legacy was, to some extent, taken up in the work of Antony Gormley who produced metal casts from the human body (often his own), siting them in unexpected locations such as beaches. When, in 1998, Gormley's huge public sculpture 'The Angel of the North' was erected outside Gateshead in the North of England, Gormley fully emerged as Moore's heir in terms of his attempt to produce humanist emblems for the industrial age.

in the journal *Documents*, copies of which Bacon later owned, Bataille had established a sense of the human as not so much elevated above, but rather coexistent with, the bestial. 'On great occasions', he wrote, 'human life is concentrated bestially in the mouth... the stricken individual... frantically lifts up his head, so that the mouth comes to be placed... in the extension of the vertebral column, that is to say the position it normally occupies in the animal constitution.'[2] As Dawn Ades has shown, Bacon's recurring images of the wide-open mouth in paintings from 1948 to 1955, deriving also from Eisenstein's film *Battleship Potemkin* and Poussin, encapsulate this viewpoint.[3] However, this quotation equally illuminates Bacon's remarkable animal depictions, which tend, ironically, to receive less attention than those of humans [**33**]. Preferring photographs to actual models—often from the late nineteenth-century photographer Muybridge—Bacon followed futurist or Duchampian precedents in incorporating motion into these images. Photographic traces of spasmodic animal movement were translated into flicks or flurries of paint.

Paradoxically, though, Bacon was a traditionalist, painting with the bravura of Velasquez or Rembrandt in an age increasingly attuned to media imagery. In interviews he elaborated on the brinksmanship required to 'trap' images, often via photographic mediation, at the point where they encoded the very pulse of nervous energy. This desire, as he said, to 'return the onlooker to life more violently'[4] should be distinguished from his occasional use of explicitly violent subject matter, reflective of post-Holocaust human pessimism. In later paintings such as *Study for a Portrait of Lucian Freud (Sideways)* (1971), intensities of paintwork, articulating or cancelling the figures they represent, are located in large swathes of Matisse-like colour or raw canvas, crossed by elegant linear arcs, which read as schematized interiors. Sparse props, often incongruously streamlined furnishings, accompany Bacon's figures. He had been a successful designer of modernist tubular steel chairs and rugs in the 1930s. However different his intentions from Moore's, his figures are frequently offset against the utopian uniformities of high Modernist abstraction and design. On this level at least there may be a residual humanism.

As a painter of the isolated figure, Bacon also evinced a fiercely individualist artistic position. In this he was similar to the younger Lucian Freud, who, eschewing Bacon's reliance on photographs or memory, opted for an unremitting painterly interrogation of the live model. His hyperrealist style, partly reliant on the *Neue Sachlichkeit* (new objectivity) of German art in the 1920s, can be seen in his 1951 *Interior* at *Paddington* [**34**]. His razor-sharp, hallucinatory realism was inherently at odds with left-wing injunctions towards forms of socially committed realism; such a position in any case seemed untenable to many, and Albert Camus's *The Rebel*, translated into English in 1953, helped foster anti-bourgeois convictions in artists, in the absence of political faith in Communism. By 1959 the critic John Berger, who had previously supported socially oriented art, acknowledged that an individualistic revelation of the real constituted in itself ideological opposition towards the status quo.[5] Like the Expressionist-oriented painters Frank Auerbach and Leon Kossoff, who emerged in London in the late 1950s, Freud became increasingly immersed in the pragmatics of a perceptual and emotional struggle with the motif. An underlying respect for hard-won

33 Francis Bacon

33 Francis Bacon

Study of a Baboon, 1953

Bacon habitually used unprimed canvases which allowed him to drag his paint across the weave, producing raw, textured marks. He dispensed with preliminary drawing (although a few preparatory drawings have recently come to light) and occasionally utilized chance processes, such as throwing paint-filled sponges at the canvas, in order to suggest images. The materials used for his central motifs normally differed from those used for the backgrounds. Oil paints, thinned with turpentine or enhanced with pastel, were used for the former, acrylics or emulsion house paints for the latter.

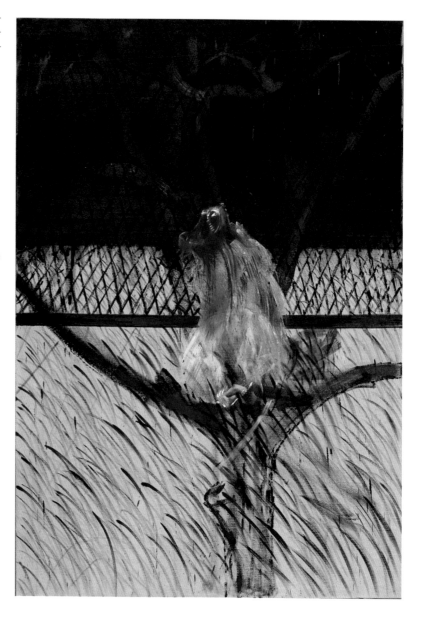

34 Lucian Freud

Interior at *Paddington*, 1951

The spiky yucca plant has the same intense presence as the haunted, Sartrean young man. All details are given equal weight, suggesting that the democratizing plenitude of photographic vision has some role for Freud.

observational skills and a basic suspicion towards the modernist cult of innovation went hand in hand with disdain for the public 'message'.

The individualist ethics of the School of London were rooted in the reception of existentialist principles from France. These were mainly transmitted to artists through the work of Alberto Giacometti, a Swiss-born sculptor who had been a surrealist up until the mid-1930s and then converted, dramatically, to working from life. Giacometti's mythical status was founded on legends of his driven persona as much as his anxiety-laden work. Whereas Moore's sculpture essentially derived from carving, Giacometti was a modeller who obsessively kneaded and whittled his spindly clay figures until they distilled complex or contradictory spatial apprehensions. His influential interpreter

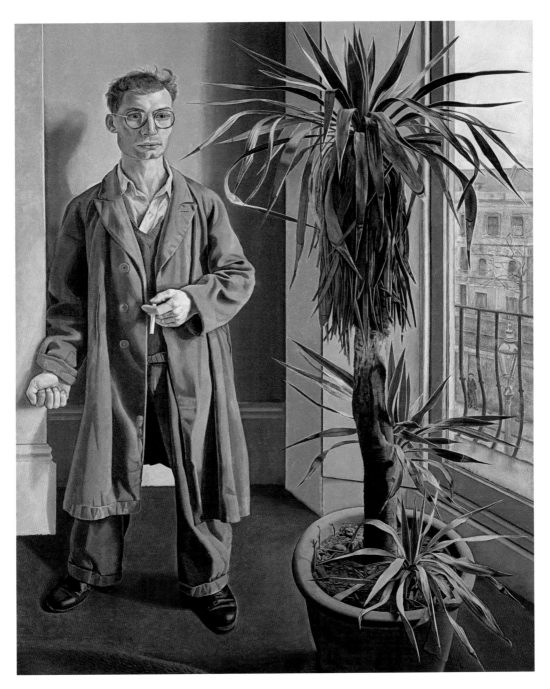

from 1941 onwards, Jean-Paul Sartre, described this process: 'He knows that space is a cancer on being, and eats everything; to sculpt, for him, is to take the fat off space.'[6] Implicitly questioning the reassuring givens of perspective, Giacometti repeatedly attempted to express the fragile contingency of his perceptual relations to his models, describing, for instance, how a model in his studio 'grew and simultaneously receded to a tremendous distance'.[7] The immobility of the figure in a drawing of 1955, in which lines bind the joints of

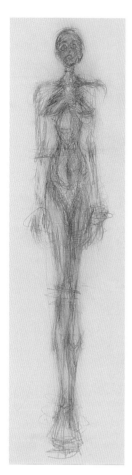

the body like wire [**35**], indicates that Giacometti's thinking was also inflected by Maurice Merleau-Ponty's *Phenomenology of Perception* (1945). Writing much later, the psychoanalyst Jacques Lacan might almost be registering the frozen, hieratic look on this figure's face when, glossing Merleau-Ponty, he describes 'the dependence of the visible on that which places us under the eye of the seer... this seeing to which I am subjected'.[8]

The period 1948–53 saw Giacometti establishing himself with dealers in both Paris and New York, and his British reputation, largely an outcome of the critic David Sylvester's advocacy, was consolidated with an Arts Council exhibition in 1955. In that year another French sculptor, Germaine Richier, achieved considerable critical impact in London with an exhibition at the Hanover Gallery. The 'masculine' qualities of her bronzes—their unabashed dialogue with Rodin's full-scale figures, their rugged, scarred surfaces and violent deformations—troubled critics, in Britain as in France, not least because of set assumptions about the imagery expected of women artists [**36**]. However, the work Richier produced in the late 1940s and early 1950s possibly had a greater formal impact on others than that of Giacometti. The latter's angst could be appropriated, but hardly his style. By contrast, Richier's morbid allegory, and the anti-humanist implications of her animal and insect imagery, had some take-up in the spiky, skeletal forms of British sculptors such as Lynn Chadwick, Reg Butler, and Eduardo Paolozzi. Exhibiting collectively at the Venice Biennale of 1952, they were said to manifest a 'Geometry of Fear' by the veteran critic Herbert Read. This was an evocative coinage. Britain acquired nuclear weapons in that year, following the example of the Russians in 1949.

Whether European figuration of the 1950s saw man as embodying the principles of existential choice, popularly available in Sartre's pamphlet *Existentialism and Humanism* (1946), or of bestial irrationality, as in the Bataillean concerns of Bacon, this period saw the demise of a related notion—the artist as tragic genius. Certainly, isolated or eccentric figures abounded. In many ways the frenetic late drawings of the former surrealist Antonin Artaud, produced just after the war had ended and comparable to works by Fautrier or Wols discussed in Chapter 1, had set the tone for this apotheosis of the *artiste maudit*. Hospitalized at the psychiatric asylum at Rodez in France during 1943–6, Artaud identified himself with Van Gogh, producing self-images manifesting a fierce desire to burst the bounds of identity. Asserting the rights of the body over the mind, Artaud wrote: 'The human face is temporarily, / and I say temporarily, / all that is left of the demand, / of the *revolutionary* demand of a body that is not yet and was never in keeping with this face.'[9] Frantic, he gouged out the eyes of one self-image, in an attempt to reach his internal other.[10] A slightly later self-image, its surface bruised and blotched from reworkings, exudes a hard-won dignity [**37**].

Artaud's drawings, linked as they were to his writings, have only recently gained recognition. However, by the end of the 1950s, when MoMA in New York surveyed the figuration of the period in its *New Images of Man* exhibition, intense subjectivism was beginning to look dated. Peter Selz, in the exhibition catalogue, asserted that 'the act of showing forth these effigies takes the place of political and moral philosophy'.[11] Forgetful of

Having originally been
taught by a pupil of Rodin
and by the Paris-based
sculptor Antoine Bourdelle,
Richier produced work in a
classical vein before the
Second World War. After the
war her work changed
markedly. Her figures
appeared traumatized.
Often they seemed to be
emerging from a larval
condition. Their limbs
looked strangely amphibian.

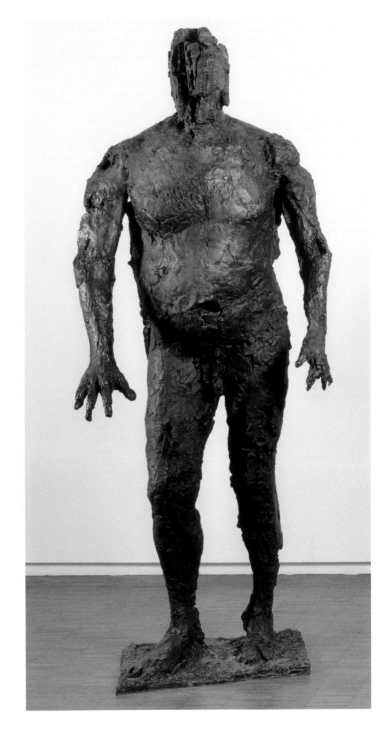

the fact that Abstract Expressionism's glory and failure had rested on these
terms, and seemingly insensitive to the difficult moral decisions that had
recently informed European individualism, he made figuration look complicit with America's neutralized political status quo. A few years later, in

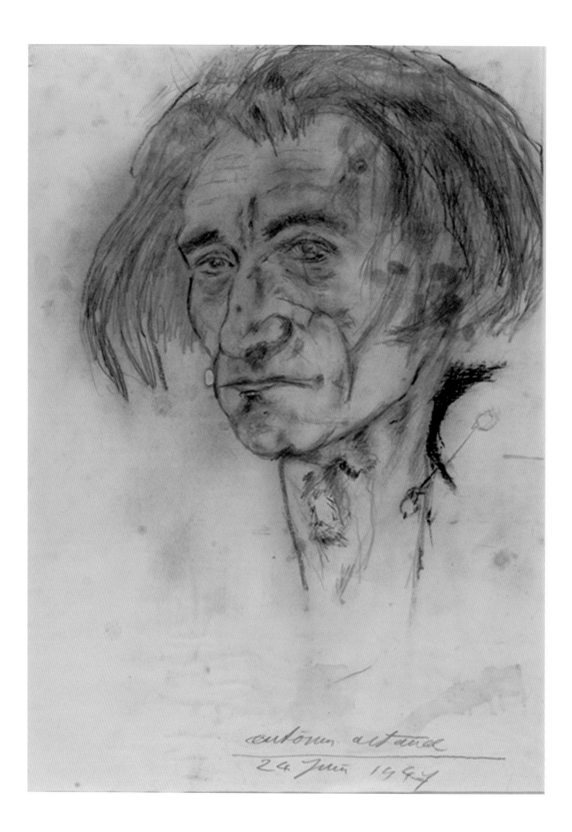

antonin artaud
24 Juin 1947

Artaud's late drawings have been a comparatively recent discovery. His poetry and writings on the theatre were better known previously. In the latter respect, his notions of catharsis had a decisive impact on the Body Art of the 1970s (see Chapter 6). After the Second World War, and long spells of confinement in asylums, Artaud marked his return to Paris with a legendary performance at the Vieux-Colombier theatre in 1947. With some of the great literary figures of the day sitting in the audience, he emitted screams, curses, and guttural incantations.

France, one of the doyens of post-Structuralist philosophy, Michel Foucault, was to claim that the humanist notion of man, on which Selz's claims had ultimately rested, was merely an outcome of bourgeois liberal ideology. 'Man', Foucault claimed, 'is an invention of recent date. And one perhaps nearing its end.'[12] The notion of a deep-rooted artistic subjectivity was similarly in crisis.

Art and commodity: New Realism

In the late 1950s France changed dramatically. The Algerian uprisings of mid-1954, leading to the independence of that country in 1962, signalled the end of French colonial power. Simultaneously American financial aid, under the Marshall Plan, set in motion a massive acceleration of state-led modernization, hand in hand with a new consumer ethos. By American standards the boom in consumption was modest: in 1961 one in eight people in France owned a car, compared to three in eight in America, but cinema in particular propagated images of the luxury-filled utopia to come. The literary theorist Roland Barthes was among the first to respond to the plethora of semiotic codings operative within this new advertising-led culture. His *Mythologies* of 1957, a collection of previously published essays, wittily discerned deep-seated social prejudices and aspirations at work in mass imagery—the latest detergents, women's magazines, margarine, the face of Garbo. Artistic responses were ambivalent. The idea of appealing to an increasingly mobilized and class-variegated audience spoke to an anti-elitist avant-garde dream. At the same time artists had to compete with a fast social turnover of imagery and a decline in their audience's attention spans. Galleries could hardly compete with cinemas.

The *Nouveau Réaliste* (New Realist) movement partly responded to this, although the group as a whole was of less consequence than its individual members: Yves Klein, Arman (born Armand Fernandez), Jean Tinguely, and Daniel Spoerri pre-eminently. Group solidarity was briefly achieved when their main critical advocate, Pierre Restany, issued a manifesto in April 1960 asserting that, since easel-painting was moribund, a 'passionate adventure of the real' was called for. Broadly speaking, this constituted a long-overdue French reassessment of Dada, particularly the Duchampian readymade. In 1959 Duchamp, on a visit to France, met Tinguely and Spoerri. Subsequently his spirit presided over a cluster of international exchanges between the New Realists and the American Neo-Dadaists, Johns and Rauschenberg. It was in America that several of the New Realists cemented their reputations (French galleries were slow to respond to new trends), but their name was quickly appropriated, and their achievements assimilated into America's burgeoning Pop tendency, when they were shown alongside the likes of Warhol at *The New Realists* exhibition at Sidney Janis's New York gallery in 1962. (They had also been represented in *The Art of Assemblage* at MoMA the previous year.) After this, and in the wake of Klein's premature death in June 1962, the group gradually dissolved. However, their responses to consumerism were prescient, not least because they reflected a wariness of the tokens of capitalism.

Representative examples were Arman's series of *Accumulations*—boxes filled with identical readymade objects in various states of wear and tear, which responded to issues of overproduction and built-in obsolescence, distilling a poetics of premature ageing and flawed uniformity [**38**]. In dialectical fashion Arman offset his *Accumulations* with his *Poubelles* ('trash cans') consisting of transparent containers filled with garbage. This trash, incidentally, found its own level through the anti-aesthetic utilization of gravity as an organizing principle, but nevertheless had exact social origins; titles included *Household Rubbish* (1960) and *Small Bourgeois Trash* (1959). In October 1960 Arman and his friends filled Iris Clert's Paris gallery with refuse. The work's title, *Le Plein* ('Full Up'), astutely responded to an equally notorious and carefully stage-managed event of two years earlier by Arman's friend, Yves Klein. This consisted of the emptying and whitewashing of the same space, under the title *Le Vide* ('The Void'). Klein's mystical gesture was a manifesto of immateriality, a concept central to his thinking. Arman countered this with the all-too-material detritus of mass production.

A materialist poetics was further manifested in the output of Daniel Spoerri. Combining the readymade principle with a respect for the laws of chance stemming from Dada, Spoerri began to produce *Tableaux-pièges* ('Snare-pictures') in the late 1950s. These pieces, initially reflecting his own impoverished lifestyle, dealt with consumption of a rudimentary kind. The leftovers of a (usually modest) meal on a tabletop—plates, cutlery, as well as crusts and so on—would be permanently affixed in position, and the entire ensemble hoisted vertically to hang on the wall. In 1962 Spoerri adapted the principle to book format in *An Anecdoted Topography of Chance*. At the back of the book, an elaborate numbered diagram maps the debris on a table in his hotel room on 17 October 1961. Using this, the reader reconstitutes the histories of humble objects, aided by the author's associations and a series of footnote annotations by Spoerri's associates in the Fluxus movement (see Chapter 4). The entry for a pin begins: 'Pin from a spectacularly folded new grey sports shirt, bought at the Uniprix on the Avenue GÉNÉRAL LECLERC for 20 francs, after being insulted by the salesgirl because I didn't know my size.'[13] This may be a humorous harbinger of taxonomic practices within Conceptual Art. However, Spoerri's attention to the minutiae of human waste constitutes an obliquely critical response to his times. Underlying this is a certain nostalgia, which bypasses the harder realities of art's changing relation to its public.

The commodification of spirituality: Yves Klein

Of all the New Realists Yves Klein most acutely registered the inexorable changes in art's societal role. He was a mixture of self-appointed messiah and self-aggrandizing showman. Like Salvador Dalí, he set out to sell himself. That he appeared to sell off the hard-earned freedoms of avant-gardism, not least its spiritual reserves, has troubled many commentators.

Klein was almost childishly romantic, a lover of cults and rituals. Aged twenty, he became devoted to Rosicrucianism, having contacted a Californian sect immersed in the principles of Max Heindel's *The Rosicrucian Cosmoconception* (1937). Their beliefs—which were only tangentially related to those of the hermetic seventeenth-century Rosicrucian Brotherhood—emphasized an evolution from the current materially bound epoch to a future age of pure spirit. They saw empty space as spiritually replete, whilst matter constituted

38 Arman

In Limbo, 1961

Whilst implicitly
acknowledging the
Surrealism of Cornell [20],
Arman possibly evokes
Barthes's mournful vision
of commodified toys as
expressed in the latter's
book *Mythologies* (1957).
Barthes wrote that in the
consumerist era, rather than
becoming worn through
affection, the mechanical
doll disappears 'behind the
hernia of a broken spring'.

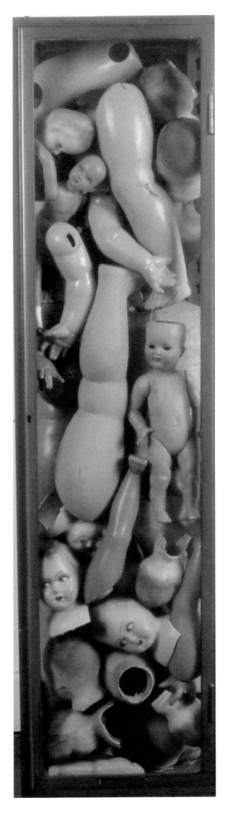

crystallized space. It was the responsibility of initiates to enlighten their brethren. Klein thus conceived of himself as the prophet of a liberating 'immateriality'. His *Le Vide*, mentioned earlier, obviously embodied the notion of a spiritually energized emptiness. (Zen Buddhism, which Klein became aware of on a trip to Japan in 1952–3, similarly embraces 'nothingness'. Cage and Rauschenberg, it will be recalled, were utilizing Zen principles in America at this time.) Similarly, Klein's late photo-manipulation *The Painter of Space Hurls Himself into the Void* [39] pictured the artist as the avatar of human potentiality: Heindel's followers envisaged an age when men would levitate. To add to all this, Klein loved Catholicism and religious fetishism; he was a lifelong devotee of Saint Rita of Cascia.

Conversely, Klein loved fakery and the artificial. Like Duchamp and the post-Abstract Expressionist generation in the US, he distrusted the arbitrary integrity of the Expressionist gesture. He encapsulates a growing tiredness

39 Yves Klein

Single Day Newspaper (November 27th 1960), incorporating a photograph captioned *The Painter of Space Hurls Himself into The Void*

Klein's leap took its place among texts advertising an imaginary *Theatre of the Void*. The image wittily pitted Klein's artistic apotheosis against other newsworthy material of the day. The first Soviet and American space launches had occurred during 1957–9, whilst Klein pre-empted the first man in space, the Russian Yuri Gagarin, by six months.

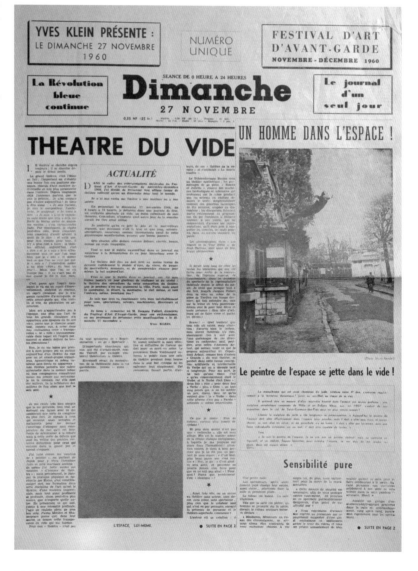

in France with the existentialists' rhetoric of 'authenticity'. The space in *Le Vide* was thus liberating rather than physically oppressive, as in Giacometti's sculptures. As someone nonetheless wishing to communicate truths, Klein cultivated an aesthetic predicated on dandyish equivocation. Towards the end of his life, stung by American criticism that his work was 'corny', he turned this into a virtue, asserting the need for an 'EXACERBATING AND VERY CONSCIOUS ARTIFICIALITY with a touch of DISHONESTY'.[14] A similar show of duplicity had underpinned his strategic entry into the art world. Having dabbled intermittently with monochrome painting, Klein had brought out a small booklet, *Yves Peintures*, in 1954. It purported to illustrate works of 1951–4 produced in various cities. In fact the plates were not photographic reproductions of pre-existing paintings but sheets of commercially inked paper.

There is an open play on authorial presence and reproducibility in this gesture. However, when Klein actually started to produce his fully fledged *Monochrome* paintings in 1955, the verbiage of spirituality came to the fore. Having experimented with various colours, he stuck permanently with the colour which would be connotative for him of the 'boundlessness of space'— ultramarine blue. The single-colour canvas was undoubtedly innovatory, although Malevich's Suprematist abstractions were forerunners, whilst Rauschenberg had recently produced his *White Paintings* in New York. Klein conceived of his use of pure colour as a kind of victory over the competing claims of line, thus reviving a classic seventeenth-century French debate between the 'Rubenistes' and the 'Poussinistes'. Simultaneously he claimed that he refused 'to bring [colours] face to face in order to make such and such an element stronger and others weaker', thereby adumbrating a doctrine of the 'non-relational' which would be espoused later by American abstractionists (see Chapter 5).[15] Klein also pioneered new techniques, such as the use of a house painter's roller and of a binder to impart a powdery quality to his chromatic surfaces, thus greatly enhancing their optical expansiveness. However, the fact that this blue quickly became Klein's trademark—he patented it as *I.K.B.* (*International Klein Blue*), saw it as ushering in his 'Blue Period' (*à la* Picasso), and took to calling himself 'Yves the Monochrome'— reintroduces the notion of charade or, more precisely, self-commodification.

In 1957 Klein had a key exhibition at the Galleria Apollinaire in Milan. He showed eleven blue monochromes, all unframed and uniform in size and facture. They were sold at variable prices, established after Klein's consultations with individual buyers. Klein was to argue that the purchasers had discerned qualities unique to the works, mystically registering the levels of 'pictorial sensitivity' imbued in each by the artist. However, there is again a complex switching between seemingly irreconcilable positions: the idea of the authentic expressive/spiritual exchange between artist and viewer and an acceptance that art objects are material commodities. The implications of the latter position would be succinctly expressed in a Pop context in 1962 when Andy Warhol showed thirty-two images of Campbell's soup cans at the Ferus Gallery, Los Angeles, identical but for labels conforming to the available range of flavours. Unlike Klein, Warhol priced them all the same. Clearly Klein epitomized a prior historical juncture where the theologically related model of the creator–artist began to conflict with a technologically based model reflective of changing societal modes of production. His principles shifted to gratify a new audience primed to expect that their unique desires—their spiritual needs, even—would be assuaged by standardized products.

It is here that critics discern Klein's bad faith. In later ritualistic performances of 1959 he signalled a shrewd economic sense. He set up transactions where wealthy buyers purchased not paintings but 'Immaterial Pictorial Sensibility' itself, for which they paid in gold leaf. Having received printed receipts from Klein they were enjoined to set fire to them, since, as the artist frequently asserted, outward manifestations were merely the 'ashes of his art'. Hence the buyers ironically attained literal immateriality—a fairly standard product, it might be argued—whilst Klein kept half of the gold. Thierry de Duve sees Klein as committing a crime against his avant-garde legacy—in marxist terms, substituting 'exchange-value' for 'use-value'.[16] However, if we absolve Klein from being entirely mercenary, he exemplifies a kind of hysterical reaction—both to art's interface with a commodity culture and to a decline in the notion of the artist as someone able to speak, disinterestedly, 'for mankind'.

Symptomatically, Klein wanted to renounce individuality and sensitize the interpreter/consumer, yet retain the authorial mystique of the artist. His performances, which help to announce a new genre of post-war art, exemplify this. The *Anthropometries of the Blue Age* [**40**], performed at the Galerie Internationale d'Art Contemporain in Paris in March 1960, both parodied and confirmed the inflation of the creative ego, seen as linked, inextricably, with masculinity. While a chamber orchestra played his Cage-influenced *Monotone Symphony* (a work consisting of one note held for twenty minutes), Klein, wearing a tuxedo, instructed several naked female helpers, described by him as 'living paintbrushes', to imprint their paint-smeared

40 Yves Klein

Anthropometries of the Blue Age, performance, 9 March 1960

This performance exemplifies Klein's participation in the masculinist tradition of the dandy. The self-contained male, renouncing biological productivity (symbolized by the fecundity of the paint-covered women launching themselves at virginal paper surfaces), ultimately reproduces 'cleanly' via art.

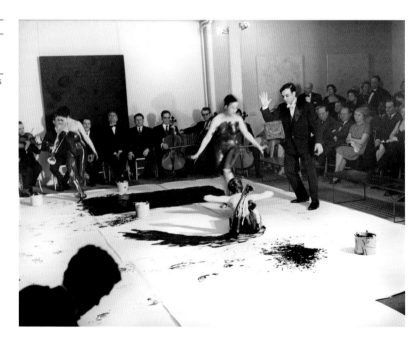

bodies onto paper laid on the floor. Klein made much of not dirtying his hands with paint, and officiating at the 'birth' of his work. No doubt he was ironizing Pollock's ejaculative action paintings, which were also horizontally oriented and avoided touch. (Hans Namuth's dramatic photographs of Pollock painting were widely circulated in the 1950s.) Closer to home, Klein had reason to mock the showy public painting demonstrations of the 'Lyrical Abstractionist' Georges Mathieu, who, in 1956, had produced a 12- by 36-foot (3.7- by 11-metre) painting, full of expressive bravado, at Paris's Théâtre Sarah-Bernhardt. By appropriating the indexical traces of his models, which he predictably saw as embodying life-energy, Klein instigated a new non-autographic mode of artistic production. Rauschenberg had, however, experimented with the indexicality of photography around 1950, producing life-sized photograms of the body of his then wife, Sue Weil, on blueprint paper. (These were reproduced in *Life* magazine in April 1951.)

Klein's penchant for fakery remains puzzling. His most striking performance gesture, *The Painter of Space Hurls Himself into the Void*, was an exercise in contrivance. Presciently recognizing the crucial role played by photography in the way a time-bound performance comes to be constructed for posterity, Klein got his collaborator, Harry Shunk, to create three photographic montages which skilfully transformed a relatively safe jump into a tarpaulin manned by judo friends into an awesome ascension. One of these was published as part of a brilliant spoof newspaper produced for one day only—Sunday 27 November 1960 [**39**]. Although this newspaper was only placed on a few news stands for photographic purposes, its production establishes that Klein was happy to assimilate his spirituality to the logic of mass circulation.

The body's economy: Piero Manzoni

If the ostensible spirituality of much of Klein's output appears compromised, it is useful here to look to an artist who, in many ways, acted as Klein's shadow, producing unambiguously acidic materialist counter-propositions to the French artist's excesses. Piero Manzoni was a Milan-based artist who, in the mid-1950s, was deeply affected by the work of that city's senior avant-garde presence, Lucio Fontana. Manzoni inherited Fontana's liberation from aesthetic constraints, symbolized for instance by the latter's innovatory environmental installations of the early 1950s utilizing looping neon light fittings. He also made alliances with like-minded younger artists in the *Gruppo Nucleare* (Nuclear Group). In early 1957 Manzoni saw Klein's Milan *Monochrome* exhibition, described above, and began a series of *Achrome* paintings in which he bled the mysticism, along with the colour, out of Klein. He aimed, as he said, to purge space of any image whatsoever, to arrive at a point zero. Notwithstanding the link, again, to Rauschenberg's *White Paintings*, Manzoni's *Achromes*, whilst being uniformly colourless, assumed many guises: bread rolls in regimented rows or outgrowths of fibreglass mounted on board, squares of canvas machine-stitched together, straw miraculously piled in a box-shaped mass. Frequently they were mummified in kaolin (porcelain clay) and therefore vaguely reminiscent of Jasper Johns's contemporary embalmed emblems. (Johns had produced all-white *Flags*, *Numbers*, and *Alphabets* which were shown in Italy in 1958–9.)

Manzoni's 1959–62 output became increasingly self-referential. Like Klein, he dealt with the anomalies of godlike creativity in the commodity era, but internalized these effects with analytical precision. His art correlated exactly with his abbreviated, peripatetic existence. On his travels between European cities he signed others as *Living Sculptures*, providing mock-bureaucratic certificates of authentification. His *Lines*, begun in 1959, constituted lines of varying lengths, the maximum being 7,200 metres, painted on scrolls of paper or card and then placed in cardboard tubes or canisters with descriptive labels. One of these labels, pasted on a solid wooden cylinder, announced a 'line of infinite length'—a parodic invitation to sublime reverie and a clear exemplar for later Conceptual Art. Manzoni also drew ruthlessly on his bodily resources. He produced a number of *Artist's Breath* works consisting of balloons filled with his 'divine pneuma'. Attached to wooden bases, they poignantly deflated. He made plans to preserve his blood in phials. Most notoriously, he filled ninety cans of *Merda d'artista* (artist's shit) in 1961.

Closely related to Duchamp's provocative readymades (especially the urinal), these cans of excrement possibly respond to the French iconoclast's absurd, scurrilous equation, 'ahhre est à art ce que merdre est à merde' (art/

ahh is to art as 'shitte' is to shit), in which a verbal pun on 'les ahhres' (meaning 'down payment' in French as well as aurally connotative of relief) was probably intended.[17] They suggested that, socially, art objects were on a par with supermarket commodities, a reading strengthened by a remarkable mock-advertising photograph in which Manzoni posed with one of his 'products' ready-canned on the 'factory floor' [41]. Italy, it should be noted, underwent its 'economic miracle' between 1958 and 1961.

Manzoni stipulated that his cans were to be sold by weight according to the current price of gold, referencing Klein's use of gold leaf in the *Rituals for the Relinquishment of the Immaterial Pictorial Sensibility Zones* described above. He thereby invoked the alchemical transubstantiation of base matter into gold, but stripped of Klein's romanticism. In the *Merda d'artista* Manzoni's incipient mysticism was also undercut by the body's economy. Freud had talked of children, during the 'anal stage', withholding their faeces or bestowing them like gifts on their parents. This clearly correlates with the anti-aesthetic nature of Manzoni's gesture—its unresolved relation to a parent culture. On one occasion, however, Manzoni came close to Klein's love of Catholic ritual. On 21 July 1960, in Milan, he conducted a pseudo-eucharistic performance in which an audience was invited to consume hard-boiled eggs which had been marked with the artist's thumbprint (he consumed one himself in a form of symbolic self-absorption). This probably had social implications. After the election of Pope John XXIII in 1958 there was a push for Roman Catholic revival in Italy, fuelled by falling church attendances. But the subtle interrelations in Manzoni between Catholic/alchemical imagery, the iconography of body remnants/souvenirs, and a broader testing of society's aesthetic tolerance again argue for a deep-rooted affinity, beyond the work of Klein, with that of Duchamp.

It will be recalled that Duchamp had used a transubstantiation metaphor, consolidated in *Etant Donnés*, to convey his sense of a new reciprocal exchange between the work of art and its spectator. Like Manzoni, Duchamp had mined his body's resources, and art historians have argued that he possibly had alchemical interests; it is far from coincidental that the most notorious proponent of this view, Arturo Schwarz, opened a bookshop in Milan in 1954 (and later a gallery) which Manzoni frequented. All in all, the European Catholic backgrounds of Duchamp, Klein, and Manzoni equipped them with an ambivalent switching between irreverence and respect for the 'theology of matter' in an age of brute materialism. They mapped out a different route from the Modernist art object from American artists such as Johns and Rauschenberg, although Duchamp's presence in New York was crucial for the latter pair. For Europeans the changing status of the artist, and the birth of a new contract between artist and audience, could quickly assume a metaphysical dimension. Images of martyrdom and rebirth were liable to be invoked. The example of Joseph Beuys in Germany is a case in point.

The artist–hero: Beuys and West German art

In performance events of his later career such as *Coyote* [42] Joseph Beuys was to outdo Klein by presenting himself as a shamanic figure, communing with an animal formerly deified by the American Indians in order, symbolically, to

41 Piero Manzoni

The Artist with 'Merda d' artista', at Angli Shirt Factory, Herning, Denmark, 1961

This provocative image of Manzoni with one of his cans of excrement could be seen as a rejoinder to photographic images of tormented artists at work in their studios. Hans Namuth's photographs of the intense-looking Jackson Pollock at work on his drip paintings would have been well known to Manzoni.

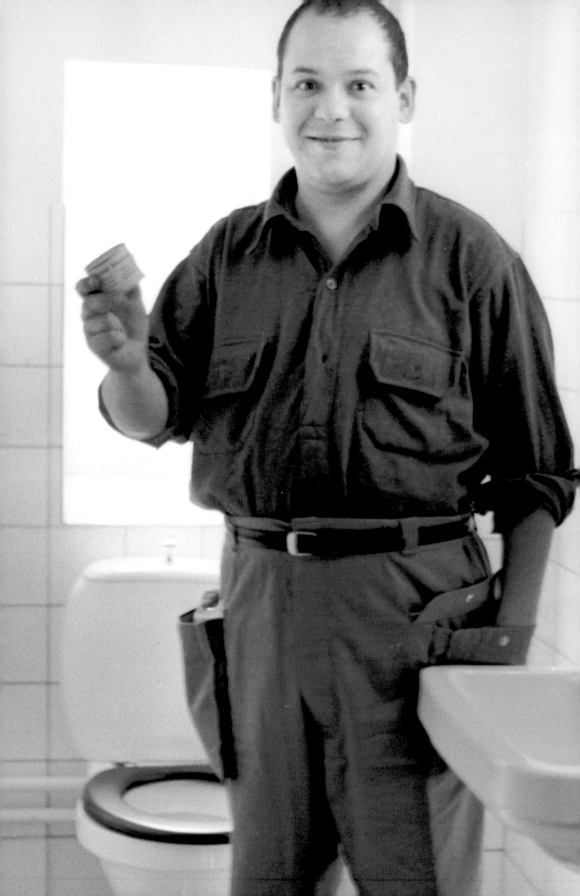

recover a lost relationship for the materialist West. In this he set himself apart from ordinary humanity. He, too, fictively assumed divine status.

He stood apart also from the broad line of development of post-war art in West Germany. Separated from its ideologically opposed other half, West Germany emerged slowly from conditions of outer devastation and inner demoralization. The tradition of avant-gardism had been obliterated. The Nazis had favoured a debased classicism and hidden or destroyed the 'degenerate' art of modernism. The legacies of the Bauhaus, or Dada and Surrealism, were slowly recovered; Kurt Schwitters's retrospective was held in Hanover in 1956, Max Ernst's in Cologne in 1963. There was some take-up of *informel* and *tachiste* currents, mainly from France, in the early 1950s, notably in works by Ernst Wilhelm Nay. However, when, in 1959, Kassel put on its second *Documenta* exhibition (the first of these important events, dedicated to forging a new dialogue with European and American art, had taken place in 1955), Nay's work was programmatically placed next to Jackson Pollock's rather than that of French painters. The exhibition director, Arnold Bode, no doubt wished to assert comparability in terms of aesthetic power, but the power was unequal in other respects. Under NATO (the North Atlantic Treaty Organization, formed to counter the Soviet bloc), West Germany was increasingly beholden to America for

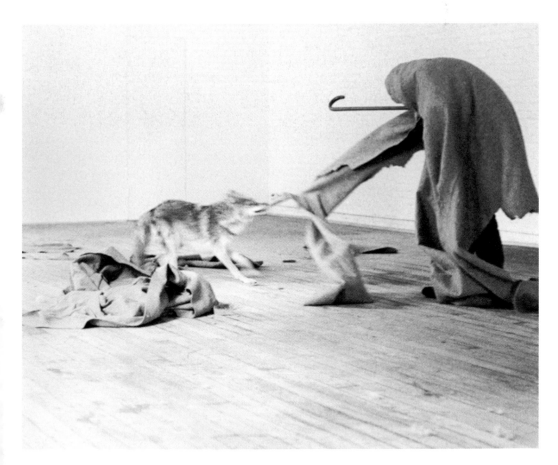

the delicate matter of its military rebuilding, quite apart from general economic recovery. Unfortunately Nay, like other European abstractionists, ended up looking second-rate alongside the Americans. From this point on, West German artists became involved in a complex struggle to recover their identities as modernists.

On the one hand there was a desire for internationalism, a need to shake off the recent past and to assert a new idealism. The Zero Group, which fully emerged in Düsseldorf in 1958, formed close links with European anti-*informel* trends; Klein was an important contact. Similarly, in the early 1960s locations symbolically distanced from the previous cultural centres—Wiesbaden, Wuppertal, Darmstadt, as well as Düsseldorf and Cologne—saw the establishment of experimental Fluxus events in which younger German musicians and artists mingled with visiting Americans to develop interdisciplinary Cage-inspired practices (see Chapter 4). However, it might be argued that the painful questions of national reappraisal, which in any event were rendered problematic by pre-war nationalism, were merely postponed in such instances. A certain turn towards figuration in Berlin, to be discussed shortly, possibly faced up to immediate anxieties. The most distinctive alternative, however, was provided by Beuys, not least in terms of his anachronistically heroic pose. The fact that Beuys had a highly ambivalent relationship to America, and it to him, was bound up with this.

Based in Düsseldorf, where he became Professor of Sculpture at the Academy of Art in 1961, Beuys first came to prominence in the course of Fluxus events of 1962–4, a context which suited his impatience with aesthetic formalism and desire for dialogue. However, when the latter turned to confrontation, as at Aachen Technical College in 1964 when he was assaulted by right-wing students, Beuys decided on a quasi-religious path. Having trained academically as a sculptor, he had taken to using unorthodox materials by the early 1960s: battered hunks of wood or metal, industrial relics, disused batteries, wax, and felt. Time-scarred surfaces and organic matter reflected the range of his speculations, which were resolutely anachronistic. Beuys had no truck with consumerism; he saw humanity as out of touch with itself. He was fascinated by natural history, mythology, alchemy, Paracelsus, and particularly the thought of Rudolf Steiner, the founder of anthroposophy, who had previously influenced Kandinsky's spiritualized abstraction.

Steiner's 1923 lectures *About Bees* provided Beuys with an idiosyncratic aesthetic starting point. Steiner had seen the bee colony as a model for human development. Its ability to generate the molten fatty material of wax and thence to produce the crystallized system of honeycombs became a trigger for Beuys's process-oriented sculptural theory which involved an interplay between fluid and fixed principles, governed by permutations of heat. This in turn would reflect for him the transformative potential of human beings and inform his later utopian concept of 'social sculpture', in which public dialogue itself became the means of dissolving cold, entrenched forms. His 'lectures', involving convoluted diagrams scrawled on blackboards, would eventually constitute the core of his practice.

In physical terms, Beuys's thought is well illustrated by *Filter Fat Corner* of 1963 [**43**]. In what is essentially an installation, the ambient room temperature

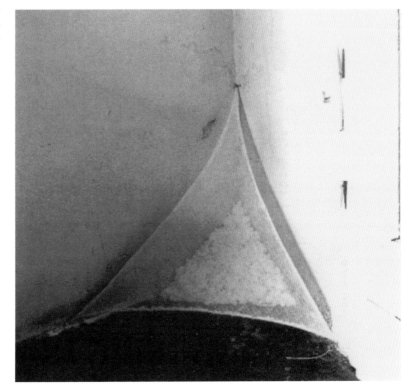

The work consisted of a triangular gauze filter stretched across a corner into which lumps of fat had been packed. Apart from alluding to physical metamorphoses brought about via osmosis, processes of refinement and purification were evoked. In a sense, Beuys continued to investigate the implications of Duchamp's *Large Glass* [**18**]. In his notes for the *Glass*, Duchamp had imagined subtle transformations of energy and matter occurring as his mechanical entities interacted.

is enlisted as the means of potentially liquefying a mass wedged into an inescapable geometric structure. The symbolism may seem literal but Beuys's inventiveness as a sculptor should not be underestimated. In the 1960s the American minimalist Robert Morris was to revisit the same formal dynamic in his move from geometry to 'Anti-Form' (see Chapter 5), and the *Fat Corner* also found an echo in a Morris installation [**69**]. Beuys's visual language was not, however, unprecedented. The Italian sculptor Medardo Rosso had used beeswax in the late nineteenth century, and the Russian constructivist Tatlin had designed constructions to utilize corners. Beuys's famous *Fat Chair* (1964), in which a potentially unstable mass of fat is banked up on a fixed geometric base, structurally shadows Duchamp's *Bicycle Wheel* of 1913 which consisted of a movable upper element and a stable readymade 'pedestal'. The principle of the readymade pervaded Beuys's art generally, but with his slogan of 1964, 'The Silence of Marcel Duchamp is Over-rated', Beuys asserted that Duchamp, now out of the avant-garde mainstream, withdrew aristocratically from the democratizing possibilities of his readymades. By contrast, Beuys appropriated an old utopian rallying cry: 'Everyone an artist'.

Beuys has been taken to task here for misunderstanding Duchamp. The art historian Benjamin Buchloh claimed that, for all his rhetoric of social emancipation, Beuys's artistic position was deeply conservative, reactionary even. Far from altering the status of the object within art discourse, as Duchamp had, Beuys had subscribed to the most 'naive context of representation of meaning, the idealist metaphor: *this* object stands for *that* idea, and *that* idea is represented in *this* object'.[18] Beuys's iconography was certainly narrowly codified, not least according to autobiographical factors which encouraged spectators to excavate his intentions rather than consider his broader allusions. Apart from borrowing from Steiner's ideas, his use of fat recalled a plane crash experienced while flying for the Luftwaffe in the Crimea in the winter of 1942–3. Beuys claimed that he had been saved by a nomadic tribe of Tatars who, sympathetic to the Germans after persecution by the Soviets, 'covered my body in fat to help it regenerate warmth, and wrapped it in felt as an insulator to keep the warmth in'.[19] In fact this episode was fabricated, partly on the basis of a dream. Photographs published later showed Beuys standing relatively unscathed next to his aircraft, recalling Klein's contrivances. There had also been precedents in German art for the creation of rebirth myths: Max Ernst claimed to have 'died' with the start of the First World War, coming back to life in 1918. Whatever the truth of the matter, the materials that had facilitated this rebirth were invoked constantly by Beuys as metaphors for spiritual healing. One of his most compelling sculptures, *Infiltration Homogen for Grand Piano* (1966), consisted of a piano completely covered in felt. Part of a larger performance or 'Action', it was an oblique tribute to children deformed as a result of their mothers' use of the anti-nausea drug thalidomide. Eloquently speaking of the inner reserves of suffering, it cleverly humanized John Cage's *4´33˝*.

In further Actions of 1963–5 Beuys's signature materials acted as props in pseudo-rituals. In *The Chief* (1963–4), performed in galleries in Copenhagen and Berlin, he lay for nine hours in a felt roll with two dead hares attached to his head and feet, the felt supposedly insulating him from external concerns and facilitating a shamanistic communication with the animals. The hare, mythologically linked to notions of transformation and thought to have special access to the earth's energies, reappeared in *How to Explain Paintings to a Dead Hare*, performed at the Schmela Gallery, Düsseldorf. With his head covered in honey and gold leaf, connotative of alchemical change, Beuys spent three hours in 'conversation' with a dead hare, since 'even a dead animal preserves more powers of intuition than some human beings with their stupid rationality'.[20] Beuys's arrogation of superior telepathic powers reached its high point in *Coyote* [**42**], as noted earlier in the chapter. Here, during a week-long interaction between man and animal at René Block's New York gallery, a 'psychological trauma point' was supposedly tapped into.[21]

Whether Beuys's audiences, and particularly his American one in this case, felt the benefit of his shamanism is a moot point. His invocations of primal regeneration, as expressed by himself as charismatic mediator, raised suspicions that, rather than tending to West Germany's recent historical wounds, he was unconsciously recycling the Wagnerian/Nietzschean archetypes beloved of National Socialism.[22] Beuys's politics, however fundamentally impractical, were far removed from this. His social libertarianism led to his dismissal from his professorship at Düsseldorf in 1972 due to a policy of unlimited admission of students, and in 1974 he and the writer Heinrich Böll instigated the *Free International University*. Further concerns with ecological issues, paralleling the rise of the Green Party in West Germany in the early 1980s, were expressed in the initiation of 7,000 *Oaks*, a symbolic 'urban greening' project, begun at Kassel as part of *Documenta 7* in 1982. The widespread planting of trees, next to basalt column markers, took five years to complete, although Beuys himself died in 1986.

Such idealism won him a big following, but his reception in America, where his metaphysics fell foul of native pragmatism, was never secure—a situation ironically registered by Beuys in his subtitle for *Coyote*: 'I like America and America likes me'. Although he made strenuous efforts to win favour in the US (he received the accolade of a Guggenheim exhibition in New York in 1979), Beuys was mistrustful of American materialism. He spoke for a generation of middle Europeans whose self-determination (a key Beuysian concept) was undermined by the imposition of alien values before they were able properly to rediscover their own. Artistically, Beuys virtually equated American materialism with formalism—a kind of Modernist aesthetic packaging shorn of the symbolic density he favoured. (Once again, Morris's dislodging of Beuys's forms from their meanings may bear this out.) The upshot of this was that, ironically enacting the rebirth of the artist, in an era broadly pledged to witnessing the death of the author, Beuys was a conduit for the rediscovery of their identities, vis-à-vis American cultural hegemony, by artists working in West Germany. In Düsseldorf particularly, where his teaching was massively influential, he was a formative, if eccentric, influence on the likes of Gerhard Richter and Sigmar Polke (see Chapter 4).

Whilst Düsseldorf was responsive, however ambivalently, to New York, Berlin in the early 1960s looked back to the German Expressionist legacy, with its emphasis on the autographic mark. Antipathetic towards abstraction and *tachisme*, artists turned the powerful impact of MoMA's *New American Painting*, shown in Berlin in 1958, to their own advantage. The gestural aggression of Pollock was wedded to a treatment of the figure derived from sources such as Die Brücke and Max Beckmann. In a city which saw the creation of the Berlin Wall in 1961, artists felt alienated and deeply mistrustful of political ideologies. Georg Baselitz, who had moved from East to West Germany in the mid-1950s, exemplified this in grotesque, dismembered images of the body, implicitly repudiating both the armoured body-type of official Fascist art and the heroic worker-images endorsed under the Socialist Realism of East Germany. The provocative obscenity of early pictures such as *Die Grosse Nacht im Eimer* (*The Big Night Down the Drain*) [44] led, in 1963, to a West German attorney having paintings removed from Baselitz's first one-man show. The savagely apocalyptic *Pandemonium Manifesto*, produced by Baselitz in 1961 in collaboration with the painter Eugen Schönebeck, dredged up images from a disturbed collective psyche: 'the sacrifice of the flesh, bits of food in the drains, evaporations from the bedclothes, bleeding from stumps and aerial roots'.[23]

Later works by Baselitz, and fellow Berlin painters such as Markus Lüpertz, would be read in the 1980s as signs that, despite successive attacks on the authorial voice in the art of the 1960s and 1970s, to say nothing of attacks on art as an institution, the heroic, internally divided image of the artist was still intact. In that sense they perpetuated the angst-ridden humanism of Artaud discussed earlier. However, these conditions could only

The exposed genitalia in
Baselitz's uncompromising
paintings and graphics of
this period are essentially
attempts to bring into
the open, to make public,
the effects of official
cover-ups and repressed
emotions in post-Holocaust
West Germany. Three years
earlier Günter Grass's
novel *The Tin Drum* had
exploited images of retarded
childhood to allegorize the
darker aspects of the
German psyche.

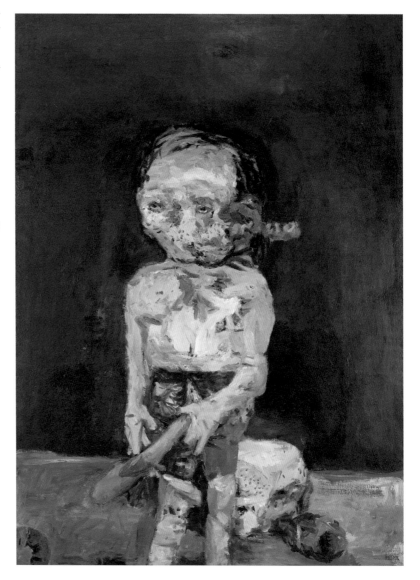

legitimately persist in the light of Germany's unique historical position.
Elsewhere the dynamics of post-war history, as we shall see, meant that the
implications of mechanical reproduction, consumer-oriented markets, and
changing artist–audience relations irrevocably altered the terms within which
not only art, but also 'the artist', could be conceived.

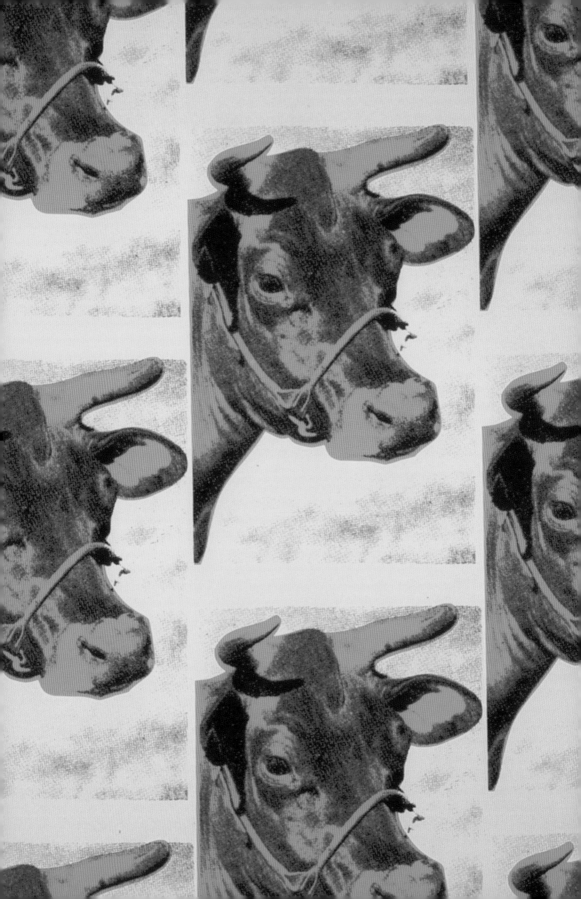

Blurring Boundaries

Pop Art, Fluxus, and their Effects

By the late 1950s consumerism and mass culture (film, television, advertising) were all-pervasive. For Modernism's advocate Clement Greenberg this was profoundly negative, amounting to an onslaught of kitsch. As explained earlier, he believed that, to retain their integrity, the arts had to protect themselves against the debased variants on their accomplishments that advanced capitalism generated for the masses.

It is significant, however, that when he wrote *Avant-Garde and Kitsch* in 1939, Greenberg's elitist opposition of formal culture to kitsch was motivated by the spectre of totalitarian uses of mass propaganda in Germany and Russia and the suppression of avant-gardes. In an important essay Thomas Crow argues that Greenberg appreciated that the emergence of the avant-garde had necessarily been tied to the birth of mass culture in the nineteenth century and that, although he chose to privilege the former, he saw them as mutually defining. Following the logic of this, Crow establishes that the avant-garde had always sought a 'necessary brokerage' between high and low cultural forms, borrowing images from popular culture and relocating them both to reinvigorate its own idioms and to forge alliances with other subcultures, often with different class loyalties.[1] In the US, Rauschenberg and Johns had used mass-produced imagery in ways that destabilized Greenberg's Modernism and, on occasions, signalled illicit gay affiliations. However, they did not theorize their position vis-à-vis high and low forms. By contrast, the London-based Independent Group (IG) had, as early as 1952–3, established the criteria for what became a fully fledged Pop aesthetic, openly embracing kitsch.

Pop culture and mechanical reproduction: the Independent Group

The IG came together in London through the ICA (Institute of Contemporary Arts). Founded in 1946 by British advocates of Surrealism such as Roland Penrose and Herbert Read, the ICA was identified with mainland European experimentation as opposed to the Neo-Romantic and realist currents in 1950s British art. The IG constituted a loose alliance of artists, architects, photographers, and art and design historians who, with the ICA's encouragement, organized a highly eclectic programme of lectures in 1952–5 on topics such as helicopter design, science fiction, car styling, advertising, and recent scientific and philosophical thought.

The IG's academic latitude was underpinned by a radical belief that culture should connote not the heights of artistic excellence but rather a plurality of social practices. They therefore identified themselves with capitalism's cultural consumers. The main critic in the group, Lawrence Alloway, argued against humanist-led values of uniqueness in favour of a 'long front of culture' characterized by a continuum of artefacts from oil paintings to 'mass-distributed film and group-orientated magazines'.[2] This openness to culture at large informed the first IG usages of the term 'Pop' around 1955. (Alloway was to move to America in 1961 and to champion a more narrowly painting-based Pop Art, as discussed shortly, but it is important to appreciate the sociologically inclined origins of the term.)

The IG's breadth of reference was dramatized in two early events. The first, now accorded an originary mythic status, was a surrealistic epidiascope lecture delivered in 1952 by the Scottish-born sculptor Eduardo Paolozzi which galvanized colleagues with its flood of heterogeneous imagery from pulp and commercial sources. The materials shown, a set of collages with the generic title *Bunk* [45], were not even considered art by Paolozzi until 1972 when they were incorporated into silkscreen designs. The second event was the exhibition *Parallel of Life and Art*, the beginning of an important sequence conceived by IG members, installed at the ICA in 1953 by Paolozzi in collaboration with the architects Alison and Peter Smithson and the photographer Nigel Henderson. This consisted of dramatic non-hierarchical juxtapositions of photographs from sources as diverse as photojournalism and microscopy [46]. Although fine-art images were included (Pollock, Dubuffet, Klee), they were clearly reproductions, submitted to a form of cultural levelling by means of a common grainy texture.

This exhibition subordinated the authentic artistic gesture to the principle of reproducibility. It therefore dramatically expanded art's parameters while fuelling the destabilizing of authorial agency noted in Chapter 3. The IG's immediate inspirations were books such as Amédée Ozenfant's *Foundations of Modern Art* (1928) or Sigfried Giedion's *Mechanization Takes Command* (1947), which were prized for their photographic juxtapositions of art and technology rather than their modernist rhetoric. However, the IG's acknowledgement of photography's ubiquity brought them close to the conclusions of the marxist critic Walter Benjamin, who, in the 1930s, had analysed photography's societal role in undermining authorial origins. In his seminal essay, *The Work of Art in the Age of its Technical Reproducibility*, Benjamin argued that the 'auras' art objects once possessed by virtue of their specific locations or 'cult value' had 'withered away' in mass society at the hands of reproductive technologies. (He also believed that, in substituting 'a plurality of copies for a unique existence', technical reproducibility created the conditions for a politicized (socialist) art for the masses.[3])

The IG were not alone in recognizing that the visual sphere had been colonized by technology; Rauschenberg was simultaneously presenting traditionally artistic imagery (brushstrokes, reproductions of artworks) as part of a continuum of culturally produced signs, although he did not commit

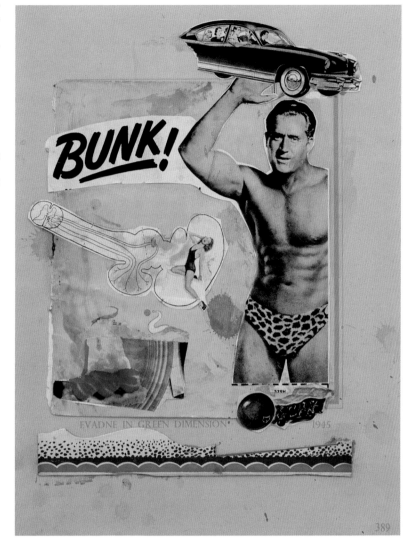

himself solely to photographic imagery until the early 1960s [**60**]. Steinberg's
critical interpretation of Rauschenberg, discussed in Chapter 2, bore similarities with Benjamin in suggesting that whereas works of art had once
seemed to be 'natural' analogues for human experience, Rauschenberg's 'flatbed' pictures declared themselves to be synthetic cultural constructs. That
Steinberg characterized this shift as 'post-Modernist' marks a significant
historical moment, with far-reaching consequences, as will be seen. In the
case of the IG, a proto-postmodern attitude underpinned their departure
not only from the humanism of ICA elders such as Herbert Read but from
contemporary British painters who were also reliant on photography, such
as Francis Bacon. From the 1960s onwards artists who saw photography as
indexed to shifts in the cultural functioning of images would increasingly
question humanist/individualist positions.

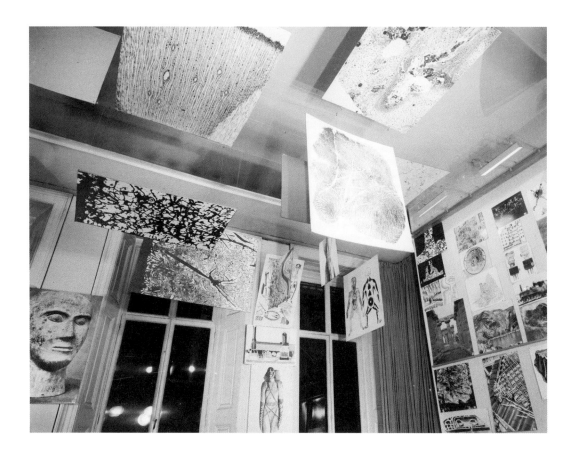

46 Independent Group

Parallel of Life and Art, photograph of exhibition installation, ICA, London, September–October 1953

In this early Independent Group exhibition, photographs of varying sizes were attached to the gallery walls. Others were suspended by wires from the ceiling. Analogies were set up between various structures deriving from technology, science, art, and the natural world. Revisiting the spirit of the New Vision photography of the 1930s, which had been associated pre-eminently with the Bauhaus teacher László Moholy-Nagy, the exhibition helped broaden attitudes towards visual culture in Britain.

'The aesthetics of plenty': Pop Art in Britain

If the IG implicitly accepted Benjamin's cultural prognosis, they hardly followed his political agenda. With the exception of Henderson, they belonged to the first working-class generation of artists, and were commercially or technically trained rather than grammar-school-educated. Nevertheless, whilst the British writer Richard Hoggart argued for a reaffirmation of vernacular British working-class culture in the face of decadent Americanization in his 1957 book *The Uses of Literacy*, the IG openly celebrated Americana, avoiding political side-taking. In Alloway's terms, they endorsed an 'aesthetics of plenty' at a time when Britain was attuned to scarcity; post-war rationing was not lifted until 1954 and packaging on goods was uncommon. In this dour climate it is understandable that they looked to the consumerist diversity of a post-Depression culture. Broadly speaking, they welcomed the shift in power from the state to the marketplace, but it was unclear at times where their sympathies lay. For instance, in 1960 the artist Richard Hamilton argued controversially that the mass audience should be 'designed' for products by the media rather than the other way round.[4] However, whilst the IG's advocacy of American-led consumerism separated them from the wary Europeans discussed in Chapter 3, they did not lack irony.

In this respect Duchamp was again a formative influence, on both Hamilton and Paolozzi. Although Hamilton admiringly mimicked the 'presentation

Hamilton's housewife muse
is conjured from a winking
eye (the small plastic object
attached at the top left),
a shape in shallow relief
suggestive of an apron,
and a sinister toaster-cum-
vacuum-cleaner, its
functioning obligingly
indicated with dots (an
allusion to both advertising
conventions and Marcel
Duchamp's early mechanistic
paintings). She hovers
next to a fridge whose
contents are schematically
represented. Glamorous
denizens of the kitchen such
as Betty Furness, the 'Lady
from Westinghouse', were
television celebrities in
the US.

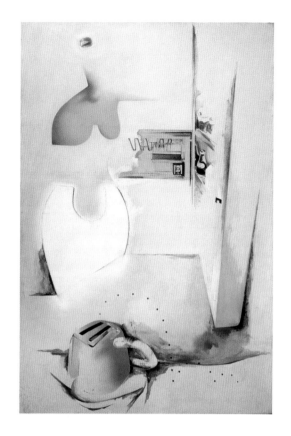

techniques' of design stylists in images such as *Hers is a Lush Situation* (1958), in which elements of a Cadillac advertisement fuse with painterly allusions to female anatomy, a key resource was Duchamp's more sinister vision of woman/machine conflations in the *Large Glass* [**18**]. Hamilton was later to make a replica of the shattered original, but his *$he* of 1958–61 [**47**] inherits not only its diagrammatic organization from the *Glass* but also its ambivalence to socially constructed femininity. *$he*'s fragmentary images evoke the American housewife of the period. Hamilton asserted that his aim was to update 'art's woman', who was 'as close to us as a smell in the drain…remote from the cool woman image outside fine art'.[5] His targets were de Kooning or Dubuffet [**9**], but his cool, aproned alternative is far from liberated: the toaster suggests routine mechanical copulation, and there is blood on her shiny floor. In certain of Paolozzi's collages male sexuality is interrogated [**45**]. Brawn triumphs over machine as Charles Atlas holds a car aloft. The car in turn connotes Henry Ford, whose verdict on history, recalling Paolozzi's generic title for such collages, was that it was 'bunk'. Ultimately male sexuality, as linked to technological progress, appears to be debunked.

This wavering between affirmation and parodic foreboding is further dramatized by an exhibition normally thought to epitomize IG ideas concerning interdisciplinarity between areas of art practice—*This is Tomorrow* of 1956, consisting of twelve pavilions set up in the Whitechapel Gallery by artists/designers. Strictly speaking, it was not an IG manifestation, since several pavilions involved contributions by artists/designers working in constructivist or abstract modes. However, two pavilions clearly expressed the polarities in IG attitudes. The first of these was designed by Hamilton in collaboration with John McHale and John Voelcker. It assaulted the senses, anticipating the environmental Happenings shortly to emerge in America. Outside the pavilion a 16-foot (4.9-metre) Robbie the Robot (from the film *Forbidden Planet*) was juxtaposed with an image of Marilyn Monroe. Inside, spongy floors emitting strawberry-scented air freshener, a jukebox, and a reproduction of Van Gogh's *Sunflowers* (then the best-selling postcard at London's National Gallery) vied for attention. This celebratory side of Hamilton incidentally informed his famous collage, *Just What Is It That Makes Today's Homes So Different, So Appealing?* (1956), a cornucopia of consumer dreams crammed into a living room, which was reproduced in the catalogue of the exhibition. The word 'pop', wittily incorporated into the collage on a lollipop held by Charles Atlas over his 'bulge', momentarily connoted sensual gratification. (Hamilton wrote a famous letter to the Smithsons enumerating the qualities possessed by popular art such as sex, expendability, and glamour.[6] It is ironic perhaps that his subsequent output as a Pop artist would often be allusive and intellectualized.)

By contrast, the second distinctive IG pavilion in *This is Tomorrow*, by Paolozzi, Henderson, and the Smithsons, was a poignantly desolate affair. It consisted of a rudimentary living-space-cum-garden-shed, far removed from Hamilton's dream home, presided over by an extraordinary photocollage by Henderson conforming to his interest in a human image 'stressed' by photographic manipulations (and linked stylistically to Paolozzi's ravaged-looking 'Brutalist' sculpture of the period) [48]. The floor was ironically spread with tokens of family life—a rusted bicycle, a battered trumpet—whilst littered stones and clay tiles reminded Reyner Banham, the design historian of the IG, of excavations after a nuclear holocaust.

The disparity between the pavilions points up two ways of reading the IG. Dick Hebdige sees them as devoted to a democratizing 'politics of pleasure' and thereby (to recall Crow) signalling subcultural affinities with those who regularly consume culture rather than loftily contemplate it. Alternatively, the art historian David Alan Mellor points out that in many ways the IG's iconography of robots and science fiction was complicit with the 'Tory Futurism' of the period.[7] A Conservative government had been returned to power in Britain in 1951, and by the late 1950s their propaganda of 'the Leisure State' was inextricably bound up with bright images of a technological future, backed up by a nuclear arms programme. The flip side of popular pleasures, it seemed, was catastrophe.

Hamilton taught at London's Royal College of Art in the late 1950s, where Peter Blake and Richard Smith produced figure-based and abstract Pop variants respectively. In 1961 Royal College products such as David Hockney, Derek Boshier, Patrick Caulfield, and the older, American-born R. B. Kitaj came to prominence at the *Young Contemporaries* exhibition. Hockney, brought up in working-class Bradford, exemplified the freedoms of expanded educational provision as well as the growing affluence of the early 1960s. Unconcerned with the semiotic analyses of IG forebears, he imported their ethic of surface style into his painting, but kept to personal or domestic themes. Paintings of 1960–2, in a *faux naïf* style deriving from

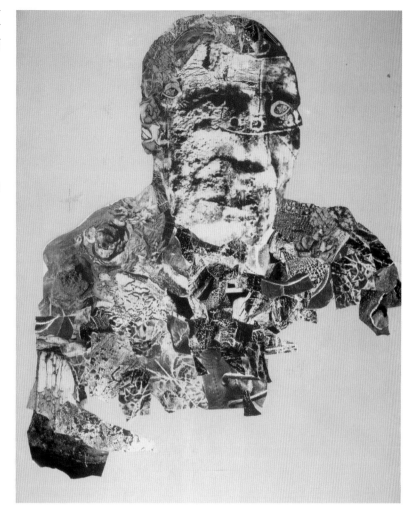

Dubuffet, dealt openly with his homosexuality at a time when it was crim-
inalized in Britain. Like Hamilton, he looked to America, moving to
California in 1963, but his libidinal liberation went hand in hand with fey
stylizations which could appear vacuous, as in the tourist-brochure eroticism of *Sunbather* (1966) [**49**]. Lawrence Alloway was to set such tendencies in British Pop against the superior 'density' and 'rigour' of New York's
burgeoning Pop aesthetic.[8] Whilst Caulfield's work later stood up to the
formal resolution of American art, Hockney's feyness was part of a camp
discourse set in motion by Johns and Rauschenberg (and subsequently
Warhol) to deflate a hard, masculinist Modernism via the domestic or
decorative. His ubiquitously reproduced *A Bigger Splash* (1967) wittily ups
the stakes in the attack on the Abstract Expressionist mark, lamely asserting
a northern English virility.

Hockney's sexual openness was at one with the experimental lifestyles
of 1960s youth culture in Britain. The birth-control pill, invented in 1952,
radically affected sexual morality, although sexist attitudes prevailed among
men, to be countered by the rise of feminism. (The American feminist Betty

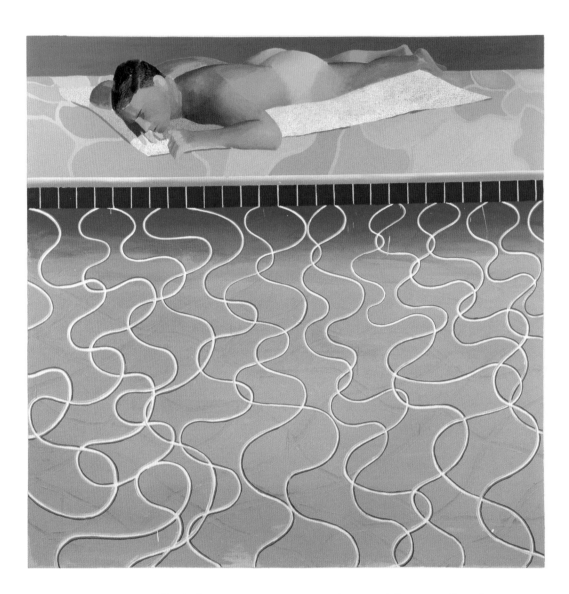

Friedan's *The Feminine Mystique* of 1963 and Germaine Greer's *The Female Eunuch* of 1970 were highly influential publications.) Allen Jones notoriously explored sexual fetishism in a Pop idiom (e.g. *Girl Table*, 1969) whilst Pauline Boty, a recently rediscovered female Pop artist, parodied permissiveness in *It's a Man's World II* (1965–6), with its painted fragments from soft-porn magazines.

When Harold Wilson's Labour government came to power in late 1964 the mythology of Swinging London was born. In this climate high and low cultural forms increasingly cross-fertilized, as symbolized by the cover of the 1967 LP record *Sgt. Pepper's Lonely Hearts Club Band* by the Beatles. Designed by Peter Blake in collaboration with his first wife Jann Haworth, it fuses the nostalgia for British folk culture (fairgrounds, circuses, etc.) of his early Pop paintings with the druggy countercultural iconography of the period. If, in 1962, the German marxist Adorno, in line with Greenbergian Modernism,

Sunbather, 1966

Hockney was originally attracted to Los Angeles by John Rechy's homoerotic novel, *City of Night* (1963). Hockney subsequently celebrated its homosexual subculture in images of naked men emerging from, or basking next to, swimming pools. At a submerged level the eerie stillness of these images may communicate some unease with the good life. Frank Perry's 1968 film *The Swimmer* examined the despair underlying aspects of California's sunny swimming-pool culture.

Art education in Britain

The Independent Group, and the exhibitions associated with it, were important exemplars for British art education. The two stylistic impulses showcased in the *This is Tomorrow* exhibition—its Pop and abstract/constructivist sides—eventually converged in the development of new notions of art-school training. Bauhaus-derived ideas of 'basic design' (emphasizing analytic investigations of visual structures and materials) were fused with an openness to photography and mass-media imagery. The 1944 Education Act had extended art training to talented working-class students, initiating a massively expanded professionalization of the visual arts. In the mid-1950s Richard Hamilton, working alongside his constructivist-oriented colleague Victor Pasmore at King's College Durham (later the University of Newcastle upon Tyne), set up a pioneering one-year Foundation Course, followed by Tom Hudson and Harry Thubron at Leeds College of Art. This quickly became standard practice in art colleges. IG attitudes to culture also helped broaden higher education conceptions of art history, paving the way for cultural studies programmes in British polytechnics in the late 1970s.

could assert 'politics has migrated into autonomous art',[9] some forms of art had blithely migrated into the sphere of mass-produced pleasure.

'The gap between art and life': Happenings, Fluxus, and anti-art

British assaults on high/low cultural distinctions were paralleled in America during 1958–64 by attempts to close what Rauschenberg once described as the 'gap' between art and life. These took the form of experimental Happenings and Fluxus manifestations, pledged to artistic interdisciplinarity in defiance of conventional painting and sculpture. As further extensions of a performance genre dating back to the Black Mountain happening of 1952 (see Chapter 2) and thence to Dada, both were committed to Cage's decentring of the artist's ego, favouring live artist–audience interaction as opposed to the aesthetic closure of Greenberg's aesthetics. Future adherents attended Cage's unorthodox classes on music at the New School for Social Research, New York, in 1958–9. They included Allan Kaprow, the ideologue of Happenings, and George Brecht and Dick Higgins, who were to throw in their lot with a further devotee of avant-garde music, the Lithuanian-born George Maciunas, the future promoter of Fluxus events.

Whilst they shared a desire to reconfigure artist–audience relations through disorienting transgressions of media boundaries, the tendencies differed fundamentally. Happenings such as Kaprow's seminal *18 Happenings in 6 Parts* (1959) were put on in New York by visually trained artists whose experimentalism was tied to the promotional concerns of specific venues, notably the Judson Memorial Church, with its pioneering *rapprochement* between religion and modern art, and the Reuben Gallery, where *18 Happenings* took place. Happenings therefore took the form of complex sensory environments, bordering on theatre in terms of vestigial narrative content and the use of props, but soliciting spectator participation. Jim Dine's *Car Crash*, a response to a spate of car accidents in which friends had died, reactivated trauma via a barrage of poetically allusive actions, images, and sounds [**50**].

Such activities represented an extension of Rauschenberg's *Combines* (Rauschenberg himself was involved in performances, often in league with

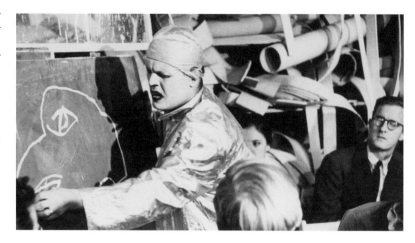

Merce Cunningham's dance company, during this period) wedded to a reinterpretation of Pollock (see the end of Chapter 1). By contrast, typical Fluxus performances such as Emmett Williams's *Counting Song* (1962), in which he simply counted the audience, were predicated on the itinerant performance patterns of musicians or poets. They usually dispensed with fussy staging and centred on rudimentary experiences, recalling Cage's advocacy of silence. Fluxus also inherited his mysticism. The term, as elaborated in Maciunas's manifesto of 1963, recalls the Greek philosopher Heraclitus in endorsing the principle of flux: 'Act of flowing: a continuous moving on or passing by…a continuous succession of changes.' George Brecht thus devised sparse, open-ended 'event scores' courting elementary or indeterminate processes; *Three Aqueous Events* of 1961 consisted of three words: ice, water, steam.

Alternatively, Fluxus events could be behaviourally or socially challenging. In 1962, in a concert in Wiesbaden, West Germany, the Korean-born Nam June Paik performed *Zen for Head*, an interpretation of a composition by the experimental musician La Monte Young which involved him drawing a line on a strip of paper placed on the floor using his head and necktie dipped in ink and tomato juice. Three years later Shigeko Kubota, one of several female participants in Fluxus, translated this event's bloody connotations into female flows with her *Vagina Painting*, implicitly counterposing the body's productivity to the intellectualism symbolized by Paik's use of his head, although she in fact employed a brush attached to her underwear [**51**].

Fluxus had no fixed aesthetic agenda. It was precariously held together via Maciunas's organizational zeal. Whereas Happenings constituted a 'local' phenomenon, responding to New York's in-house art debates, Maciunas had international ambitions for Fluxus. Having come up with the logo while assisting with a publication of La Monte Young's scores and running his AG Gallery in New York in 1960–1, he moved to Wiesbaden in West Germany to work as a designer for an American air-force base, quickly rallying like-minded talents to his cause. The first event to take place under the Fluxus banner, the *Fluxus Internationale Festspiele Neuester Musik*, therefore occurred in Wiesbaden in September 1962, when Paik performed the action described above. This was followed by a number of densely packed festivals throughout Europe. The resultant international co-minglings, recalling the structural

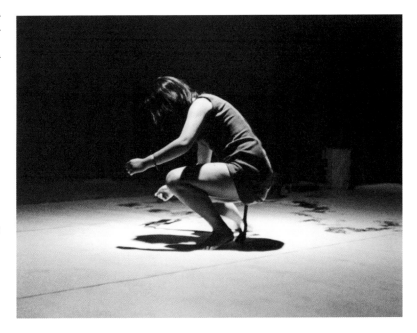

dynamics of the European-American Dada alliances of 1916–23 and providing a model for conceptualism to follow slightly later, led to the establishment of various outposts centred on charismatic practitioners/publicists (e.g. Ben Vautier in Nice, Willem de Ridder in Amsterdam, Wolf Vostell in Cologne). In autumn 1963 Maciunas's return to New York shifted the emphasis back to America. By the end of 1964, however, the network's fragile unity was ruptured when Maciunas supported Henry Flynt's picketing of a New York concert by the German composer Karlheinz Stockhausen on the grounds that, as 'Serious Culture', it was fundamentally imperialistic.

Flynt's passionate conviction that 'Serious Culture' was predicated on forms of cultural exclusion was bound up with his sympathies for America's Civil Rights Movement, dedicated to raising public awareness of the oppression of black Americans, and brought to a head with the march on Washington headed by Martin Luther King in August 1963. Flynt's and Macunias's activist responses to social inequality were further exemplified in a *Fluxus Policy Newsletter* of the previous year in which Maciunas had advocated civil disruption.[10] However, such hard-line approaches alienated Fluxus members such as Brecht, who saw the movement as consciousness-changing rather than interventionist, whilst Kaprow, from the Happenings camp, deemed them 'irresponsible'.[11] Although Fluxus nominally continued into the 1970s, it now became factionalized. Its oppositional tendencies nevertheless introduced a powerful note of anti-(art-)institutional negativity into the 1960s (a legacy once more from Dada). Whilst destruction was the subject of formative Fluxus events (for instance Paik's notorious *One for Violin Solo* (1961) in which, having slowly raised the said instrument overhead, he slammed it down with full force), iconoclasm surprisingly had a distinct flowering in Britain.

The anti-art mood in Britain was to be memorialized by an enigmatic suitcase, a distant relation to Duchamp's *Boite-en-valise*. Produced by John

This is an installation which
closely follows a promotional
photographic montage for
de Ridder's distribution
company. The location
recorded in the original
montage was actually the
artist's living room in his
home in Amsterdam with his
friend Dorothy Meijer posing.
Among the Fluxus products
on view, the Japanese-born
Ay-O's *Finger Box Set*, in the
open briefcase at centre
right, demonstrates the
further permutations of
Duchamp's *Boîte* [17].

Latham, an assemblage artist who achieved brief international success early
in the 1960s with his sprayed book ensembles, it contained the physical
remains, and the documented consequences, of a strange ritual entitled *Still
and Chew*. Latham's students from Saint Martin's School of Art in London
were invited to his home in August 1966 to communally chew up the pages
of Clement Greenberg's *Art and Culture* (1961), borrowed from the college
library. The resultant pulp was then 'brewed' and bottled before being returned
to the library, after which, unsurprisingly, Latham lost his job. Antisocial or
not, the gesture clearly made a point, not least in relation to the Modernist
aesthetics then embodied at Saint Martin's in the works of Anthony Caro's
successors (see Chapter 5). *Art and Culture* contained essays by Greenberg
such as *Avant-Garde and Kitsch* which, as explained earlier, endorsed aesthetic exclusivity. By parodically testing it against bodily needs, Latham
encapsulated a generational shift towards inclusiveness.

An ally of Latham, the German-born Gustav Metzger, followed this up
a month later with his *Destruction in Art Symposium*, attracting nearly one
hundred international iconoclasts to London, many with Fluxus links, to
reflect on artistic/performative destruction in relation to nuclear devastation.
Metzger had pioneered such concerns in 1961, when he had sprayed acid onto
nylon sheets on the banks of the Thames. However, histories have tended to
ignore such British activism in favour of a single orgy of destruction, Jean
Tinguely's *Homage to New York*. This massive agglomeration of auto-destructive
machinery, set up in the sculpture garden of MoMA in March 1960 as the
French New Realist's entrée into New York's Happenings scene, had consumed itself in flames before being extinguished by the city's fire brigade.

If Fluxus advocated anti-art, it also, paradoxically, commodified itself.
Its acolytes patented a remarkable variety of multiple-edition objects which
Maciunas, a one-man cottage industry, then manufactured, issuing exhaustive
price lists filled with quirky typefaces. On offer were small boxes such as
Water Yam (1963), containing Brecht's event scores, or *Flux Clippings* (1966),
containing Ken Friedman's toenail/bunion clippings. Alternatively Robert
Watts's sheets of *Flux-stamps* (1963) subverted the official postage system,
as well as functioning as covert propaganda. In 1964 Maciunas set up a
Fluxshop in his Canal Street loft in Manhattan. Although spectacularly
unsuccessful, it spawned European offshoots such as Willem de Ridder's
European Mail-Order Warehouse/Fluxshop. An installation based on a photograph advertising this [**52**], complete with a female 'commodity', shows the
quantity of *Fluxkits* and *Flux Year Boxes* that came to be produced. All in
all, such ventures amounted to a marxist recognition that the dynamics of
commodity circulation needed to be addressed if art's finance-based institutions were to be challenged. Ironically, of course, much Fluxus 'mass-
production' was pledged not to profit-making but to the elimination of
artistic auras, to reprise Walter Benjamin's terms.

A telling corollary to this aspect of Fluxus can be found by returning to
Happenings. In 1960–2, Claes Oldenburg, a Yale-educated artist with wealthy
Swedish origins, made New York's impoverished Lower East Side the site
of a kind of self-analysis. He constructed an environment, *The Street* (1960),
which, in its Reuben Gallery showing, consisted of shards of stiffened cardboard and burlap hanging from the ceiling, evoking urban detritus. This

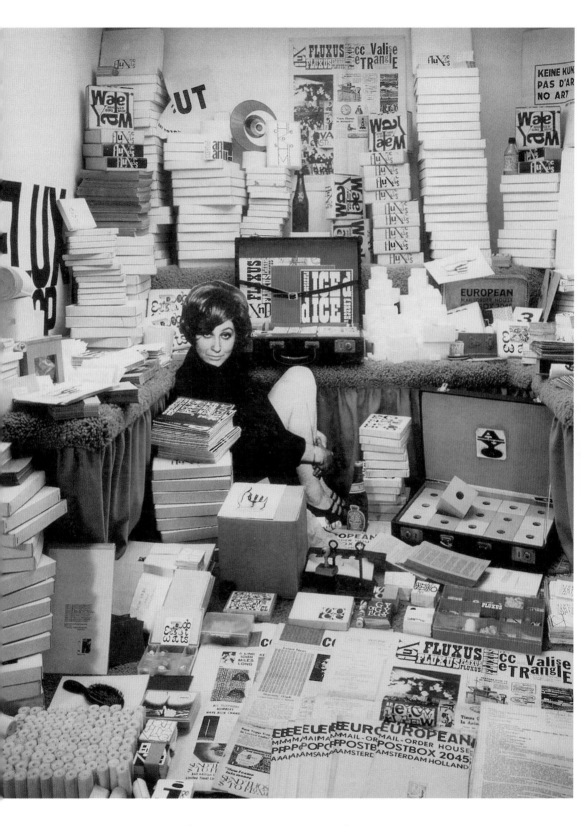

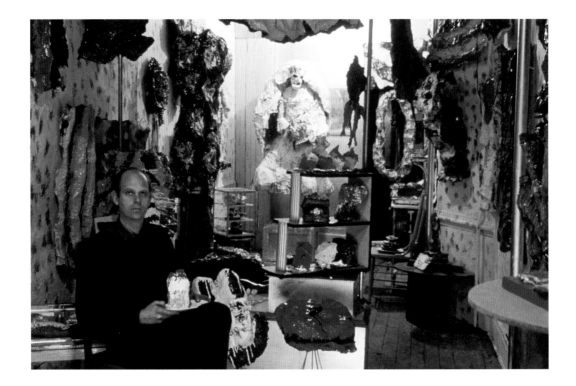

53 Claes Oldenburg

The Store, 1961

A grotto filled with misshapen, paint-dripped travesties of goods, Oldenburg's *Store* was a temple to vulgarity. In it he recreated the merchandise he passed in New York's Lower East Side on his way to his own premises: erotic underwear, slices of pie or cake from delicatessens. One key creation, visible at the back of this photograph showing the artist posing with his produce, was the 'Bride Mannekin', a sardonic response to shop-window models in bridal outfits.

then became the location for a Happening titled *Snapshots from the City*, a sequence of vignettes, briefly illuminated, in which he enacted psychodramas, identifying with city bums. Oldenburg next created an alter ego for himself, a metamorphic transvestite character whose name, Ray Gun, came to evoke Oldenburg's repressed phallic desires for a further creation, 'The Street Chick'. These characters, allegorizing Oldenburg's longing for class mobility, appeared in performances of the *Ray Gun Theater*, itself an offshoot of an attempt to infiltrate Lower East Side life in the form of the *Ray Gun Manufacturing Company*, otherwise known as *The Store*, with premises at 107 East Second Street.

This in effect became Oldenburg's challenge to capitalist modes of art distribution. In its back room he produced a profusion of roughly crafted plaster sculptures, approximating to consumer desirables such as clothing or food, splashily painted *à la* Abstract Expressionism. These were then sold by the artist at the front at prices not far above those of their real-life equivalents [53]. In a familiar tale of assimilation, rather than selling to baffled locals they attracted shrewd buyers such as MoMA and the offer to move the *Store* uptown to Richard Bellamy's Green Gallery, whose advance payment soaked up Oldenburg's net losses on the project. By the mid-1960s Oldenburg's work was also undeniably uptown, the epitome of Pop chic. His homages to consumer fantasies, such as the kapok-filled hamburgers with their Magrittean enlargements of scale, were kitted out first in canvas 'ghost' versions, then in sexy vinyl. Reminders of a harder New York, such as the *Soft Drainpipes* of 1967, obeying a libidinal logic, went flaccid. And the prices naturally escalated.

Pop Art in America: Lichtenstein and Warhol

Fluxus's *rapprochement* between aesthetic and everyday experience went hand in hand with attempts to circumvent the workings of the market. By contrast, American Pop's contemporaneous merging of elite and mass culture was underwritten by the business acumen of dealers riding a booming economy. The movement emerged suddenly in 1962 when critics such as Gene Swenson, attuned to an iconography of urban signage by Johns and Rauschenberg, seized on Lawrence Alloway's earlier 'Pop' coinage to characterize paintings in a spate of exhibitions by James Rosenquist, Roy Lichtenstein, and Andy Warhol. The movement was not so much self-generated as market-created by dealers such as the Italian-born Leo Castelli. Its birth was also accompanied by the phenomenon of instantaneous accreditation by museums, Alloway's *Six Painters and the Object* at the Guggenheim Museum in 1963 being particularly prescient. By 1964, whilst the careers of individual participants flourished, the movement as such was over. Heralded by mass-circulation magazines such as *Time* and *Life*, it had generated a new media-led hunger for artistic novelty.

Turning to the art itself, New York Pop stepped up Johns's and Rauschenberg's critique of Abstract Expressionism's bombast through a cool impersonality. Rauschenberg's early 1960s silkscreen paintings [**60**] appear convoluted alongside the colourful, emblematic images of Lichtenstein and Warhol. Borrowing the compositional clarity of contemporaneous abstraction [**65**], they employed single images, ready-designed from pre-existing commercial sources, in enlarged or repeated formats [**55**]. Lichtenstein's brushstroke paintings of 1965–6 [**54**] upstaged Johns's earlier parodies of Abstract Expressionist painterly largesse, translating its spontaneous flourishes into a formulaic graphic design idiom and turning 'expression' into one culturally mediated sign among others. His comic-strip images of the 1960s explored the stock signifiers of American mass culture. Square jaws connoted maleness, blonde hair and tears femininity. Gender roles were further demarcated into the spheres of combat (Lichtenstein's men are often at war in unspecified Asian locations, hinting at American involvement in Korea or Vietnam) and the domestic bedroom (women invariably agonize over

---

The makings of Pop: the American art market

The Italian-born dealer Leo Castelli, assisted by his talent scout Ivan Karp, was pre-eminent in marketing American Pop Art. Having already snapped up Johns and Rauschenberg for his gallery (see Chapter 2), Castelli took on Lichtenstein in 1961, followed by Rosenquist and Warhol three years later. He extended his operations to Europe via a collaborative deal with his ex-wife Ileana Sonnabend, the daughter of a wealthy Romanian industrialist, who opened a Paris gallery in 1962.

When Rauschenberg won the Grand Prize at the Venice Biennale in 1964, aided by a string of strategic European exhibitions and Castelli's promotional machinations before the event, it was clear that the art world's financial capital was now New York. Wealthy collectors set the pace; Ethel and Robert Scull, their fortune based on a taxi empire, reportedly paid $45,000 for Rosenquist's multi-panelled *F-III* of 1965. When, in 1973, their collection was sold, at several thousand per cent profit, a dizzying escalation in post-war art prices was established.

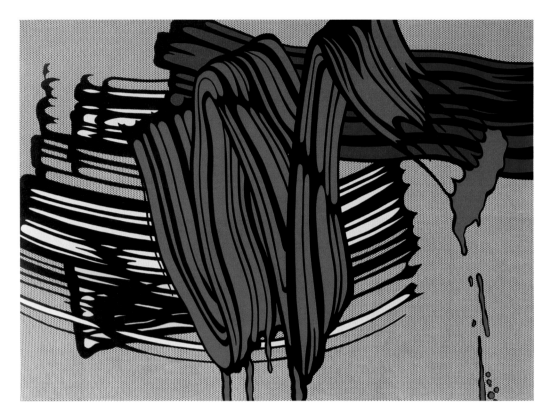

54 Roy Lichtenstein

Big Painting VI, 1965

Whilst clearly representing a critique of free expression, Lichtenstein's 'brushstrokes', like most of his other Pop works, had an exact comic-book source. They initially derived from a strip entitled 'The Painting' published in Charlton Comics' *Strange Suspense Stories* no. 22 of October 1964. Elements of this strip were originally incorporated, in a redesigned format, in Lichtenstein's *Brushstrokes* of the same year.

love affairs). Skilfully transferring the Ben Day dots of the printer's screen and the stylizations of comic-book graphics into more satisfying abstract designs, Lichtenstein asserted that his aim was to unify his source materials visually, thus appeasing Modernist detractors scornful of debased 'copying' from kitsch.

By contrast, Warhol mercilessly debunked Modernist protocols. Whilst his homosexuality was not widely acknowledged until after his death, he blithely used the related sensibility of camp as his main weapon. Defined by Susan Sontag in a famous essay of 1964 as 'love of the unnatural: of artifice and exaggeration', a 'good taste of bad taste', it had permeated Warhol's earlier output as a successful illustrator in the 1950s.[12] He had, for instance, produced stylish gold-leaf collages of shoes specially personalized for celebrities, before moving from the commercial to the fine-art sphere. His first exhibition of works in the latter idiom was decidedly camp. In 1961, paintings derived from commercial graphics were displayed behind a scattering of fashionably clad mannequin 'shoppers' in the window of Bonwit Teller's, an upmarket women's clothes store. The ensemble teasingly fused the dynamics of (male) high-art production and (female) mass-culture consumption, such gender connotations having been in place since the mid-nineteenth century, and persisting in Greenberg's art/kitsch opposition, according to Andreas Huyssen.[13]

In 1962 Warhol embarked on his iconography of consumerism—the screen-printed rows of dollar bills and Coca-Cola bottles on large canvases or the paintings of individual Campbell's soup cans that were shown at his first solo exhibition at Los Angeles's Ferus Gallery. The 'stacking' of his 'products' in rows implied a submission to the routinization of supermarket-era shopping as well as mimicking the techniques of mass production. (Parallels exist with slightly earlier gestures by Manzoni and Klein: see Chapter 3.) Warhol pragmatically turned mechanization's threat to artistic autonomy into an aesthetic rationale, talking of wanting to be a machine, and pursuing the industrial metaphor to the extent of employing assistants to print his silk screens in his 'Factory'. This essentially masculine managerial stance, which updated art-historical workshop practices (e.g. Rubens), sat oddly alongside his campness.

Through aligning himself with female consumption, Warhol came close to Duchamp, who had represented himself in drag on a perfume bottle [25], but Warhol's taste was more flamboyantly vulgar, especially when it came to opposing Abstract Expressionism's virility. His *Cow Wallpaper* [55], its ungainly bovine profiles appearing incongruously rural alongside his urban subjects, repudiated a whole lineage of 'bullish' imagery in twentieth-century art ranging from Picasso's *Guernica* to Motherwell's *Elegies* [12]. At the same time, in producing wallpaper—the very incarnation of the domestic and decorative—he parodied the broodings of Modernists over where abstract paintings ended compositionally, revelling in the philistine perception of such works as 'wallpaper'. (The American critic Harold Rosenberg once denigrated certain forms of Abstract Expressionist art as 'apocalyptic wallpaper'.[14])

55 Andy Warhol

Cow Wallpaper, 1966

Warhol's wallpaper initially decorated a room at Leo Castelli's New York gallery in April 1966. Another room was devoted to his floating *Silver Clouds* (helium-filled silver pillows).

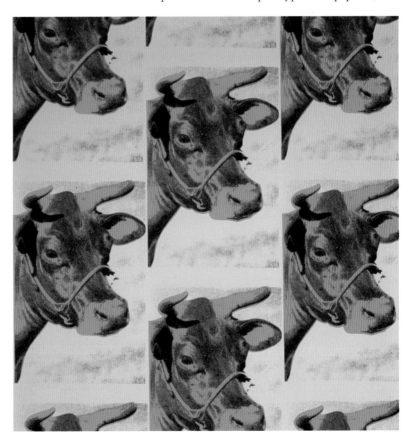

Warhol's anti-Modernist position informed his most celebrated depictions: of Marilyn Monroe and Elizabeth Taylor. These celebrities were as much gay icons as objects of male heterosexual desire, not least because of their publicized sufferings in heterosexual relationships, and in his silk-screen-printed portraits of 1962–3 the garish inks virtually functioned as make-up, creating drag-queen connotations. Warhol was plagued by personal cosmetic insecurities. An early painting called *Before and After* (1960) was adapted from a newspaper advertisement dramatizing the transformation of a woman's nose from aquiline to ski-slope via plastic surgery; Warhol himself had had a 'nose job' in 1957. Applying silk-screen inks like cosmetics, he ironically attended to Modernist painting's 'complexion'—its concern, in Greenberg's terms, with maintaining surface integrity. Warhol famously asserted that to know him, his audience simply needed to look at the surface of himself or his work; there was nothing more.

In cosmeticizing Modernism Warhol brilliantly replayed certain conditions surrounding the foundational construction of the 'modernist' artist (for the two usages of the term, see Chapter 1). In his essay *The Painter of Modern Life* (1863), the French art critic Charles Baudelaire had argued that what distinguished the (male) artistic advocate of modernity was a marrying of the aristocratic spirit of the dandy with that of the *flâneur* in the desire to 'distil the eternal from the transitory' out of urban flux. In a section entitled *In Praise of Cosmetics* he extolled the artifice of make-up as an analogue for his aesthetic credo. Its ability to 'create an abstract unity in the colour and texture of the skin' was said to approximate 'the human being to the statue, that is to something superior and divine'.[15] Warhol's Marilyn was turned into a divinity in precisely these terms, although his *Gold Marilyn* of 1962, consisting of a solo head placed on a gold-painted field, also evoked Byzantine icons. The fact that Warhol was a fervent Catholic suggests a mobilization of fetishistic religious impulses equal to Klein's or Manzoni's. Certainly Warhol's carefully distanced persona and the voyeuristic establishment of a freak show of hangers-on at his Factory positioned him as Pop's dandy par excellence.

Warhol's voyeuristic tendencies surfaced most clearly in the *Disasters* series (1962–4). The *Marilyns*, produced shortly after her suicide, anticipated these works in dramatizing how mass culture threads private tragedy through its machinery. (The repeated frames of the *Marilyn Dyptich* [1962], some with the image over-inked or virtually invisible, connoted film, a medium to which Warhol turned in 1963.) Deriving initially from a stark newspaper headline '129 die in Jet' (the subject of a 1962 painting), the *Disasters* series ironically revived an important genre of Neoclassical 'history painting': the heroic death. Warhol, however, programmatically placed allusions to celebrity deaths, such as Monroe's or President Kennedy's (registered via the grief on his wife Jackie Kennedy's face), on a par with those of 'unknowns'—the harrowing *Suicide Jumps* and *Car Crashes* [**56**]. The latter constituted dystopian reflections on the symbol of American affluence in the wake of Jim Dine's earlier Happening [**50**]. Other works in the series, the *Electric Chairs* and the *Tunafish Disasters*, dealt with unknowns who momentarily achieved fame precisely through death. All in all, death was presented as a social leveller.

Democratizing processes were often the subject of Warhol's fey pronouncements. He noted approvingly that when Elizabeth II drank the Coca-Cola offered by President Eisenhower, it tasted the same to her as to the man in the street. In a famous utterance he conflated the conformities of commodity culture with an alien political credo: 'I want everybody to think alike…Russia is doing it under government…Everybody looks alike and thinks alike, and we're getting more and more that way.'[16] The conflation reflected the way American media representations of ideological rivalry between the US and Russia hinged on the supposedly egalitarian benefits of capitalist commodity output (as in reports of the 'kitchen debate' between America's Vice President Nixon and Russia's President Khrushchev in 1959). But Warhol's embrace of sameness potentially had moral valency. In an important essay Thomas Crow argues that the restatement of identical images in the *Disasters* series reminds us, poignantly, of the daily repetitiveness of tragedy.[17] It might equally be asserted, in line with Warhol's observation that 'when you see a gruesome picture over and over again, it doesn't really have any effect', that he was commenting on the affective numbing brought on by repeated exposure to the mass media.[18] Alternatively, critics have seen Warhol as cynically capitulating to alienation effects. Hence the disjunctive colouration (and titling) of certain images—*Lavender Disaster* (1963), for instance, in which multiple electric chairs appear in toilet-roll hue—possibly amounts to his commodifying of voyeurism, rendering it decorative.

Whatever one's viewpoint, Warhol's reruns of media intrusions shadow structural changes in American national consciousness brought about through the mass witnessing of traumatic spectacle on TV (the filming of Kennedy's assassination in 1963 was a vivid demonstration of this new collective phenomenon).[19] In this sense his recognition of technology's increasing mediation between the public and private spheres was exemplary, and his wholesale importation of photographic processes into the fine-art arena, symbolized by the decision to 'paint' using photographic stencils just before Rauschenberg's move in the same direction [**60**], represents a key historical juncture. It implicitly underlined Benjamin's sense of photography's sociocultural destiny, as discussed earlier, creating a precedent for later conceptually oriented art. In the latter respect, Warhol's utilization of a low, journalistic photographic genre can be correlated with the more resolutely amateurish, or deadpan, uses of photography in the work of a Pop contemporary from Los Angeles, Ed Ruscha. In *Twentysix Gasoline Stations* (1963) [**57**], the first of a series of self-published books, Ruscha undercut the rarefied *livre d'artiste* tradition via the creation of an artless visual itinerary of the petrol stations on Route 66 between Los Angeles and Oklahoma, a forerunner of the Bechers' later taxonomies [**93**].

Ruscha's book also presented a cool take on the poeticized mythology of the American highway synonymous with Jack Kerouac's 1950s Beat novels and Robert Frank's related 'art photographs'. Warhol's recoding of reportage photography into fine-art terms probably played off earlier photographic history. In the 1940s the New York photographer Weegee, hailing from a similar working-class immigrant background to Warhol, had made his name in the commercial arena, opportunistically photographing grisly car

---

56 Andy Warhol

Five Deaths Seventeen Times in Black and White, 1963

The use of serial repetition here, as in other early Warhol works, relates interestingly to minimalist uses of repetition (see Chapter 5). The reciprocally ironic relation between Warhol and the minimalists came to a head in 1964. Warhol exhibited a series of *Brillo Boxes*, consisting of large wooden boxes covered with silk-screened commercial logos, at the Stable Gallery, New York. He must have been aware of Robert Morris's anonymous cubic structures of the period. Late that year Morris exhibited his austere geometric forms at the city's Green Gallery [**69**].

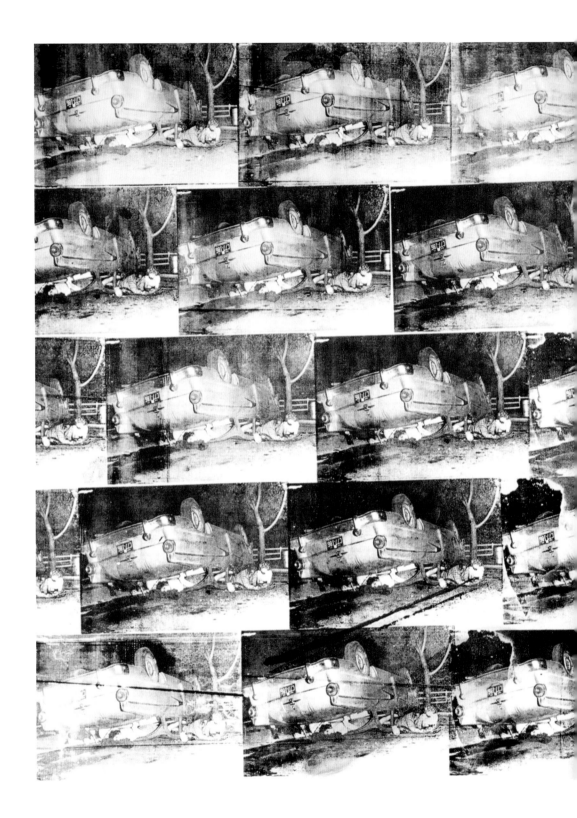

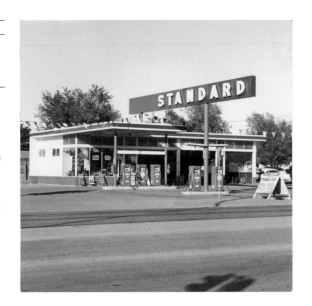

57 Ed Ruscha

Standard, Amarillo, Texas, from *Twentysix Gasoline Stations* (artist's book), 1963

Ed Ruscha produced a sequence of photographic books in the 1960s. Other examples, equally deadpan in nature, were *Some Los Angeles Apartments* (1965) and *Every Building on Sunset Strip* (1966). They deftly transposed the documentary vernacularism of American photographers such as Walker Evans into Pop terms.

accidents for newspapers, before being turned into an 'art photographer' when MoMA bought and exhibited his work in 1943. In the late 1940s, when Warhol first lived in New York, Weegee's book *Naked City* was a bestseller, heralding its author's later self-promotion as 'Weegee the Famous'. The recoding of his morally ambiguous work, to say nothing of his negotiation of the interface between commerce and art stardom, may well have provided Warhol's model. Crow notes that images from Warhol's *Disasters* series often possess a dark film noir aura, such that we might well be witnessing events of the 1940s, and the image of a suicide victim used in *1947 White* (1963) actually dated from the year in that title. Interestingly, certain of Warhol's commercial logos were nostalgically anachronistic. His Coca-Cola lettering derived from early in the century.[20]

Weegee's intrusive photographs often exploited the traumatized blanking-out of accident victims in a state of shock [**58**]. Warhol in fact used 'blanks' in a more literal way, accompanying several of his *Disasters* with monochrome panels [**56**]. Frequently overlooked in analyses, these acknowledged the contemporary abstractions of Ellsworth Kelly or even Barnett Newman (by the mid-1960s Warhol's work was in dialogue with contemporaneous abstraction, especially minimalist repetition; see Chapter 5), while providing a form of antithetical stasis or 'blanking-out' in relation to the images. They may well be metaphors for the sublime—the experience of awe in the face of overwhelming external forces that the Abstract Expressionists Newman and Rothko, drawing on eighteenth-century aesthetics, talked of wishing to evoke in their abstract fields. For once, it seems, Warhol may have seen some virtue in Modernism. However, his sublime, as we shall see, was intrinsically 'postmodern'. He calls for yet further reappraisal, not just as a prophet of the author's disappearance behind codes of representation (although, ironically, Warhol's authorial presence actually increased as surely as the auras of his images decreased), but as a moralist of sorts, or even a form of therapist, anaesthetizing us against the effects of traumas to come.

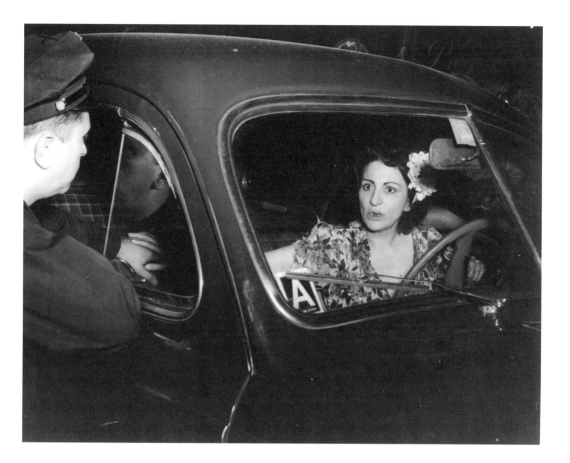

58 Weegee

'Sudden Death for One...Sudden Shock for the Other...', photograph first published in the New York evening newspaper *PM Daily,* 7 September 1944

The freelance newspaper photographer Arthur Fellig, better known as 'Weegee', was notorious in New York in the late 1930s for being the first to arrive at any scene of crime, arrest, or tragedy. Generally he worked late at night or early in the morning, and his images are characterized by the use of photographic flash. At the turn of the 1940s he occasionally lectured at New York's 'Photo League', forging links with the 'art photography' world.

Pop and politics: the US and West Germany

In general, American Pop luxuriated in the abundance of the Kennedy era (1960–3), as exemplified by Tom Wesselmann's and Mel Ramos's paintings juxtaposing glamorous nudes with brightly packaged foodstuffs. But James Rosenquist, like Warhol, occasionally registered its shallowness. He had trained commercially as a billboard artist, working close-up on enormous advertising hoardings which later predisposed him towards the use of abstracted fragments of imagery. In *Painting for the American Negro* [**59**], a response to civil rights issues, a slice of cake, connotative of consumer pleasures, is given a political inflection: it seems to hint at the social stratification implied throughout the painting. Cake had made another appearance in Rosenquist's earlier *President Elect* (1960–1). This time it was proffered by a ghostly hand emerging from the newly elected President Kennedy's face and emblematizing what Rosenquist feared would be 'empty promises'—cake for the masses, to recall Marie Antoinette. By contrast, Rauschenberg lauded Kennedy's vigorous statesmanship in several silk-screen paintings, as exemplified by the repetition of the pointing hand in *Retroactive 1* [**60**].

As the American dream soured during the 1960s, Rosenquist encapsulated the changing mood in *F-III* (1964–5), a fifty-one-panel mural in the tradition of Picasso's politically motivated *Guernica*, depicting images of doom (an atomic

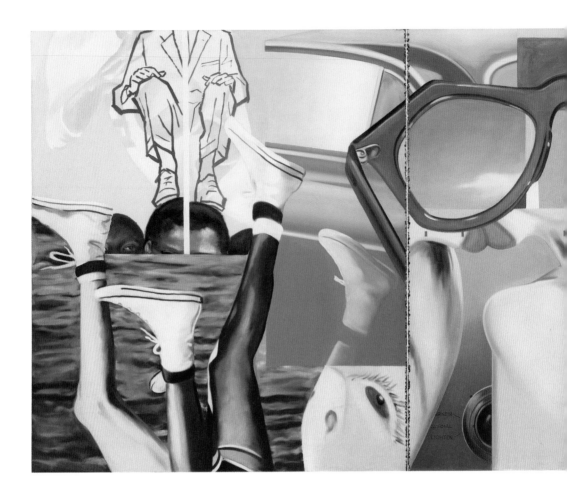

59 James Rosenquist

Painting for the American Negro, 1962–3

Rosenquist's paintings made use of bizarre, filmic jumps in scale and content, hinting at buried narratives. In the top–left corner the lower half of a seated businessman is depicted in an illustrational mode. His feet, possibly awaiting the services of a shoeshine boy, are firmly planted on the head of an illusionistically painted back man. Further along, an enlarged head (perhaps that of a black activist or the car's chauffeur) is rendered anonymous by the slice of sandwich cake in the final frame.

explosion) and desire (yet more cake) intercut with an ominous image of an F-111 bomber. Planes of this type were instrumental in America's increasing involvement in the Vietnam War, as overseen by Kennedy's successor Lyndon Johnson. In fact they proved expensive design failures and thus appropriate symbols for an escalating Cold War conflict, ostensibly fought to uphold the freedom of South Vietnam against neighbouring communist aggressors, but evolving into an unwinnable war of attrition, which dragged on until 1973. Despite the equation it drew between political expediency and economics (Rosenquist commented that the prosperous lives of American arms-industry workers were predicated on death), Rosenquist's bomber was seductive enough to be installed in an entire room of Castelli's gallery and to be sold to fashionable collectors (see text box on the American art market).[21]

If Rosenquist's politics were compromised by his Pop gloss, a more abrasive form of social commentary was conducted throughout the 1960s by the Los Angeles-based assemblage artist Ed Kienholz. Kienholz had helped consolidate West Coast Pop's distinctive 'funk' idiom with the establishment, in 1957, of Los Angeles's important Ferus Gallery, in collaboration with the curator Walter Hopps. By the turn of the 1970s his response to nearly two decades of racial tension, epitomized by riots in Los Angeles's

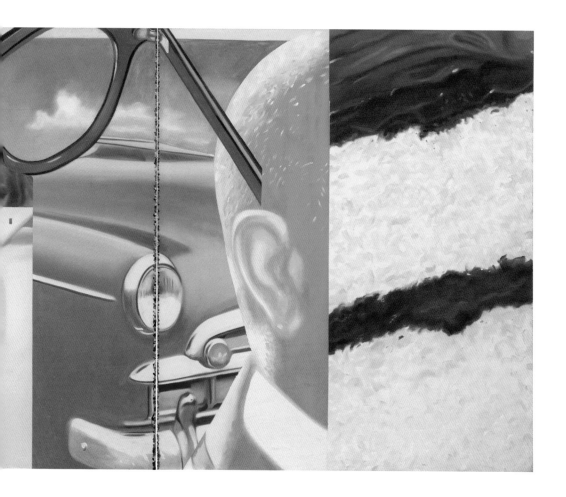

Watts district in 1965 and in hundreds of other cities in 1967 and 1968, was a stark tableau first shown at *Documenta 5* in Kassel, West Germany, in 1972. It consisted of life-sized mannequins and related props. Its imagery was nightmarish. Lit by the headlights of their parked cars, six white men, their faces hidden by rubber Halloween masks, systematically emasculated their black victim, while his white date cowered, vomiting, in the truck from which he had been dragged [**61**].

By 1970 America's domestic troubles had become compounded by proliferating anti-war protests. These reached a peak when President Johnson's Republican successor, Richard Nixon, bombed North Vietnamese bases in neutral Cambodia. Pop had long been supplanted as a movement, but it is significant that its idioms could still be mobilized by an outsider commenting on the US's international power game. This was the frequently overlooked Brazil-born artist and poet Öyvind Fahlström, who was to settle in Sweden but spent much of the 1960s shuttling between that country, Italy, and America. His *CIA Monopoly* [**62**] of 1971 sardonically comments on the US Central Intelligence Agency's intervention in global affairs. If Kienholz aimed to outrage his viewers, Fahlström invites them to 'play'. The magnetic pieces on his board are movable, positing some degree of social/political participation

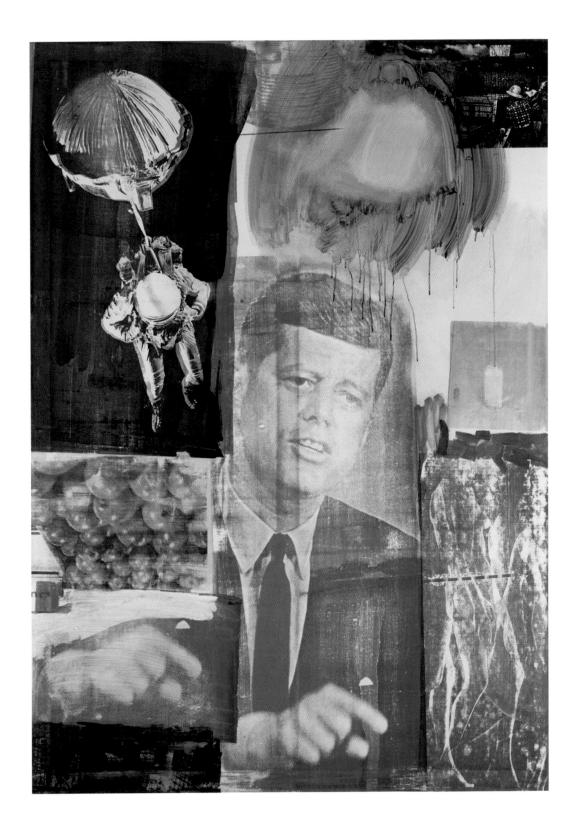

60 Robert Rauschenberg

Retroactive 1, 1964

Rauschenberg's silk-screened canvases bearing images of Kennedy were produced after the president's assassination, although Rauschenberg had ordered the screens before the event. Kennedy's populist rhetoric of space conquest (in 1969 the US was to put the first man, Neil Armstrong, on the moon) thus becomes elided with an image of his deification; the parachuting astronaut at top left doubles as an angel.

61 Ed Kienholz

Five Car Stud, 1969–72

Ruthlessly forgoing aesthetic or metaphorical niceties, Kienholz's grotesquely theatrical scenario compels the viewer to witness what he termed a 'social castration'.

for the viewer. With Warhol in semi-retirement after the trauma of his shooting by Valerie Solanas in 1968, few home-grown exponents of Pop, whatever their commitment to a vernacular art, had any such stomach for sociopolitical commentary.

If Fahlström implicitly criticized American Pop's political silence from within, two Germans conducted a different dialogue with it from afar. Gerhard Richter and Sigmar Polke had moved to West Germany from the East before the erection of the Berlin Wall, settling in Düsseldorf, where, apart from assimilating Fluxus's anti-formalist ethos, they saw reproductions of Pop works by Lichtenstein and Warhol around 1962–3. These offered alternatives to a set of restrictive aesthetic options: the Socialist Realist modes in which they had originally been indoctrinated, the abstraction that was being touted as West Germany's aesthetic corollary of American Modernism's 'freedoms', and the atavistic return to quintessentially German Expressionist roots favoured by Berlin artists. Predisposed by their backgrounds to assume the hidden hand of ideology in art's productions, they gravitated towards Pop's intrinsic irony, its distanced appraisal of the way cultural information is processed. Nonetheless, an early manifestation of their position, the performance event *Life with Pop—A Demonstration of Capital Realism*, makes it clear that they were more intrinsically self-reflexive than their American counterparts.

The 'Capital Realism' (which later became 'Capitalist Realism') of the above event's title succinctly posited a German Pop idiom which was not so much the liberated converse of Socialist Realist academicism as the reflection of another ideology. The event itself, which took place in a furniture store, consisted of Richter and a further collaborator, Konrad Lueg (later to run a

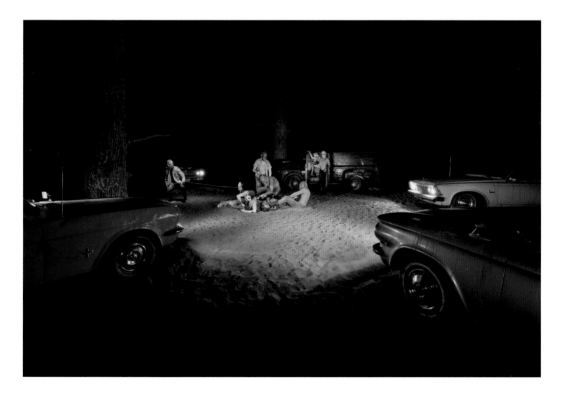

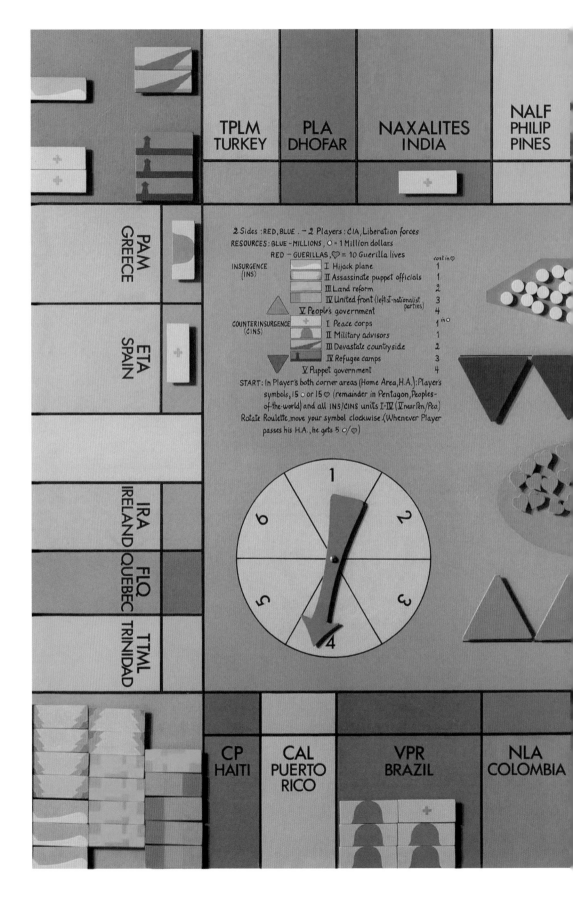

TPLM
TURKEY

PLA
DHOFAR

NAXALITES
INDIA

NALF
PHILIP
PINES

PAM
GREECE

ETA
SPAIN

IRA
IRELAND

FLQ
QUEBEC

TTML
TRINIDAD

2 Sides : RED, BLUE . – 2 Players : CIA, Liberation forces
RESOURCES : BLUE – MILLIONS, O = 1 Million dollars
RED – GUERILLAS, ♡ = 10 Guerilla lives

			cost in ♡
INSURGENCE (INS)		I Hijack plane	1
		II Assassinate puppet officials	1
		III Land reform	2
		IV United front (leftist-nationalist parties)	3
	V People's government		4
COUNTERINSURGENCE (CINS)		I Peace corps	1 in O
		II Military advisors	1
		III Devastate countryside	2
		IV Refugee camps	3
	V Puppet government		4

START: In Player's both corner areas (Home Area, H.A.) : Player's
symbols, 15 O or 15 ♡ (remainder in Pentagon, Peoples-
of-the-world) and all INS/CINS units I-IV (V near Pen/Peo.)
Rotate Roulette, move your symbol clockwise. (Whenever Player
passes his H.A., he gets 5 O/♡)

1
2
3
4
5
6

CP
HAITI

CAL
PUERTO
RICO

VPR
BRAZIL

NLA
COLOMBIA

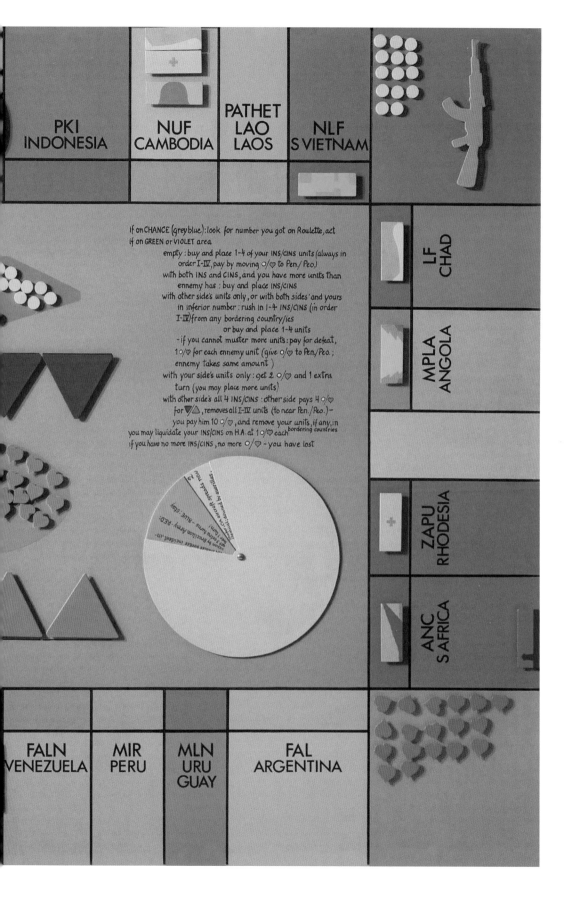

gallery as Konrad Fischer), sitting in a mock living room in which both they and a range of bourgeois living accessories were raised on pedestals. Surrounding objects included Winston Churchill's recently published memoirs and a television broadcasting a programme on the Adenauer era. (The performance took place on 11 October 1963, the date of Konrad Adenauer's resignation as West Germany's chancellor.) In an adjacent space spectators passed by papier-mâché figures of Kennedy and the art dealer Alfred Schmela. All in all, the artists ironically presented themselves as complicit in the complacency engendered by Adenauer's 'economic miracle'.

In subsequent paintings by Polke, deliberately inept versions of American Pop techniques ironically signalled West Germany's secondary cultural/economic status vis-à-vis America. In his *Rasterbilder* works he subverted Lichtenstein's stylization of printer's dots by exploding his photographic motifs into molecular fields. The elements of these fields achieved a distracting autonomy—some dots were half-formed, others merged. In the case of *Bunnies* [63], this atomizing of the image implied a critique of capitalism's marketing of female sexuality: the closer the (male) spectator peers at these Playboy 'Bunnies', the more they 'break up', their mouths dispersing in red showers. Commenting on his dots, Polke amusingly linked their perverse behaviour to his personality, acknowledging an obvious pun on his name: 'I love all dots. I am married to many of them. I want all dots to be happy. Dots are my brothers. I am a dot myself.'[22]

Less anarchic by nature, Richter similarly used photographs as readymade subjects, often working from family snapshots, although *Eight Student Nurses* (1971), the images of eight victims of a Chicago murderer, drew on Warhol's investigations of media-induced morbidity. Unlike Warhol, however, Richter produced painted simulations of photographs, blurring the outlines of their imagery to create out-of-focus effects, as though thematizing irresolution, both in terms of memory, as befits a response to photographed subjects, and in terms of the distinction between painting and photography. In the latter respect, his later paintings from photographs of dead members of the Baader–Meinhof gang, a group of terrorists who committed suicide in Stammheim prison, Stuttgart, in 1977 after the attempted hijacking of a plane by their supporters had failed [111], function dialectically in relation to Warhol's memorializations of heroic death (see above). For Richter it was precisely *painting's* continuing ability to embody historical consciousness, in the light of *photography's* usurpation of the business of recording, that was at issue.

Such concerns (which will be further explored in Chapter 7) show Richter departing from Pop, but it is relevant here to anticipate another aspect of his later career—the split in his work between photorealist images, which in the Baader–Meinhof works have an obliquely ironic relation to the heroicizing public imagery of Socialist Realism (the terrorists were communist opponents of the West German regime), and abstractions [113]. It is as if this split in his work reproduced the historical rift between Socialist Realist and abstract Modernist positions, hinging on the question of art's public responsibility, that he had been compelled to negotiate through moving to the West.

Recalling the start of this chapter, Greenberg's horror of kitsch—the principle which Pop so fervently embraced—had initially been bound up with an abhorrence of the aesthetic consequences of Stalinism, namely

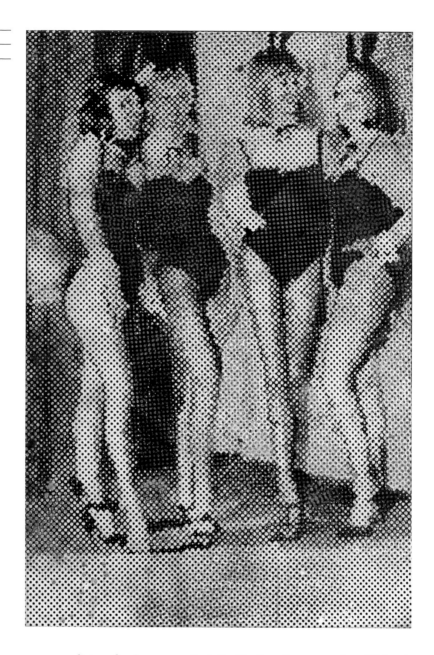

propagandist art for the masses: Socialist Realism. In a sense, then, Richter's eventual response to Pop was to retreat from its embrace of kitsch, recovering the historical conditions from which it, as the antithesis of Greenberg's Modernism, had grown. In doing this he, and Polke also, return us to the central premises of post-war avant-gardism, discussed in Chapter 1. However daring Pop's levelling of high and low cultural distinctions, its aesthetics were ideologically rooted: it was as 'American' as Greenberg's Modernism. In that sense, it constituted 'Capitalist Realism', as far as Polke and Richter were concerned; a form of propaganda, as the case of Rosenquist demonstrates, for values it was not always comfortable with.

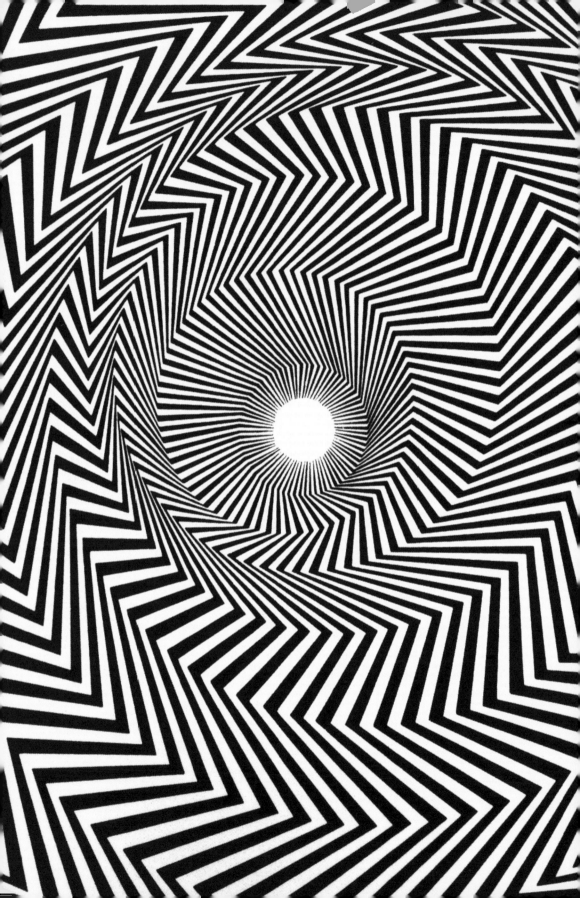

Modernism in Retreat

Minimalist Aesthetics and Beyond

5

Clement Greenberg's Modernism was a source of antagonism for most of the artists discussed in Chapters 2–4. Their weapons of defiance were the bodily, the readymade, the mass-(re)produced, the kitsch, and the aesthetically hybrid. At the turn of the 1960s Modernism's rhetoric of aesthetic purity had reached a pitch. However, it could only be comprehensively challenged if, as well as being set against the social realities it spurned, it was found wanting in its own abstract terms. Aesthetic dilemmas demanded solutions. This chapter will show how practices of abstraction mutated from the early 1960s onwards, gradually recovering vestiges of figuration and human content.

The non-relational: Reinhardt, Stella, Judd

In America the output of two painters of the early 1960s, Ad Reinhardt and Frank Stella, manifested telling ambiguities from a Modernist standpoint. Ad Reinhardt, the senior of the two, with a career stretching back to the late 1930s, carved out a particularly intractable position for himself. On the one hand, he possessed the hallmarks of a staunch Modernist. He deplored any confusion between art forms, fiercely advocated a philosophy of 'art as art' predicated on relentlessly negativistic itineraries of all the things art was not,[1] and in his 'black paintings' of 1955–67 practically banished compositional incident from a sequence of unyielding monochromes. On the other hand, Reinhardt had no time for Modernism's avatars, the Abstract Expressionists. He regarded their paintings as impure marriages of abstraction and Surrealism, satirizing their Jungian sympathies in one of the cartoons savaging the art-world art that he published in the 1950s, the punningly titled *A Portend of the Artist as a Yhung Mandala* (in ARTnews, 1956). This jibe notwithstanding, Reinhardt was deeply sympathetic towards various forms of mysticism. The sombre iconicity of his 'black paintings', from which Greek cross structures slowly emerge against faint bluish or reddish haloes, attests to this.

Reinhardt's art-world purges were given impetus by the lukewarm reception he received from Clement Greenberg. In the early 1960s this Modernist critic was wary of the uninflected object-like quality of Reinhardt's 'black' canvases. Having previously espoused values of painterly all-overness and flatness (as discussed in Chapter 1), Greenberg was now retreating from their logical extremes, observing that 'a stretched or tacked-up canvas already

Detail of 73

exists as a picture—though not necessarily as a successful one'.[2] In line with his advocacy of painters like Morris Louis, he increasingly stressed the optical incident within the pictorial field rather than its overall cohesion. Yet it was precisely the latter self-referring quality that younger artists in New York, such as Don Judd, Sol LeWitt, and Frank Stella, prized in Reinhardt. Stella's own 'black paintings' of 1958–60, which set his career in motion, were almost calculated to confirm Greenberg in his critical reorientation.

Stella's works took the critic's earlier dogma of formal self-containment to a deadpan conclusion. Expunging any residues of Abstract Expressionist emotionalism and seizing on Johns's use of systematic pictorial rationales [29], Stella deduced the internal logic of paintings such as *Die Fahne hoch!* [65] from their nature as objects. The unvarying 2-inch- (5-cm-) wide bands of black that filled the canvases were thus derived from the width of their stretchers. The slivers of bare canvas that were left behind paradoxically functioned as 'drawing', echoing the framing edges of the supports and setting up centrifugal or centripetal ripples. Such images seemed to obey structural necessity rather than aesthetic whim. But Stella, of course, made minimal decisions as to how to extract necessity from his formats. This flew in the face of the Modernist idea that painting imposes a fixed set of aesthetic limitations.

In subsequent sequences of work Stella dramatically moved from painting in a Modernist sense towards 'objecthood' (to pre-empt Michael Fried's later terminology). In the aluminium-coated shaped canvases of 1960 the paintings' reverberative internal patterns were dictated by notches cut into the corners or sides of the supports, or by holes puncturing the centres. Their aluminium surfaces encouraged the art historian Robert Rosenblum to characterize them as 'irrevocably shut metal doors',[3] an association underlining both their self-containment and the artist's stated desire to repel attempts to 'enter them' visually.

In the face of such drastic metamorphoses, the Modernist critic Michael Fried, torn between loyalties to Greenberg and to Stella (he was a close friend of the latter), attempted to cast such works in Modernist terms. He claimed, for instance, that the reflected light from the aluminium canvases counterbalanced their tendency to function as objects by creating an optical shimmer.[4] He and other Modernist commentators such as William Rubin were spared further explanatory acrobatics when, having pursued his endgame with painting to the extent of producing polygonally shaped canvases in 1963, in which the redundant centres of the paintings were completely removed, Stella changed direction. His enormous *Protractor* paintings of 1967–8 now reintroduced complex internal relationships between arcing bands of colour. For a time at least he appeared to have entered the Modernist fold, alongside other 1960s exponents of 'hard-edge' abstract colour painting such as the highly influential Ellsworth Kelly [64]. However, in the 1970s Stella's surprising turn to a kind of parodic or baroque gestural painting marked him as terminally ambivalent.

The resolution with which Stella squeezed both content and formal rhetoric out of his works temporarily diverted any discussion of his emotional investment in them. The titles of his early 'black paintings' have led, however, to considerable speculation concerning hidden agendas. *Die Fahne*

64 Ellsworth Kelly

Blue on White, 1961

Although Kelly is broadly linked to post-painterly or hard-edge abstraction in the US, his work in the 1950s was often perceived as 'European' in sensibility. This work, both in terms of the exploration of shape and the use of the colour blue, evokes Henri Matisse's late paper cut-outs of 1952–3. Curves are among Kelly's signature stylistic features. The formal content of this work consists of the interaction between the sensuous curved elements at the top and the white background, which appears to cut into the lower portion of the blue mass. Sensory experiences of nature, such as glancing at the sky, or twisting a leaf between the fingers, are invoked. By the early 1960s Kelly, like Frank Stella, made increasing use of shaped canvases, but his lyricism contrasted with Stella's more logical, proto-Minimalist approach. Often Kelly's large shaped canvases were set against gallery walls in such a way that the wall or the architectural setting functioned as the ground for his vibrant planes of colour.

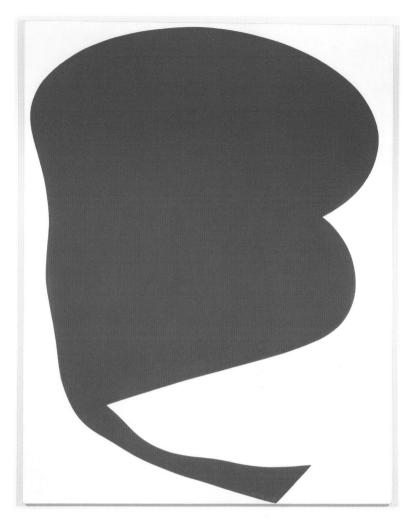

hoch!, for instance, translates as 'Raise the Flag!', a phrase from a Nazi marching song which doubles as an ironic nod towards Jasper Johns [**28**], and, given Stella's imputation of aggressive motives to those pictures, it has been argued that they encode a fascination with fascistic forms of domination.[5] En masse, however, the titles catalogue so many connotations of blackness (for instance, references to jazz hang-outs and a transvestite club in Harlem) that they probably simply reflected Stella's identification with New York's seamier side. He was at emotional rock bottom when the works were produced, and may well have seen them as continuous with a tradition of black paintings deriving from the gritty, noir ambience of 1940s film and photography [**16**]. In this, Stella was a precedent for the Warhol of the *Disasters* [**56**]. This comparison may be extended to another similarity between these apparently dissimilar figures—a conception of art output as akin to industrial production.

It is here that readings of Stella as preoccupied by metaphors of dom-ination gain some purchase. Basically, it has been argued that, as the 1960s progressed, Stella's works, whether Modernist or anti-Modernist in orienta-tion, came to acquire the impersonal clarity of corporate logos.[6] This argument may not be as reductive as it appears. Moves by American corporations from international to multinational status during this period may have insidiously informed the way ambitious artists, conscious of America's new-found hegemony in the Western art world, seized the advantage of having instantly identifiable brand identities within an expanding art market. It is revealing perhaps that Leo Castelli, Stella's dealer, once characterized his shiny aluminium canvases as 'cash registers'.[7] Certainly by the late 1960s Stella, like Warhol, had embraced a managerial ethos, employing assistants to cope with the demand for his wares and effectively splitting artistic creativity into executive and production modes.

Whether or not Stella is to be seen as a cipher for larger economic forces, it is interesting that when he, along with fellow artist Don Judd, theorized the move to a new impersonal aesthetic, in an important interview of 1966, the rhetoric of American cultural supremacy played its part.[8] It is necessary here to say something about Judd. Initially a painter, Judd had come to believe, in the wake of Stella's productions, that both painting and sculpture were inherently illusionistic and should be superseded by the creation of what he called 'specific objects' in literal space.[9] His production of this new artistic genre, which took the form of single or repeated geometrical objects, was part of a broader move towards minimalism, to be discussed shortly. The objects, which were uninflected, hollow, and occasionally subdivided internally according to part-to-whole ratios, were fabricated by workmen at factories, according to his specifications, in materials ranging from cold-rolled steel to Plexiglas [66]. In articulating their position, Stella and Judd made much of the fact that their new works were 'non-relational'. This meant they were structurally self-evident and pragmatically ordered according to a principle of 'one thing after another', thereby shaking off the fussy 'relational' characteristics of much previous art.

What they took to be relational was epitomized by the work of the British sculptor Anthony Caro, then being promoted by Greenberg and Fried in a notable softening of their pro-Americanism. Caro had transferred his loyalties from Henry Moore to US Modernism in the late 1950s by absorbing the example of the American sculptor David Smith. In the 1940s and 1950s Smith had utilized the industrial process of welding to produce imposing steel or other metal structures, thereby establishing the practice of construction, pioneered by artists such as Picasso and the Russian constructivists earlier in the century, as the pre-eminent post-war sculptural principle. Revitalizing British sculpture through the importation of Smith's techniques, Caro boldly dispensed with the American's assumption that sculpture should be oriented vertically from a base. Smith's links to an older Abstract Expressionist generation had predisposed him towards residues of figuration, even in his most apparently abstract works [67], but Caro made a radical shift to horizontally oriented abstract sculptures. Occupying large areas of ground, they were painted in the bright colours of American Post-Painterly Abstraction in order to counteract their weight and make their elements 'hover' above the ground. Fried in particular lauded Caro for achieving a purely non-referential Modernist sculptural syntax in which part-to-part relationships were orchestrated to cohere, as the spectators circled the works, in moments of optical exultation [68].

It was this balancing of relational parts that Stella and Judd disliked. Judd's own objects acknowledged construction as a technical paradigm,

66 Donald Judd

Untitled, 1969

Judd's industrially manufactured, modular pieces, developed from 1966 onwards, were stubbornly empirical investigations of specific materials and visual effects. He shunned mystification and openly declared the nature of his structures. The interiors of his boxes were normally exposed or could be viewed through coloured Perspex. Colour was often inherent in the materials he selected, but he sometimes coated his metal pieces with metallic motorcycle paints so that colour appeared to be at one with the surface rather than 'applied'.

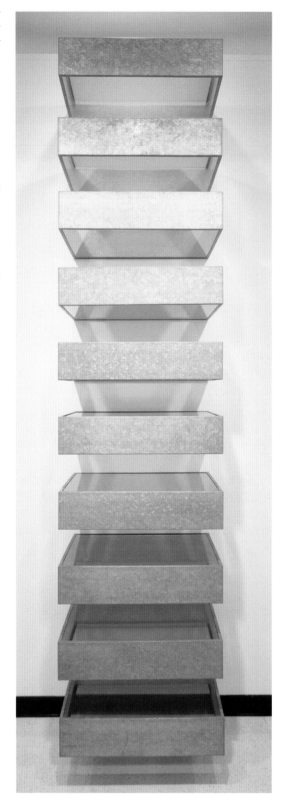

Lectern Sentinel, 1961

Smith's series of *Sentinel* sculptures, which were begun in 1956, were placed in the landscape surrounding his studio at Bolton Landing in upstate New York. Given their clear figurative associations, they appeared to survey or guard the terrain. In this example, the overlapping and angling of the welded stainless-steel plates brilliantly hint at the classical motif of *contrapposto*, whereby the body is slightly twisted through the employment of a resting and a supporting leg.

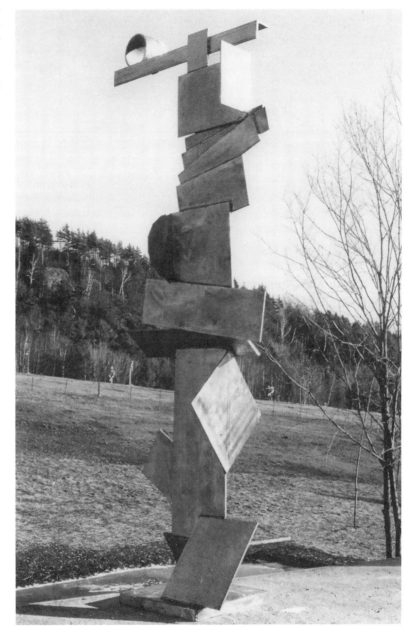

but completely rejected a composed or 'arty' look. For Stella and Judd relational art was intrinsically Modernist, but it was also seen as tethered to European sensibility, which is where the aforementioned cultural chauvinism comes in. Thinking largely of European geometrical abstraction, Judd asserted in a 1966 interview with Stella and himself that European art was 'over with': the new American art was characterized by a direct and powerful presentation of 'whole things', whereas European art was 'rationalistic'. However ambivalent he was about Modernist values, he was

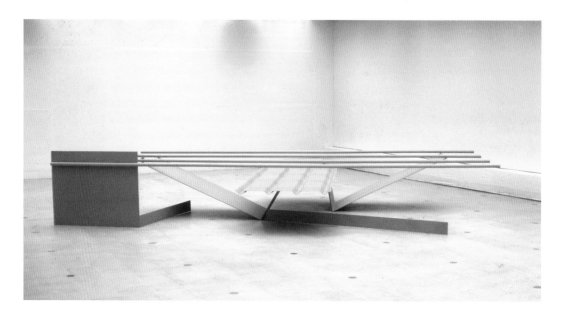

68 Anthony Caro

Prairie, 1967

The rods in Caro's sculpture
seem to float uncannily
above the ground, appearing
merely to touch the plates
from which they are
cantilevered. Caro enhanced
this effect by painting them
a lighter yellow than the
structure beneath, whose
corrugations, travelling
in a different direction,
nevertheless rhyme visually
with the rods.

flexing America's art-world muscle in the way that Greenberg and New York's MoMA had in the 1950s.

If the above appears to tilt the discussion in favour of Judd's pristine objects embodying the technological sublime (in other words, an awed capitulation to the sheer authority of America's spreading technological and corporate might), it is worth investigating Stella's and Judd's claim that non-relational works of art were in some way a release from rationalism—a principle that might, initially, appear to be synonymous with authoritative exposition and clarity. By looking now to the wider minimalist milieu, a rather different picture emerges.

Minimalism and anti-rationalism

The 'Minimal Art' tag was derived from the title of a 1965 essay on the withdrawal of manual effort from aesthetic output by the British philosopher Richard Wollheim.[10] Its connotations of reductive paring-down, however, were rejected by all of the key figures who came to be identified with it after a spate of solo shows in 1963–4: Don Judd, Robert Morris, Carl Andre, and Dan Flavin. Other labels such as 'Literalism' or 'Primary Structures', the latter the title of the key exhibition of these artists at New York's Jewish Museum in 1966, were no more helpful. As Judd asserted, the reductionist interpretation of minimalist art was predicated on what was thought to be missing from the objects when works such as his were kept uncomplicated precisely in order to isolate specific and positive qualities. Reduction alternatively implies a calculated attempt to reach an essential core. In this respect the work of many minimalists implicitly denied any rationalist or idealist accession to 'meaning'. Judd's ordering systems were anti-rationalist, he claimed, because the logic of 'one thing after another' obviated the need for aesthetic decisions. In the case of Robert Morris, though, the principle of anti-idealism went deeper.

In the early 1960s Morris had been involved with the moves towards a simplified, task-oriented style of dance which his then wife, Simone Forti, and dancers such as Trisha Brown and Yvonne Rainer developed at New York's Judson Memorial Theatre. In its openness towards interdisciplinarity this tendency paralleled contemporaneous Merce Cunningham/Rauschenberg and Fluxus performances. In sculptures of the period Morris explored Duchampian preoccupations with the body and gendered identity [**27**], as noted earlier. These concerns naturally found their way into the fairly elaborate dance events he organized between 1962 and 1965 such as *Site* (1964, with Carolee Schneemann) and *Waterman Switch* (1965), but the convergence between sculpture and dance had been economically suggested in Morris's first performance, *Column*, at the Living Theatre in New York in 1961. The 'performer' in the piece was a grey-painted 8-foot (2.4-metre) plywood column which stood on an empty stage for three and a half minutes. Manipulated externally by strings, it then fell to the floor, where it remained for the same period before the performance ended. The piece conflated anthropomorphic allusions to male sexuality (as subsequently explored in *I-Box*) and current moves in sculpture from a (virile) verticality to a stress on horizontality [**67, 68**]. In 1964–5, Morris began to use such geometrical forms in the context of minimalism, but his sense of their metaphorical possibilities clearly separated him from Judd.

This is not to say that Morris was unconcerned with the problem of maintaining the sense of the wholeness of his geometrical forms. However, in his contemporaneous *Notes on Sculpture* he evinced an interest in how such 'whole objects' were actually perceived by spectators, playing off the concept of the 'good gestalt' (a term used by psychologists to designate the whole or regular structures we are predisposed to search for in visual configurations) against the fact that our bodily based experience of objects, even the most regular ones, is inevitably partial or contingent. We may be able to conceptualize 'cubeness', but we can only experience actual cubes in time from certain angles and distances. We oscillate, as Morris put it, between the 'known constant and the experienced variable'.[11]

In real terms, this led Morris to the controlled perceptual conditions involved in works like *Untitled (Three L-Beams)* of 1965. These large, identical L-beams were placed in sitting, lying, and balancing postures, like three platonic Graces. The spectator's experience of them as visually different had to be reconciled with the fact that their natures were identical. Much has been made of Morris's interest at this time in Merleau-Ponty's *Phenomenology of Perception* (1945), in which the philosopher was at pains to strip the body's primordial apprehensions of spatial, temporal, or sensory stimuli from the tyranny of predetermined axiomatic truths. Morris's Green Gallery exhibition of 1964–5 [**69**] might almost be described as a phenomenological gymnasium, its aesthetic apparatus designed to tone up its audience's eyes, bodies, and minds. What is clear is that Morris's work '[took] relationships out of the work and [made] them a function of space, light and the viewer's field of vision'.[12]

In moving from Judd's non-relational interests to Morris's phenomenological ones, a split within minimalism emerged between a desire to see art

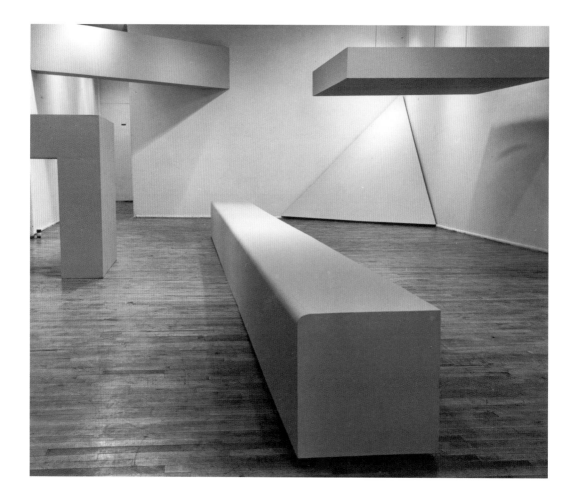

objects achieve ultimate self-sufficiency (thereby pushing the Modernist credo to its limits) and a desire to see such objects defined by their ambient conditions.[13] The latter position, which Morris partly inherited from the Duchampian emphasis on the role of the spectator, constitutes a radical break with Modernist assumptions, undermining the autonomy previously claimed for works of art. Minimalism here becomes deeply relativistic, supportive of the view that art can only acquire value or worth in relation to external factors, such as its social or institutional setting. Such a view sets distinct limits on the artist's ability to control meaning, recalling Barthes's theorization of the loss of authorial agency.

This issue of loss of agency can be differently exemplified in the art historian Rosalind Krauss's reading of the anti-rationalism of another artist associated with minimalism, Sol LeWitt. Discussing his *Variations of Incomplete Open Cubes* (1974), a modular structure composed of 122 wooden units demonstrating all the permutations produced by systematically removing the various sides of a cube, she shows how an apparent logicality flips into obsessive compulsion.[14] Although LeWitt's productions clearly responded to minimalist preoccupations, such that this project echoes Morris's play on the 'known constant' discussed above, he was to present himself as one of the first practitioners of Conceptual Art in articles of 1967 and 1969 with statements such as, 'The idea becomes a machine that makes the art'.[15] This principle informs the wall drawings that LeWitt embarked on from 1968 onwards. Revealing a minimalist predilection for impersonality, they were designed for specific locations but were frequently carried out by draughtsmen on the basis of succinct instructions from LeWitt—for instance, 'circles, grids, arcs from four corners and sides' [70]. Strict adhesion to such prescriptions, with no clear sense of how they would unravel *in situ*, led the interpreters to produce unexpectedly labyrinthine or eccentric visual structures. Again, the strange coexistence within minimalism of authorial removal and aesthetic autonomy is touched upon.

LeWitt's abandonment of control, his deployment of pragmatic systems to undermine rationality, would appear to argue against the earlier points made about minimalism's tacit complicity with America's power base. However, the loss of agency which he seems glad to submit to may be read as the symptomatic underside of that coin. In this sense, minimalism emerges as the aberrant child of booming industry and mass production, its fixations on strong *Gestalts* and repetitive systems bespeaking a pragmatism internalized and, in many cases, gone awry. Forcing Modernist aesthetics to breaking point, minimalism vacillated between an awe for the totality of power and a sense of powerlessness. In the latter respect it was closer to America's disaffected countercultures of the mid-1960s than might be supposed.

'Art and Objecthood': Fried and his detractors

In June 1967 the critic Michael Fried published an essay of pivotal importance entitled *Art and Objecthood*, which staunchly defended the Modernist cause against minimalism (he called it 'Literalism' in the essay).[16] Greenberg had already disparaged the minimalist object two months earlier for being too gratuitously 'far-out' and intellectualized, no more readable as art than 'a door, a table, a sheet of paper'.[17] Essentially Fried expanded this view that minimalist works did not distinguish themselves sufficiently from mere objects, arguing that the real test of a work of art was that it 'suspend its own objecthood'. Modernist art was now charged with the strenuous task of 'compelling conviction' pictorially, which meant overcoming the limitations of literal shape through the mystique of 'opticality'. (We saw earlier how he attempted to make this stick in the case of the recalcitrant Stella.)

Thinking mainly of Robert Morris [69], Fried asserted that minimalism committed the cardinal sin, from a Modernist viewpoint, of borrowing another discipline's effects. In the case of minimalism, theatre appropriately supplied the effects. Minimalist objects were said to rely for their uncanny anthropomorphic sense of 'presence' precisely on being like presences waiting to be met (and completed as artworks) by spectators entering the gallery space. Theatrical staging and duration, Fried argued, were integral to their functioning, and in danger of usurping their raison d'être entirely. Whilst the presence of such objects made spectators conscious of their own physicality, the superior Modernist works of Caro possessed an absorbing *presentness*, momentarily freeing spectators from self-awareness. One effect was profane, the other transcendent. Concerned that the turn to minimalism

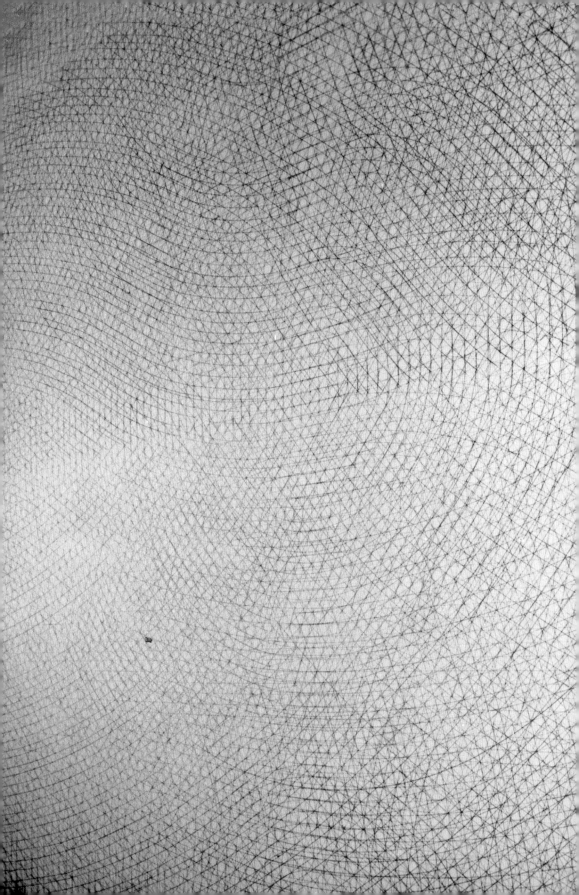

70 Sol LeWitt

Circles, Grids, Arcs from Four Corners and Sides, 1973 (detail)

In the early 1960s LeWitt had largely devoted himself to producing modular open cube structures made from wood. His wall drawings represented a continuation of his interest in pushing systems to their limits, but also made a radical contribution to the history of drawing. Drawing has traditionally been thought a peculiarly private activity for artists, a way of trying out ideas, preparing for more finished works in other media. LeWitt both removes himself from its production, providing it with a conceptual basis, and turns it into a public art. In a sense these works are modern descendants of fresco paintings.

might threaten the idealist values bound up with the latter, Fried famously declared that Modernist art and 'theatricality' were 'at war'.

They had been skirmishing for years, and Chapter 6 will demonstrate that theatricalities of various orders won out in the 1970s. But Fried was correct in recognizing that a great deal stood to be lost. If factors such as the height or position of a spectator became entangled with the functioning of a work of art, how could secure, universally valid value judgements be made about its success or otherwise? Too many variables were in play. New criteria for legitimating art's societal status would follow and the cultivated humanist art criticism, predicated on the possession of a 'good eye' that Fried practised, would be in jeopardy. Clearly there was an ideological basis to Fried's fears. This point can be further elaborated by considering the minimalist Carl Andre.

Andre's sculptural aesthetic was heavily indebted to the early twentieth-century Romanian sculptor Constantin Brancusi, particularly his *Endless Column* (1937), in which modular zigzag elements were stacked vertically, implying infinite extension both upwards and downwards. Andre similarly employed standardized units in sculptures from the early 1960s onwards, utilizing prefabricated elements such as sheets of metal or bricks and arranging them, as did his friend Frank Stella, in self-evident, numerically determined structures. In *Lever* of 1966, which consisted of a line of 139 abutted firebricks, he claimed to have brought Brancusi's column down to earth: 'Most sculpture is priapic with the male organ in the air. In my work, Priapus is down on the floor.'[18] This enactment of the 'fall' of sculpture logically led him to consider the terrain it covered. His *Floor Pieces* [71] were thus compressed pedestals from which spectators, who were encouraged to walk on them, could look beyond art. In *Art and Objecthood* Fried discussed an anecdote recounted by the sculptor Tony Smith in which, driving along the New Jersey Turnpike, Smith had sensed a kind of elation at the endlessness of the experience. Smith's yearning for an experiential state that could not be 'framed' not only epitomized the lure of theatricality for Fried but betokened the art object's complete dissolution. And, although he did not say as much, if the object disappeared, so would its role as item of exchange-value.

This leads on to the politics embedded in the physical aspects of Andre's *Floor Pieces*. The artist asserted that part of his intention was to sensitize his

71 Carl Andre

Magnesium Square, 1969

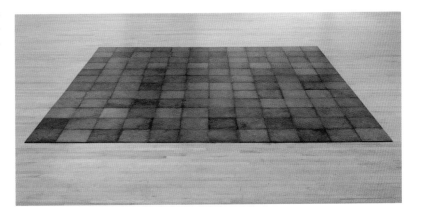

spectators to gravity. The properties of the materials he used—lead, copper, aluminium, and so on—would thus be transmitted through his audience's feet. This bias towards physically based sensations extended to a materialist conception of art itself. He claimed that his work was 'atheistic, materialistic and communistic', the last because its non-hierarchical structures, based on bringing 'particles' into alliance rather than corralling parts into a whole via processes such as welding, were somehow 'accessible to all men'.[19] It is ironic that Andre's works later aroused widespread hostility. In 1976 the revelation that the Tate Gallery in London had bought part of Andre's brick work *Equivalents I–VIII*, as orchestrated by Britain's popular press, led to philistine attacks on the spending policies of Britain's public galleries from general public and art establishment alike.[20] But the marxist/materialist ideology informing Andre's aesthetics separated him, and many of his artist associates,

72 Agnes Martin

Flower in the Wind, 1963

In her consistent use of grids Agnes Martin participated in a tradition in twentieth-century art stretching from the Cubists and Mondrian to her minimalist contemporaries. The grid was a non-hierarchical and non-referential structure. It asserted the flatness of the picture plane, echoing its framing limits while implying an indefinite structural extension of the picture beyond its limits. For Martin this had metaphysical connotations, whereas for the Minimalists its associations were essentially literal and pragmatic.

from Fried's conservative humanism, however surely his works later became items of exchange-value. The politicization of the late 1960s avant-garde will be discussed in Chapter 6, but Andre's role in the formation of the Art Workers' Coalition in 1969, which subsequently protested against the art establishment's tacit assent to war in Vietnam, should be noted in passing.

Materialist ideologies by no means pervaded all of the art associated with minimalism. The American painter Agnes Martin, who became identified with the movement when her works were exhibited in the *Systemic Abstraction* show at New York's Guggenheim Museum in 1966, sought spiritual absolutes. An enormously self-reliant artist, from a Presbyterian background, she produced taut but tremulous graphite lattices on lightly painted fields. These were intended to evoke luminescence or immateriality and lighten the 'weight' of the squares that enclosed them [**72**].[21] Martin's mystical denial of ego ran the risk of conforming to prevalent stereotypes of female passivity, but it also prevented critics from reducing her work to the personal or biographical, as will be seen to have happened in the case of Eva Hesse.

Martin's quietism provides a striking contrast with another female abstractionist who emerged in the late 1960s, in the context of the British response to Modernism—Bridget Riley. Sculptural abstraction in Britain had been galvanized, in more senses than one, by the 1965 *New Generation* show at London's Whitechapel Gallery, which established Caro's painted constructions as paradigmatic for a generation of sculptors, notably Phillip King. In terms of abstract painting, however, London rather lagged behind New York's example, despite the initial promise of Robyn Denny's and Bernard Cohen's paintings in the wake of the 1960s *Situation* exhibition. Minimalist aesthetics were likewise slowly assimilated. Riley, however, carved out a profoundly distinctive path with her assertive, optically disorientating paintings.

Although her work had superficial parallels with the formulaic illusion-inducing paintings of the Hungarian Victor Vasarely, the basis of Riley's work in naturalistic starting points (such as the effects of wind in long grass), or in physical sensations, provided her work with greater metaphorical range. The invasive energy of certain images [**73**] quickly led to threatened male critics complaining of unfeminine 'aggression'. She achieved international prominence in 1965 when she was featured, alongside her compatriot Michael

---

Minimalism and the masculine

The abstractionist Agnes Martin's desire for what she once described as 'impotence' might be seen as implicitly criticizing minimalism's flirtation with power, reminding us that, however radical its anti-idealist rhetoric, minimalism was fundamentally a male movement. In this respect the art historian Anna Chave has noted a preponderance of phallic metaphors among its male practitioners. The sculptor Dan Flavin's breakthrough to his signature use of fluorescent tubes was thus the *Diagonal of May 25th 1963*, a strip light, angled at 45 degrees, which corresponded, as the artist once averred, to the 'diagonal of personal ecstasy'. Carl Andre's claims that his works brought Priapus down to earth seem relevant here, but it could well be maintained that, as with Robert Morris's *Column*, discussed in the last section, a *parody* of sculptural virility was involved, presaging new conceptions of male artistic identity.

Kidner, in the *Responsive Eye* exhibition at New York's MoMA, following this up by winning the prize for painting at the 1968 Venice Biennale, but her work often aroused suspicion.

This was partly due to the way Riley became synonymous with the fashionable cult of 1960s Op Art. Arriving in New York for the *Responsive Eye* exhibition, she was appalled to see how quickly her motifs had migrated onto dresses in shop windows, and attempted unsuccessfully to sue for copyright infringement. More damaging was the vitriol of American critics. Incensed that the curator of *The Responsive Eye*, William Seitz, had had the temerity to place the likes of Riley next to American abstractionists such as Morris Louis, Rosalind Krauss—a critical ally of Fried—asserted that Riley's species of 'opticality' was pure gimmickry in comparison with the superior Modernist variety, no more worthwhile than exercises in perceptual illusion produced by students.[22]

Krauss's hierarchy of opticalities has its ironies. Following a shift of allegiance to a counter-Modernist position in the 1970s, she would eventually champion the historical importance of Duchamp's path-breaking experiments with optical illusion, in the form of his *Rotorelief* discs of 1935. When rotated on a machine, certain of these set up pulsatile oscillations between inward and outward expansion. Krauss therefore came to see them as exemplifications of an impulse in twentieth-century art away from Modernism's lofty disembodied visuality—which made no attempts

73 Bridget Riley

Blaze 1, 1962

Riley's Op paintings of the early 1960s were exclusively in black and white although, as her critical mentor the psychologist Anton Ehrenzweig noted, they could generate disembodied sensations of colour. She was to begin incorporating colour into her work from 1966 onwards, exploiting dazzling chromatic contrasts.

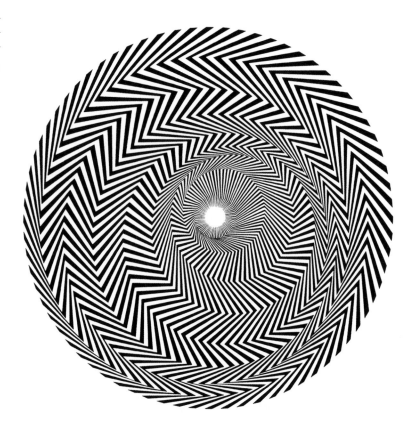

to meet spectators' visual 'desires'—and towards the gratification of somatic fantasies.[23] Riley's illusions were not pledged to undercutting the sovereignty of retinal art in quite the same way as Duchamp's, and a trend towards Kinetic Art in the 1960s would take up, in its own quasi-scientific terms, his exploration of actual movement. Her contribution to challenging Modernist proprieties has, however, been obscured by the vagaries of critical debate.

In America the promotion of Modernist opticality on the East Coast also deflected attention from work dealing with the mechanics of perception by West Coast artists. Robert Irwin and James Turrell's Light and Space Movement, formed in Los Angeles in the late 1960s, was dedicated to sensitizing spectators to the mysteries of natural light. Such effects took some stage-managing and Turrell eventually dedicated himself to creating *Sky Window* installations, consisting of rectangular apertures in the ceilings of rooms, through which ineffable changes in the sky's luminosity or chromatic density could be experienced. From 1977 onwards he laboured on his huge Roden Crater project, transforming the interior of a volcanic cinder cone in Arizona. Works such as these were intended to engender experiences of ethereal other-worldliness rather than carnal excitation or convulsion. But it is clear, not least from Krauss's change of direction, that aberrant forms of opticality would eventually join forces with theatricality in rendering Fried's Modernism insensitive to changing needs, and hardly as timeless as he imagined.

Anti Form and body metaphors: Hesse and Bourgeois

In the mid-1960s minimalism functioned as a kind of purgative, ridding sculpture of surplus aesthetic and metaphorical baggage, but its austerity almost begged to be undercut. In 1968, therefore, Robert Morris published a text, titled *Anti Form*, which was widely taken to signal a refutation of minimalism's assumptions. That a short article by an artist possessed such clout is symptomatic of a widespread acceptance of artists as theoretical legislators in the later 1960s. This went hand in hand with a changing sense of art's academic status. Artists increasingly moved between humanities disciplines. Morris, for example, had studied psychology and philosophy in the early 1950s; Don Judd, who published extensively as an art critic, had studied philosophy at Columbia University.

In *Anti Form* Morris argued that, rather than being preconceived, sculpture should follow the dictates of process. Seriality should be abandoned in favour of randomness and materials should be allowed to find their own forms in response to principles such as gravity.[24] Renouncing geometry, he himself scattered materials such as threads or metal scraps in amorphous masses on gallery floors or, having cut strips into large sheets of felt, hung them from hooks so that the strips cascaded to the floor. Given that he and Carl Andre had regarded their practices as imbued with anti-virile metaphors, this change of tack might be interpreted as a means of softening minimalism's hard masculinist edges. (It is far from coincidental that Morris illustrated *Anti Form* with one of Oldenburg's 'soft sculptures'.) Dissolution was a cultural condition in 1968. As we shall see, the gallery system was under attack, and Morris was pledged to undermining its rigidities, as well as his own. However, if Morris feminized his practice, it is ironic that a female

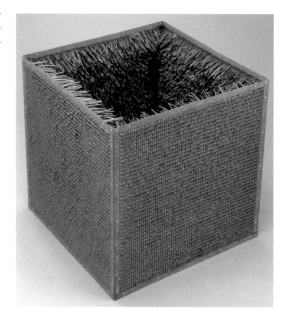

curator, Lucy Lippard, had already set the desublimation of minimalism in motion.

In 1966 Lippard had curated an important exhibition entitled *Eccentric Abstraction* at New York's Fischbach Gallery, dedicated to work which addressed the tactile or the visceral rather than the cerebral. Under this rubric she particularly promoted the work of the German-born artist Eva Hesse. Familiar with minimalist ideas through her friendship with Sol LeWitt, Hesse had recently begun exploring the underside of the movement's fetishization of unyielding surfaces and systems. In 1968, for instance, she produced two versions of *Accession*, consisting of perforated Minimalist cubes threaded with thousands of pieces of plastic tubing which provided them with bristling interior lives [**74**]. These pieces had obvious bodily connotations, but the dialectic of mutually defining principles that they embodied clearly pre-empted Morris's move to *Anti Form*.

The biological associations of Hesse's work invariably existed in counterpoint to her emphasis on the literal nature of materials. Lippard underlined this, observing that, in 'eccentric abstraction', 'a bag remains a bag and does not become a uterus, a tube is a tube and not a phallic symbol. Too much free association on the viewer's part is combatted by formal understatement.'[25] Hesse in fact stressed that absurdity was often her most pressing theme. This was exemplified by *Hang Up* of 1966, in which an enormous loop of metal wire, extending from a frame bandaged in cloth, flopped out into the viewer's space as though paradoxically disgorging the frame's emptiness [**75**].

Whatever existential dilemma it embodied, *Hang Up*'s figuring of emptiness begs to be interpreted in emotional terms, and psychoanalytical accounts of Hesse's work have posited the death of her father in the year it was produced, which reactivated memories for her of her mother's suicide, as a key determinant for subsequent works.[26] However, such analyses tend to construct Hesse as a peculiarly inward artist, more attuned to psychological

Hang Up, 1966

Constructed according to Hesse's specifications by her then husband, the sculptor Tom Doyle, and her friend, the conceptualist Sol LeWitt, *Hang Up* combines a number of contradictory elements: painting and sculpture, pictorial space and real space, emptiness and expansiveness. The painted 'frame' is tonally gradated from dark to light grey, as is the wire that extends from it some 10 feet (3 metres) into the spectator's space. This tonal fluctuation lends further instability to what is already an unstable, or paradoxical, visual experience. At the time the work was produced, Hesse was interested in the existential writings of Samuel Beckett, whose *Waiting for Godot* she saw as paralleling her own sense of the comic absurdity of existence. She was also affected by Ad Reinhardt's renunciative art and writing.

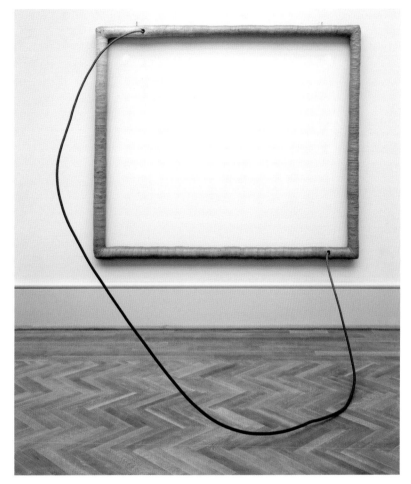

nuances, by virtue of her sex, than her male peers. They are given piquancy by the fact that Hesse died tragically young from a brain tumour, but interpretations which see her work as mired in morbidity, such that her use of cheesecloth dipped in latex has been said to evoke diseased skin, have served her badly. Hesse's success stemmed from her ability to seize educational opportunities such as a scholarship to Yale University, which in turn allowed her to surmount contemporaneous social taboos against women departing from the domestic sphere. Her journals bear witness to the pressures of maintaining a dual identity as a woman and an artist: 'I cannot be something for everyone... Woman, beautiful, artist, wife, house-keeper, cook.'[27]

Biographical drama tends to detract from Hesse's historical significance. In many ways she maintained a more frank and inventive relation to the history of sculpture than her male counterparts. Hesse's breakthrough to a mature style was partly a response to seeing Beuys's process-oriented works during a period spent in Germany in 1964–5. By contrast, Morris virtually repressed his debt to Beuys (although it resurfaced in his utilization of felt). Similarly, Hesse implicitly acknowledged that, just as Pollock's painting

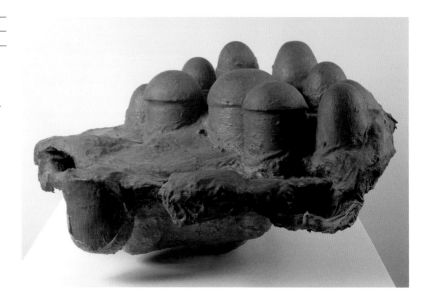

had spawned a genre of performative art, so it now stood as exemplary for sculpture. Although Morris's *Anti Form* article significantly reinterpreted Pollock's drip paintings as being about the behaviour of materials rather than Modernist opticality, it was Hesse who, in her last *Rope Pieces* of 1969–70, translated Pollock's painterly skeins into two highly evocative hanging sculptures. One, utilizing fibreglass over string, had the delicacy of a spider's web, whilst the other, in latex, threatened to absorb the spectator in its tangles.

If Hesse's formal originality got overlooked, her reintroduction of body metaphors into abstract sculpture initially overshadowed the contribution of an older French-born artist, Louise Bourgeois. She had been using a material that became associated with Hesse, liquid latex, to create visceral, biomorphic sculptures in the early 1960s [**76**]. But although Lippard showed her work alongside that of Hesse in *Eccentric Abstraction*, Bourgeois remained relatively unappreciated until the early 1980s. Before leaving France for America in 1938 she had been affected by Surrealism's emphasis on psychoanalytic investigation. Whereas Hesse publicly made little of the psychological content of her work, aware perhaps of the dangers discussed above, Bourgeois gradually revealed that a complex psychobiography informed her output. Such openness went hand in hand with the increasing politicization of women artists, accompanied by changed aesthetic values, in the 1970s (see Chapter 6).

The troubled early history that informed Bourgeois's work involved the fact that her father had installed his mistress in the family home, systematically undermining the self-esteem of his wife and daughter. Bourgeois's intensely ambivalent feelings towards him would be given expression in disturbingly direct works such as the installation *Destruction of the Father* (1974), a conglomeration of globular forms both sprouting from and overhanging a long 'table', based on a cannibalistic patricidal fantasy. In smaller carved or modelled sculptures she developed a lexicon of mutating 'part objects'— split-off parts of the body, neither securely male nor female, active or passive, onto which feelings of seduction or repulsion, pain or pleasure, could be projected.

Her persistence in using a relatively anachronistic sculptural language, partly rooted in surrealist reworkings of 'primitivist' sources, seemed increasingly pointed in the 1980s and 1990s as the Modernist imperative towards formal innovation lost its grip. She was understood as speaking in the subversively unsublimated bodily terms which (masculine) Modernism, with its abhorrence of surrealist eroticism, deemed extra-aesthetic.

Minimalist legacies: sculpture, film, public art

In December 1968 Robert Morris organized an important exhibition under the 'Anti Form' aegis called *9 at Castelli's* in the warehouse of Leo Castelli's gallery. Although Hesse was included, the successes of this exhibition were Richard Serra and Bruce Nauman, whose works explored relationships to their bodies that were more mechanistic and cerebral. Serra's use of industrial materials to carry out actions such as rolling, folding, and splashing drew on the working-class industrial roots he shared with Carl Andre, exhibiting a pronounced masculinist ethos. In *Casting*, carried out in situ at Castelli's, Serra threw molten lead into the angled junction between the floor and wall of the space, pulling the resultant castings away when they hardened and repeating the action to produce a series of 'waves'. This concern with physical operations led him to examine the way forces were brought into equilibrium by rudimentary leaning or propped structures. In *Corner Prop* (1969) a 2-foot- (0.6-metre-) square cube of lead was supported against a wall, over 6 feet (1.8 metres) above the ground, by means of a slender lead pipe. With such heavy materials problems of balance were decidedly literal rather than 'pictorial', and the sense that the works might collapse provided spectators with an uncomfortable frisson, directly addressing their bodily presences.

Time was an active principle in Serra's work and he therefore made several short films, such as *Hand Catching Lead* (1968) [**77**], in which repeated images of a hand attempting to catch a falling piece of lead create a hypnotic rhythm, making the spectator conscious of the filmic process. Film's intrinsic qualities as a medium rather than as a vehicle for narrative had been explored earlier in the century by artists such as Hans Richter and Man Ray. However, it was not until the turn of the 1960s, largely as a result of the advocacy and commitment of the Lithuanian-born critic and film-maker Jonas Mekas in New York, that the 'underground' films of figures such as Stan Brakhage, Bruce Conner, and Andy Warhol came to represent an alliance between film and experimental practices in other artistic media. By the late 1960s the abstract possibilities of the medium were being explored in the 'structuralist' films of the American Hollis Frampton and the Canadian-born Michael Snow. The latter was a friend of Serra, and his film *Wavelength* (1967), consisting of a continuous zoom through his apartment lasting forty-five minutes, heavily affected the sculptor, who promoted it vigorously on a trip to Europe in 1969. This kind of cross-fertilization between artists, which further extended to Serra's friendship with the minimalist composer Philip Glass, was typical of the times, paralleling a questioning of disciplinary boundaries that had been given impetus by Fluxus.

Bruce Nauman, based in Los Angeles, also turned to film (and videotape), although more as a means of recording a sequence of performances, carried

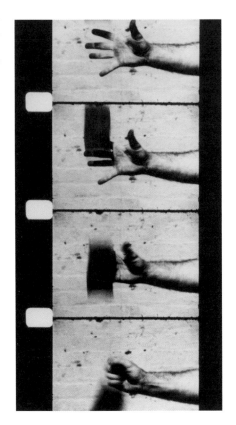

out in the isolation of his studio, that examined sculptural, conceptual, and bodily interactions. In one he bounced two balls between the floor and ceiling of his studio. Another showed him walking, with hands clasped behind his neck, towards and away from the camera along an uncomfortably narrow 20-foot- (6-metre-) long corridor. In a third he staked out the perimeter of a square marked on the floor with balletic steps dictated by a metronome's beat [**78**].

Nauman's interrogation of his bodily identity owed much to a heady cocktail of reading. Samuel Beckett and the *Gestalt* psychology and phenomenology that had affected Morris were formative influences. So was the philosophy of Wittgenstein, with its scepticism as to language's ability to broker between public and private systems of meaning. In a sequence of sculptural objects, partly indebted to Duchamp, whose example for West Coast artists was particularly vivid after his retrospective in Pasadena in 1963, Nauman sent language's metaphorical and descriptive functions spinning into collision. Its role as name (and identity) was submitted to the principle of anamorphosis in a work consisting of neon tubing, *My Last Name Exaggerated Fourteen Times Vertically*, of 1967 [**79**]. Stretching out the implications of his signature with the detachment of a laboratory investigator, Nauman succinctly articulated a male artist's self-alienation in direct counterpoint to what has been said about Hesse's or Bourgeois's ability to metaphorize their bodies/identities within their objects.

78 Bruce Nauman

*Dance or Exercise on the
Perimeter of a Square*
(film), 1967–8

Carried out for the camera
alone, Nauman's
performances of the late
1960s often dealt with the
artist's confinement in his
studio. This was ironic given
that elsewhere art was
shrugging off its traditional
solipsism and taking to the
streets [**82**]. In a sense,
though, Nauman was testing
himself against humanist
models of the body and
philosophical introspection.
This work could almost be a
post-existential satire on
Leonardo da Vinci's famous
humanist emblem of man
circumscribed by geometry.

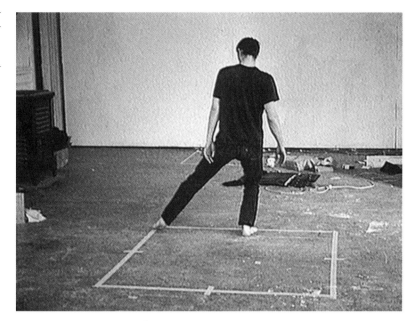

79 Bruce Nauman

*My Last Name Exaggerated
Fourteen Times Vertically*,
1967

This relates to another work
of 1968, *My Name As
Though It Were Written on
the Surface of the Moon*,
also in neon. The latter,
slightly more legibly, reads:
'bbbbbbrrrrrruuuuuucc-
cccceeeeee'. It has been
suggested that it may
have been a response to
photographs sent back to
earth by five lunar orbiters
launched by the US between
1966 and 1968.

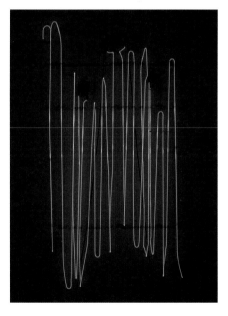

Nauman's use of neon was not unprecedented. The minimalist Dan Flavin
was an obvious reference point. The conceptualist Joseph Kosuth had also
investigated Wittgensteinian tautologies regarding language and representation in neon works such as the self-descriptive, blue-lit *Five Words in Blue
Neon* (1965). However, Nauman's ironic allusions to the numinous connotations of light put him more in line with European contemporaries such
as the Italian *Arte Povera* artist Mario Merz, who revivified assemblages of
mundane objects through the insertion of neon tubes. Neon also connotes the
public dimension, via advertising, and in later works of the 1980s Nauman

ironically brought it into proximity with private erotic imagery. *Hanged Man* (1985) once again deals with male sexuality. Two overlapping neon circuits alternately flash on and off. One represents a live, hanging stickman with enormous limp phallus; the other depicts him hanged, with an erection. Such sadistic (or masochistic) allusions to games and torture, coupled with the theme of surveillance, would further dominate the video works Nauman produced in the late 1980s and 1990s.

It is clear that Nauman's cluster of body-related metaphors increasingly eluded a fixed artistic medium. More than Serra, therefore, his concerns in the late 1960s crossed over from sculpture into the spheres of Conceptual and Performance Art, which will be discussed shortly. Modernist aesthetics had reached a cul-de-sac, compromising the expressive resources of sculpture and painting, whilst the logic of Morris's minimalism pointed beyond traditional forms. Breathing space had to be sought in less heavily colonized visual practices. This situation persisted until well into the 1970s, and sculptural metaphor, as investigated by the likes of Hesse and Bourgeois, would be revisited on the back of a return to figuration. This development can briefly be indicated by looking at British sculpture.

In the late 1960s Anti Form's main exponent in British sculpture, defying all that Caro stood for, had been Barry Flanagan, who produced quirky ensembles of rope and sand-filled hessian sacks. In the 1970s Richard Long kept post-minimalist principles alive through his informal placement of stones or sticks in landscape locations. In an earlier work, *A Line Made for Walking* (1967), which was recorded in a photograph, he hardly intervened as a maker, simply treading a mark into a field. But these works ultimately embodied a romantic desire to escape aesthetic confinement. It was not until the end of the 1970s, in the work of a new generation of sculptors including Tony Cragg, Richard Deacon, Edward Allington, Anish Kapoor, and Bill Woodrow, that the sculptural object as such, in relation to human or urban themes, reassumed importance.

This group came to prominence in a key exhibition of 1981, held in London and Bristol, entitled *Objects and Sculptures*, which paralleled contemporaneous exhibitions of painting signalling a new zeitgeist (see Chapter 7). Their work varied considerably. Kapoor, an Indian-born artist, reflected something of Britain's ethnic diversity in the 1980s in exotically shaped moulded objects, placed on the floor and covered with brilliantly coloured chalk powder redolent of his country of origin. Cragg and Woodrow were drawn to the industrial landscape. The latter's *Twin Tub with Guitar* (1981) involved him cutting out and constructing a metal 'guitar' from a twin-tub washing machine, to which it remained umbilically linked. In a form of post-minimalism surrealism, he instituted alliances between unrelated objects via an industrial/consumerist logic. Less taken with overtly social themes, Deacon evoked poetic associations between ears, eyes, and animal forms in open structures constructed from girders of laminated strips of wood. The 'skins' of his large shell-like structures were often visibly patched together with materials such as sheet metal, corrugated iron, or linoleum [80]. This fusion of aesthetic form and metaphor would have been unthinkable without precedents such as Robert Morris or Eva Hesse. (Deacon frequently invoked Don Judd and Carl Andre.)

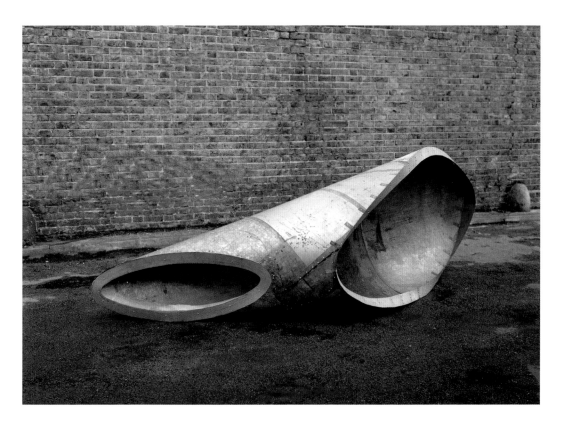

In the 1990s Rachel Whiteread was to carry out a more overt reassessment of the minimalist inheritance in very different terms. Her casts of the negative spaces surrounding objects with strong human associations such as baths or bathroom sinks had a precursor in one of Bruce Nauman's enigmatic sculptures, *A Cast of the Space Under My Chair* (1966–8). However, Whiteread pushed the emotive connotations of casting through myriad variations of material and colour, registering the poignancy of the dialectic between presence and absence. Her remarkable *House* (1993) [**81**] was cast from the inside of a house in Bow, London, from which the exterior was subsequently peeled away. The house had been the sole survivor of a line of Victorian terraced houses, slated for demolition, which symbolized the last vestiges of a working-class community now dispersed among housing schemes. Although it had never been envisaged as a permanent fixture, Whiteread's ghostly monument to the former dwelling spoke eloquently of the erasure of human and social memory and aroused mixed but intense public controversy before its removal by the local council.

A loose connection exists between this case and the controversial demolition of an earlier site-specific sculpture, Richard Serra's *Tilted Arc* (1981). In that instance Serra's 120-foot- (37-metre-) wide steel-plate wall had been commissioned for a civic location on New York's Federal Plaza, a pedestrian area flanked by government offices. Serra's provocative intervention in the space, which compelled pedestrians to change direction and follow his sculpture's trajectory, led to a court case in which the government body

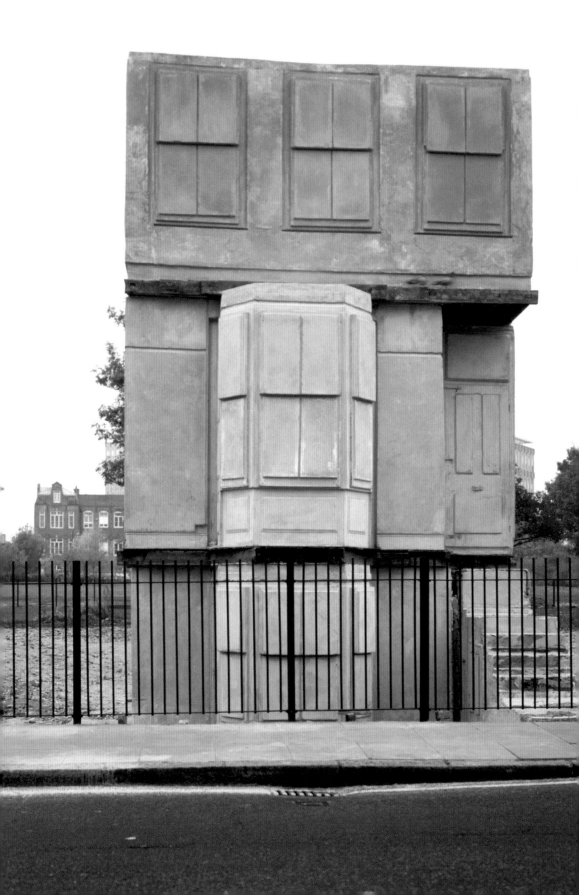

81 Rachel Whiteread

House, 1993

Rachel Whiteread's *House* revived a taste for outrage previously brought to the fore in Britain by the Tate Bricks saga. Before its completion in October 1993 it had attracted little press interest. In November of that year, however, a combination of Whiteread winning the Turner Prize and the decision by the Neighbourhood Councillors of Bow that the work should be demolished led to a massive dispute. Defenders of the work argued that an English taste for iconoclasm, dating back to the dissolution of the monasteries, was being rekindled.

that had commissioned the work secured its removal. The critic Douglas Crimp drew attention to aspects of the state's case against *Tilted Arc*, which claimed that it ran the risk of deflecting explosions onto government buildings opposite and impeded adequate surveillance of the area beyond. Such, he noted, were the state's expectations of the public.[28]

Two of the most challenging post-minimalist sculptures sited in the public domain have thus been destroyed. Whilst public sculpture has taken diverse forms since the 1960s, in several American and European cities Claes Oldenburg's upscaled Pop icons, such as the 1976 *Clothespin* in Philadelphia, have displaced Henry Moore's reclining figures as the most acceptable compromises between civic aspiration and artistic avant-gardism. In the cases of Serra and Whiteread, it appears that the metaphors left in play once Modernist aesthetics had been discredited proved too plainly redolent of the insecurities that social modernization, symbolized by the notoriously dysfunctional housing estates and soulless city centres of the 1960s and 1970s, had wrought in the social psyche. If minimalism had once proved ambivalent about technology and state power, as argued earlier, it had engendered the metaphorical resources to question such monolithic principles.

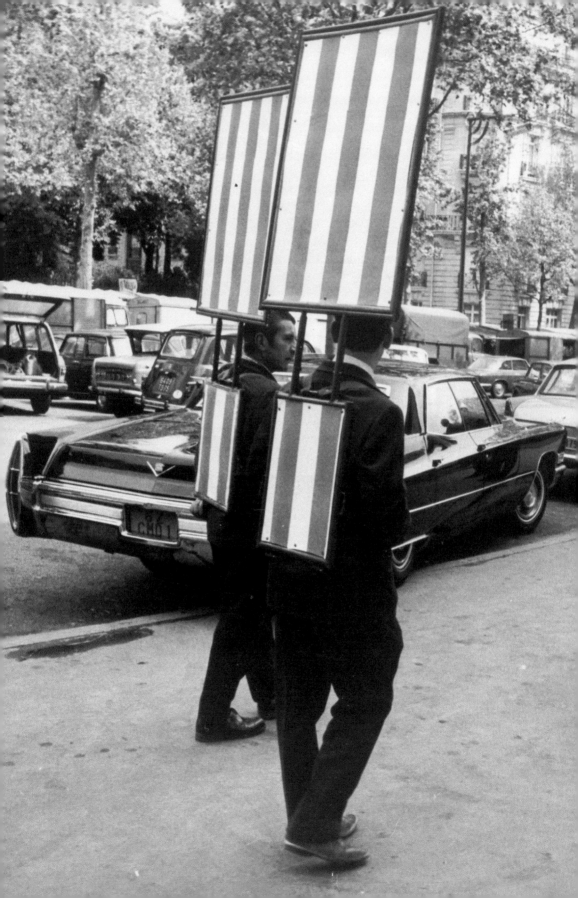

The Death of
the Object
The Move to Conceptualism

6

A curious photograph shows sandwich men walking through the streets of Paris [**82**]. They are bearing signboards displaying the stripe motifs of the French artist Daniel Buren. The image suggests directionless protest. Modernist abstraction had reached an impasse in the mid-1960s and Buren was one of many artists who felt that the entire framing or institutional conditions for avant-garde art needed to be redefined. Buren's seemingly innocuous abstractions were therefore part of a strategy. Inserted in various environments, the stripes would assert that, for all its vaunted aesthetic autonomy, Modernist art is defined by context. Paintings, especially Modernist ones, normally rely on the museum, or gallery, for their 'visibility'. Out on the streets of Paris such objects become vulnerable, invisible even. Or so Buren, envisaging the 'end of painting', hoped.[1]

The sandwich men's impotent militancy was doubly ironic. The year was 1968, now fabled as a time of political dissent across Europe and America. Over the next few years artistic tendencies such as *Arte Povera*, Land Art, Conceptual Art, and Performance Art interrogated not just aesthetic but social and cultural preconceptions. In dealing with them in this chapter, it makes sense to begin by examining a strand of politicized art linking the immediate post-1945 years to 1968 and its aftermath.

1968: political radicalism and counterculture

Although the artistic avant-garde was hardly central to the radicalism of 1968, it was certainly part of the foundations for it, particularly in France and neighbouring countries. In this respect the model of pre-war Surrealism, with its international networks and marxist commitments, was of key significance and its activist legacy needs to be plotted. From 1948 to 1951 certain artists sympathetic towards Surrealism's politics had joined forces as CoBrA, a name derived from fusing the opening letters of Copenhagen, Brussels, and Amsterdam, the cities where its members worked. This group included the Danish-born Asger Jorn, the Belgian Christian Dotremont, and the Dutch artists Karel Appel and Constant (Constant Anton Nieuwenhuys). Their output as painters relied heavily on the earlier 'automatism' of surrealists such as Joan Miró, but what made them distinctive was a collectivist group dynamic which saw the establishment, for instance, of a commune in Bregnerod, outside Copenhagen, in 1948–9. For a brief interlude before the onset of the Cold War their ideals of communal free expression represented

Detail of 82

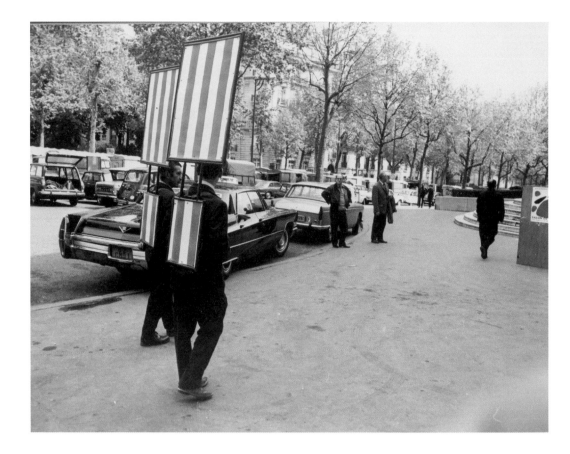

a utopian alternative to the heroic individualism of American Abstract
Expressionism and the conformism of pro-Stalinist realism.

In France, Surrealism's idiosyncratic blending of revolutionary rhetoric
and aesthetic innovation found its most spirited post-war echo in an incen-
diary movement called Lettrism, active from around 1950 and led by Isidore
Isou, a self-promoting messiah of radicalism. However, in many ways this
movement's emphasis on anarchic fragmentations of language was closer to
Dada, which had helped pioneer experimental typography and sound poetry
over thirty years earlier. Lettrism is perhaps best seen as an instance of
countercultural provocation, a bridge between Dada and the youth cults of
the 1960s and 1970s.

Lettrism's assaults on language linked it to another French movement,
Nouveau Réalisme (see Chapter 3), and particularly to the practice of
'décollage' developed by the likes of Raymond Hains and Jacques Villeglé.
Décollage involved tearing sections from compacted layers of posters or
billboard advertisements to bring about collisions of imagery and lettering.
It could be seen as a symbolic form of urban vandalism, a declaration of
solidarity with those anonymous authors of graffiti markings and defacings
who had earlier inspired the photographer Brassaï [10]. Implicit was a critique of the way public space was being rationalized to facilitate the passive
consumption of advertising and other imagery by a mass audience. In this

sense, its perpetrators were pledged to undermining the burgeoning culture industry soon to be celebrated by certain Pop artists.

Similar impulses percolated through various left-wing art formations and were finally given theoretical advocacy by a group integrating aesthetics and politics called the Situationist International, founded in 1957. The main theorist of that group was Guy Debord. Departing from the classical marxist emphasis on the primacy of production, he argued that everyday life, with its alienating work routines and stultifying restrictions, needed to be interrogated as rigorously as class relations. Once again this placed him in the tradition of surrealist thought.

The situationists denounced the myths of social freedom and satisfaction promoted by forms like advertising, asserting that such representations merged into a monolithic 'spectacle'. (Debord's key book, published in 1967, was titled *The Society of the Spectacle*.) They devised two strategies for undermining its control. One was the playfully disruptive principle of *dérive* (drift), which might involve situationists mapping alternative routes through the city in accordance with their desires rather than civic prescriptions. The surrealists had similarly followed the dictates of what they called 'objective chance'. The other, *détournement* (diversion), involved the rearrangement and derailing of existing routines and sign systems. The latter principle informed works by two artist associates of the group, the Italian Giuseppe Pinot-Gallizio and Asger Jorn, formerly a member of CoBrA. Pinot-Gallizio hijacked the principle of the production line to create 'industrial paintings' by the yard. Jorn's *Modifications* consisted of scrawled interventions on banal second-hand oil paintings [83]. Celebrating kitsch, Jorn simultaneously revitalized hackneyed aesthetics. He wrote: 'Painting is Over. You might as well finish it off. Detourn. Long live Painting.'[2]

83 Asger Jorn

Le Canard Inquiétant, from *Modifications* series, 1959

Modifications such as this were only one aspect of Jorn's output. During his early CoBrA period he produced raw, expressionistic paintings bearing scrawled imagery relating to child art. The *Modifications* attest more clearly to his political beliefs. They recall, yet again, an aspect of Duchamp's practice—this time his 'adaptation' of the *Mona Lisa* (or rather a reproduction of it) via the incorporation of the letters 'L.H.O.O.Q'. However, despite the visual dislocations Jorn brought about, he implicitly valorized the work of unknown artists.

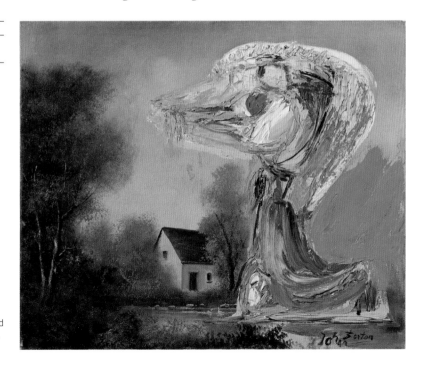

By 1962 Debord had steered Situationism away from its artistic alliances,
although he himself had produced films and worked collaboratively with
Jorn on experimental books. The aesthetic sphere was now disparaged as
merely another branch of the spectacle. Politics took centre stage and the
group played some part in mobilizing the French student strikes in 1968,
particularly at Nanterre University, where, aware of precedents in Germany
and Italy and exasperated by poor conditions and an antiquated administration, the students first took militant action. In May their colleagues were
to be joined by striking workers in bringing much of Paris to a standstill,
forcing President de Gaulle's government to a point of crisis.

In these circumstances it is hardly surprising that art's very nature and
underlying assumptions were questioned. Daniel Buren, whose stripes, borne
by sandwich men, opened this chapter, was part of international conceptualism, a tendency in art then at its height. His stripes, standardized at a width
of 8.7 centimetres and printed on varying surfaces, reflected its prioritization
of idea over process, to say nothing of its radical questioning of art's dependence on notions such as authorial origins and institutional placement. But
conceptualism was largely formalized in America and Britain and will be
discussed in those contexts in due course. As a French artist, Buren was
partly working in the tradition of Situationism, as he later confirmed.[3] One
photograph shows one of his works on a billboard, partially obscuring a flyer
relating to Nanterre's 1968 eruptions. In many respects he stands alongside
two apparently different artists from mainland Europe whose outputs,
however much they became annexed to conceptualism, ultimately stemmed
from European activist roots, although not specifically situationist ones—
Marcel Broodthaers and Hans Haacke.

Institutional critique: Broodthaers and Haacke

Marcel Broodthaers, based in Belgium, took up visual art in 1964, having
previously been a poet. His relations to it were to be profoundly ambivalent.
He had been involved in a spin-off group from CoBrA and the Belgian
Communist Party in the 1940s and 1950s and was critical of the commercial

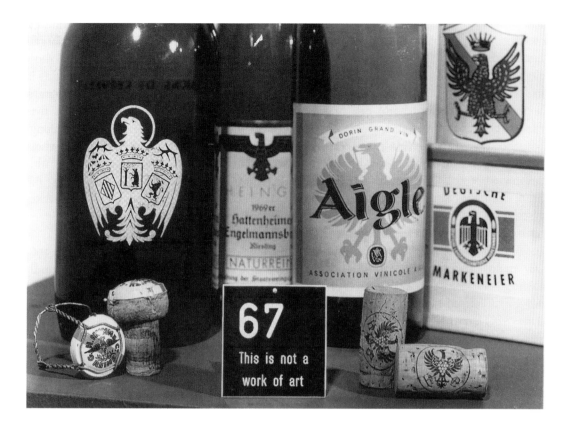

67
This is not a
work of art

motivations of much 1960s avant-gardism, particularly US-style Pop. For him the marxist notion of 'reification' (the illusory sense that social relations or values are immutable, which extends to capitalism's implantation of abstract values in material goods) was art's defining principle. His characteristic works involved esoteric exposés of the arbitrary relationships between objects and signs, in the tradition of the Belgian surrealist René Magritte's famous depiction of a pipe with the words 'This is not a pipe' inscribed beneath. In 1965, for instance, he took two human femur bones, one male and one female, and painted them the colours of the Belgian and French flags respectively, obliquely commenting on the way national characteristics are often thought, like gender, to be innate.

In 1968 Broodthaers participated in a sit-in by artists at the Palais des Beaux-Arts in Brussels. This inspired his most explicitly political project—a sardonic dismantling of the notion of the museum and its functions. It took place between 1968 and 1972 in a series of enigmatic events and installations manifesting different 'sections' of a fictitious museum. Possibly the most elaborate section, the *Department of Eagles*, displayed in the Kunsthalle in Düsseldorf in 1972, consisted of vitrines containing diverse representations of eagles, produced in art, craft, or commercial contexts and dating 'from the Oligocene to the present' [**84**]. The objects were accompanied by signs asserting 'This is not a work of art'. Acknowledging Magritte as well as Duchamp's readymades, the declarations implied that museums obscure the ideological functioning of images via the imposition of spurious value judgements or taxonomies. Eagles have often symbolized the transcendence of material reality but, like certain museum collections, they have also signified imperial might.

Whilst Broodthaers posed complex questions about cultural meaning, the German-born Hans Haacke revealed his socialist affiliations more unambiguously in his institutional interventions. Given the dramatic nature of America's Republican backlash in the immediate post-1968 period, it is not surprising that he carried these out in New York. The year 1968 had been a turning point in left-wing hopes in the US with the assassinations of Robert Kennedy and Martin Luther King. In Chicago Mayor Daley ordered brutal police reprisals against demonstrators protesting against the pro-Vietnam position adopted by the Democratic Party. In 1970 President Nixon pushed on with the war, extending it to Cambodia. This time opposition was met with the killing and wounding of student demonstrators by the National Guard at Kent State University and Jackson State College. Haacke's response to all this was to install a visitors' poll as his contribution to an exhibition entitled *Information* at New York's MoMA. It directly asked museum-goers whether they would vote for Nelson Rockefeller as Republican governor of New York State if he supported Nixon's military actions. The majority answered in the negative. Rockefeller was a prominent trustee of the museum.

American artists also targeted New York's museums. The Art Workers' Coalition, which Carl Andre helped to form in 1969, mounted two anti-Vietnam demonstrations in MoMA, whilst in May 1970 Andre and Robert Morris headed an 'Art Strike' against the powerful Metropolitan Museum of Art, demanding that it close for one day to draw attention to recent atrocities. Although the museum resisted, other institutions supported the cause. Yet however much reactionary politics cemented international bonds among avant-gardists, it took a spate of intense wrangling between the combined forces of Haacke, Buren, and Broodthaers and America's art establishment to delineate the ideological rifts most clearly.

The wrangling centred on the Solomon R. Guggenheim Museum. In 1971 it staged the sixth in a series of international exhibitions designed to demonstrate a liberal responsiveness to avant-garde developments. Daniel Buren was invited to exhibit. Part of his contribution consisted of a huge stripe painting hung from the skylight inside the building so that it plunged down the central well encircled by the famous spiral ramp of the gallery. It thereby drew attention to what Buren perceived to be the peculiarly coercive and mesmerizing effects of the architecture, which he felt diverted people's attention from the works on display. On this occasion it was necessary to compete with the museum itself to make his work 'visible'. In the event the Guggenheim's administration physically removed the work. This was ostensibly because it impeded the viewing of other site-specific work by American minimalists, but given that New York's press had started to buzz with conservative fears about the anti-institutionalism condoned by liberal arts organizations, the museum probably simply used this as a pretext. Buren had touched a sensitive nerve.[4]

This was confirmed when Haacke's forthcoming exhibition was cancelled. It was to have included documentation that the artist had unearthed in the New York County Clerk's Office relating to the corrupt dealings of the Shapolsky family, slum landlords who owned large quantities of Manhattan real estate. Although Haacke's exhibition was subsequently shown elsewhere, its cancellation provoked Marcel Broodthaers to withdraw from a Guggenheim show of European artists in 1972 and to send an elliptical open letter to fellow contributor Joseph Beuys criticizing him for continuing to participate.[5] In 1974 Haacke delivered a parting shot. He exhibited listings of the corporate and business interests of the Guggenheim Board and Trustees in a group exhibition held in the Stefanotty Gallery, New York. As with much of his future output, the interests underpinning art's supposedly neutral institutions were systematically exposed in a dry, pseudo-bureaucratic presentational style. All in all, this amounted to open warfare. In the revealing words of the Guggenheim's director Thomas Messer, Haacke's Shapolsky project had represented 'an alien substance that had entered the art museum organism'.[6] Perhaps what was at stake was a return of the repressed. The European refusal to separate art from politics was infiltrating the very networks which had once groomed Modernism for export.

The above narrative suggests that, whilst Surrealism has now become assimilated into the system it opposed, its activist post-war heirs have provoked significant moments of crisis. The art theorist Peter Bürger was damning in his assessment of artistic radicalism since 1945, arguing that, whereas avant-gardes of the early twentieth century sought to dissolve distinctions between art as a specialized sphere and other areas of social life, post-war tendencies such as American Neo-Dada merely professionalized nonconformism, turning the avant-garde itself into a social institution.[7] Buren, Broodthaers, and Haacke at least modify this view.

A coda is provided by the work of the American Gordon Matta-Clark (son of the Chilean surrealist Roberto Matta), who carried out quasi-situationist incursions into the city's fabric up until his death in 1978, literally cutting into and piercing condemned buildings. This 'anarchitecture' involved him, on one occasion, slicing a building in two halves, and revealing, like an anatomist, the inner processes of one of the 'suburban and urban boxes' that he deemed responsible for 'insuring a passive, isolated consumer' addicted to privacy and private property [**85**].[8] There is no doubting what Matta-Clark opposed, but the alternatives were less clear. After the Prague Spring had been crushed by the Russians in late 1968, Communism looked more repressive than capitalism. Chinese Maoism, although popular in the 1960s with a number of leftist intellectuals, was similarly discredited.

In 1971 Matta-Clark co-founded *Food*, a cooperative restaurant in New York, as both an artwork and a social facility, anticipating the personal and local politics of that decade. In line with the thought of French post-marxist thinkers such as Louis Althusser and Michel Foucault, ideology increasingly came to be seen as all-pervasive, at work in the very institutions in which human beings are socialized. As left-inclined artists began to examine their assumptions about gender, race, or ecology, there developed an increasingly nuanced sense of the system to which they were opposed. Political options seemed less black and white.

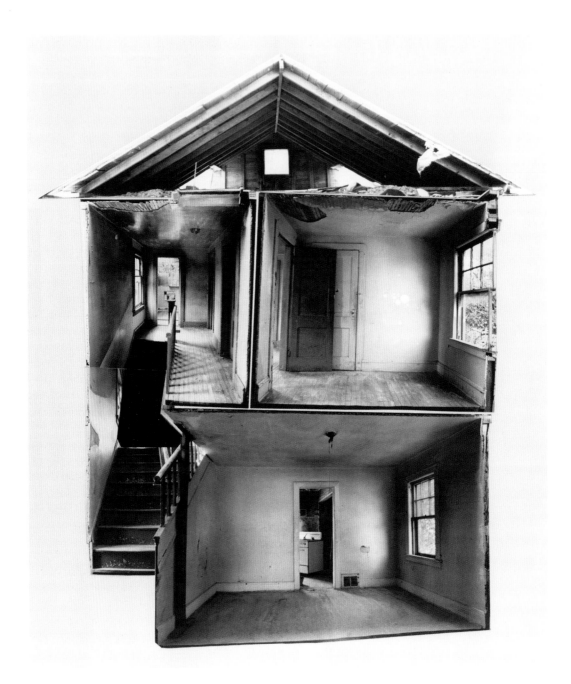

Art into life: *Arte Povera*

Europeans like Buren and Haacke raised doubts about the liberalism of New York's art establishment, but they worked within it, implicitly accepting its central position in the art world. In Europe the pull of American aesthetics continued to be resisted in certain quarters. In the mid-1960s Italian artists who were to become grouped under the *Arte Povera* (Poor Art)

85 Gordon Matta-Clark

Splitting, 1974

This collage makes use of photographs of a project carried out by Matta-Clark in Englewood, New Jersey, which involved him splitting apart a house that was due for demolition. Having divided the house in half by making two parallel cuts through it and removing the intervening section, Matta-Clark then split it by removing part of the foundations on one side and tilting that half of the building backwards.

umbrella tended to regard minimalism as narrowly prescriptive. Anticipating the way minimalism would itself open up issues of context and anti-form and looking back to the precedents set in their own country by Lucio Fontana and Piero Manzoni, figures such as Michelangelo Pistoletto and Greek-born Jannis Kounellis set about challenging Italy's tradition-bound view of aesthetics. Pistoletto produced large, polished stainless-steel sheets which incorporated the reflections of spectators within partially filled-in painted scenarios. (*Vietnam* of 1965 inserts the viewer between demonstrators carrying an anti-war banner.) Kounellis's *Untitled* installation of 1967 featured a live macaw sitting on a perch in front of a monochrome abstract painting, its colours outstripping those of art.

In 1967 this trend was seized on by the critic Germano Celant, who codified it as *Arte Povera* in an exhibition in Genoa. He would subsequently promote it internationally. In prose bristling with vitalist metaphors, he argued for the distinctively heterogeneous, non-didactic nature of the new Italian art. The artist was seen as someone who 'mixes himself with the environment, camouflages himself…enlarges his threshold of things' and who, unlike his over-theorized American counterparts (although that was not actually stated), 'draws from the substance of the natural event—that of the growth of a plant, the chemical reaction of a mineral…the fall of a weight'.[9] In many ways the exemplar for this neo-Romantic construction was Joseph Beuys, and the German artist's symbolically energized fragments of stone and lumps of wax or metal would find their way into works by *Arte Povera*'s main practitioners: Pistoletto, Kounellis, Gilberto Zorio, Giovanni Anselmo, Mario Merz, and Luciano Fabro.

It is important, however, to see *Arte Povera* as reflecting a set of specifically Italian circumstances. Between 1967 and 1969 confrontations in Italy between students and police were far more numerous and violent than those in France. In late 1968 the chaos was compounded by protracted industrial disputes. Terrorist bombings by groups such as the Red Brigades punctuated the early 1970s. Amid such events *Arte Povera*'s forms gain a particular poignancy. Motifs and materials connoting a rich cultural heritage were often juxtaposed with objects suggestive of social disparity or hardship. In his *Venus of the Rags* (1967), for instance, Pistoletto forced a classical statue into confrontation with an enormous mound of rags. A particularly suggestive image is Luciano Fabro's *Golden Italy* of 1971, one of a series of hanging sculptures representing a map of Italy hung upside down by its 'leg', like a carcass [**86**]. Industrial expansion in the wealthy north of Italy had seen mass migration from the poorer south in the 1960s, reinforcing the traditional polarization of the country's two halves. Fabro's work in gilded bronze seems, symbolically, to reverse regional fates.

Fabro's *Golden Italy*, with its suggestions of a transmutation from base matter into gold, has thematic links with Jannis Kounellis's alchemical imagery. This artist's desire to transform the material conditions of art would produce spectacular gestures such as the temporary housing of twelve live horses at the Galleria L'Attico in Rome in 1969 [**87**], but in other installations he used veiled alchemical allusions such as propane-gas flames, setting up historical links with Klein and Beuys (see Chapter 3). Fabro's metaphorical reversal of his native land's fortunes also suggests parallels

86 Luciano Fabro

Italia d'oro (Golden Italy),
1971

Fabro made his first
sculpture in the *Italia*
series in 1968. Dozens of
variations followed in
subsequent years. Another
theme established in 1968
was that of Feet. This
involved the artist producing
a series of bizarre sculptural
installations in which large
'feet' or 'claws', often in
glass or polished metal,
functioned as the bases for
free-standing fabric
'stockings', frequently made
of silk. Fabro may have been
commenting obliquely on
the Italians' well-known
predilection for elegant and
expensive clothing.

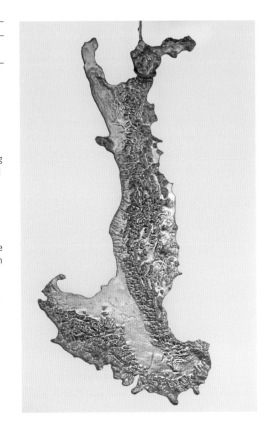

with Mario Merz. The latter's 'igloos', dating from 1968, consisted of hemispherical metal-ribbed structures covered with materials ranging from broken glass or slate to branches. They evoked nomadic lifestyles, sustained by the land's basic resources. As such they embodied what Germano Celant described as a 'moment that tends towards deculturization, regression, primitiveness...towards elementary and spontaneous politics'.[10] Far removed from the marxist analyses of Haacke, they connoted a similar distrust of galleries and aesthetic confinement.

Primordial returns: Smithson, Land Art, and language

As already stated, many exponents of *Arte Povera* eyed American minimalism with suspicion. However, one US artist schooled in minimalist principles shared their concerns with organic metamorphoses and the interrelations of landscape and history, namely Robert Smithson. As one of the first exponents of Land or Earth Art, he was committed to working with the spaces, materials, and fluctuating conditions of the physical world. In this he represented the apotheosis of all that the Modernist critic Michael Fried, with his warnings of art's surrender to 'theatricality', had argued against.

Smithson had strong political motivations and, in line with Haacke and Buren, he talked in 1972 of wishing to explore the 'apparatus' he was 'threaded through'.[11] By this he meant the gallery system with its hunger for artistic commodities, but he saw this as merely an extension of the larger post-industrial phase of capitalism. Whilst he fell in with American sculpture's

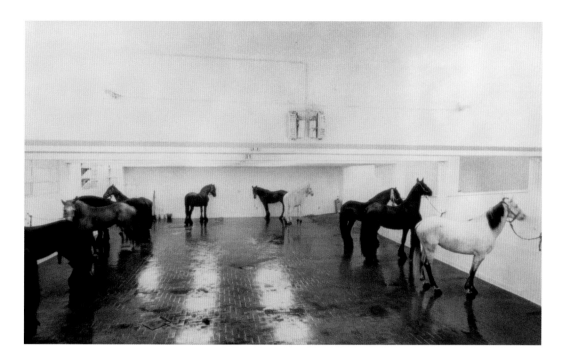

87 Jannis Kounellis

Horses (Galleria L'Attico, Rome), 1969

Carried out partly to confront the economic interests on which galleries are based, this installation took place over a three-day period. The artist chose horses of various breeds and colours, associating them symbolically with energy and power. At the same time he set up ironic art-historical associations with equestrian statues or the horses in the allegorical and mythological paintings of the Italian Renaissance.

orientation towards anti-form or process, in dialogue with minimalism's fixed structures, his synoptic viewpoint prevented him from perceiving this as simply another aesthetic step forward. If anything, it represented a move backward. Process for him was annexed to entropy, the principle whereby ordered systems undergo exponential deterioration or unravelling. Minimalism's geometries were thus placed under an ecological spotlight. In order to feed the needs of increasing consumer turnover, the industrial order that minimalism had fetishized sanctioned the despoliation of more and more land. Smithson's response was to create impermanent earthworks in sites blighted by industrial waste, drawing attention to cyclical interactions of order and disorder. Reversing *Arte Povera*'s alchemical logic, he nurtured a vision of a return to base matter, a reassertion of nature's rights over man's.

His most famous work, *Spiral Jetty* (1970), embodies these entropic principles. It grew out of wasteland at the edge of the Great Salt Lake in Utah where unsuccessful attempts had been made to extract oil from tar deposits. At a cost of about 9,000 dollars, provided by New York's Dwan Gallery, a crew of workmen with trucks extended a strip of the mainland into the lake's pinkish water, forming a spiral measuring 1,500 by 15 feet (457 by 4.6 metres). Photographs foster the impression that the structure still exists, but it is now submerged. In any case its location was never easily accessible to spectators.

This was a paradox which Smithson exploited. He underlined the fictive dimension of the piece by reconstituting it in various registers ranging from written and photographic documentation to a film [**88**]. The fact that spectators were obliged to reconstruct the piece conceptually opens onto a related aspect of Smithson's output, his punningly titled 'non-sites'. These mainly consisted of metal bins containing mineral samples which, when

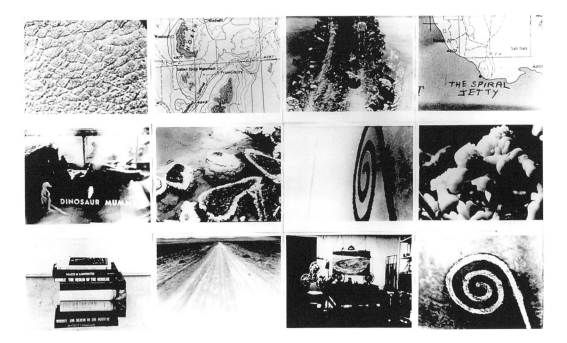

located in galleries, made available to 'sight' deposits from external 'sites'. This dialectic would be echoed by the British land artist Richard Long, who, from the late 1960s onwards, created geometrical formations from materials such as rocks, sticks, or mud on gallery floors or displayed maps and photographs, inviting his audience's imaginative reconstruction of his activities in the landscape.

In his non-sites Smithson ironically situated his work at a midway point between presence and absence. As information was given, so it was drained away. The dissolution informing his practice was at times virtually apocalyptic. He was a prolific writer, producing numerous essays before his tragic death in a flying accident in 1973. In an account in which he recalled the filmic ideas provoked in situ by *Spiral Jetty*, he described a sunstroke-induced vision: 'Following the spiral steps we return to our origins, back to some pulpy protoplasm....My eyes became combustion chambers...the sun vomited its corpuscular radiations.'[12] This kind of atavistic regression on Smithson's part seems, as with several previously discussed artists, to have direct resonances with the thought of the French writer Georges Bataille. In an essay of 1930 entitled *Sacrificial Mutilation and the Severed Ear of Vincent Van Gogh*, Bataille had talked of Van Gogh's insanity as bound up with an obsession with staring at the sun. It is perhaps no coincidence that, as part of his sun-blasted vision, Smithson fantasized 'Van Gogh with his easel on some sun-baked lagoon'. Elsewhere this radical sense of dissolution fed into a view of language as liable, like geological structures, to fissuring: 'Words and rocks contain a language that follows a syntax of splits and ruptures. Look at any word long enough and you will see it open up into a sea of faults, into a terrain of particles.'[13]

As will become clear later, Smithson's apprehension of the disjunctions between linguistic signifiers and their referents places him with Rauschenberg

Stills from the Spiral Jetty Film (Panel A), 1970

These are frames from Smithson's half-hour-long film based on his *Spiral Jetty.* Shots taken of the dusty road on the way to the site of the work were intercut with images of the blazing sun, the earth-moving equipment used to create the structure, images referring to prehistory (models of dinosaurs), sections of maps, and aerial views of the *Jetty* itself (bottom right). The deliberately disorientating effects were compounded by filming from a circling helicopter. Other Land-related projects of the period provoked dizzying perceptual experiences. In Britain, the Boyle Family (Mark Boyle, Joan Hills and their children Sebastian and Georgia) carried out a 'World Series' project, begun in 1968. It involved choosing sites at random (via collaborators throwing darts at unseen maps of the world), travelling to the sites (wherever they might be) and producing fibreglass reliefs from them. These hyper-real fragments were hung on gallery walls.

89 Ian Hamilton Finlay

Wave Rock, 1966

Alongside his own production of visual poetry, which took the form of silk-screen prints as well as inscribed objects, Finlay was significant for his involvement in the small press publishing activities associated with the alternative poetry movement of the 1960s. In 1961 he co-founded the Wild Hawthorn Press with Jessie McGuffie and in 1962 the magazine *Poor. Old. Tired. Horse.* This was to run until 1968. Such enterprises helped to open up a relatively insular Scottish culture to international influences.

or Warhol, at a point of transition from a Modernist paradigm, predicated on aesthetic (and experiential) essences, to a 'postmodern' one. However, the importance he accorded to language also links him to contemporaneous conceptualist trends and, more broadly, to the 'concrete' and performance poetry of the 1960s. Concrete poetry, involving explorations of the abstract visual possibilities of language, had been pioneered in 1956 by the Swiss poet Eugen Gomringer and would be realized most fully in three-dimensional terms by the Scottish artist Ian Hamilton Finlay. In *Wave Rock* (1966) Finlay made palpable Smithson's disintegrative pairing of landscape and language. Sandblasted onto glass, words visually enact the principles of fixity, fluidity, and erosion to which they are semantically tied, whilst the fluctuations of light through the object reinforce the theme that is 'written' into it [**89**]. At this time 'sound poetry', with its roots in Dada and French Lettrism, was also being variously developed by the likes of Ernst Jandl in Austria, Henri Chopin in France, and Bob Cobbing in Britain. Such linkages help indicate how, at the end of the 1960s, artistic disciplines themselves were continually dissolving and merging.

Despite thematic parallels with Smithson, Ian Hamilton Finlay was to develop a very different mode of land-based art in 'Stonypath', the garden in Lanarkshire, Scotland, that he began in 1967 and continued to develop until his death in 2006. At war with modern philistinism, Finlay looked back in his garden to both the iconography and the intellectual probity of French Revolutionary Neoclassicism, maintaining that 'certain gardens are described as retreats when they are really attacks'.[14] Although Finlay's garden incorporated disconcertingly modern conceits such as a stone bird table in the form of a battleship, it was largely populated by allusive epigrams inscribed on buildings or stone tablets. In many respects it embodied the eighteenth-century principle of the 'picturesque', borrowing its construction of the 'pastoral' from paintings by Poussin or Claude Lorrain, with their classical follies offset by open vistas and secluded copses. In eighteenth-century aesthetics the picturesque was routinely counterposed to the notion of the sublime, which involved uncultivated nature being passively experienced as

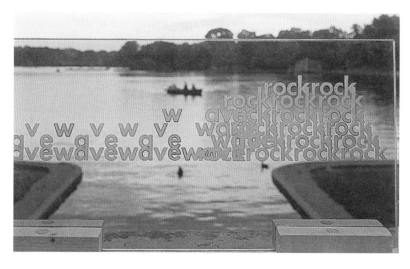

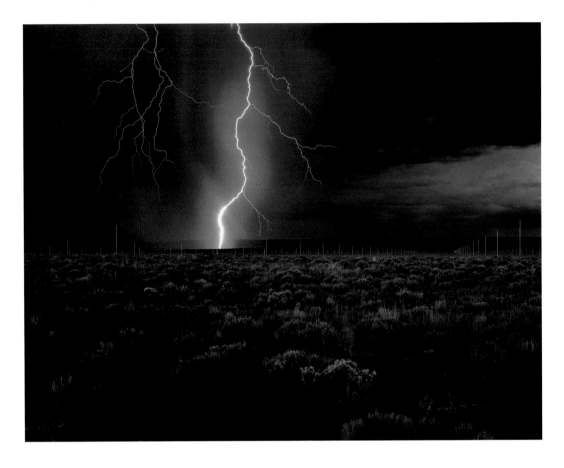

something overpowering and unfathomable. Since, as mentioned earlier, the sublime had its place in Abstract Expressionism, it is not surprising to find it reappearing in the American Land Art of Smithson's contemporaries, providing a sharp contrast not only with Finlay, but with much British Land Art.

It should be noted first, though, that American Land Art differs from British variants simply in terms of the quantities of land available to it. One non-American artist who exploited this was the Bulgarian-born Christo. Associated with French *Nouveau Réalisme* in the 1960s, he subsequently became famous for collaborating with his wife Jeanne-Claude in the 'wrapping' of sites ranging from part of the coastline of Sydney, Australia (1969), to the Reichstag in Berlin (1995). In 1976 he produced *Running Fence*, in which he ran 18-foot- (5.5-metre-) high sections of white fabric along metal runners that snaked for 24½ miles (39 kilometres) along the north Californian landscape before plunging into the ocean in Marin County. The American artist Michael Heizer worked on a similar scale, supervising the removal of thousands of tons of earth in *Double Negative* (1969–70) to produce two 'cuts' facing each other across the chasm of the Mormon Mesa in Nevada. However, scale alone does not produce sublime effects. The American Walter De Maria demonstrated what could be done with his *Lightning Field* of 1977, in which 400 stainless-steel poles were planted in an area of approximately 1 square mile (2.6 square kilometres) near Quemado, New Mexico, a location noted for its high incidence of electric storms. De Maria thus coaxed these forces into completing his work [**90**]. There is perhaps a sense, though, of a coercive appropriation of power, an enactment of fantasies which Smithson had resisted.

It is interesting to note finally that, as his contribution to the 1977 *Documenta 6* exhibition in Kassel, West Germany, De Maria hired a Texan drilling rig to sink a metal rod (or rather, 167 20-foot (6-metre) rods screwed together) into the earth to produce his *Vertical Earth Kilometer*. Afterwards the top of the rod, flush with the ground, was all that marked the spot. This might be said to invoke a kind of conceptual vertigo, a sense of the invisible sublime in the tradition of Manzoni's *Line of Infinite Length*. However, its invasive, technocratic dimension was pointed up by the British performance artist Stuart Brisley, who had originally been allocated the site which De Maria occupied. Recapitulating previous instances of European artists' unease with America's aesthetic hegemony, Brisley excavated a pit nearby, living on-site in rudimentary fashion for two weeks. His digging yielded up bones and rubble from the Second World War. Meaning was elicited from below rather than imposed from above.

Dematerialization: Conceptual Art

Walter De Maria's *Vertical Earth Kilometer* typifies a conviction, pervasive by the mid-1970s, that thought was as much an artistic material as any other. Critics certainly perceived the conceptual to be the dominant zeitgeist. In her important chronicle of the period 1966–72, Lucy Lippard saw it as unifying practices such as Land Art and anti-form in a wave of 'dematerialization', predicated on resistance to galleries and the market.[15] Wholesale applicability aside, the term 'Conceptual Art' had been specifically employed by the Fluxus artist Henry Flynt in 1961 and by Sol LeWitt (see Chapter 5). Its full ratification came, however, in an essay of 1969 by the American Joseph Kosuth entitled *Art After Philosophy*. Here Kosuth identified Duchamp as a historical pivot. Art before him, he claimed, had been hampered by its physical embodiment. After the Duchampian readymade, advanced art's quest consisted in posing 'analytic propositions' as to what art might be. Its essential nature was therefore conceptual.[16]

Kosuth was making a bid to raise the theoretical stakes in the aftermath of minimalism. He also took the opportunity to place himself, alongside the British artists Terry Atkinson and Michael Baldwin, as the first producer of authentically 'analytic' Conceptual Art in 1966. Certainly his *Art as Idea as Idea* series (1966–8), comprising photographically enlarged dictionary definitions of words such as 'meaning', was among the first works of the 1960s to assert a strict identity between verbal concept and artistic form. However, his reading of Duchamp was narrowly focused on the issue of nomination (the conferral of art status). It might be argued that, in reducing artworks to tautologies (self-definitions), he was simply reiterating a Modernist credo of formal autonomy. Conceptual purity now stood in for optical refinement.[17] He thus ignored questions of art's relations to spectators, institutions, or dominant modes of production that had led to a more politicized post-Duchamp sensibility elsewhere. As will be shown, it was not until the early to mid-1970s that Anglo-American conceptualism fully caught up with the political mood of 1968.

This should not detract from the uncompromising nature of many of the propositions, whether strictly analytic or not, generated by late 1960s American conceptualists. The dethroning of the art object bred a kind of puritan iconophobia. Written declarations or documentary information were offered to audiences in lieu of sensual pleasures. Lawrence Weiner's short statements gave open-ended instructions for sculptures that did not require actual realization; 'A square removed from a rug in use' (1969) is one example. In certain instances, literal dematerialization was practised. Douglas Huebler announced, in the catalogue to an exhibition curated by Seth Siegelaub to be discussed below, that since the world was full of objects, to which he pointed his audience using maps and diagrams, he would not add more. The same year John Baldessari's *Cremation Piece* (1969) declared that the artist had 'cremated' his accumulated art production, adding the assurance that he felt better for it, and Robert Barry sent out announcement cards to the effect that 'March 10 through March 21 the Gallery will be closed'.

Questions naturally arose about how such recalcitrant gestures should be distributed. Dan Graham's strategy of placing his art productions in commercial magazines such as *Harper's Bazaar* offered an important exemplar. In *Homes for America* (1966)—inserted in *Arts* magazine—he produced a documentary-style survey of post-war housing, which at the same time could be read as an oblique reflection on aesthetic (minimalist) standardization and its social corollaries. Publications increasingly became outlets for conceptual proposals. Seth Siegelaub's key curatorial venture in New York, *January 5–31 1969*, consisted simply of a catalogue which gallery-goers were invited to read. As far as the critic Lucy Lippard was concerned, such modes of dissemination gave art an unprecedented fluidity. She extended this to artists themselves. No longer reliant on 'belated circulating exhibitions', they could carry their wares in their heads or pockets. With improved transcontinental travel, this provided a way of 'getting the power structure out of New York'.[18] An international art community based on the free exchange of ideas fleetingly emerged. As with Fluxus (see Chapter 4), satellites to New York such as Art & Language in Britain or Jan Dibbets in Holland established themselves, although conceptualism had broader repercussions, with strongholds becoming established in Latin America, Japan, and Australia. However, by the early 1970s it was becoming clear that the markets had caught up. Robert Barry, seemingly the least recoupable artist, found his ephemera being collected by Herbert and Dorothy Vogel in New York.[19] Similarly, conceptualism became museum art. Harald Szeeman's innovatory exhibition *When Attitude Becomes Form* at the Kunsthalle, Berne, in March–April 1969, began a process which was further consolidated by *Information* at MoMA, New York, in 1970 and *The New Art* at London's Hayward Gallery in 1972.

Much as conceptualists railed against such assimilation, they were curiously attracted to bureaucratic language. The redundant aesthetic formulas of Modernism were transformed into a babble of systems and statistics. On 4 January 1966, for instance, the Japanese-born On Kawara started to

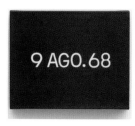

91 On Kawara

9 AGO. 68, 1968

Each of On Kawara's *Date Paintings* is individualized to some degree. Typefaces vary, as do the colours. They are always horizontal in format but each one corresponds to one of eight predetermined sizes.

produce 'date paintings' on an almost daily basis. As tokens of his continuing existence they took the day's date as their subject matter [**91**]. He also produced a ten-volume book which listed one million years counting back from 1971, the year it was produced.

The case of the British Art & Language group is particularly interesting in relation to this tendency. Its founding members Terry Atkinson, Michael Baldwin, David Bainbridge, and Harold Hurrell felt that the increasingly discursive nature of art obviated the need to produce objects. Theory about art could in itself be considered art. They therefore produced a journal, *Art-Language*, first published in 1968, which set about dismantling Modernist rhetoric. Its vocabulary was perversely obscure in order to resist cultural commodification and to test the 'competencies' of readers rendered intellectually flabby by a surfeit of 'opticality'. But to whom exactly was it addressed? An air of intellectual sanctimony clung to it. Information theory was newly in vogue around this time and avant-garde art naturally experimented with its idioms. In the summer of 1968, while Paris was witnessing the return of barricades, the ICA gallery in London put on a show entitled *Cybernetic Serendipity*, which explored computer applications within the arts. The year 1972 saw Art & Language, now expanded to include a New York contingent, install a computational system of sorts entitled *Index 01* as their contribution to the Kassel *Documenta* exhibition. It consisted of eight metal filing cabinets on four grey blocks surrounded by walls papered with an index. Spectators were invited to cross-reference some 350 texts assembled by group members to determine levels of logical congruence or discrepancy. They thus participated in the group's sifting of ideological cant.

It could be argued that *Index 01* was insufficiently ironic in its replication of the structures of state administration. The art historian Benjamin Buchloh has detected a kind of doublethink at work in such projects. He argues that, whatever their working-class roots and marxist sympathies, artists such as Art & Language were unwittingly establishing their radical kudos using the signifiers of the (middle) managerial class to which they had in fact acceded.[20] On the alternative view, as cultural producers Art & Language dissolved their status as individual artist-geniuses in a model of collectivity, while radicalizing an audience habituated to passive contemplation.[21] In the latter respect Art & Language were particularly influential in placing theory on the agenda in Britain's notoriously conservative art schools, having pioneered a controversial course at Lanchester Polytechnic, Coventry, in 1969–71. From this point on, few self-respecting art tutors or students could persist in seeing art as unmediated expression.

The rise of semiotics: Burgin and conceptualism

Other British conceptualists saw Art & Language's allegiance to analytic philosophical procedures as verging, like Kosuth, on covert formalism. Victor Burgin in particular saw photography as a means to a more productive social engagement. He was aided in this by the French writer Roland Barthes's *Elements of Semiology*, published in English in 1967. Barthes's contribution to literary theory had partly consisted in adapting the findings of the Swiss linguist Ferdinand de Saussure whereby, in language, the relation between 'signifier' (word or utterance) and 'signified' (the thing to which it refers) is shown to be fundamentally arbitrary. To give a simple illustration, 'cat' refers to a feline animal in so far as it differs from 'bat'. Meaning is constituted via a shuffling of available linguistic components. It is in no sense innate in things, but constructed. This means that it can also be permeated by changing ideologies. In one essay, Barthes analysed a photograph of a black soldier apparently saluting the French flag. Beyond signifying patriotism, he saw it as encoding a second order of signification arising from its placement on the cover of the conservative magazine *Paris Match*. In this context it connoted 'imperialism', reassuringly implying black assent to French rule at a time when the Algerian conflict had destabilized France's colonial position.[22]

The assimilation of such ideas led to an easing of the conceptualist embargo on visual imagery, and representations now stood to be investigated as repositories of social information. In this respect, Burgin partly conceived his role in educational terms. Along with theorists from disciplines such as film studies and sociology, he helped pioneer Cultural Studies as an alternative to Art History in British polytechnics. The prevailing assumption was that fine-art productions were no more worthy of analysis than other cultural artefacts. Burgin gave such principles practical embodiment. *Possession* of 1976 [**92**] was a mock advertisement, produced in an edition of 500 and fly-posted around Newcastle upon Tyne. It deftly redeployed the genre's linguistic and photographic tropes to show how the longing for 'possession', on which advertising plays, assumes incompatible economic and gender relations.

For Burgin, then, photography was primarily a social sign system whose operations needed to be exposed. This attitude was shared by the Californian conceptualist John Baldessari, who, having gradually moved from text to photo-based work through the 1970s, produced photo-assemblages in the mid-1980s which disrupted the integrity of photographic space or narrative by recombining or reshaping images from sources such as films or newspapers, deleting areas, and adding colour overlays. Such active inroads into visual currency echo the situationist-style institutional interventions that were discussed earlier. Baldessari was not overtly political, but other conceptualists based in California in the early 1970s, such as Martha Rosler and Allan Sekula, eventually embarked on stringent critiques of photographic reportage conventions from a left-wing standpoint. Burgin's practice should also be seen as broadly informed by the trade union militancy in Britain in the period 1970–4. Given this climate of left-wing activism, one notable feature of *Possession* was its author's unusual embrace of (limited) mass distribution (although Dan Graham's earlier *Homes for America* could also be recalled). In terms of conceptualism's overall trajectory, Burgin was effectively rematerializing art in public space after Daniel Buren had symbolically dissolved it [**82**]. Ironically his mock advertisement's unmasking of societal mechanisms remained similarly 'invisible' given that, in a survey, only one person in seven claimed to understand it.[23]

Burgin came to feel in the late 1970s that works such as *Possession* failed because they assumed that it was possible to speak ironically from a vantage point that was outside ideology. In line with Barthes's doctrine of the demise of the author, he came to perceive the author-position not so much

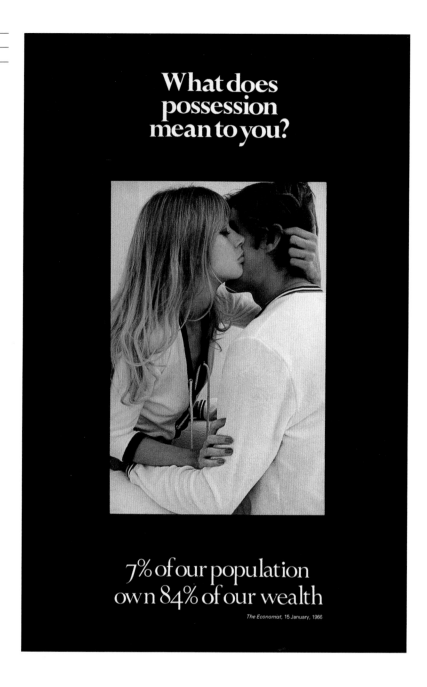

as stable, a fount of social insight, as constituted out of a plurality of socially determined assumptions. This point of view led him, in the late 1970s, to explore his own gender position in works which double back on their dominant masculinist cultural viewpoint. However, in acknowledging the socializing and enculturating voices that both formed and informed his practice, Burgin implicitly posited an audience willing to make an investment in reconstituting his role as author. This paradox persisted through much of the full-blown postmodernist art production that Burgin's work presaged.

Conceptualism provided photography with a long-sought-after centrality within fine art, but privileged its normally downgraded amateur or documentary modes over its attempts to appear 'arty'. The German artists Bernd and Hilla Becher thus utilized a documentary look in their suites of photographs of industrial buildings such as blast furnaces, mine-heads, or cooling towers [**93**], unifying individual types within classes via a standardized frontal presentation and low horizon line. They appeared to be creating pseudoscientific taxonomies in a specifically German photographic tradition extending back to August Sander. However, their play on variations within a category also suggests a parody of the minimalist interplay between the 'known constant' and the 'experienced variable' (see Chapter 5).

The Bechers were to have an enormous impact on German photographers such as Thomas Ruff, who, in the late 1980s, subtly nudged their documentary idiom back towards pictorialism. In this way conceptualism channelled its iconophobia (its disdain for the insistent visual/authorial 'presence' in much Modernist art) back into forms which, while being powerfully visual once more, could nevertheless invoke photography's claims to social transparency. As will be seen, Jeff Wall's work, in particular, consolidated this tendency in the late 1980s [**124**].

Gender positions: feminism and art

Victor Burgin's male self-questioning paralleled the rise of radical feminism. As the 1970s progressed, women powerfully contested the cultural stereotypes attached to traditional childbearing or domestic roles. In many ways Burgin's work responded to that of Mary Kelly, an American artist based in Britain, whose work systematically used conceptualist devices to probe the social foundations of gender conditioning. However, Kelly's work departed significantly from overtly separatist feminist practices. These, as exemplified by the Californian Judy Chicago, celebrated the rediscovery of an essential 'feminine' consciousness. To understand first what Chicago stood for, it is worth examining *The Dinner Party* [**94**].

This enormous installation, which drew record crowds when first exhibited at San Francisco's Museum of Modern Art in 1979, consisted of a triangular table with places set with ceramic vulvas and embroidered runners for thirty-nine imaginary female guests. These, along with 999 additional female invitees, whose names were written on floor tiles as part of the installation, were mainly artists and writers from the past. The work had two central functions. It rehabilitated talents overlooked or disparaged in male-oriented constructions of history, tying in with a reorientation of art history in the 1970s associated with writers such as Linda Nochlin in America and Griselda Pollock in Britain. At the same time its emphasis on 'applied arts' productions drew attention to women's frequently anonymous cultural participation, questioning aesthetic hierarchies.

Male critics responded rather predictably. Robert Hughes, for instance, described the work as 'mainly cliché…with colours worthy of a Taiwanese souvenir factory'.[24] The point was that decorative excess, bordering on kitsch, was being deliberately flaunted in the face of a renunciative, masculinist modernism. 'Sisterhood' replaced the image of the alienated male outsider. Along with the artist Miriam Schapiro, Chicago set up a Feminist Art

93 Bernd and Hilla Becher

Typology of Water Towers (one of six suites of nine photographs), 1972

The Bechers' photographs of industrial structures, which they began in 1959, belong to the genres of documentary photography, sculpture, and industrial archaeology simultaneously, as well as having status as Conceptual Art. Although resolutely sober in format, the suites of images often contain a surprising humour. Standing next to their peers, unpromising industrial structures acquire distinct personalities.

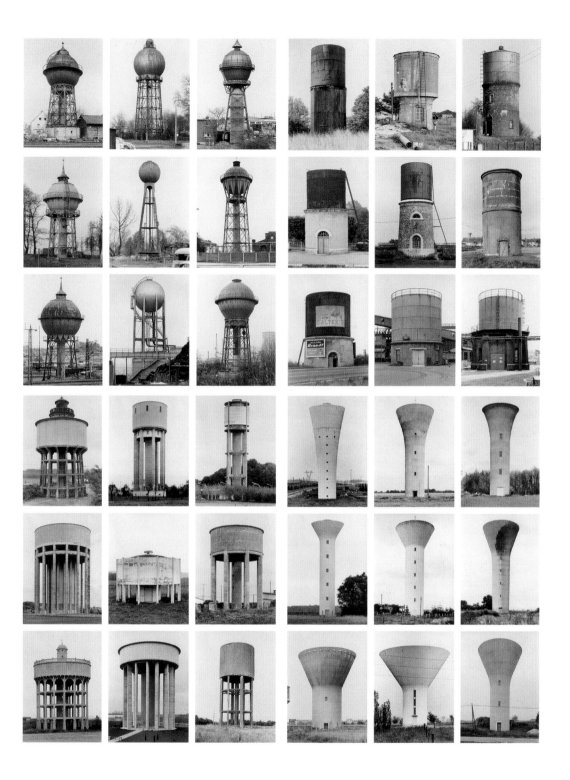

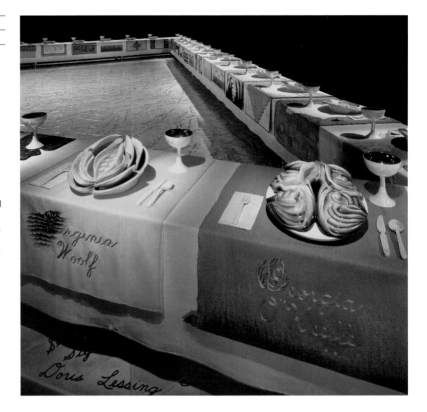

94 Judy Chicago

The Dinner Party, 1979

Each of the ceramic plates adorning the table in this installation was individualized. In this photograph, the Georgia O'Keeffe plate on the right owed something of its original design to her *Black Iris* paintings of the mid-1920s. The plate dedicated to the reclusive Calvinist poet Emily Dickinson appropriately had ruffles of pale pink, whilst that dedicated to the Italian baroque painter Artemisia Gentileschi was surrounded by billowing folds evocative of the drapery in her paintings.

Program at the University of California in 1971, which led to *Womanhouse*, a collaborative project in which teachers and students occupied an abandoned house, creating environmental works exploring domestic creativity. At the same time artists such as Faith Ringgold, a black American whose feminism was also informed by racial marginalization, contributed to the continuity of folk practices such as quilt-making. However, it should be noted that, although *The Dinner Party* was realized with the aid of numerous helpers, Chicago retained sole authorship of it. She diligently displayed her co-workers' names, but kept certain hierarchies in place.

A controversial aspect of the work was its vulvic iconography. This was part of a genre of 'central-core' imagery, promoted by critics such as Lucy Lippard, which aimed to dislodge the cultural primacy of the phallus, rehabilitating the sign of women's biological 'lack' (to invoke Freud's discredited terms) as the symbol of their creativity. The work possibly echoes Louise Bourgeois's cannibalistic installation *Destruction of the Father*, discussed in Chapter 5, which was shown in New York in 1974, the year *The Dinner Party* was begun. But there is a sense in which Chicago turns Bourgeois's symbolic consumption of the patriarch into celebratory female self-consumption, which clearly has erotic undercurrents. The nature of the work's address thus becomes ambiguous. Indeed, many women found it reductive, implicitly returning them to biology.

This was certainly Mary Kelly's view. Her *Post-Partum Document*, produced between 1973 and 1979, was concerned with recording her relationship with her son during his weaning, but pointedly renounced corporeal

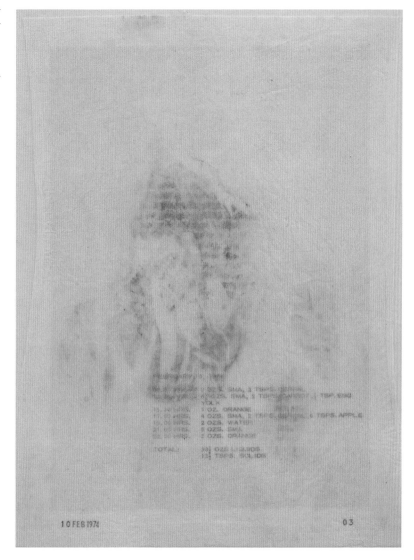

imagery in favour of 135 framed items such as diagrams, texts, and traces from the body (faecal smears on nappy liners) [**95**]. Polemically countering the essentialist view that gender is biologically determined, *Post-Partum Document* grew out of Kelly's participation in a London women's group dedicated to examining the sexual division of labour. With childrearing as her theme, she became deeply affected by Juliet Mitchell's book *Psychoanalysis and Feminism* (1974), which introduced English speakers to post-Freudian accounts of the dawning of gendered subjectivity. Most influentially, it explained how the French psychoanalyst Jacques Lacan had reinterpreted Freud's unconscious rite of passage, the Oedipus Complex, as allegorizing the unequal accession of boys and girls to patriarchal language. He had thus made socializing forces of Freud's notorious anatomical markers of sexual identity—penile possession and lack. The phallus became symbolic rather than literal. Using such ideas, Kelly produced a painstaking record of maternal separation. After a pre-Oedipal phase during which mother and child were united, her son's linguistic initiation gave him a 'positive' relation to the phallus while she was returned to the condition of lack originally inscribed by her gender.

Kelly's work brilliantly tracked gender's linguistic basis. One of the six sections of the work records early conversations between mother and child. Shown his own reflection in the mirror, the child introjects the paternal position: 'da/da-/da-da'. Elsewhere the work raises fascinating questions about the relation between creativity and procreativity. Interrogating the psychoanalytic platitude that, in raising babies, women compensate for their phallic lack, Kelly hypothesized a form of female fetishism, turning her child's imprints, clothes, or gifts into compensatory tokens which were exhibited in taxonomic style. These fetishes asserted that, far from succumbing to imaginary identifications, women could attain symbolic distance from procreation, becoming cultural as well as natural producers.

Apart from provoking feminist objections that it capitulated to male-centred theory, Kelly's work was considered dauntingly abstruse. Her defenders appealed to the Brechtian ideas promoted in Britain in the 1970s by *Screen*, a politicized journal dedicated to film theory. In the 1930s Bertolt Brecht had mounted marxist arguments for an anti-realist art which, rather than naturalizing societal norms, which were profoundly unnatural, made its audience conscious of its devices.[25] However, the Kelly-inspired 'scripto-visual' art that followed such precepts, showcased most prominently in the exhibition *Difference: On Representation and Sexuality* at New York's New Museum of Contemporary Art in 1984, could be seen as having a moralizing undercurrent. Visual pleasure, associatively linked to a world where men traditionally did the looking whilst women's bodies were objectified, was considered suspect.[26] This politically correct attitude tied in with Kelly's moratorium on bodily depictions.

A broader undermining of humanist content in late 1970s art was fuelled by English translations of writings by the French post-structuralist philosopher Jacques Derrida.[27] Derrida saw a 'metaphysics of presence' as endemic to Western thought. His 'deconstructive' strategy, aimed at eroding the bourgeois certainties bound up with this, consisted in revealing how the self-sufficiency (and authority) of many concepts is illusory. In defining themselves against their opposites, concepts often contain residues of what they refute. Meanings are never stable, but in continual slippage. The notion of 'presence' in itself provides a good candidate for deconstruction, since 'presence', in defining itself against 'absence', admits to a lack (in this sense 'lack' inheres in *all* human subjectivity). In line with these ideas, Kelly's work, like that of Victor Burgin, turned the author into a phantom-like entity, never fully available to the viewer. At the same time, functioning as Burgin did in a critical capacity, she argued against the reliance on 'presence', now deemed symptomatically modernist, in 1970s Body Art.

Questions of 'presence': Body Art and Performance

The concept of Body Art, which had first been articulated (as 'body work') in an article of 1970 by the critic Willoughby Sharp,[28] ostensibly designated a genre of live performance, following modes established by precursors such

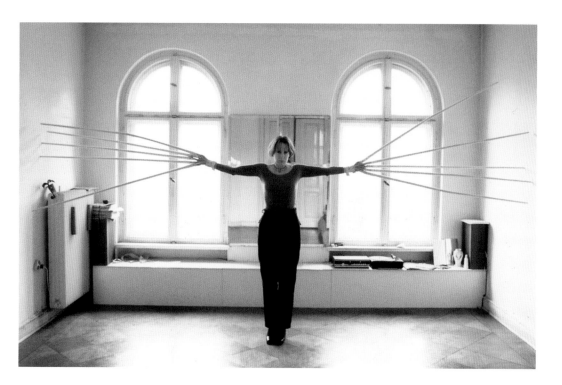

as Yves Klein or the Fluxus performers, in which artists used their bodies as their materials [**51**]. Mary Kelly asserted that such apparently radical activities compensated audiences for the dematerialization being practised elsewhere. The comforts of artistic presence were provided in abundance, she argued, however transient the context.[29] In effect, the form relied, like Land Art, on photographic mediation. Examples range from Bruce Nauman's recordings of his audienceless 'performances' [**78**] to the films in which the German artist Rebecca Horn investigates the possibilities of peculiar body extensions, cross-fertilizing nineteenth-century medical prosthetics with the nursery terrors of Heinrich Hoffmann's *Struwwelpeter* [**96**]. However, even in photographic form, Kelly felt that the literal presence of the artist heralded a newly auratic, and commodifiable, art. Whatever the truth of this, it could be argued that photographic documentation, precisely by being *after the fact*, dramatized the insufficiency of the sense of presence that performance was able to summon up both for artists and their audiences. As a genre, performance oscillated between being experientially available and poignantly lacking. It therefore placed identity in a Derridean 'gap'.

An interesting instance of this involves Rudolf Schwarzkogler, an artist linked with one of the earliest groups of Body Artists, the Viennese Actionists. Aiming to unblock the repressed emotions underlying Austria's post-Fascist amnesia, the Actionists owed much to the influential doctrines of the French surrealist Antonin Artaud's *The Theatre and its Double* (1964), in which he had called for a cathartic theatre, overcoming the form's past reliance on text through ritualistic gestures and vocal exertions (Derrida naturally saw this as haunted by a nostalgia for presence).[30] From late 1962 onwards the group's key members, Hermann Nitsch, Günter Brus, and

Otto Muehl, staged Dionysian ceremonies which frequently involved disembowelling animal cadavers. Schwarzkogler, however, mainly appeared in harrowing photographs, notably ones which apparently showed him bandaged in the aftermath of a self-castration. It is clear now that such scenarios were contrived. Schwarzkogler mocked up his experiential agonies with a collaborator's body as his stand-in.

Kelly's worries about Body Art mainly derived from masochistic or narcissistic female versions, where women could be seen as unwittingly submitting to patriarchal oppression or courting male objectification. In the case of the Paris-based Gina Pane, who inflicted wounds on her body, turning it into an emblem of suffering, such concerns may have been justified. However, in that of the American Hannah Wilke, who defied what she termed 'Fascist Feminism' by posing in photographs according to media stereotypes of desirable femininity, it may be that she was parodically acting out femininity as a form of masquerade, exposing the artifice of gender.[31] Such strategies rendered objectification impotent, bereft of a suitably passive object. Adrian Piper, an African-American artist, addressed interpersonal social assumptions from a different angle, dressing up as a man in her *Mythic Being* performances of 1972–5 in order to explore, in the course of walking New York's streets, experiences of confrontation, rejection, and ostracism. The distortions of self-image brought on through racial stereotyping were pointedly expressed in a self-portrait by Piper of 1981 [**97**].

Carolee Schneemann, an American artist whose 1960s performances such as *Meat Joy* (1964) had contributed decisively to the translation of 'action painting' into performance terms, developed an aesthetic out of the active as opposed to the passive female body. Her *Interior Scroll* [**98**], first performed in Long Island, New York, in 1975, involved her standing before an audience and gradually unravelling a scroll from her vagina. From this she read a parodic account of a meeting with a 'structuralist film maker' who had criticized her films for their 'personal clutter' and 'persistence of feelings'.[32] In a sense Schneemann's performance dealt with the internalization of criticism, but it could also be aligned with an essentialist feminist interest in *écriture feminine* (female writing). This form of French feminist theory, espoused by writers such as Hélène Cixous, posited female access to a pre-Oedipal (hence implicitly anti-patriarchal) language of bodily pulsations. The painter Nancy Spero produced a number of frieze-like paintings on paper bound up with this notion in the 1970s, alternating texts connotative of both 'male' and 'female' speech with repeated printed motifs of the goddess figures who were being rediscovered by feminists. Other artists actively used bodily secretions or traces in the manner suggested, although not strictly accomplished, by Shigeko Kubota [**51**]. The Cuban-born Ana Mendieta, working in America, produced earthworks (titled *Siluetas*) which poignantly suggested the imprint of her body on the landscape. The author's simultaneous presence and absence were again at issue.

Turning to Body Art by male practitioners, a prevalence of masochistic ordeals demonstrated that, at least by virtue of feeling pain, their authors most definitely existed. The Californian Chris Burden performed a number of carefully planned but self-endangering actions. In *Shoot*, performed at F-Space Gallery in Santa Ana, California, in 1971, he arranged for a male

*Self Portrait Exaggerating
My Negroid Features*, 1981
As an African-American
who is able to pass as
'white', Piper has written
eloquently of the social and
institutional prejudices that
surface when she divulges
her racially mixed identity.
In a text entitled 'Flying'
of 1987 she wrote: 'I am
the racist's nightmare . . .
I represent the loathsome
possibility that everyone is
'tainted' by black ancestry.
If someone can look like
me and sound like me who
is unimpeachably white?'
(quoted in *Adrian Piper*,
New York: Alternative
Museum, 1987, as reprinted
in Ikon Gallery catalogue,
Birmingham, 1991, p. 26).

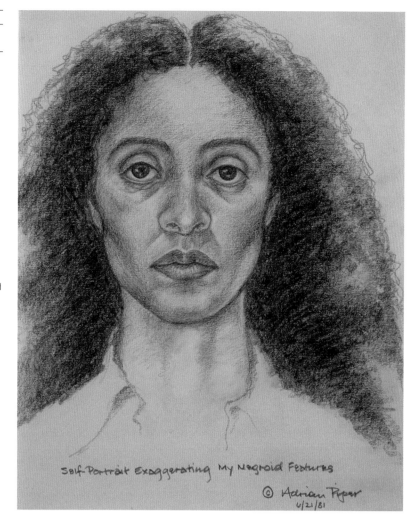

Self-Portrait Exaggerating My Negroid Features

© Adrian Piper
6/21/81

friend to shoot at him, sustaining a deep arm wound [**99**]. The New York-based poet Vito Acconci produced less aggressive works. His *Step Piece*, performed for month-long periods in 1970, saw him stepping on and off a stool daily at the rate of thirty steps a minute for as long as he could manage. His progress was duly recorded in dry documentary style. Comparing male 'body works' with those by women, men often pitted themselves against themselves, metaphorically testing social expectations of invulnerability, whilst women challenged cultural conditioning head-on, becoming active rather than passive.

A notorious work by Acconci reflects a gradual blurring of fixed gender positions. *Seedbed* (1972) involved Acconci masturbating under a ramp in a gallery. As he imagined his audience, his groans were relayed into their space by loudspeakers. Invisibly dominating the gallery space while simultaneously being (pleasurably) 'walked over', Acconci set up a fascinating interplay of empowerment and masochism, ironizing the dynamics of his masculine creativity and control.

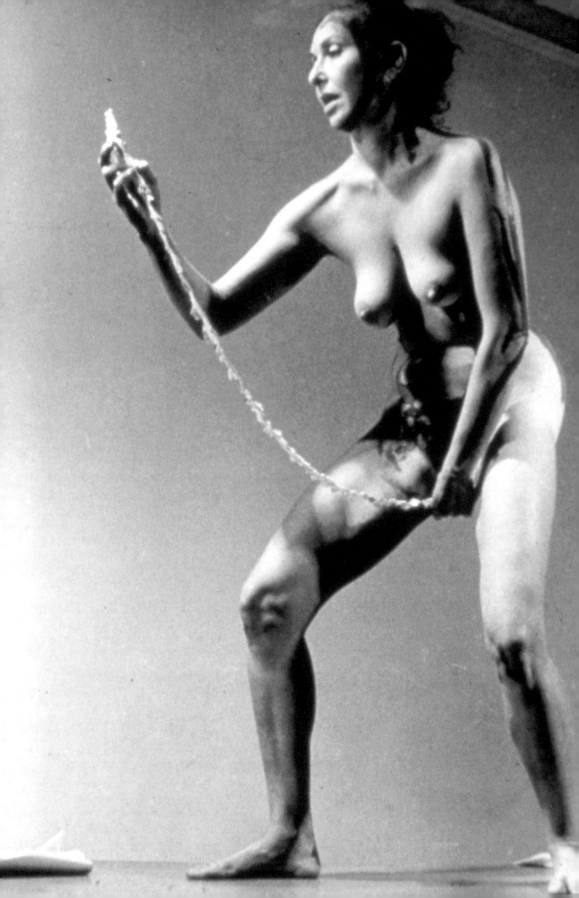

Works by male American body artists rarely made overt social reference. Burden's performances can now be interpreted as mapping the brutalization of the social body onto the private one, but actual parallels with politically motivated instances of self-immolation, such as that of Jan Palach in Prague in 1969, are tenuous. Social responsiveness was more the province of the British performance artist Stuart Brisley. His *10 Days*, first performed in Berlin between 21 and 30 December 1972, involved the artist sitting at a table daily at mealtimes and being served with food which he refused. The food was left on the table to rot. On the tenth day he crawled the length of the table through the debris, before presenting his 'new self' at a banquet for friends. Although no explanation was offered, the event's response to Christmas festivities seemed pointed when Third World famine was constantly in the news.

By contrast, Gilbert and George, whose symbiotic partnership began in 1967 at London's Saint Martin's School of Art, showed a dandyish irresolution towards social protest. Their famous *Singing Sculpture* (1969) was riven with contradictions. Wearing anachronistic suits, they posed as 'Living Sculptures' with a table as their pedestal. Their gold-painted faces echoed Joseph Beuys's earlier performance persona, but they had nothing of his shamanic idealism. As they circled robotically to the music-hall nostalgia of a recording of Flanagan and Allen's *Underneath the Arches*, they appeared to annex the dreamy resignation of its tramps to the futility of the characters in Samuel Beckett's influential play *Waiting for Godot*. In the mid-1970s, they began the sequence of large, multi-panelled photo-installations which continue to the present. Appearing in their works as besuited witnesses of social deprivation and intolerance, they seemed like donors in secular altarpieces or Victorian philanthropists visiting hell [**100**]. Like Warhol, they were *flâneurs* of a kind but lacked street credibility and seemed unsure how to maintain social distance. In the 1980s this led to strange visual conjunctions. Homoerotic, religious, and nationalistic iconographies rubbed shoulders uneasily.

Another British artist trained at Saint Martin's, Bruce McLean, explored sartorial concerns in a more theatrical mode. Between 1971 and 1974 he and several friends presented themselves as *Nice Style*, the 'World's First Pose Band', a group dedicated to parodying the posing of rock stars. An obvious self-consciousness about the artificiality of performance, as filtered through mass-media channels, was apparent. By contrast, the self-styled Genesis P-Orridge from Manchester participated, albeit warily, in Britain's late 1970s punk rock scene with his four-piece, electronically oriented band *Throbbing Gristle*. P-Orridge, along with his girlfriend Cosey Fanni Tutti, had mounted a provocative exhibition under the enigmatic *Coum Transmissions* banner at London's ICA in 1976. Titled *Prostitution*, it included bloodied tampons and images of Tutti posing in pornographic magazines. Press outrage, in the wake of the 'Tate Bricks' scandal earlier that year (see Chapter 5), inevitably followed. Between 1975 and 1981 the lyrics accompanying Throbbing Gristle's pounding, discordant music further investigated unsettling and taboo subjects. *Zyklon B Zombie*, a single of 1978, derived its title from the gas used by the Nazis in their extermination chambers.

98 Carolee Schneemann

Interior Scroll, performance, 1975

The performance work for which Schneemann first rose to prominence was *Meat Joy*, a sixty-to eighty-minute piece of 1964 which, although elaborately scripted, had something of the character of an orgy, with its male and female semi-naked participants writhing on the floor manipulating raw fish, dead chickens, wet paint, and ropes. The later *Interior Scroll* was still highly sexualized. Schneemann likened the scroll she removed from her vagina to an 'uncoiling serpent'.

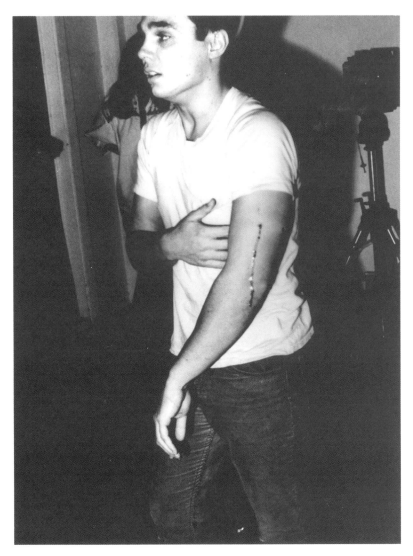

99 Chris Burden

Shoot, 1971

Shoot involved the artist having a .22 gun fired at him from a distance of about 15 feet (4.6 metres). Rather than experiencing the detached spectacle of a shooting—as was common from watching TV in early 1970s America—Burden's audience was forced to comprehend the traumatic actuality of such an event. The bullet had been intended to miss, but Burden in fact sustained a deep wound. Burden performed a series of similarly dangerous actions around the same time. Discussing *220,* performed at F-Space in Santa Ana, California, in October 1971, he noted: 'The gallery was flooded with 12 inches [30 cm] of water. Three other people and I waded through the water and climbed onto 14-foot [4.3-m] ladders, one ladder per person. After everyone was positioned, I dropped a 220 electric line into the water. The piece lasted from midnight until dawn, about six hours. There was no audience except for the participants.' The piece ended when, early in the morning, Burden's wife came to turn off the circuit breaker outside the building. (See Chris Burden and Jan Butterfield: 'Through the Night Softly', *Arts*, 49, no. 7, March 1975, pp. 68–72.)

Whilst Throbbing Gristle embraced the technologies bound up with the 1970s music industry, they were antagonistic towards the mass media at large. In America, Performance Art allied itself more wholeheartedly with technology and spectacle. This was the case with the elaborate operas and multimedia productions of Robert Wilson and Laurie Anderson respectively. In the latter's *United States Parts I–IV* (1983), the author's voice, fed through an electronic 'harmonizer', mimicked the 'Voice of Authority'. The elliptical anecdotes it recounted succeeded in dissolving any secure sense of an authorial presence behind the words. Back projections, tape recordings, and music further contributed to a seductively sinister *Gesamtkunstwerk*.

In other areas of 1980s art the long-standing dialogue between photography and performance tilted decisively in favour of the former, prioritizing

100 Gilbert and George

The Alcoholic, 1978

Gilbert and George's presence in their pictures can be seen as an extension of their early Living Sculpture activities. They often stand apart from the other imagery in the pieces as though acknowledging the artifice involved. Moral issues are frequently raised. *The Alcoholic* seems essentially compassionate, but in one notorious work, *Paki* of 1978, they flanked a young Asian man. Their images were flooded in red whilst he remained in black and white. Whether they were guardians or oppressors seemed unclear.

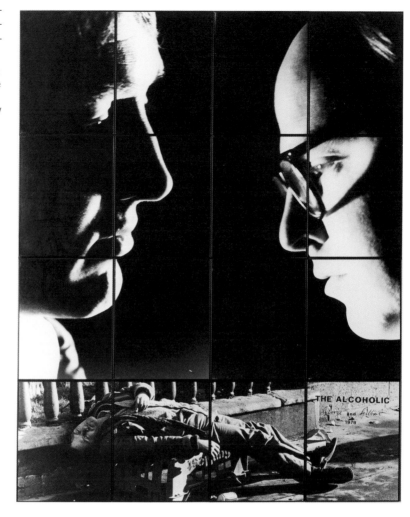

performance's fictive nature over its capacity for presence. This postmodern turn is exemplified by Cindy Sherman, to be contextualized more fully later, who 'performed' herself acting out other female personae in photographs. Both 'Cindy Sherman' as author and the existence of any originary performances were opened up to doubt [**101**]. A similar concern with masquerade featured in photography and film in the 1990s. A notable example is the work of Matthew Barney, whose persona in his films, not just in terms of gender but also species identity, was shown to be manifestly constructed [**130**].

If Mary Kelly had worried that Body and Performance Art would summon up a new artist-subject to gratify bourgeois needs, it seems that much of it succeeded in rendering this subject elusive and unfixed. However, whether the work mounted any real challenge to the artist's status within commodity culture remains open to debate. Much Performance Art of the 1970s, in line with the other tendencies discussed in this chapter, implicitly repudiated the art object's position within capitalism. But, as will be shown, rather than dematerializing itself further, art at the turn of the 1980s largely underwent a rematerialization. It might be concluded from this that the post-1968 avant-garde project, however innovatory its forms, simply failed. In fact, as Chapter 7 explains, it had to weather a political and cultural sea change.

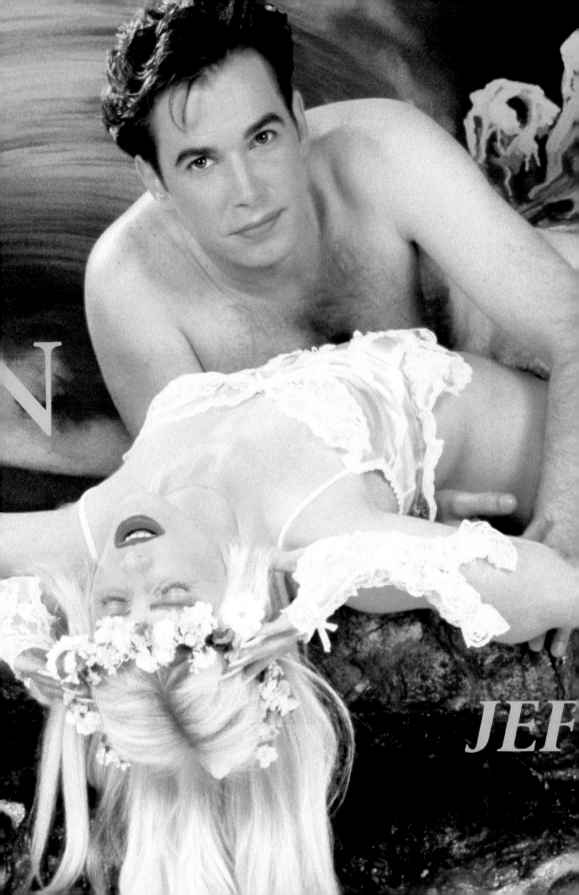

JEF

Postmodernism

Theory and Practice in the 1980s

7

Historians generally regard the years 1973–4 as a turning point in the post-war economic fortunes of Europe and America. After a golden age which had lasted from 1950, an era of instability set in. Rising oil prices, in the aftermath of the Arab–Israeli war, caused Europe's economies to become inflated and to go into recession in 1973–4 and again in 1979–83. Different financial conditions led to changes in industrial organization. The previous Fordist model of integrated production began to give way to flexible (e.g. short-term) contracts, the decentring of output ('outsourcing' of plants), and increased mobility of capital across international markets. Companies expanded globally as service industries such as computing replaced the old manufacturing concerns. All in all, a phase of late capitalism appeared to be underway. Whereas previous monopoly or imperialist phases of capitalism had been linked to cultural modernism, late capitalism was to be seen as synonymous with a 'postmodern' epoch.[1]

One of art's key changes was the loss of any overall sense of an avant-garde project. If this book has taken the self-referring Modernist aesthetics of Greenberg and Fried to be the horizon against which post-war avant-gardes defined themselves, the social and economic changes of postmodernity bred a pluralist cultural ethos in which artistic practices proliferated without any agreed goals. Art objects became cultural products among others, rather than catalysts for social or aesthetic values. Some practices certainly maintained the oppositional stances of the period around 1968. But it became harder for art to achieve any adversarial distance from the social mechanisms into which it was merged. This chapter will frequently return to that struggle.

Theories of the postmodern

The notion of the postmodern had had some currency among cultural theorists in the early 1970s. The American-based literary critic Ihab Hassan applied the term to a swathe of artistic experimentalists ranging from Duchamp and Cage to writers such as Thomas Pynchon. By 1985 Hassan had established criteria for distinguishing postmodernist works from their modernist counterparts. For instance, the latter were said to privilege depth and determinacy whilst the former prioritized surface and indeterminacy.[2] Such crude oppositions are far from watertight. Recalling the dual definitions of modernism outlined in Chapter 1, indeterminacy could easily be seen as a modernist concern, indicative of responses to social modernization. By the same token, it is Modernism (capital M), as defined by Greenberg, which most clearly privileged origins or essences, whereas late modernists, such as

Detail of 117

Yves Klein, often undermined authorial presence. Whilst certain opponents of Modernism may certainly have been proto-postmodernists (Rauschenberg, as noted earlier, was perceived as such by Leo Steinberg in 1972), a more sophisticated model of cultural change is required to make the term meaningful.

Another early exponent of the notion was the British architectural critic Charles Jencks. In *The Language of Post-Modern Architecture* (1977) he announced grandly that modern architecture had 'died' in St Louis, Missouri, on 15 July 1972 at 3.32 p.m., when much of the notorious Pruitt–Igoe housing scheme was dynamited.[3] Celebrating the demise of the austere functionalist ethos of modernist architecture, he argued polemically for an eclectically postmodern play of stylistic quotations cross-fertilizing modernist forms with previous historical idioms. His model was primarily aesthetic but by the 1980s it was linked to a neo-conservative rhetoric which trumpeted the virtues of increased choice in a less socially stratified society. The crucial shift from an aesthetic to a societal model of the postmodern came, however, with the French philosopher Jean-François Lyotard's *The Postmodern Condition*, first published in 1979.[4]

Lyotard's book replaced the play of styles with a thoroughgoing cultural relativism. According to Lyotard, the 'grand narratives' that had informed Western societies since the Enlightenment (in other words since the eighteenth century, when European philosophers such as Kant and Rousseau had laid the intellectual foundations for modernism) could no longer sustain credibility. These abstract systems of thought, by which social institutions validated themselves, were infused with ideals of social perfectibility or progress. (In terms of modern art, Greenberg's aesthetic Modernism might be considered a grand narrative of sorts.) Societies now generated a profusion of 'language games'. Institutions and businesses spoke to differing social interests, differing desires and concerns.

These ideas chimed in with the political changes of the period. The year 1979 saw Margaret Thatcher accede to power in Britain, followed, in 1981, by Ronald Reagan in America. This sharp swing to the political right heralded policies of economic deregulation and an allied relativization of values. Thatcherism, for instance, promoted the idea of an 'enterprise culture' predicated on personal (and entrepreneurial) initiative rather than social cohesion. These were hardly Lyotard's politics. His philosophies derived from marxist roots. Yet the bitter lessons learnt from 1968 and post-Stalinist repression had suggested to him that Marxism was unworkable. It was another unwieldy grand narrative. Like the French philosopher Michel Foucault, Lyotard welcomed the dissolution of the Enlightenment legacy. The micro-politics of groups such as ecologists or feminists seemed preferable to monolithic causes.

Lyotard's views ran counter to those of another influential philosopher of the left, the German Jürgen Habermas. In a lecture in 1980 Habermas acknowledged that modernist ideals seemed unsustainable but argued nevertheless for a continuation of the Enlightenment project. For him, art, science, and morality had to remain as specialized narratives while last-ditch efforts were made to create bridges between them.[5] In so far as the notion of avant-garde opposition to normative culture persisted in the years to come, Lyotard's and Habermas's positions broadly underpinned differences of standpoint. But if artists were to endorse either postmodernist pluralism or modernist totality, how were they to separate themselves from the historical process? If culture is in a postmodern phase, then art must inevitably be symptomatic of this. The American literary critic Fredric Jameson certainly thought so. His highly influential essay of 1984, *Postmodernism, or the Cultural Logic of Late Capitalism*, argued that culture's destiny was inextricably bound to capitalism's.[6]

Jameson asserted that aesthetic and commodity production had become indistinguishable. Technologies of reproduction (such as television) had replaced technologies of production. Art was increasingly sponsored by commercial companies, leading to a new interdependence of art and advertising. Subsequent commentators noted that avant-gardism was now a commercial signifier rather than a deeply rooted position. Social levelling had caused shifts in class values. The refined cultivation of the aristocracy or the principled militancy of the working classes, to which the avant-garde had once appealed, had become absorbed into an undifferentiated consumerist philistinism. Since enshrined academic principles and moral pieties also no longer posed any opposition, to whom could the avant-garde speak? As we shall see, gender and identity politics continued to be key issues for artists, but such concerns were socially decentred.

The main thrust of Jameson's analysis, however, was an account of the mindset underlying the cultural products of postmodernism. Using Warhol as an early example, he talked of an emotional numbing or 'waning of affect' as characterizing postmodern subjectivity. Whereas modernism had frequently invoked the artist's inner depths as a bulwark against an alienating external world, a 'new depthlessness' seemed to haunt recent art. Artists now manipulated visual surfaces and codes, assuming that their sensibilities were formed out of representations rather than prior to them in any sense. Most dramatically, Jameson adapted the thought of the French social theorist Jean Baudrillard to evoke the 'schizophrenic' effects of an autonomous sphere of social sign production where signifiers had become detached from their referents and existed in free play as derealized simulacra.[7] Artists were left with a 'rubble of distinct and unrelated signifiers' and an accompanying loss of temporal coordinates.[8] A culture of retro styles confirmed the loss of authentic historical awareness. Similarly, whilst parody had been a weapon of the beleaguered modernist, pastiche, described by Jameson as 'speech in a dead language', was now the order of the day.

These are dramatic claims, more applicable perhaps to the experience of Los Angeles or Las Vegas than certain parts of Europe. When, slightly later, the theorist David Harvey related such effects to insidious forms of space-time compression, brought on, for instance, by the way global communications collapse space into an accelerated temporal dimension, they seemed more feasible.[9] However, one way of testing Jameson's theories is to measure them against the art that directly preceded them.

The American artist Cindy Sherman, earlier described as postmodern, is relevant here. Emerging in New York in the late 1970s with Pop, conceptualism, and Body Art as her expressive resources, her first important works, a sequence of sixty-nine *Untitled Film Stills*, were produced between 1977 and

101 Cindy Sherman

Untitled Film Still #6, 1977

Sherman poses as a woman daydreaming. She holds a mirror, a clichéd symbol of vanity, in one hand. Momentarily her blank stare triggers a disturbing double take. She becomes a victim of crime in a police photograph, 'killed' by the voyeuristic, mechanical gaze of the camera.

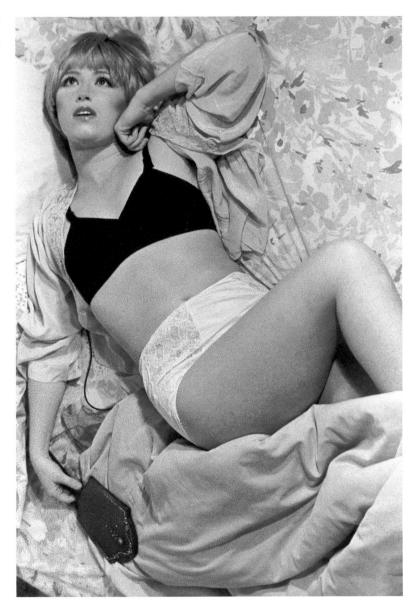

1980 [**101**]. Ideally they should be seen en masse since she appears in all of them, threading her persona through codes of clothing, lighting, setting, and composition filched from 1950s American B-movies. Appearing as a film star lookalike, a flirtatious college student, a defiant housewife, she tips her hat to feminist debates, establishing femininity as a construct rather than something innate. But it is Sherman's implicit assertion that representation itself is already precoded (via cinematic tropes in this instance) that seems to gel with Jameson's talk of pastiche, surface effects, and disconnected signifiers. Sherman's images are uncannily simulacral, referable to no external origins. Photography thus becomes the ideal postmodernist medium, freezing the ostensibly real as a sign.

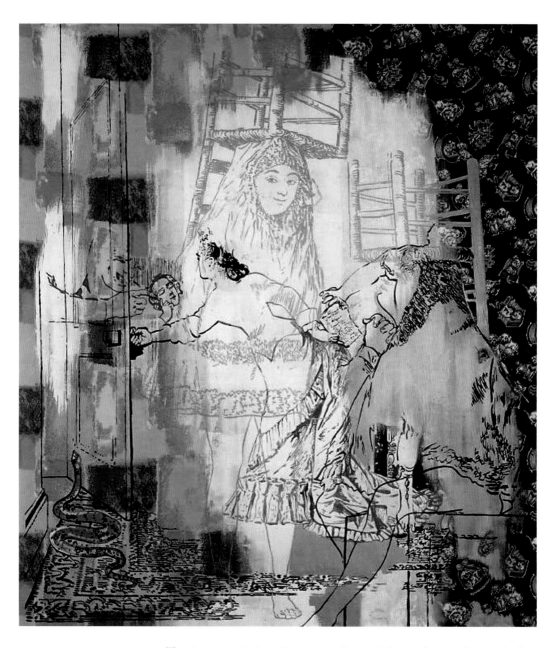

Turning to painting, the postmodern epithet is frequently attached to Sigmar Polke, previously discussed (in Chapter 4) in relation to German Capitalist Realism [**63**]. Looking at *This Is How You Sit Correctly (after Goya)* [**102**] of 1982, it is possible to see how his earlier appropriations of mass-media imagery subsequently became intermingled with diverse high-cultural allusions. Against a background featuring a collision of two varieties of decorative fabric, one abstract, the other sprinkled with saccharine animal motifs (possibly for a child's room), Polke has overlaid fragmentary, irresolute linear quotations. This mode of layering imagery was partly borrowed from the French dadaist Francis Picabia, whose *Transparencies* of the 1920s, consisting of linear overlaps of disparate motifs, had a distinct vogue in the early 1980s. The American painter David Salle, who was directly affected by both Picabia and Polke, set elliptical fragments of 1950s textile design into grisaille fields of soft-porn imagery, floating nebulous and deliberately crude graphic notations from Old Master paintings over them. Polke's melding of public and private, decoration and fine art, also harks back to Rauschenberg's *Bed* [19]. However, whilst Rauschenberg's discursive jumps were mediated by a formal logic, Polke's cultural fragments seem irreconcilable. The effect is very much that of Jameson's 'rubble of distinct and unrelated signifiers'.

It seems clear, then, that postmodernist theory, or Jameson's at least, identified a shift of artistic mood. But to what extent *was* the art of the early 1980s merely symptomatic of a new cultural condition? If, on Jameson's account, the loss of a 'depth model' in art reflected capital's deeper inroads into social formations, to what degree were artists self-reflexive about such seemingly dire circumstances? One possibility, entertained by Jameson, is that postmodern sensibility was itself often experienced as a form of elation or euphoria, and his related notion of a 'postmodern sublime' will be dealt with in due course. For the moment, it can be asserted that postmodern art in the early 1980s broadly resolved itself into two camps. First there were those who were content to surrender to the free play of the signifier, even in its most lurid consumerist garb. Alternatively, there were those postmodernists who set about reassessing modernism, utilizing Duchampian, situationist, or conceptualist strategies to open up fault lines in the capitalist spectacle.

The latter option posed certain difficulties. In theory Polke's dazzling mergers of high and low imagery ought to amount to a socially critical position because he was profoundly sensitive to the historical preconditions for cultural fragmentation. (His work would later incorporate the kind of alchemical allusions that Beuys and Kounellis had used as metaphors for a residual spiritual agency.) But if one characteristic of the postmodern is art's structural dissolution into the wider culture, Polke's mergers possibly replicate such assimilation. On this count, he would belong to the former camp. The question returns, how was art to attain oppositional distance?

The return to painting

The dilemma posed above was dramatized in the early 1980s through the interplay of painting and photo-related practices. Painting first demands consideration. Broadly speaking, it had fallen out of critical favour in the 1970s. The Modernist cult of abstraction had looked increasingly inappropriate to the times, although, as will be seen, important figurative painting was still being produced. By the turn of the 1980s a full-scale revival of figuration, informed by lessons learned from abstraction, was underway. Not only was it promoted in large exhibitions, but its return coincided with a temporary shift in art-world domination from America to Europe. The defining exhibitions were *A New Spirit in Painting* at London's Royal Academy in 1981 and *Zeitgeist* in Berlin in 1982. Their European curators made passionate claims for a reaffirmation of humanist concerns, sensing that conceptualism's ascetic intellectualism had signalled the end of a historical trajectory. In the catalogue for the London show one of its organizers

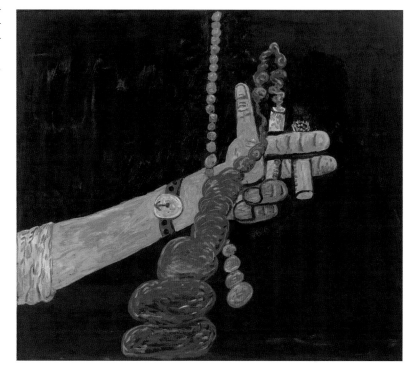

asserted that 'the subjective view, the creative imagination, has come back into its own'.[10]

One of the early discoveries of this revival was Philip Guston, whose work had already provided a catalyst for what critics in late 1970s New York dubbed 'New Image Painting'. Guston had initially been linked to Abstract Expressionism, shifting dramatically to figuration in the mid-1960s. Deciding that his previous output had been dishonestly geared to specious notions of purity, Guston spent the 1970s setting down the insistent, graspable facts of his daily moods, obsessions, and insecurities. His lexicon of crude, idiosyncratic images borrowed their stylizations from 1940s American cartoonists such as Al Capp or Basil Wolverton (figures who also influenced the 1960s underground comic-book artist Robert Crumb) [103].

Another rediscovered American painter was Leon Golub. Since the 1950s Golub had been developing a scarred and lacerated figuration, responding to issues such as the use of napalm in the Vietnam War, but his reputation was consolidated when he exhibited his *Mercenaries* and *Interrogations* in 1982. Depicting a world of brutalized males, paid to carry out human violations at the political margins, Golub avoided a moralizing position. His mercenaries and interrogators swap banter among themselves and gaze out of his pictures as though assuming our complicity in their actions [104]. Sometimes a bound or gagged victim is present. Golub painted the works on the floor, dissolving build-ups of paint with solvents and then scraping the surface with a meat cleaver. Paint adheres in the weave of his canvases as though corruption were etched into the creases of his protagonists' clothes, the laughter lines around their eyes.

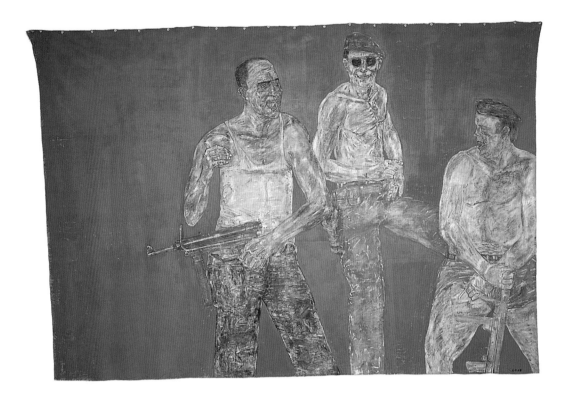

Mercenaries II, 1979

Set against huge fields of red oxide on mural-sized, unstretched canvases, Golub's figures' frozen poses fleetingly echo those on Greek pottery, but they travesty classical faith in the body.

Although Guston and Golub became visible internationally, as did Julian Schnabel, who will be discussed shortly, American artists did not figure particularly prominently in the European promotion of the painting revival. In many ways the phenomenon provided a means for ambitious European curators to revenge themselves on two decades of American art-world hegemony. In 1982 the German *Documenta 7* exhibition at Kassel, curated by Rudi Fuchs, was dominated by new figuration from Italy and Germany. The French critic Pierre Restany perceived an 'anti-American Kulturkampf' taking place.[11]

The new Italian painting was dubbed the *Trans-avantgarde* by the critic Achille Bonito Oliva, who promoted it in a book of 1980, arguing that the presumption of difficulty and singularity of purpose in avant-gardism had been supplanted by a cultural nomadism and eclecticism.[12] The perfect exemplar of this was the painter Francesco Clemente, who moved restlessly between Rome, New York, and Madras at the turn of the 1980s, incorporating a heterogeneous range of sources in his narcissistic and poetically allusive images. Clemente's style was broadly expressionistic but, like several contemporaries, his magpie borrowings from past and present art looked to the example of the early twentieth-century Italian painter Giorgio de Chirico, whose late output, with its bizarre amalgams of classicism and modernism, suddenly found favour. As noted earlier, Picabia's late work was also rehabilitated, whilst exhibitions of Picasso's final expressionistic paintings, produced between the late 1950s and his death in 1973, consolidated assumptions that, after phases of doctrinal purity, the modernist masters had rekindled their creativity via idiosyncratic, excessive imagery.

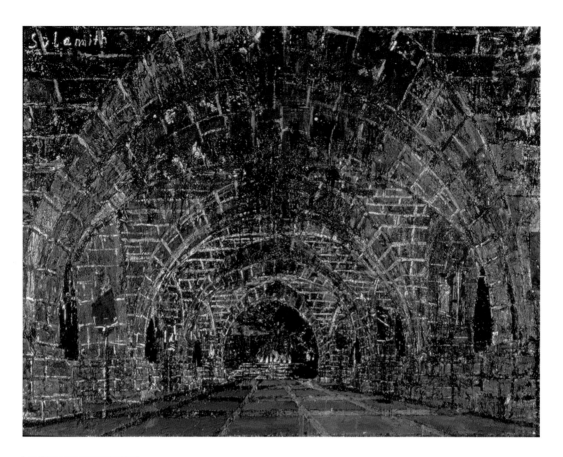

It was in West Germany that a prevailing mood of eclecticism resolved itself into what most resembled a common painting style, with a brooding Neo-Expressionist idiom becoming dominant. As noted at the end of Chapter 3, painters such as Georg Baselitz and Markus Lüpertz had long been concerned with keeping German Expressionist traditions alive, but the younger Anselm Kiefer, a pupil of Joseph Beuys, drew on his teacher's example to deal self-consciously with Germany's recent cultural and political history. In his landscapes thick accretions of black paint, mixed with sand, straw, or ashes, simultaneously emblematized his own artistic desire to renew painting and referred to the way retreating armies burn land to render it unusable. Whilst American critics such as Donald Kuspit lauded Kiefer, alongside other German painters, for heroically 'lay[ing] to rest the ghosts... of German style, culture and history so that people can be authentically new',[13] German-born critics such as Andreas Huyssen were more cautious of the artist's apparent invocation of Teutonic myths linking the regeneration of the *Volk* with the soil.[14]

Kiefer's evident fascination with Fascist architecture was similarly ambiguous, but in *Sulamith (Shulamite)* (1983) [105] it served to evoke atonement. The title derives from a poem by an ex-concentration-camp internee, Paul Celan, in which Nazi and Jewish archetypes are juxtaposed in the repeated refrain 'your golden hair Margarete / your ashen hair Shulamith'. In the painting the blackened brickwork of the depicted interior, which was based on a Fascist architectural scheme honouring the 'Great German Soldier', transforms it metaphorically into an enormous oven.

Painting's new-found preoccupations with national identity and with recycling previous stylistic tropes were attacked in a polemical essay of 1981 by the art historian Benjamin Buchloh, who noted that regression to nationally distinct artistic modes in twentieth-century art, such as the classicizing *rappel à l'ordre* in French art in the 1920s, had often accompanied swings to the political right.[15] Buchloh's critique tended to gloss over anomalies. For instance, a German painter such as Jörg Immendorff, whose revivalism involved the 1920s *Neue Sachlichkeit* (New Objectivitiy) idiom of German painters such as George Grosz, clearly manifested an edgy unease with Germany's political divisions, as in his *Café Deutschland* series, rather than any yearning for national belonging. But Buchloh's analysis did draw attention to the way that, after an internationalist, left-oriented conceptualist phase, the return to figurative, nationally identifiable styles suited an art market attuned to Reaganism.

National styles, tied to newly valorized painterly signatures, became highly desirable. In Europe the institutional triumphalism surrounding the 'return to painting' quickly dissipated as its commercial backers went global. In 1983 the Cologne dealer Michael Werner, who had helped to establish German Neo-Expressionists such as Baselitz and Lüpertz, cemented business links with Mary Boone, the New York dealer responsible for the success of their American counterparts. (The couple married in 1986.) It might be argued that invocations of national identity in, say, Kiefer symbolized resistance to such homogenizing global arrangements. But the sheer impetus of the early 1980s market meant that few ambitious artists could extricate themselves from the ideological paradoxes it generated. Many blithely played along. One outstanding example, to return to Mary Boone, was one of her protégés, the American painter Julian Schnabel.

When Schnabel's first exhibition sold out before its opening at Mary Boone's gallery in February 1979, it was taken by many to be an augury. An essentially derivative painter, Schnabel brashly revived the rhetoric of the macho artist–genius, specializing in painting fractured images over large surfaces covered with objects such as smashed crockery. His meteoric success owed much to Charles and Maurice Saatchi, the then owners of the global advertising agency Saatchi & Saatchi, with Charles, as art collector, becoming the embodiment of new patterns of commercial patronage. Bulk-buying the work of selected artists or movements, Saatchi strategically dropped them when necessary. A case in point was the Italian *Transavanguardia* painter Sandro Chia, whose career suffered accordingly. In the case of Schnabel, the fact that the Saatchis owned nearly all of the works shown in his Tate Gallery exhibition in 1982 raised doubts about their role in prematurely canonizing relatively undeveloped talents.[16]

The backlash against painting: photo-related practices

In 1983 Hans Haacke, previously discussed (in Chapter 6) in the context of conceptualism, parodically turned his hand to oil painting. In *Taking Stock (Unfinished)* [106] he surrounded an image of Margaret Thatcher, one of the political enablers of the current art boom, with a decor connotative of her regard for 'Victorian values', framing the painting in appropriately grand style. Behind Thatcher the artist depicted a bookcase containing leather-bound volumes. These are shown to contain details of company reports, including those of the Saatchis. The heads of the brothers are further emblazoned on two cracked plates on the top shelf of the bookcase, signifying their links with Julian Schnabel. The Saatchis' agency had advised both the British Conservative Party and Thatcher on matters of public image before their election victories in Britain in 1979 and 1983. Haacke thus supplied the 'evidence' confirming the new painting's complicity with political and economic interests.

Haacke's implied criticisms were shared by a sector of New York's cultural establishment which had grown up with post-1968 conceptualism. In 1976 the critics Rosalind Krauss and Annette Michelson had founded a magazine whose title, *October*, invoked the militancy of the Russian avant-garde after the 1917 revolution. Their commitments were broadly towards conceptualist uses of photography, backed up by the heavy theoretical artillery of semiotics and post-structuralist philosophy. Taking Barthes's notion of 'the death of the author' as a given, Krauss theorized photographs, alongside other visual artefacts such as body casts, as examples of an indexical order of signs, which constituted direct traces or imprints of reality. In this they differed from iconic or symbolic signs, which required the mediation of the artist's hand. Since Duchamp had shown a predilection for indexical signs, he came to represent the historical touchstone for opposition to the nascent fetishization of the painterly mark.[17] Photography thus became for the 1980s what the readymade had been for the 1950s and early 1960s in terms of antagonism to painting. In 1977 a further *October* collaborator, Douglas Crimp, curated a key exhibition of photographically produced works at New York's Artists Space gallery entitled *Pictures*. Exhibitors such as Sherrie Levine and Robert Longo re-photographed and re-presented imagery from an increasingly invasive world of visual signs. Such strategies were again underwritten by post-structuralist conceptions of the artist/author as someone who shuffles existing texts and signs, renouncing the possibility of creative originality.

By the early 1980s younger critics such as Craig Owens and Hal Foster had gravitated towards *October* and were arguing for an art that was strategically deconstructive rather than symptomatically postmodern, like the new painting. These critics largely supported practices which echoed those of situationist-influenced conceptualists such as Daniel Buren. They therefore

106 Hans Haacke

Taking Stock (Unfinished), 1983–4

In this painting Haacke's use of allegorical detail has an ironic air of academic exactitude. For instance, the marble sculpture of Pandora, pointedly placed on the Victorian table next to Margaret Thatcher, is based on one produced in 1890 by the British sculptor Harry Bates and owned by the Tate Gallery, London.

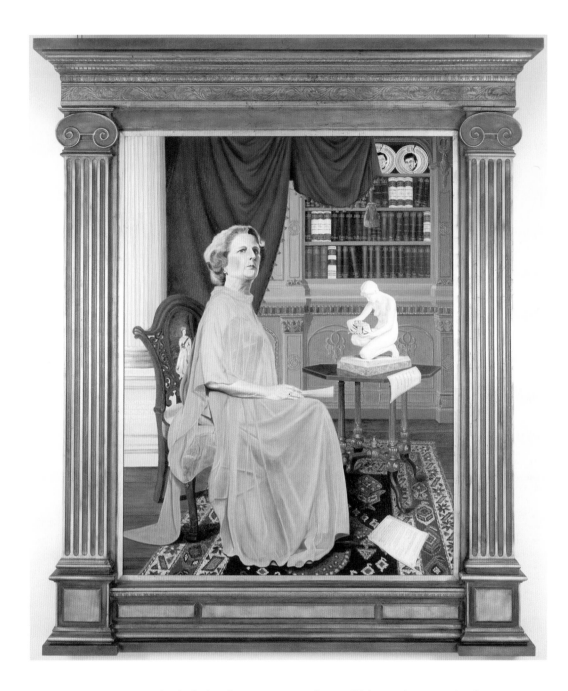

backed the American artist Jenny Holzer, who specialized in inserting highly ambiguous printed statements into the public domain. Her *Truisms* (1977–8) consisted of long lists of conflicting homilies or injunctions (such as 'An elite is inevitable' or 'Any surplus is immoral') which seemingly questioned the possibility that univocal viewpoints could issue from either an authorial or a public sphere. These lists were affixed to buildings or lamp posts, whilst single statements subsequently appeared on T-shirts, their meanings dramatically modified in relation to the wearer's gender.

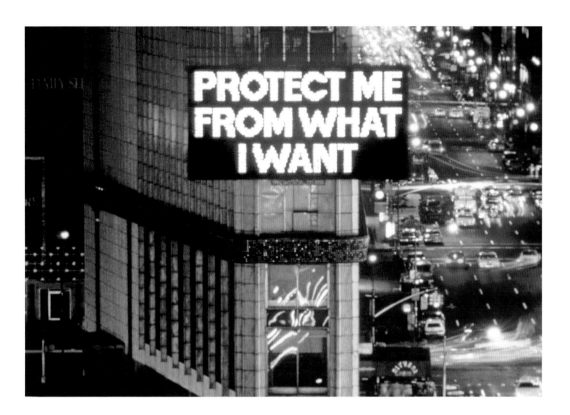

From *Survival*, 1983–85
(installation view selection
from *The Survival Series*,
Times Square, New York,
1985)

Holzer has used a diversity of
means to disseminate her
messages. These have
included posters, plaques on
buildings, T-shirts, bus
tickets, park benches,
baggage carousels at
airports, LED screens in
shopping malls or sports
stadiums, television, radio,
and billboards. In 1989 her
slogans and statements
appeared on LED strips
following the circular motion
of the spiral ramp at New
York's Guggenheim Museum.

From 1982 onwards Holzer periodically paid to have messages flashed across electronic billboards. Hence, in 1985–6 the message 'Protect me from what I want' (part of her *Survival* series) hovered above Times Square [**107**]. No doubt hurrying shoppers paused confusedly, as the voice of authority (or advertising) ventriloquized their insecurities.

Another American artist, Barbara Kruger, used similar strategies, recapitulating Victor Burgin's parodic advertisements with striking juxtapositions of photography and text echoing 1920s and 1930s political photomontages and typographics by John Heartfield and Alexander Rodchenko. Like Holzer's, her texts hijacked an authoritarian voice but levelled accusations at nameless adversaries from the viewpoint of the oppressed or marginalized. In *Untitled* (1981) a photograph of a carved female bust is captioned 'Your gaze hits the side of my face', cleverly reversing the Medusa myth to convey the immobilization of women in social spaces dominated by male looking. As this work implies, as Kruger took possession of the voice of power, so she, at some level, became possessed. She inevitably became entrapped both in representation and in the mass media's machinations. This was dramatized in different terms in 1987 when she appeared on the cover of the magazine *ARTnews*. Whether Kruger was aware of it or not, this magazine had been carefully selected by a major American bank as a vehicle for advertising to potential clients with 'portfolios of $5 million or more'.[18] It seems, then, that oppositional postmodern artists, in ceding their agency to other voices, ironically fell prey to Jameson's postmodern merging of art into commerce.

The *October* critics nevertheless attempted to distinguish a 'postmodernism of resistance' from a 'postmodernism of reaction',[19] making ambitious claims for the former's departure from modernist assumptions. Craig Owens, for instance, perceived an 'allegorical impulse' at work in the way certain artists since Rauschenberg had effected crossovers between aesthetic mediums or appropriated cultural imagery to establish that meanings were contingent rather than fixed. Rosalind Krauss further argued for a decisive shift from modernist notions of authenticity and originality.[20] Krauss's thinking may well have been stimulated by the example of Duchamp's ironic play on the original and the copy in his editioned readymades of the 1960s. Certainly Sherrie Levine, an artist who came to prominence in Crimp's 1977 *Pictures* exhibition, became Krauss's protégée precisely by (almost literally) recasting Duchamp [**30**].

Levine also re-presented other works such as photographs by the American Depression-era photographer Walker Evans. Her apparently rudimentary strategy raised fascinating questions. For instance, Evans's documentary aesthetics were partly predicated on a notion of transparency, whereby the plight of the subjects of his photographs (the downtrodden Southern sharecroppers and their families of the 1930s) supposedly predominated over any awareness of the photographer's style. In effect the opposite was the case: pragmatism and stoicism came to be identified with the name 'Walker Evans'. In usurping Evans's authorship, Levine ironically focused attention back on the 'subjects' of his photographs, making the images curiously transparent again. Another artist concerned with appropriating imagery was Richard Prince. In re-presenting images of cowboys extrapolated from advertisements for Marlboro cigarettes, he effaced his authorial presence while obliquely preserving an ironically macho identification between himself, as artist, and the romantic outsider-figures of the cowboys [**108**].

All in all, Prince's and Levine's decentring of authorship, like that of Holzer or Kruger, spoke of the impossibility of being outside representation.

108 Richard Prince
Untitled (Cowboy), 1991–2
Prince's early appropriations from advertising, of which this is an example, have interesting connections with his later practice. After 1985 Prince started to employ verbal jokes in his works. They were often silk-screened as texts across the centres of large, single-colour canvases alluding to Modernist abstractions. The character of the jokes, which usually reflected 1950s, Middle American, 'blue-collar' values, often had an undercurrent of malevolence. Many of them dealt with infidelity. From the evidence of his earlier appropriations, Prince himself was a fugitive, teasingly untrustworthy artist.

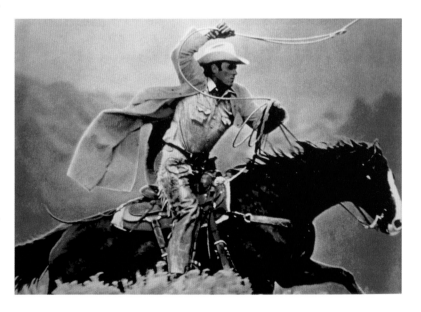

However, in terms of the workings of the art world, this translated into capitulation as much as resistance. By 1986 Sherrie Levine followed the likes of Schnabel in showing at Mary Boone's chic New York gallery. Deconstruction of authorial presence did not lead to artists deconstructing their own authority. Postmodern authorship in fact became an increasingly exotic affair, as audiences became adept at unpicking authors from the codes in which they were camouflaged. This was backed up by a highly professionalized critical and academic discourse and a publishing industry quick to cash in on the inverted intellectual snobbery that 'critical postmodernism' often inadvertently engendered. In relation to conceptualism's principled avant-gardism, oppositional postmodernism often smacked of mannerism.

The 'postmodern sublime': permutations of photo-painting

If attempts to assert the moral superiority of photo-related practices over painting rang hollow, it was arguably when photography and painting converged that the most challenging forms of postmodern art resulted. In 1981 the artist and critic Thomas Lawson asserted that, whereas the art promoted by the journal *October* sometimes appeared smug in its marginality, painting, with its greater public visibility, perversely held out greater critical potential. Demanding a kind of blind faith, it could attain a degree of irony that photography's more straightforwardly declarative imagery lacked.[21] Lawson mainly cited the work of the American David Salle, but may easily have had in mind artists such as Malcolm Morley, Eric Fischl, and Gerhard Richter. In their different ways, they continued to affirm a discredited medium. However, rather than reviving past rhetorical strategies in the manner of the Neo-Expressionists, they acknowledged that painting had to interface directly with photography and its conventions.

This applies most obviously to Malcolm Morley. A British-born painter who had worked in America since 1958, Morley had pioneered a form of 'Photorealism' (also dubbed 'hyper-' or 'super-realism') in America in the mid-1960s, producing images such as *SS Amsterdam in Front of Rotterdam* (1966) which were painstakingly transposed from photographs. In the early 1970s other artists achieved critical and commercial success from related practices. Painters such as Philip Pearlstein, Chuck Close, and Richard Estes translated the pictorial plenitude of photographs into glossy painted surfaces, densely encoded with visual information. At the same time the sculptor Duane Hanson made uncanny direct-cast replicas of live figures, painting them illusionistically and dressing them in actual clothes.

As Photorealism became fashionable, however, Morley grew frustrated with his seamless surfaces. This is dramatized in *The Ultimate Anxiety* (1978) [109], in which a depiction of a train cuts incongruously across an image transposed from a postcard reproduction of a painting by the Venetian master Francesco Guardi. This work relates to other 'catastrophe' pictures Morley produced at this time such as *The Day of the Locust* (1977), in which a Pop-like replication of the cover of the Los Angeles *Yellow Pages* appears to be eaten away from the inside by swarms of imagery. Morley produces a refreshingly direct response to the cultural relativism of his times. But he also dramatizes the peculiar sense of dislocation which arises as different orders of representation intrude upon one another.

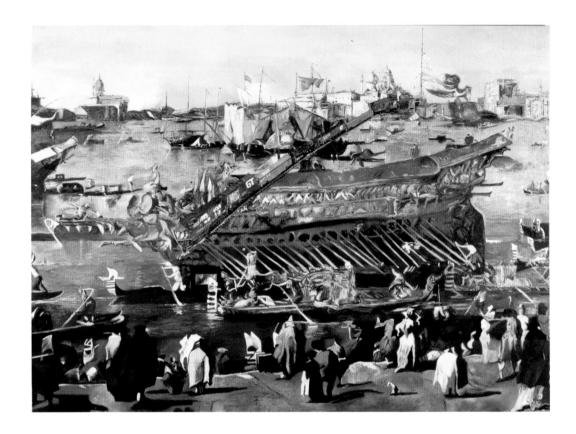

The American artist Eric Fischl's painterly realism might appear anachronistically descriptive, but his works were also riven internally by divergent modes of representation linked to photography and film. The flat literalness of Fischl's paint-handling, along with certain compositional devices, partly derived from the 1920s and 1930s American realist painter Edward Hopper, whose work was widely exhibited in 1981. However, Fischl translated Hopper's poetic vision of Middle American ennui into an examination of suburban neuroses and repressions. Arresting narratives in mid-flow, he obliged his spectators to become entangled in morally ambiguous scenarios, anticipating David Lynch's film *Blue Velvet* (1986).

This sense of imminent implosion was closely informed by Fischl's pictorial strategies. Combining disparate figures derived from sources such as photographs taken on nudist beaches, he sought a 'seamless look constituted by fragments'.[22] In *The Old Man's Boat and the Old Man's Dog* of 1982 [**110**] Fischl revisited Théodore Géricault's famous painting *Raft of the Medusa* (1819), which had commented obliquely on corruption in early nineteenth-century French government. Its subject aside, Fischl's work communicates moral breakdown in the way its photographically derived, voyeuristic fragments almost fail to cohere. Unlike Géricault he cannot achieve a unified public statement. His realism is vitiated by technologies oriented towards visual distraction and discontinuity.

As pointed out in Chapter 4, the German painter Gerhard Richter similarly looked back mournfully on painting's loss of public function in his

110 Eric Fischl

The Old Man's Boat and the Old Man's Dog, 1982

Fischl's works invariably contain narratives with undercurrents of social dysfunction or malaise. Here a group of decadent, inexperienced seafarers have abandoned themselves to the mercies of a beer-swigging 'Old Man' who appears oblivious to a storm brewing in the distance.

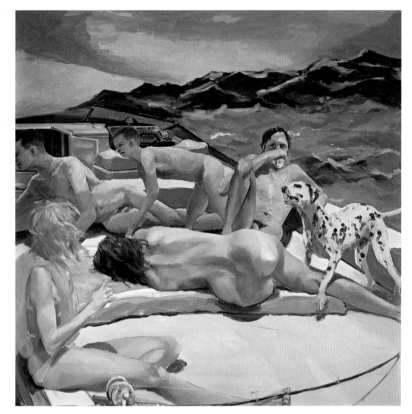

October 18, 1977 (1988), a cycle of fifteen paintings which mimicked the appearances of blurred black-and-white photographs [**111**]. Richter had initially produced 'photo-paintings' just before Malcolm Morley in the 1960s. However, in contrast to Morley, his works frequently possessed a metaphysical cast which aligns him with a lesser-known American-based artist, the Latvian-born Vija Celmins. Celmins's drawings of the late 1960s and early 1970s dealt with issues of proximity and distance. Taking photographs of limitless phenomena, such as the ocean or the star-filled sky, as her models, she translated such ungraspable subjects into finite blocks of graphic description, which call for close-up inspection [**112**].

This oscillation between an informationally saturated surface and an elusive subject assumed a political edge in Richter's *October 18, 1977*. The cycle dealt with the apparent suicides, ten years previously, of members of West Germany's militant Red Army Faction. Having lived under a Stalinist regime in Eastern Europe, Richter abhorred ideological dogmatism. Nevertheless he felt some sympathy for the terrorists as misguided heirs of the idealism of 1968.[23] Aware that photographs had originally been instrumental in implanting ideologically tinged images of the terrorists in the German public's mind, Richter submitted such imagery to his painterly blur. As though reversing the terms of Fischl's reworking of Géricault, he filtered photographic imagery through a former technology of public address (the depictions of dead terrorists echoed previous paintings such as Manet's *Dead Toreador* of 1864). At the same time, by obliging his spectators to adjust their positions in relation

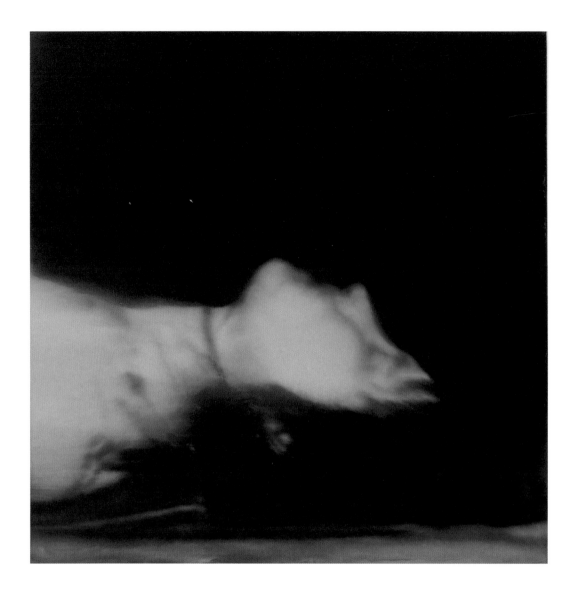

*Dead, from October 18,
1977* series, 1988

to his blurs (in order to 'focus' them), he implied that, just as painting and photography were making competing demands from within the same object, so ideology's claims were unresolvable. This might be linked to Fredric Jameson's influential essay on postmodernism, cited earlier, where its author drew attention to a peculiarly postmodern modality of the sublime, rooted in the philosopher Kant's thought, whereby representation appears stretched to inconceivable limits by technology.[24] Once a container for public conscience, painting becomes, in Richter's hands, replete with photography, a technology often employed to collapse critical distance.

In the mid-1980s Richter produced abstract paintings [**113**] as well as realist photo-paintings. As argued earlier, he appeared here to be recapitulating the ideological options underpinning post-war modernism in so far as his own transplantation from Eastern to Western Europe had been paralleled by an

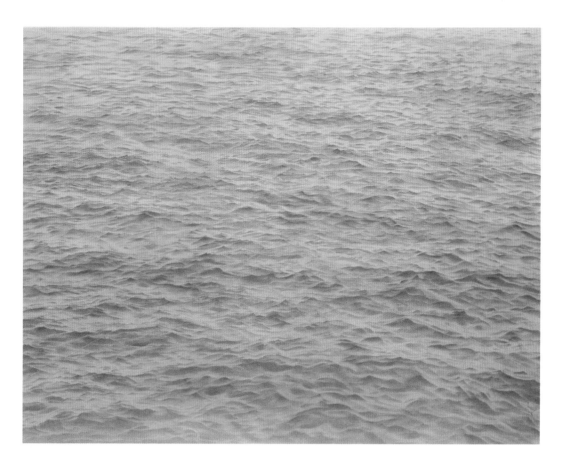

112 Vija Celmins

Untitled (Ocean with Cross #1), 1971

Born in Riga in 1938, and transplanted to America in 1949, Celmins became well known in the 1990s. Her strangely detached, unlocated subjects suggest a radical retreat from the concerns of modern life. Perhaps they relate to her early rootlessness. However, in the 1960s her photo-paintings often dwelt on highly specific, violent incidents. Fire was often involved, as in *Burning Man* (1966), showing a man in flames escaping a car crash. Her expanses of water possibly suggest such horrors have been exorcized.

imperative to favour abstract artistic modes over realist ones. Significantly, in 1979–80 the British conceptualist collective Art & Language, who had previously been opposed to the seductions of the painterly, physically merged communist-style realism and abstraction in their series *Portraits of V. I. Lenin in the Style of Jackson Pollock* [**1**]. Their ingenious double-images, described at the start of this book, parodied the nascent return to (figurative) painting. Whilst the modernist project was widely being pronounced as passé, Art & Language demonstrated that history is deeply embedded in the forms that representation takes. This repudiated the prevailing pluralist ethos whereby historical modes were simply deemed available for co-option.

Richter's abstractions also appeared to mock the modes of expressionist brushwork blithely revisited by Neo-Expressionist contemporaries. However, Richter complicated matters here by asserting that his abstractions were concerned with expressing the 'transcendental' or 'inexplicable'.[25] To clarify this, Jameson's notion of a postmodern sublime might again be pertinent. Looking at *July* (1983) [**113**], one needs to be aware that Richter had painted related abstractions in the late 1970s from photographs of his own paintings, but by this point was overlaying free brushwork onto smooth, photo-derived, abstract grounds. The effect is that of looking into some form of photo-graphically illusionistic space, in which brushstrokes, either directly applied

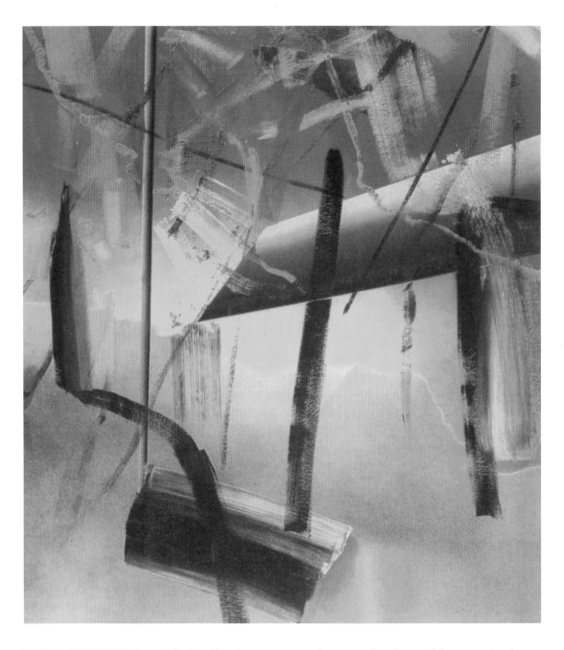

or 'depicted' in incongruous scale, usurp the places of figures or landscape features. The Surrealist Salvador Dalí once asserted that he wished to make 'hand coloured dream photographs'. However, rather than depicting dreams (which are impalpable) Richter paradoxically depicts 'expression', locating it in the lurid photo-reality envisaged by Dalí. We are given dizzying access into the very interstices of representation. As with Richter's realist photo-paintings, phases of recent art history appear to be conflated. Abstract Expressionist invocations of the sublime and Lichtenstein's brushstroke paintings [54] are brought into collision with technology. In comparison

with Art & Language's 'abstraction', the net outcome is hardly a historical dialogue. Instead, a postmodern sublime is envisioned.

Art and difference

The above suggests that, even at its most self-consciously historicist, painting of the 1980s sometimes succumbed to an apocalyptic sense of the postmodern (or what Jameson called an 'inverted millenarianism'). In this it ran the risk of appearing to languish, symptomatically, in a putative 'postmodern crisis'. This was compounded by the status of artists such as Morley or Richter, who, being male, white, and financially secure, could be interpreted as relatively immune from more pressing crises such as social marginalization or deprivation. This once more raises the question: to what extent could postmodern art claim any critical distance?

Among certain commentators, many of whom questioned the totalizing tenor of Jameson-style theory, there was a tendency to identify the theme of difference as grounds for a more ethically oriented art practice. It is important to remember that, as far back as the 1960s, post-structuralist conceptions of an internally divided, gendered human subject had undermined modernist assumptions that it is possible to invoke a universal human nature. Theorists such as Barthes, and later Derrida, had demonstrated that verbal structures in occidental cultures are built around binary oppositions: positive/negative, presence/absence, masculine/feminine, black/white. Since, in each case, one term is privileged in contrast to its negatively tinged 'other', difference becomes something inscribed both linguistically and ideologically. We have seen how this realization informed the feminist art of, say, Mary Kelly or Barbara Kruger. But further permutations of difference affect people's subject-positions in European and North American cultures, notably class and race.[26] Identity politics therefore constituted an arena for less self-referential forms of art.

Having parted company with the British Art & Language group in the early 1970s, Terry Atkinson had, by the mid-1970s, moved away from their stringent conceptualism to explore his working-class heritage in a set of 'history paintings'. In his *First World War* series (*c.*1974–81) he reinterpreted photographs of troops taken during the Great War, using a strategically 'botched' drawing style and satirical captions. He thereby encoded a critique of the way working-class labour was mobilized for capitalist warfare. By 1984–5 such explorations of ideological undercurrents were brought to bear on family photographs. *The Stone Touchers 1* (1984–5) [**114**] incorporates an ironically diligent copy of a photograph of Atkinson's children taken during a holiday in northern France. Intrigued by the rows of war graves, they are shown flanking a stone dedicated, according to the key beneath the image, to a South African infantryman. In a mock-poetic caption Atkinson asks them: 'Do you think God is a person? If he is, is he a he? If he is, is he black or white...is he a South African, or an Argentinian?' Britain's faded imperialism had recently been rekindled by the Falklands War, and South African apartheid was a pressing issue. Atkinson thus presented his suntanned children as inextricably (if unknowingly) implicated in such events.

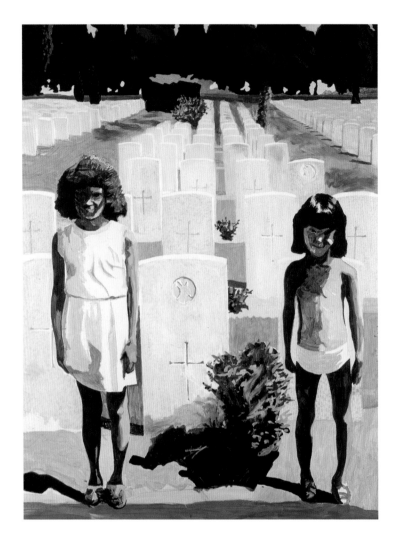

THE STONE TOUCHERS 1
Ruby and Amber in The Gardens of their old Empire
history-dressed men.

Dear Ruby and Amber,
Do you think God is a person?
If he is, is he a he?
If he is, is he black or white, or brown or yellow,
or pink or orange or blue or red, or green or purple.....?
What if he's a she?

Do you think God is a dissident? Or is he a South African,
Or an Argentinian, or an Anglo-Saxon, etc.?

Do you think he's the best knower?

If he is a she do you think all the he's would admit
she's the best knower?

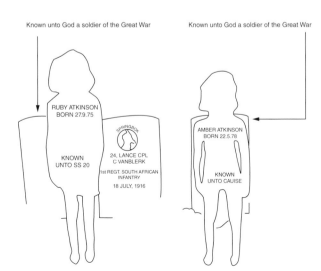

114 Terry Atkinson

The Stone Touchers 1,
1984–5

Terry Atkinson, like David
Hockney, came from a
working-class background in
Yorkshire, England. However,
his affiliations when he
eventually moved to London
were with conceptualism
rather than Pop. Whilst
conceptualism had been
international in orientation,
his 1980s output, which
dealt with subjects such as
class identity and English
attitudes to Northern Ireland,
seemed to represent a
deliberate return to
'local' issues.

Cultural identity was perhaps more urgent for the large numbers of artists whose immediate predecessors had suffered under colonial rule. The increasing visibility and empowerment of artists of 'hyphenated' cultural identity (e.g. African-American, Asian-American) are often correctly perceived as triumphs of a postmodern dispensation, but this process had barely begun. In 1984, in its *'Primitivism' and 20th Century Art* exhibition, New York's MoMA was still endorsing a relatively unreflective view of early modernism's reliance on appropriations from the West's colonial others. By 1989 a large exhibition at La Villette and the Pompidou Centre in Paris, entitled *Magiciens de la terre*, promoted a determinedly multiculturalist view of art, showing works by 100 artists from over 40 countries, many outside of the Western art ambit. It could be argued, however, that such well-meaning efforts at assimilation neutralized the specificities of cultural difference. The scars of ethnic diaspora, or subaltern status, could hardly be dispelled via symbolic gestures. For artists of mixed racial origin there was an urgent need to discover their own voices.

An exemplary figure here is the Cherokee Indian artist Jimmie Durham. Actively involved in the American Indian Movement during the later 1970s, Durham has since produced objects, performances, and installations which wittily expose the mingling of mythologization and historical disavowal that characterize white US attitudes towards Native Americans. In *Bedia's Stirring Wheel* (1985) [**115**] a car's steering wheel is wrapped in hides and star-patterned cloth and embellished with animal trophies, producing an ironic hybrid of 'primitivist' ritual object and Western conceptualist ready-made. A playful text accompanying the work proposes that it has been unearthed by a Cuban archaeologist, José Bedia, during an excavation of the 'White Planes' in AD 3290. Bedia identifies the find as 'a symbol of Office for the Great White Father' who, standing behind it, made 'pronouncements and stirring speeches'. A form of symbolic revenge on the West's technological triumphalism is envisaged.

115 Jimmie Durham

Bedia's Stirring Wheel,
1985

Durham's symbolic recoding
of the imagery of modern
America in the terms of its
native inhabitants is
interesting in relation to
Joseph Beuys's use of Native
American iconography for
purposes of symbolic
retribution [**42**]. As a
modernist, Beuys assumed
his work could possess a
certain universality of
meaning. By contrast,
Durham's postmodern
gesture acknowledges
ambiguities of translation in
the way it treats its subject.
Beuys, of course, was
European whilst Durham
actually came from a Native
American background.

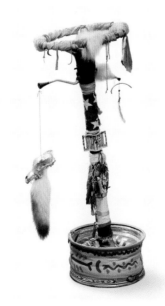

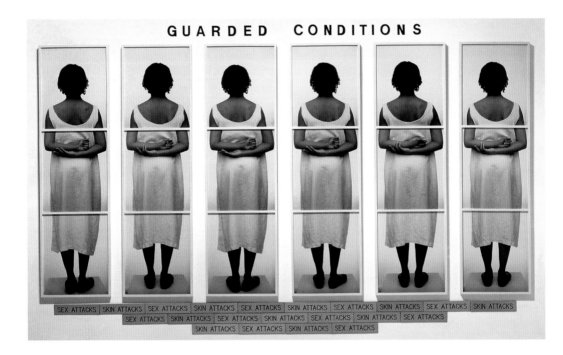

GUARDED CONDITIONS

SEX ATTACKS SKIN ATTACKS SEX ATTACKS SKIN ATTACKS SEX ATTACKS SKIN ATTACKS SEX ATTACKS SKIN ATTACKS SEX ATTACKS SKIN ATTACKS
SEX ATTACKS SKIN ATTACKS SEX ATTACKS SKIN ATTACKS SEX ATTACKS SKIN ATTACKS SEX ATTACKS
SKIN ATTACKS SEX ATTACKS SKIN ATTACKS SEX ATTACKS

116 Lorna Simpson

Guarded Conditions, 1989

The viewer of Lorna Simpson's works is compelled to shuttle between texts and images in order to construct meanings. The use of text–image conjunctions was a major component of 1980s photographic practice. In Britain Victor Burgin's teaching at the Polytechnic of Central London was particularly influential for a number of Simpson's contemporaries. These included Mitra Tabrizian, Karen Knorr, and Olivier Richon.

Racial assumptions are the butt of Durham's irony, but as Atkinson intimated, these are normally inseparable from ones involving class or gender. Depictions of African-Americans by two American-based artists prominent in the late 1980s demonstrate the complexities that accrue from this. Robert Mapplethorpe, who achieved the unlikely feat of making the modernist photography of the likes of Edward Weston function in a postmodern ambience, did so by overhauling that tradition's image of the male nude. In publications such as *The Black Book* (1986) he produced provocative, classicizing images of black males. Critics argued as to whether, as a white homosexual, he was objectifying his subjects or whether he was summoning up the spectre of a mythologized black potency to unsettle his predominantly white gallery-going audience. Whatever the case, the power of his images turned on the ramifications of 'visibility'. By contrast, Lorna Simpson, an African-American artist who employed text–image juxtapositions in a conceptualist idiom, produced a haunting series of back views of a generic black female in a shift, her identity occluded. Clearly social invisibility was being figured here, whilst Simpson's textual captions produced ambiguous supplementary meanings [**116**]. Moving from Mapplethorpe to Simpson, different configurations of race, class, and gender result from shifting relations between the artists, their subjects, and their implied audiences. In viewing such works the critical appraisal of such permutations became an ethical prerequisite.

Simulation and abjection: the late 1980s

If identity-related art inherited something of the modernist avant-garde's claims to moral authority, an entirely antithetical tendency emerged in New York during the 1980s. Encompassing artists such as Ashley Bickerton, Haim Steinbach, and Jeff Koons, its forms relied heavily on Duchampian

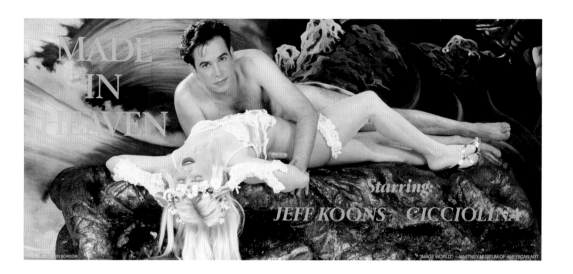

117 Jeff Koons

Made in Heaven, billboard poster, 1989

Koons followed up this poster with a series of explicit, human-scale, photo-based 'paintings' of the couple having sex. Characteristically, Koons asserted that his concerns were far removed from pornography. He had apparently gone through a moral conflict in preparing for the work, which, he claimed, would initiate viewers into the 'realm of the Sacred Heart of Jesus'. More probably he was scurrilously testing such boundaries as public/private and aesthetic legitimacy/erotic pleasure.

and post-Pop mergers between art objects and commodities. The label it acquired around 1986, 'Neo-Geo', was only really applicable to Peter Halley, a painter who coolly readjusted formal devices from Modernist abstractions to reveal latent technocratic metaphors. Halley, however, took it upon himself to theorize the tendency, partly placing it under the aegis of the French sociologist Jean Baudrillard, who, as noted earlier, perceived the ominous collapse of distinctions between reality and simulation as intrinsic to the market-led world of late capitalism.[27] With simulation as its core principle, therefore, this art was bound to antagonize artists and critics concerned with the authenticity of identity struggles.

Of all the simulationists Jeff Koons most offended against politically correct proprieties. His blithe acquiescence to consumerism was first manifested in 1980 with the presentation of off-the-shelf vacuum cleaners, in Plexiglas vitrines, as seductive items of display in the window of New York's New Museum of Contemporary Art. After a period working, appropriately enough, as a broker on Wall Street, he achieved notoriety, and considerable market success, with a series of exhibitions showing batches of work with unmistakably ironic titles: *Equilibrium* (1985), *Luxury and Degradation* (1986), and *Banality* (1988). The works on show were now carefully replicated by hired craftsmen from readymade sources, *Michael Jackson and Bubbles* (1988)—a porcelain figurine of the pop star with pet chimpanzee—being a notorious example.

Koons was a connoisseur of what the artist Barbara Kruger once termed 'the sex appeal of the inorganic': he eulogized over his vacuum cleaners' hermaphroditic ability to combine phallicism and sucking operations. Wittily turning the advocacy of kitsch into a crusade, he claimed to unburden the middle class of conditioned hypocrisies of taste. In 1989 he achieved a kind of sublimity when a billboard poster appeared which, although advertising an exhibition at New York's Whitney Museum, ostensibly advertised a film of the artist in the throes of sexual passion with his new wife, the Hungarian-born, Italy-based porn-actress and artist Ilona Staller (known as 'Cicciolina' or, in English, 'Little Dumpling') [**117**].

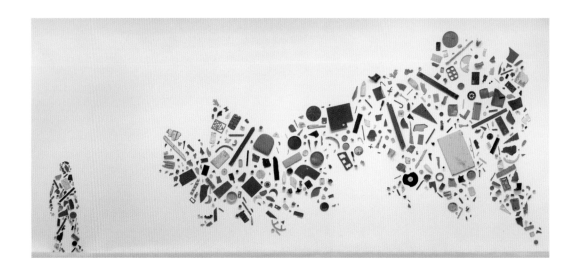

Britain Seen from the North,
1981

Born in Britain, Cragg moved in 1977 to Wuppertal in West Germany where he worked subsequently. This information adds a personal dimension to this primarily political gesture. In the early 1980s Cragg largely concentrated on themes relating to landscape and the city, but his work changed dramatically later in the decade. He became more interested in the relationships between organic and man-made forms and experimented widely with diverse materials.

In a sense, Koons was updating the moral conundrums of Andy Warhol. His sheer effrontery sits interestingly alongside rather different European responses to consumerism in the 1980s. In Britain, for instance, the sculptors Tony Cragg and Bill Woodrow, who were part of a sculptural revival discussed in Chapter 5, developed an iconography of recycling to counter the flagrant materialism of nascent Thatcherism. Cragg's *Britain Seen from the North* [**118**], an array of found plastic objects and fragments arranged to configure a person approaching a map of Britain, invokes widespread perceptions of an ideological rift between the country's north and south, subtly revising Luciano Fabro's *Golden Italy* [**86**]. By contrast, in West Germany in the later 1980s, Rosemarie Trockel added a feminist twist both to the post-Warhol aesthetic being flagged by Americans and to the influential mediations of Pop in works by senior male artists such as Sigmar Polke. Reclaiming Polke's use of fabrics for the purposes of feminine production, she produced knitted balaclava helmets patterned with repeated motifs [**119**].

Trockel's works, and even Cragg's at a stretch, could answer the requirements of an oppositional postmodernism, but American critics in particular were outraged by Koons's symptomatically postmodern flirtation with capital. The critic Hal Foster castigated Koons and others for cynically advocating the populist levelling of art and mass culture and then judiciously sidestepping the issue in favour of art's commercial advantages.[28] Furthermore, as Foster suggested in the course of an essay identifying the 'return of the real' as an emergent impulse of the late 1980s, brazen materialist excess, along with the institutional consolidation of America's political right, appeared to elicit a kind of reflex action. This manifested itself in the re-emergence of the body in late 1980s art, not necessarily as a whole, integrated entity but as something evoked by corporeal fragments and physical residues. A surfeit of capitulations and cynicism was seemingly being ejected.[29] This process came to be identified with the concept of 'abjection'.

As theorized by the French writer Julia Kristeva, abjection covers both an action, of abjecting, by which primordial experiences of the separation of inside and outside, or self and other, are re-experienced via bodily expulsions,

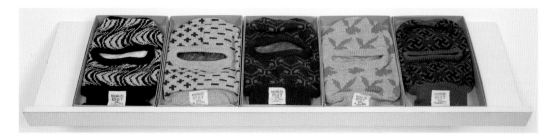

119 Rosemarie Trockel

Balaclavas, 1986

The motifs on Trockel's knitted balaclavas emblematized various issues. The 'bunnies', for instance, teasingly evoked the kind of imagery displayed in Polke's *Playboy Bunnies* [**63**], whilst the swastikas nudged taboo areas of national consciousness. However, all were reduced to the semiotic currency of 1980s shopping—the logic of the logo. Fittingly, perhaps, the balaclavas possessed a sinister edge. They had openings for eyes but not for mouths.

and a wretched condition, that of being abject.[30] Its visual corollaries ranged from the sculptures of the American Kiki Smith, in which bodies were represented as eviscerated or leaking, to certain Cindy Sherman photo-works of 1987 depicting disturbing 'landscapes' made up of human viscera or vomit, broadly connotative of conditions such as bulimia. In California a vein of Performance and Installation Art courting related themes of bodily excess and social malfunction had long been the province of artists such as Paul McCarthy and Mike Kelley. The latter's iconography of adolescent anomie, manifested in his tacky knitted hippy blankets or felt banners, matched Koons's valorization of debased taste. However, the soiled stuffed toys which he hung in claustrophobic clusters or scattered in galleries were redolent of dysfunctional families or emotional surrogacy and thus read as direct ripostes to Koons's pristine replications of toys [**120**]. Back in New York, the sculptor Robert Gober produced similarly charged stand-ins for relationships and bodily needs in his sealed plumbing fixtures, referencing Duchamp and Surrealism [**31**]. Here, however, a very specific set of contextual circumstances needs to be supplied.

During the 1980s the spread of the AIDS virus had been responsible for tragically destroying a sizeable proportion of America's male art community.

120 Mike Kelley

More Love Hours Than Can Ever Be Repaid, 1987

The title of this work powerfully conveys the emotional blackmail tied up with certain instances of toy-making or -giving. Alongside imagery relating to childhood, Kelley often explored adolescent subcultures, fads, and obsessions. His works seemed to vacillate between a celebration and a critique of the debased cultural forms and unfulfilled needs that advanced capitalist systems create.

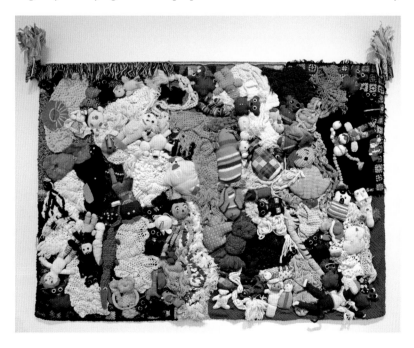

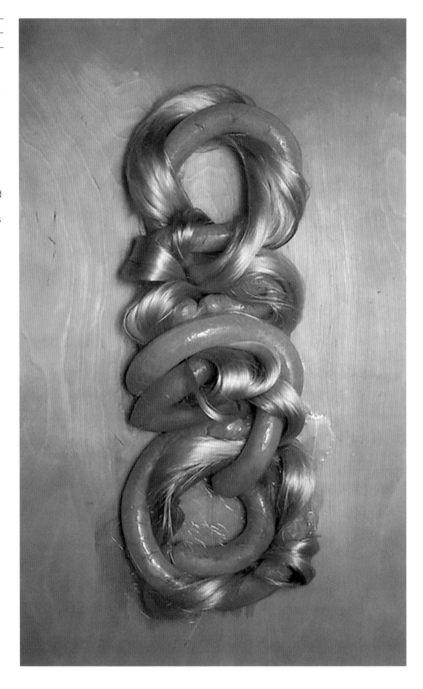

Many gay artists were therefore preoccupied with expressing the polarities of desire and mourning. In New York such representations ranged from the Cuban-born Felix Gonzales-Torres's elegiac, conceptually based billboards of 1992, showing poignantly mute photographs of two adjacent pillows with indentations, to Gober's more overt wax sculptures of male body parts with phallic votive candles sprouting from them. In 1990 a touring retrospective of Robert Mapplethorpe's sexually explicit photographs, as

The oil uncannily mirrors the ceiling of the gallery, leaving the spectator, figuratively speaking, in mid-air. Although currently installed in the Saatchi Gallery, the work was originally located in Matt's Gallery in East London. In that venue spectators had been able to view urban wasteland from the gallery's windows. The work's aura consequently seemed linked to the decline of manufacturing industries. This was lost in its later setting, where the effect was more streamlined and 'theatrical'.

described above, succeeded in provoking ringing accusations of obscenity from American conservatives. Mapplethorpe had died of AIDS in 1989 and the entire conjunction of circumstances led to a right-wing campaign against the imputed moral laxity of the arts, one outcome being a debate concerning the distribution of government funding by the US National Endowment for the Arts. It is clear, then, that the social determinants of late 1980s art were manifold.

Although nothing directly comparable could be found in Europe, the British artist Helen Chadwick echoed American concerns with the body's integrity and boundaries. Chadwick came to prominence in 1986 with the installation *Of Mutability* at London's ICA. Its main component was the 'Oval Court', a low, centrally placed platform on which blue photocopies of parts of Chadwick's body, animal cadavers, and vegetable matter were jigsawed together to produce a representation of a pool containing floating and swimming bodies. Chadwick made complex allusions to vanitas emblems and Baroque iconography, showing herself, in multiple emanations, engaged in a sensual immersion in nature's cycles of fruition and decay.[31] By the early 1990s she was producing works such as *Loop My Loop*, a back-lit cibachrome photograph of a sow's intestines intertwined with braids of blonde hair [**121**]. Such works challenged conventional dualisms such as bestial and human, base and ideal, body and mind. Ultimately, the body's internal economy

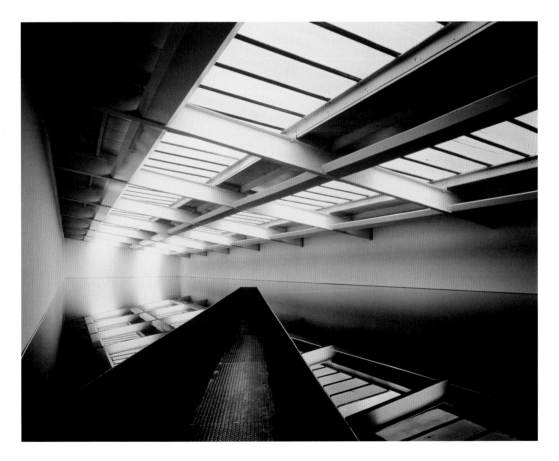

superseded the external, consumer-driven one. The impulse was perhaps solipsistic, or narcissistic, but it answered a yearning for experiential authenticity in the face of an increasingly mediated reality.

Installation as a paradigm

Many key works by Gober, Kelley, and Chadwick were installations. At the turn of the 1990s no one medium dominated Western art production, but installations were made by many practitioners at one time or another. The medium's history has been threaded through this book, with Duchamp's *Etant Donnés* and Robert Morris's Minimalist shift from a stress on the self-containment of the art object to its physical location as defining points [**69**]. Between 1987 and 1991 it served the needs of varying agendas. In 1987 the British artist Richard Wilson, who specialized in the medium, produced *20/50* [**122**], eventually installed in London's Saatchi Gallery, in which the viewer walked along a kind of enclosed jetty surrounded, at waist height, by an immense steel trough containing an expanse of impenetrable, glutinous sump oil. The effect was profoundly disorientating.

In contrast to Wilson's late modernist exploration of phenomenological paradox, 1991 saw a younger British artist named Damien Hirst produce a striking analogue for the relationship between aesthetic and lived experience. Wilson's installation had been designed for its location (it was site-specific), but Hirst's *In and Out of Love* [**123**], located in a makeshift gallery space in Woodstock Street, London, temporarily brought together a variety of disparate materials. It also required the spectator's physical movement. In an upper room the cocoons of exotic butterflies were attached to large white canvases. Heat from humidifiers and shelves of potted plants at the bases of the canvases encouraged them to hatch and flourish. In a lower room a myriad of gorgeous butterflies were embalmed on a set of brightly painted canvases.

123 Damien Hirst

a) *In and Out of Love (White Paintings and Live Butterflies)*, 1991 b) *I Love You*, 1994–5

There was a lyrical quality to Hirst's use of butterflies' life cycles, both in the 1991 installation *In and Out of Love* and the related Butterfly Colour Paintings to which *I Love You* belongs. In other thematically related works Hirst used much more brutal imagery. In *A Thousand Years* (1990) a huge steel-and-glass vitrine contained a white painted box in which flies hatched from maggots. Emerging from a hole in the box, they flew around the vitrine, laying eggs on a cow's gruesomely severed head sitting on the floor of the glass enclosure. Sooner or later the flies were destroyed by an electric fly-killer hanging from the ceiling of the vitrine.

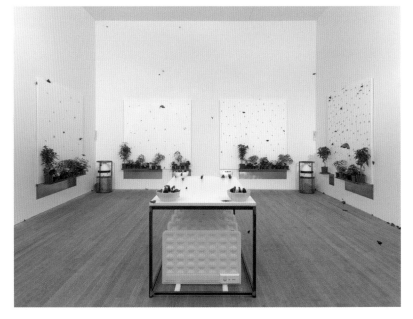

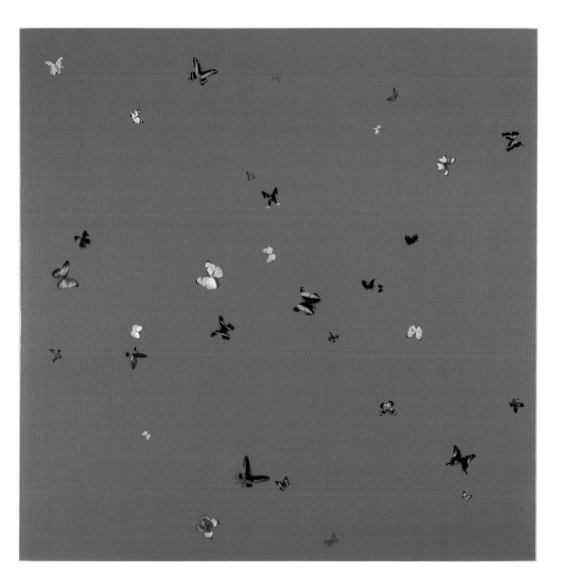

The butterflies' wings were lapped in paint, as though, as performers in a macabre poetry, the creatures had become stuck to the paintings.

What does the prevalence of installation art tell us about this period? As a medium, installation is defined by spatial location rather than by the materials that constitute it. As the above examples indicate, its physical possibilities are virtually limitless. If its defining attribute is space, this necessarily implies horizontal extension—the occupation of 'sites'. From here we might move to an observation by the American critic Hal Foster. He asserts that a key structural transformation in Western art practice since the 1960s has been a shift from what he calls a 'vertical' conception of art, whereby artists investigate the disciplinary depths of a given genre or medium, to a 'horizontal' conception, whereby art activity is conceived of as a kind of terrain on which various areas of discourse are brought together. In Foster's words, it is now the case that 'many artists and critics treat conditions like desire or disease . . . as sites for art'.[32] Installations such as Hirst's, with their urge to locate divergent feelings and issues rather than consolidate form, reflected this trend. But installation here should only be understood as a paradigm. In fact, related principles of heterogeneity also held for photography, painting, or sculpture.

This talk of multiplicity inevitably recalls the larger theme of post-modernism, often considered synonymous with pluralism. This chapter has acknowledged the stylistic revivalism and cultural relativism bound up with the subject. But it has mainly demonstrated that the underlying dynamic of the so-called postmodern era has been a tension, integral to art's practices and institutions, between a sense of historical entrapment, with all the 'symptoms' this involves, and the ethical injunction, inherited from modernism, of achieving critical distance. In a sense all the features of late 1980s art that have just been discussed could be seen as 'symptomatic'. Whatever its political commitments, identity-related art arose out of the lack of a social core; simulation art revelled in its lack of separation from the marketplace; abject art actually manifested itself in symptoms. Possibly this argues for a sense of postmodernism as a cultural logic which, as the millenium approached, was both ongoing and inescapable. However, against this deterministic view, a proliferation of symptoms could, paradoxically, be understood to betoken health. All the signs were that Western art's critical frontiers were widening.

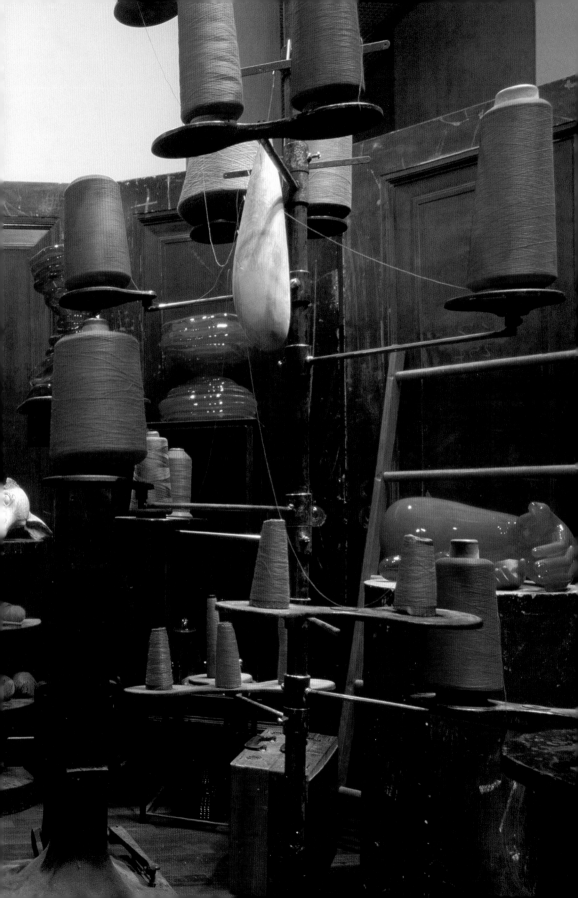

The 1990s

A New *Fin de Siècle*?

8

The Canadian artist Jeff Wall was a central influence on European and American practice of the 1990s. In 1992 he produced a work entitled *Dead Troops Talk* [**124**]. Responding to a 1980s concern with the rehabilitation of 'history painting' [**111**], it allegorized not only the decline of the Soviet Union, whose unsuccessful involvement in Afghanistan echoed America's failed intervention in Vietnam, but also Europe's growing susceptibility to religious or atavistic tendencies.[1] Whilst the Cold War opposition between capitalism and Communism had previously set the terms for post-1945 Europe, Russia's decline heralded the emergence of new historical forces.

In 1989 the Eastern bloc began splintering, reconfiguring Europe's political structure and opening the floodgates for factional struggles. The most potent symbol of all was the dismantling of the Berlin Wall in November, presaging German reunification. Suddenly Eastern European artists became visible in the West, commenting on regimes they had left and underlining the West's complacencies. A leading figure here was Ilya Kabakov. One of an influential group of Moscow Conceptualists working in the 1970s and 1980s, he quickly gained notoriety in Western Europe for his installations. These included *The Toilet*, installed as an outbuilding at Kassel's *Documenta 9* exhibition of 1992. It consisted of a full-scale replica of the dingy public toilets found in the Russian provinces, with the adjacent men's and women's sections turned into the living room and bedroom of a typical Soviet two-room apartment. It thus commented sardonically on the way collectivism in Russia was giving way to privatization and on the dislocations of public and private involved for ordinary people.

Kabakov expressed himself in an ironic language familiar to Western art audiences. This was true also of Zofia Kulik, a Polish artist who received widespread exposure in the West. In elaborately constructed photo-works she explored images of masculinity, fetishistically juxtaposing naked men in heroic or martyr-like poses with military and religious emblems, and thereby interrogating the peculiar gender archetypes produced through the overlaying of official communist iconographies onto residual Polish Catholic ones [**125**].[2] Her works have superficial similarities to works by the British artists Gilbert and George, but their thematic premises are fundamentally different. In the 1990s Western European art happily assimilated practitioners who spoke its specialized language but, as with Kulik, many artists from former communist countries were concerned with reconciling indigenous iconographies with late modernist/postmodernist forms, and thus were sceptical about the West's relatively deracinated artistic practices.

The turn of the 1990s also saw upheavals in the American art world, albeit much less radical ones. The stock market crashed in October 1987, and

Detail of 129

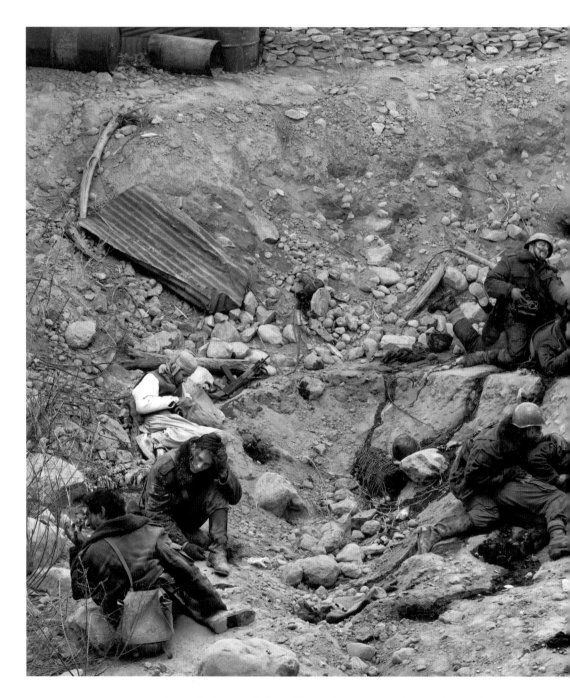

although this was followed by a short, spectacular art-buying boom, it was clear by the end of 1990 that the economic prosperity of the 1980s was over. At the same time, debates about American National Endowment for the Arts (NEA) funding, mentioned in the previous chapter, were particularly intense in late 1989 and early 1990. Conservatives in the US Senate (such as Jesse Helms) raised the disturbing spectre of state censorship.[3] A reproduction of the photographer Andres Serrano's *Piss Christ* (1987), an image of a

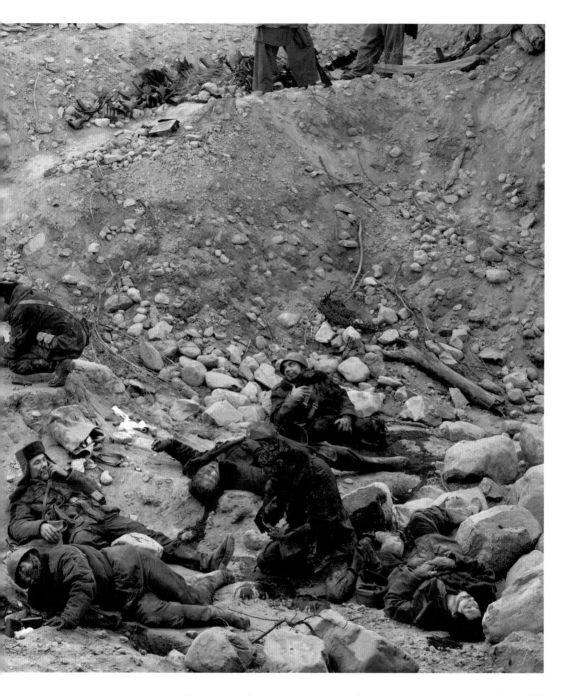

crucifix immersed in urine, was actually torn up on the floor of the US Senate. The debate had the knock-on effect of raising questions about the relationship between 'alternative' arts practices and their assumed publics. The fact was that much politically motivated art of the 1980s shown in artist-run venues supported by the NEA was actually seen by audiences who, far from having their assumptions 'disrupted', as the critical rhetoric claimed, were already committed nonconformists.[4] By the mid-1990s anomalies like

124 Jeff Wall

*Dead Troops Talk (A Vision
After an Ambush of a
Red Army Patrol near Moqor,
Afghanistan, Winter,
1986)*, 1992

This large, back-lit
photographic transparency
apparently shows soldiers
killed in mid-action. The
scene was actually mocked
up by digitally manipulating
images. In a tableau worthy
of a ghoulish horror film, a
young Muslim (centre left)
searches a Russian soldier's
possessions. He possibly
emblematizes the Islamic
fundamentalism which the
Russians were attempting to
counter in Afghanistan.

this led to a gradual withdrawal of US government arts support and a shift
from public- to private-sector sponsorship. In Britain the introduction of a
national lottery in 1993 became a means of offsetting an increasing disin-
clination to support the visual arts via public funds.

The British art revival

Paradoxically, Britain's traditional public indifference towards the visual arts
had, at the start of the 1990s, provided the impetus for an artistic revival.
In the face of limited outlets for their work, a group of students then studying
at Goldsmiths College, London, decided to turn the entrepreneurial ethos
of Thatcherism to their advantage. Late in 1988 Damien Hirst persuaded
the London Docklands Development Corporation to allow him and his
friends to use an abandoned building to stage a three-part exhibition titled
Freeze. As with later Hirst initiatives, such as *In and Out of Love* [**123**], this
pragmatic bypassing of the regular professional procedures quickly attracted
commercial interest. With the help of London dealers such as Karsten
Schubert and Jay Jopling, a roster of artists including Hirst, the sculptor/
installation artists Sarah Lucas, Anya Gallaccio, and Mat Collishaw, and
the painter Gary Hume, attained international prominence under the 'yBa'
(young British artists) banner. In Britain, artists associated with the trend
became increasingly beholden to the voracious patronage of Charles Saatchi
(see Chapter 7), thereby risking becoming typecast simply as 'Saatchi artists'.
Part of Saatchi's collection of their work, bought cheaply en masse before
prices soared, went on show in Britain in the Royal Academy's *Sensation*

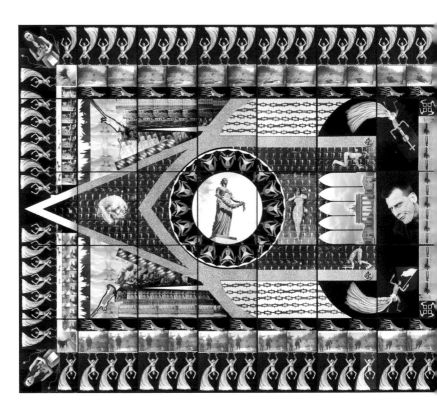

exhibition in late 1997. The success of the yBas was consolidated by numerous international solo and group shows such as *Brilliant: New Art from London*, exhibited at the Walker Art Center, Minneapolis, in 1995. In 1996 the *life/live* exhibition held in Paris demonstrated that artist-run spaces, underwritten as much by subcultural ties as by hard cash, were establishing new patterns of self-promotion by artists in Britain. This seemed to point to a wholesale adaptation to changing financial circumstances.

But was there anything distinctively new about 1990s British art? For many commentators works such as Hirst's notorious *The Physical Impossibility of Death in the Mind of Someone Living* (1991), a 14-foot (4.3-metre) tiger shark preserved in formaldehyde in an enormous glass tank, or Sarah Lucas's *Au Naturel* [126], a bawdy assimilation of lovers' anatomies to the language of the playground or building site, simply rehashed American abject art or mindlessly recycled the tropes of Dada, Fluxus, or *Arte Povera*. Tracey Emin, who, like Lucas, could be seen as annexing feminist values to the rudery indulged in by the male yBas, produced some of the most distinctive works. Her *Everyone I Have Ever Slept With 1963–1995* (1995), a nylon and polyester tent on the inside of which were embroidered patches spelling out the names promised in the title, was a clever nod to the reclamation of female craft traditions—such as embroidery—by 1970s feminists. In the notorious *My Bed* of 1998 Emin presented her own unmade bed, surrounded by the paraphernalia accrued from a depressive phase during which she had kept to it—tampons, condoms, bedroom slippers. Once again there were clear precedents: Robert Rauschenberg's *Bed* of 1955 (**19**), or John Lennon and

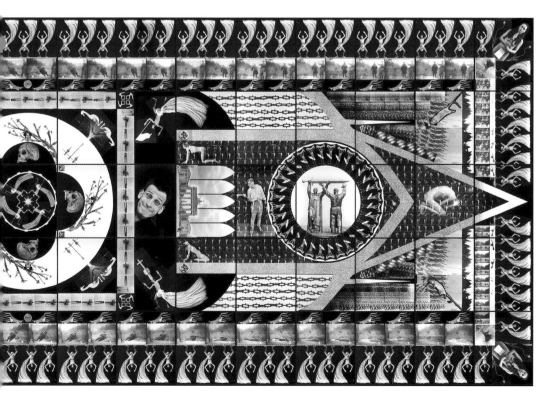

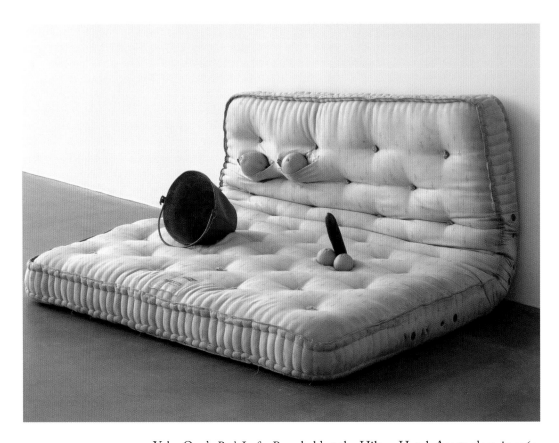

Yoko Ono's *Bed-In for Peace* held at the Hilton Hotel, Amsterdam, in 1969.
British artists were not alone in reprocessing 1950s/60s ideas. The Italian
artist Maurizio Cattelan, an emergent talent of the later 1990s, was to make
overt allusions to his country's *Arte Povera* idioms. In *Twentieth Century*
(1997), for instance, a stuffed horse was suspended high above a gallery space
as though signalling that the freedoms once symbolized by Jannis Kounellis's
live horses [**87**] now seemed utopian. As well as questioning their originality, critics in Britain also berated home-grown artists for tacitly capitulating
to the market or to the chauvinism implicit in the promotion of their work
abroad. However, it should be noted that several artists who were marshalled,
often quite perfunctorily, under the yBa banner, such as Mark Wallinger
and Gavin Turk, were profoundly critical of Thatcherism's pro-nationalist
legacy, producing work which powerfully challenged British obsessions
with national heritage and class.[5]

   In contrast to many among the critical intelligentsia, the critic John
Roberts argued that the new British art, or at least the more localized working-
class variants which he supported, possessed a number of distinctively new
attributes. Most significantly, it represented a reaction against the intellectual
obscurantism of critical postmodernism, promoting strains of strategic
'philistinism' and proletarian disaffirmation.[6] All in all, Roberts argued, a
generation seemed to be emerging which, rather than forging worthy links
between high and low cultural spheres like their postmodernist forebears,
unselfconsciously accepted the pleasures of the demotic.

Au Naturel, 1994

Lucas grew up in a working-class environment in East London, and has long employed ordinary materials and everyday idioms in her work. Early in her career, she was influenced by the American art that she saw in the late 1980s in London's Saatchi Gallery. Her grungy, abject imagery carries echoes of that of artists such as Robert Gober and Mike Kelley [31, 120]. However, her work is equally marked by a fascination with the idea of Britishness, and by a distinctly post-feminist sensibility. Rather than assuming an overtly politicized stance, she has periodically aped the laddish personae of some of her male peers. This was particularly evident when, in 1993, she ran a shop in Bethnal Green with her fellow artist Tracey Emin. Amid the merchandise were T-shirts emblazoned with sexual innuendo and propositions.

Whatever its street credibility, British art of the early 1990s often possessed a curiously anachronistic sensibility. Although Hirst's art, like that of his contemporaries Jake and Dinos Chapman, cultivated a deliberately laddish disrespect for the politically correct attitudes of the 1980s, it simultaneously harboured a quasi-Victorian fascination with death and taxonomic specimens. Hirst's 'Victorianism' is emphasized in *Away from the Flock* (1994), where the single sheep preserved in formaldehyde is a distant cousin to the straying sheep in the British Pre-Raphaelite painter William Holman Hunt's *The Hireling Shepherd* (1851). (The immensely wealthy Hirst would even end up purchasing a huge early Victorian country house in 2005—Toddington Manor in Gloucestershire, England—which he lovingly renovated.) This suggests that, like its nineteenth-century predecessor, the art of this *fin de siècle* was underpinned by a rather morbid, backward-looking sensibility. Even the prevalence of video in the 1990s, which might suggest an openness to mass-media forms or technological adaptability, partly supports this.

Video and narrative

The use of video as a medium was hardly new. The Fluxus artist Nam June Paik had experimented with television in the 1960s and the American Bruce Nauman, among others, had made artists' videos in the 1980s. Its widespread adoption in the 1990s, however, may have been bound up with its narrative potential as a time-based medium (although straightforward narration was rarely involved), suggesting a retreat from the instantaneity or simultaneity courted in much twentieth-century art.

For instance, in his *24 Hour Psycho* (1993), the Glasgow-based neo-conceptualist Douglas Gordon sought to uncover the unforeseen 'micro-narratives' lurking in Alfred Hitchcock's classic film by slowing it down to approximately two frames per second. In 1996 Gordon won the prestigious Turner Prize in London. In the related exhibition he showed the video work *A Divided Self* in which two separate monitors show a wrestling contest between two arms, one hairy and one hairless. Both arms belong to the artist. This, along with other works, could be keyed to Gordon's declared interest in a novel by the nineteenth-century Scottish writer James Hogg, *The Private Memoirs and Confessions of a Justified Sinner*, a forerunner of Stevenson's *The Strange Case of Dr Jekyll and Mr Hyde* in its concern with inner contradiction and multiplicity.[7] The video therefore requires that we unpack it conceptually, restoring narrative complexity relating to Scottish identity. There was, in fact, a markedly literary turn in much neo-conceptualism of this period. Other Scottish-based artists such as Christine Borland and Simon Starling would make use of medical case histories or arcane archival connections to produce densely layered works which require intense intellectual engagement.

Working in London, the English artist Gillian Wearing explored the disparities between people's interior and exterior lives in works such as the twenty-five-minute *Dancing in Peckham* (1994) [127], where she presented herself dancing self-absorbedly to imaginary music in a shopping centre. In other works she examined the hidden dynamics of relationships. In *Sacha and Mum* (1996) the video is played forwards and backwards so that the

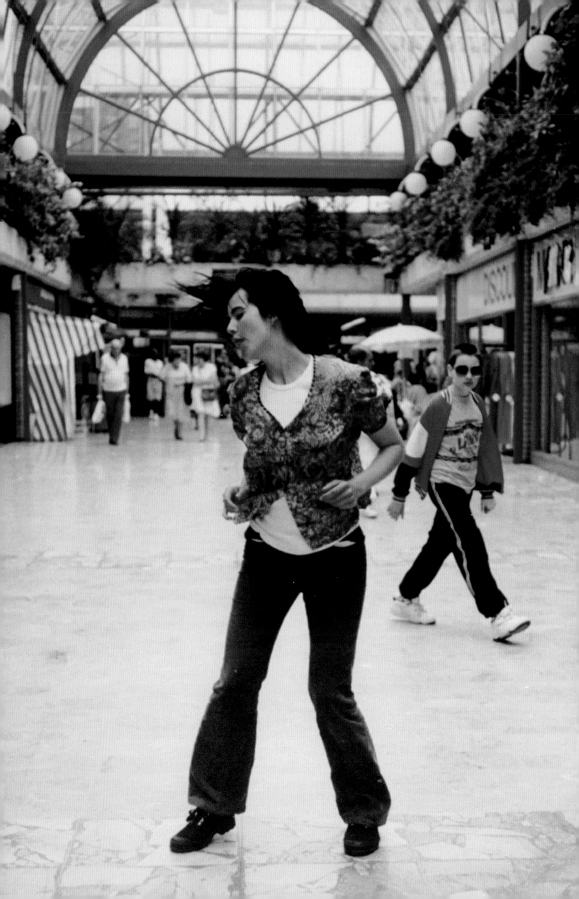

Dancing in Peckham, 1994.
Colour video with sound,
25 minutes

The idea that art can provide access to an artist's inner being is amusingly, and pointedly, repudiated here. Wearing is completely immersed in her own world. In the video, no soundtrack accompanies her dancing. She has talked about her interest in fathoming people's inner motivations as being stimulated by a series of documentaries produced in 1964–77 for Britain's BBC/Granada Television. Initially entitled *Seven Up*, they tracked the lives of a diverse group of people at regular intervals from the age of 7.

ambivalent relations between a mother and her daughter, involving the former's embraces flipping into disturbing acts of abuse, are rendered visible. Wearing's readiness to explore the potential of video as a medium of social documentation led to the ambitious three-screen video installation, *Drunk* (1997–9), which took up three walls when shown in various venues in the late 1990s. Dealing with the harrowing recording, in real time, of a group of alcoholics as they descend further into drunkenness, the work seems voyeuristic in tone, an updating of Brueghel's images of peasant life. As a documentation of inebriation it can interestingly be compared with an influential photo-installation by the American conceptualist Martha Rosler, *The Bowery in Two Inadequate Descriptive Systems* of 1974. Whereas Rosler, wary of the way documentary photography inadvertently exoticizes social 'victims', had simply juxtaposed images of the locations inhabited by skid-row alcoholics next to the colourful language by which their condition is described, Wearing registered a vicarious fascination with her drink-sodden subjects, referencing the language of the reality-TV docusoaps of the period (such as *Big Brother*). In being aligned with the morbid curiosity of the 'culture industry', her work veered towards the ethical improprieties of the yBa generation. At the same time, in exploiting video's cultural links with documentation, it exemplified the return to narration common to the art of the period.[8]

Video took widely divergent forms elsewhere in Europe and the US. The Americans Bill Viola and Gary Hill frequently invoked intense bodily or metaphysical experiences, paying close attention to the way their video installations, which typically employed multiple monitors or large screens, were set up in dramatically darkened spaces. In Hill's *Tall Ships* (1992), for example, the spectator enters a corridor where he or she is 'visited' by a series of projected human presences. Having first appeared as spots of light, they approach the spectator, as if soliciting contact, and then turn around to recede again. In marked contrast the Northern Irish artist Willie Doherty, like Gillian Wearing, exploited video's associations with practices of social surveillance and reportage, although his work was far more sober in mood. In his *The Only Good One is a Dead One* (1993) the spectator is positioned uneasily between two projections, one produced by a static camera trained on a city street at night, the other produced by a camera tracking along a country road. An Irishman's voice on the soundtrack alternates between the viewpoints of a victim and an aggressor. The spectator thus re-experiences the personal anxieties linked to the doctrinal and ideological divisions of Derry, Northern Ireland, that had once been endemic to this region.

Individualism, localism, and globalization

Such a range of video practices attests to a strongly individualistic slant in 1990s art which can be contrasted with a much-touted trend in the period towards globalization. On the one hand, internationally acclaimed figures such as the French artist Sophie Calle continued to explore postmodern themes relating to authorial positioning. In her *Double Game* project, published in book form in 1999, Calle collaborated with one of the doyens of postmodern literature, the American novelist Paul Auster. In his *Leviathan* (1992) Auster had based a character, Maria, on Calle's peculiar 'performances'

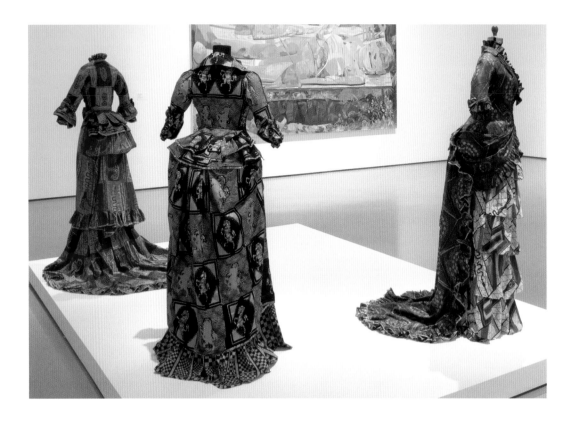

of the 1980s such as *Suite vénitienne* (1980), which had involved her surreptitiously following a partial stranger to Venice and documenting his movements photographically. In the 1990s she recomplicated these authorial switches by carrying out certain additional tasks Auster had assigned her fictional counterpart. These included strict adherence to a 'chromatic diet' involving eating foods of one specified colour per day.[9]

In contrast to such essentially solipsistic pursuits, many younger artists of the 1990s reflected new conditions of cultural hybridization and global cross-fertilization. The British artist Yinka Shonibare, who was born in England and brought up by Nigerian parents in Lagos, sought to contest the 'authentic' ethnic origins that had preoccupied many culturally displaced artists of the 1980s. Working with patterned fabrics which connoted 'Africa' but had actually begun life in their raw state in England or Holland, he produced dresses which bore witness to the cultural hybridities stemming from colonialism [**128**].

Shonibare's work implicitly endorsed a forecast by the film historian and critic Peter Wollen to the effect that, on the evidence of the 1980s and 1990s, changing patterns of international migration and tourism, along with redistributed relations between urban centres and their peripheries across Europe and the Third World, would increasingly influence, and rejuvenate, cultural forms. Warning against a too Eurocentric understanding of both modernism and postmodernism, Wollen asserted that the future would see ever-greater cultural diffusion.[10] His prediction offered a dynamic vision of cultural

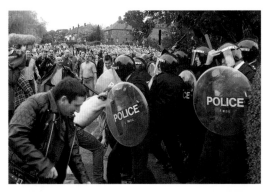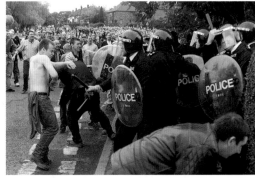

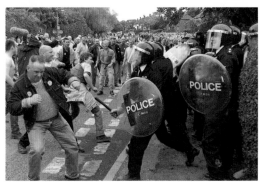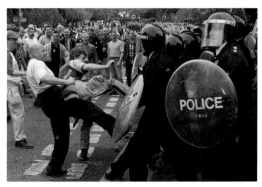

129 Jeremy Deller

The Battle of Orgreave,
2001

Deller's exact intentions in
reenacting this confrontation
are hard to gauge. On the
one hand, the event had a
virtually therapeutic effect,
allowing certain participants
to come to terms with the
traumatic nature of the
original violent struggle
between miners and police
in 1984 (some of the miners
were still extremely bitter, as
revealed in a documentary
film recording the event
by Mike Figgis). On the
other hand, the event had
something of the village
fête about it, with bands
playing and children
running around.

renewal, but it could be seen as downplaying capital's controlling grip. As the
1990s art market became increasingly globalized, other critics saw a strategic
need to shift the emphasis away from diversity towards the need for local
pockets of resistance to a market-led world system.

One of the most striking examples of an artistic practice that posited
the local as opposed to the global was that of Jeremy Deller, who came to
prominence in England at the end of the 1990s. Part social anthropologist
and part community organizer, Deller was at the forefront of what would
eventually be dubbed 'participatory art'. An idiosyncratic sound-work-cum-
performance from 1997, *Acid Brass*, exemplifies the humorous hybridity of
his practice. In it, the Williams Fairey Band, typical of the working-class
colliery bands to be found in the North of England, performed a group of
acid-house anthems, connotative of the druggy rave culture to be found in
the same region.

Deller's signature work, *The Battle of Orgreave* (2001) [**129**], although
still highly particularized in its reference to Orgreave, near Sheffield, England,
was arguably one of the most ambitious political statements of the turn of
the millennium. In 1984 some 8,000 riot police, many of them mounted,
had clashed with approximately 5,000 striking miners in the village of
Orgreave. The ensuing 'battle', in which the miners were effectively defeated,
symbolized the failure of a lengthy miners' strike and the victory of a
Conservative government, headed by Margaret Thatcher, which was intent
on breaking the power of the British trade unions. In 2001 Deller, with the
help of battle re-enactment societies and miners who had been involved in

the original conflict, restaged the battle. Although the work is riddled with ambiguities, it is clear that Deller saw himself as rewriting or correcting history in this version. The miners' defeat had been as much at the hands of the British press as of the government; reverse-editing of footage on news reports had made the confrontation appear to result from the miners' provocations rather than the decision to send in the police, thereby influencing public opinion.[11] Deller now claimed to be producing a kind of 'history painting from below', in which the truth behind the last gasp of class struggle in the UK might be revealed.[12] Arguably, despite its local reference, the work had widespread relevance. It spoke to the diminishing power of the left in Europe and America during the 1980s and 1990s, and to the effects on ordinary working people of free trade policies dictated by global imperatives.

In contrast to Deller's essay in the local-as-universal (or 'glocal'), the wider consequences of globalization were addressed in extensive and complex late conceptualist works by the American critic and photographer Allan Sekula. Sekula had been active since the 1970s as a historian and theorist of documentary photography. His analytic skills, and socialist politics, were brought to bear in a series of photographic cycles of the 1980s and 1990s, which were accompanied by lengthy, erudite publications. The photographic cycle, *Fish Story*—completed in a series of stages in the early 1990s and eventually amounting to an exhibition consisting of 105 colour photographs interspersed with 26 text panels, accompanied by a book produced in 1995—focused on the way the containerization of goods (pioneered in the US in the latter half of the 1950s) had transformed the world's economy. Asserting that new information technologies actually had less impact in facilitating the increased flow of capital than theorists of the postmodern imagined, Sekula returned to the time-honoured technology of sea transportation, showing that the flow of containerized cargo around the world was underpinned by the exploitation of workforces, creating 'a fluctuating web of connections between metropolitan regions and exploitable peripheries'.[13] In the photographs, which deliberately avoid an 'arty' look, Sekula records the cruelties wrought by 'progress' as workers become expendable and ports descend into ruin. But he is also alert to quirks of human adaptability. In one suite of photographs, produced on the coast of Mexico near Veracruz, he records the emergence of waterfront vendors, who live in disused shipping containers [**130**]. For Sekula, workers in the shipping industry are witnesses to the ethical shortcomings of our world: 'Sailors and dockers are in a position to see the global patters of intrigue hidden in the mundane details of commerce. Sometimes the evidence is in fact bizarrely at hand. *Weapons for the Iraqis in the forward hold. Weapons for the Iranians in the aft hold.*'[14]

It is clear that Sekula was far from comfortable about the way in which globalization perpetuated the social inequalities of late capitalism. As we will see in Chapter 9, the same globalizing processes were key structural determinants for the way the art world itself would develop post-millennium. Pointedly, Deller would continue to explore a committed localism. In 2000 he embarked on a 'Folk Archive' project which allowed him not only, symbolically, to cede his authorial voice to 'individuals who would not primarily consider themselves artists', but also to plunge further into a

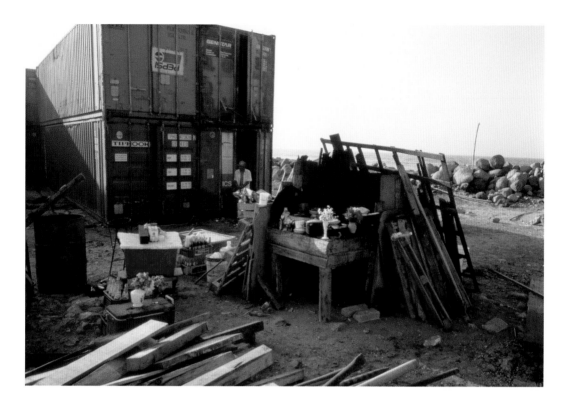

world of English eccentricity as he showcased works entered for cake and pudding festivals or facial contortions achieved at the World Gurning Championships (held at Egremont Crab Fair in Cumbria, England).[15] Whatever his socialist convictions, Deller might actually be seen as embodying the isolationist currents in Britain that had been gathering momentum since the days of Thatcher. As with the yBas, his nostalgia—which in the case of *The Battle of Orgreave* ends up memorializing an event of the recent past, one he had seen on TV as a child—might even be considered symptomatic of a retreat from the pressing immediacies of globalization, skirting close to nationalist sentiment.

Psychic resources: post-Surrealism; childhood; masculinity

If the insecurities generated by the increasingly globalized Western economy led to understandable reversions to native or local traditions, it is hardly surprising that the twentieth century's *fin de siècle* saw a marked return to the resources of the psyche, as part and parcel of what might be seen as a re-evaluation of Surrealism. In the mid-1980s the American critic Hal Foster had ventured that 'much contemporary criticism and art, much theory and practice of our postmodern present is partly, genealogically, a theory and practice of surrealism'.[16] Whilst the slant of Foster's criticism of 1990s art continued to bear this out, numerous historical exhibitions in this period suggested that Surrealism, of all the classic avant-gardes, was a driver for the prevailing zeitgeist.[17]

Louise Bourgeois, previously discussed in Chapter 5, was a presiding senior figure of the decade, exhibiting between 1991 and 1994 a series of

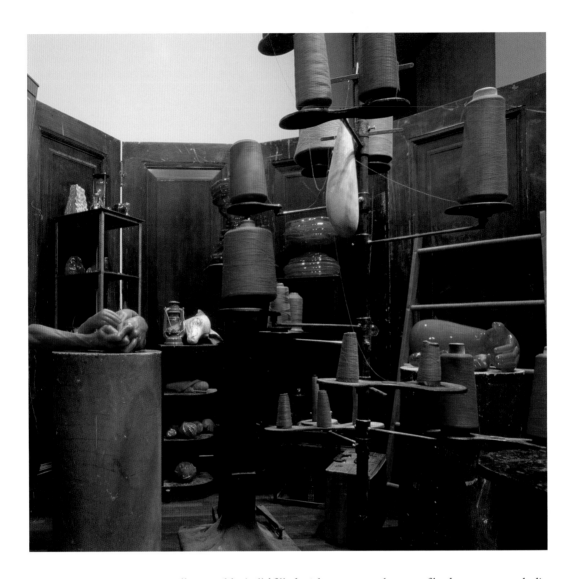

small, room-like 'cells' filled with strange sculptures of body parts or symbolic 'furnishings', and constituting further explorations of the role played in her psychic life by her parents. The project was entirely in line with surrealist exploration of the unconscious, although, given Surrealism's emphasis on the male viewpoint, it was significant that a major woman artist should be keeping its traditions alive. In 1994 Bourgeois exhibited two *Red Rooms* at Peter Blum's gallery in New York. One was designated as that of a parental couple, the other that of a child. The parents' room was impeccably neat, with a closed instrument case placed on the bed and a strange, misshapen object hanging ominously above the bed. The child's room, by contrast, was dominated by numerous spools and enigmatic glass ornaments [**131**]. Bourgeois's mother had been a tapestry restorer and had previously been invoked by the artist via spindle-like forms. In this context the vast quantity of thread seemed to signify the amount of unwinding and mending in store for the child as, growing up, it was obliged to recapitulate its origins.

131 Louise Bourgeois

Red Room (Child),
installation, 1994

The colour red, connotative
of intense passion,
predominated in the two
cramped spaces forming this
installation. One important
theme here was regressive
psychological fantasy. But
there was also a sense that
ancient knowledge was
being recovered. The
peculiar glass bottles and
flasks in many of Bourgeois's
early 1980s installations
related to alchemy. Their
scenarios also seemed to
conform to the logic of
fairy tales.

Bourgeois asserted the irreducible, ongoing primacy of human memory and the unconscious. Her art looked backward. In a very different manner, the art of the American-born British conceptualist Susan Hiller also focused on the way human beings are impelled by deep-rooted psychic and even occult forces. Childhood was again a central preoccupation of Hiller's. *Psi Girls*, a five-channel video installation of 1999, saw her presenting a series of vividly tinted movie clips of young girls performing telekinetic feats, a paean to the unleashed sexual and psychological powers of adolescent girls. Hiller's fascination with the mental formation of fantasy had, however, been most powerfully declared in an earlier installation, *An Entertainment* of 1990 [**132**]. The work comprised four synchronized video programmes consisting of footage from Punch and Judy shows filmed by Hiller at seaside locations in Britain during the 1980s. Entering a darkened space, the spectator was assaulted from all sides by fragmented images from these videos—images of Punch bludgeoning his wife and child, the hangman's gallows, a grinning death's head—that flashed up spectrally before sliding away and being replaced by others.

Such imagery could be related to social anxieties about the treatment of children in 1990s Britain. The late 1980s had seen cases of the alleged satanic ritual abuse of children gripping the public imagination (notably in the remote Orkney Islands), and Hiller's work speaks of a moment when children were imagined to be at the mercy of supernatural, archaic forces. In broader

132 Susan Hiller

An Entertainment, 1990

Discussing the almost
visceral assault on the
viewer's senses by the huge
flashing images in this
installation, Hiller herself
stated, 'I was subjecting
myself to what I saw children
being subjected to with
every Punch and Judy show'.
There was a sense that the
installation fictively situated
the spectator in the theatre
of the child's mind as it was
forced to construe images of
violence as 'entertainment'.
To quote Hiller again: 'The
child is being taught
something through the
terror of ritual.'[18]

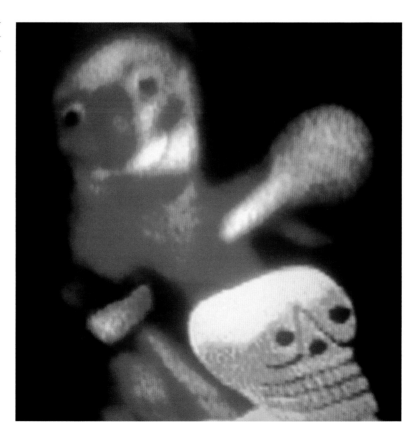

133 Matthew Barney
Still from *Cremaster 4*,
video, 1994

133 Matthew Barney
Still from *Cremaster 4*,
video, 1994

This book contains a
diversity of constructions
of artistic identity since
1945 [**37, 39, 41, 79, 97,
117, 127**]. Here the artist
aspires to a metamorphosis
which hints partly at
mythology, partly at science
fiction. However, with mock
pathos, Barney's floppy
ears and dual kiss-curls
inadequately match up to
the four horns of the ram
which the video's plot
establishes as his ideal.

terms, paedophilia was to become a significant area of public concern in
many Western democracies at the end of the twentieth century. Ironically, a
marked increase in the number of works invoking childish 'innocence' or
kitsch might be placed in this context. The toy is one of the central iconic
motifs of the late twentieth century; Jeff Koons's *Balloon Dogs* (1994–2000),
a series of 10-foot- (3-metre-) tall, mirror-polished, stainless-steel sculptures
in vivid blue, magenta, orange, red, and blue versions, have become ubiquitous
in gallery forecourts and entrances. At the turn of the 1990s, Mike Kelley
also turned the psychological ramifications of toys into a major theme
[**120**]. But why should the paraphernalia of childhood be given such exalted
status? Aside from children's security, the desire to hang on to, or extend,
childhood seemingly represents an underlying cultural fantasy of the period.[19]

If a portion of major post-surrealist 1990s art looked backwards, fix-
ated on origins, the work of other key figures of the period looked forward
ambivalently, conjuring up futuristic technological fantasies. The work of
the American sculptor and film-maker Matthew Barney made dramatic
use of available technologies in his widely discussed *Cremaster* films produced between 1994 and 1997, but, significantly, envisioned an exotic, hybridized world where technology has become not so much a tool as something
invasive. The five *Cremaster* works, which add up to approximately six hours
of viewing, involve enigmatic narratives steeped in bizarre imagery. In one
of the shortest of them—*Cremaster 4* (1994)—the plot revolves around a
hybrid satyr-cum-dandy (played by Barney) whose ambition, it seems, is
to achieve the more impressive hybridity of the Loughton Ram, one of a
four-horned species of ram from the Isle of Man [**133**]. The hero finally
attains the ram's realm (the Isle of Man itself) via a peculiar descent into
the sea followed by a journey along a form of uterine passageway (possibly
symbolizing rebirth). His libidinal metamorphoses are meanwhile symbolized by the futuristic image of two teams of motorbike-and-sidecar riders,
in matching yellow and blue leathers, who rapidly circuit the island in reverse
directions.[20]

What did Barney's strange conjunction of sportswear fetishism, technological streamlining, and surreal camp add up to? It could certainly be an
elaborately humorous parody of masculine aspirations. At the end of the
1990s Barney was effectively written off by some of the influential American
October critics as too 'immersive', too reliant on spectacular effects (too 'theatrical', to revive the language of Michael Fried).[21] They seem, however, to
have overlooked his satirical edge. There is a scene in *Cremaster 3* in which,
as part of a complex play on the recondite iconography of Freemasonry, the
artist Richard Serra ironically takes the part of the Master Mason who, as
in Masonic ritual, is symbolically deposed by the 'Apprentice' (played by
Barney himself). This is surely a parody of generational artistic (or mock-
Oedipal) rivalry. Serra represented the apogee of the post-war discourse
around modernism that was central to the *October*-style construal of post-
war art.[22] At the same time, his art was synonymous with materials and artistic
operations connotative of masculinity: large, precariously placed metal or
lead structures, as discussed in Chapter 5. Barney, by contrast, revived the
idiosyncratic materials of Joseph Beuys (an artist ambivalently received by
October critics), such as beeswax (also transposed into substances such as

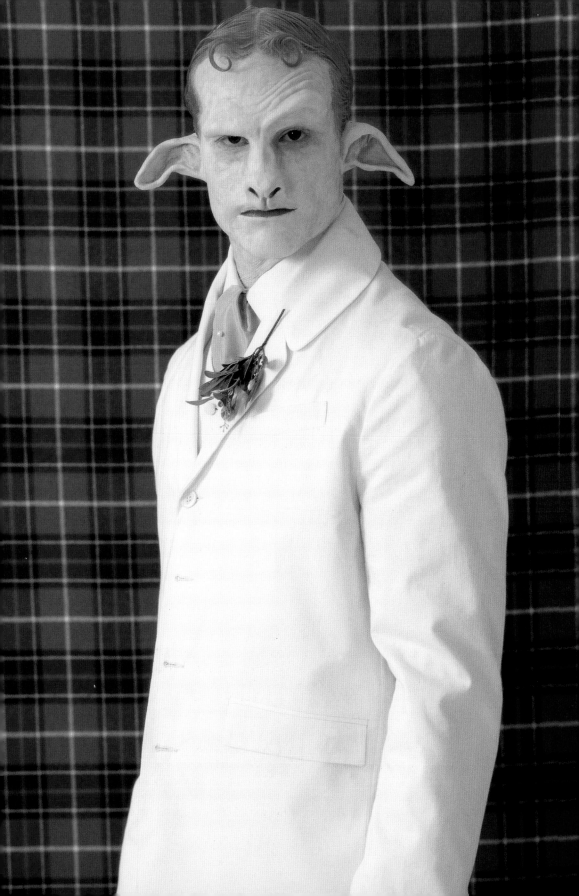

molten Vaseline, or petroleum jelly, in Barney's camp sculptural language). There is even a point in *Cremaster 3* when a surprisingly compliant Serra splashes an upright sheet of metal in ejaculatory style with beeswax/Vaseline, an amusing skit on the iconic photograph of himself of 1969 in which, wearing a gas mask and wielding a ladle above his head, he had flung molten metal in order to make castings (see Chapter 5).[23] As with *Cremaster 4*, the film thus seems to be a satire on masculinity, or more precisely the masculinist logic of avant-garde succession and supremacy, now made to seem hubristic and self-important.

In historical terms, Barney's work might be contextualized as part of a crisis of masculinity, one in a succession of such crises that have characterized Western societies since at least the early nineteenth century, although tied up in the 1990s with shifts in gender positionality arising from women's empowerment.[24] Another interesting figure in this respect is the German artist Martin Kippenberger. Based in Cologne in the 1980s, Kippenberger had steered a highly idiosyncratic artistic path, producing so-called 'bad paintings' such as *With the Best Will in the World I Can't See a Swastika* (1984), a conglomeration of variously coloured bars in synthetic-cubist pictorial space, which, in its title, amalgamated philistine attitudes to modern art with a highly questionable reference to post-war German amnesia regarding Nazism. In the 1970s Kippenberger had, for a short period, managed a famous punk club in Berlin, *S.O.36*, and was given to provocative, dissolute behaviour. He built up a 'bad boy' persona, rather like the male yBas or Jeff Koons, becoming a cult figure for young artists.

There was, however, a self-reflexive side to Kippenberger. In 1992 he had failed to be selected for that year's *Documenta IX*. Aggrieved, he went to one of the defining sites of the *Documenta*'s history, the site just outside the main exhibition venue in Kassel where Walter De Maria had sunk his *Vertical Earth Kilometer* into the earth, and placed one of his own works above the spot where the top of De Maria's rod lay flush with the ground. The work in question was a lamp post, one of Kippenberger's signature symbols, an allusion to the time-honoured prop of the drunken man [**134**]. However, as well as anthropomorphically evoking Kippenberger himself in a drunken pose, the lamp post on this occasion was bent into a pose of deference to the earth kilometre.

The brilliance of Kippenberger's gesture—combining an intrinsically sculptural idea with an in-house artistic reference—is in tune with new modalities of humorous or casual artistic address that characterize the art of this period. Further examples could be found in the sculptural and filmic practice of the Swiss artists Peter Fischli and David Weiss. Their *Sausage Series* of 1979 had been a key precursor for this humorous turn. It consisted of a series of photographs of set-ups that could have been patiently assembled by a small child at the dinner table: slices of salami doubling as piled carpets in *Carpet Shop*; upright sausages with bottle-top hats and bacon-wrapped bodies in *Fashion Show*. Another example of this mood of casual playfulness is the passport-photograph-style 'Self-portrait' which Douglas Gordon issued to the press when, as noted earlier, he won the Turner Prize in 1996. His *Self-portrait as Kurt Cobain, as Andy Warhol, as Myra Hindley, as Marilyn Monroe* offers up an unshaven Gordon sporting a hastily donned

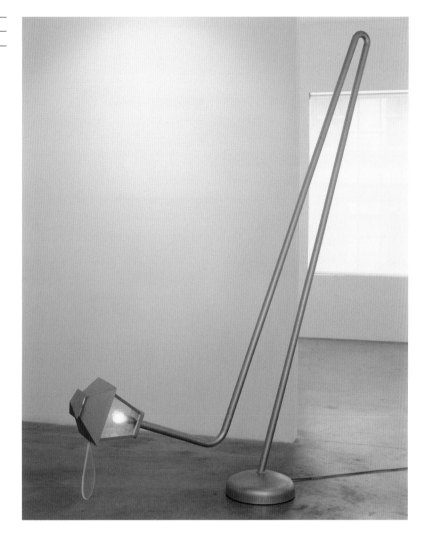

134 Martin Kippenberger
Untitled, 1992

Given that Kippenberger's sculpture was initially situated by the artists directly above Walter De Maria's subterranean *Vertical Earth Kilometer* at Kassel, the invisible rod below the ground was effectively continued upwards by the shaft of the bowing lamp post. The abeyance of the latter was given a playfully melancholic tinge by the inclusion of a Plexiglas tear hanging from the lamp itself.

peroxide-blonde woman's wig. It thereby references, in highly economical terms, the gamut of alternate personae referenced in its title, all of whom had blondeness in common, from the chilling Myra Hindley (a notorious child murderer of the 1960s) to Andy Warhol, whose 1981 gender-bending Polaroids of himself wearing a platinum bouffant wig were Gordon's likely starting point.[25] The offhandedness of the gesture is entirely characteristic of this moment. For many young artists the grand statements had all been made; this is apparent in Kippenberger's homage to De Maria. A deliberate refusal of gravitas was now the appropriate mode. However, such gestures were still aimed at those in the know, their insouciance soliciting off-the-peg intellectualism rather than aesthetic deliberation.

Fin de siècle: memory

As the twentieth century drew to a close, it is hardly surprising that art should look to themes of memory, or even nostalgia. Such themes would be present in Deller's turn-of-the-millennium *Battle of Orgreave*, as already discussed. A backward-looking impulse was also indicated by the symbolic primacy of the toy. The laddishness of Koons or Kippenberger suggested that artists themselves were failing to 'grow up', a point which might be linked to the phenomenon of 'extended adolescence' among younger people in the West.[26] (One of the least-examined assumptions of late twentieth-century art was that avant-garde innovation correlated with youthfulness. Whereas the great modernists, such as Matisse, were thought to have achieved artistic maturity with age, many artists of the 1990s peaked by the age of 30.) But just as the cult of youth dominated, so a regressive mood took hold.

Like Kippenberger, many artists reflected on what now seemed canonical statements from the recent past. A poignant example is the English artist Tacita Dean's audio-work *Trying to Find the Spiral Jetty* of 1997, which was inspired by the artist's chance discovery, whilst in America, that Robert Smithson's *Spiral Jetty*, one of the icons of Land Art (see Chapter 6) had risen to the surface of the lake under which it was submerged. The piece recorded Dean's attempt, accompanied by a friend, to reach the work by car, following instructions provided by the Utah Arts Council. However, given that she only began recording the piece some three-quarters of the way into her quest, she later fabricated the evidence of the early stages of the journey.

This provisional quality, whereby traces of the past are only partially recovered, and whereby serendipitous discoveries and a kind of meandering openness become integral to the process of working, is further developed in Dean's late 1990s film projects. In 1996 she embarked on a series of works exploring the story of Donald Crowhurst, a lone yachtsman who had briefly achieved notoriety in Britain in 1968 having entered the Golden Globe Race, consumed with the ambition to achieve the first solo voyage by boat around the world. Sadly Crowhurst was completely inadequate to the task, became radically disorientated at sea, and eventually jumped overboard. In the haunting *Teignmouth Electron* (2000), Dean documented the remnants of Crowhurst's boat, which necessitated another quest, this time to a remote location in the Cayman Islands. In the same location she encountered a further mysterious relic, the so-called 'Bubble House', which provided the title of a further film of 1999. The house had been the visionary project of a Frenchman who, jailed for financial impropriety, had failed to complete it. In Dean's words the peculiar pod-shaped shell left behind on the beach was 'a vision for perfect hurricane housing, egg-shaped and resistant to wind... with its Cinemascope-proportioned windows that look out onto the sea'.[27]

There was a pervasive melancholy to such pieces, speaking of doomed utopian aspirations, which, as Dean subsequently realized, was associatively linked in her mind with 'disappearing men' (this in different ways, links Smithson, Crowhurst, and the visionary architect of the Bubble House).[28] Whilst this chimes ironically with what has been said earlier about the vicissitudes of male identity in the 1990s, what is significant in aesthetic terms is the way that Dean worked from the basis of research or, as Hal Foster has argued, from an archival impulse.[29] This kind of artistic practice arguably lent itself to the state funding structures of the later twentieth century. In Britain and the USA diminishing funding for the arts generated increased competition for grants. Artists became adept at filling in application forms, a process which favoured a pre-planned, research-led mode of art production rather than the organic realization of felt or 'discovered' outcomes. This is not to disparage the affective power of the best of such work. Dean's practice, which allows for the intervention of what the surrealists termed 'objective chance', turns research into a poetics.

At the same time, other major figures received renewed attention on the basis of the archival and taxonomic principles underlying their work. Particular critical attention was given to *Atlas*, an enormous, ongoing collection of photographs (some source materials, some records of works, many purely personal or informational in import) compiled by the German artist Gerhard Richter. Having first been shown as early as 1972, it was a highlight of *Documenta X* of 1997, one of the last major assessments of twentieth-century American and European art prior to the millennium, curated by Catherine David. In sum, the exhibition asserted that conceptualism, with its attention to documentation and a research-based model of creativity, had been the dominant aesthetic engine for the last third of the century. Richter, a key figure of recent painting (see Chapter 7), could now be seen to tie in with this. What was more to the point, though, was the engagement with memory, both personal and communal, evoked by Richter's burgeoning archive. As the critic Adrian Searle noted, when reviewing a British showing,

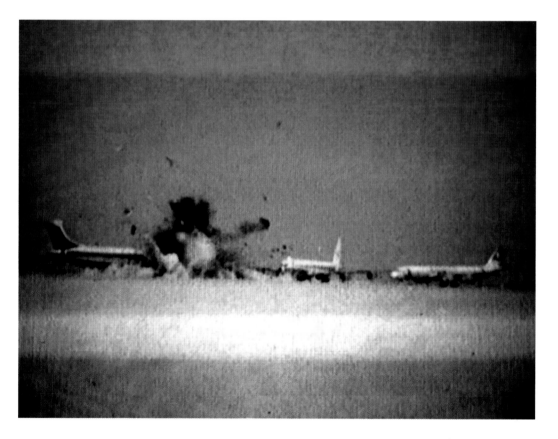

images recurred in the display 'like repetitious thoughts that won't go away'. These included 'innocent things: a toilet roll dangling in cold morning light' and 'guilty things: two women doing something with a cucumber...a Nazi hanging a boy who has almost something of a smile on his face...a photo of a train going by near the artist's studio'. Searle adds: 'Is it now possible, in Europe, to watch trains without thinking where the lines once led?'[31] As with Richter's earlier artistic practice, cultural memory seemed palpably present.

Another meditation on memory was a highlight of the 1997 *Documenta*. This was a film-essay by the Belgian film-maker and multimedia artist, Johan Grimonprez, titled *dial H-I-S-T-O-R-Y* [135]. Making use of a 'zapping' technique, derived from the experience of rapidly switching TV channels, Grimonprez edited together multiple images of Cold War-era hijackings, as shown on television news reports (most prominently the PLO-backed hijackings at the turn of the 1970s), with bizarre found footage and excerpts from personal videos. The artist asserted that his work was indirectly inspired by the Gulf War reportage of the early 1990s, which 'reduced history to a video game...catapult[ing] the camera's proximity to destruction into our living room'.[32] Punctuated by images of aeroplanes grounded on runways or dramatically exploding, the film offered a breathless hour-long array of information and imagery. If Richter's archive had spoken to the conceptualist fascination with ordering and taxonomy, Grimonprez's film had a surrealist tenor, in line with what has been said about Surrealism's late twentieth-century recurrence. This Surrealism, though, was synonymous with the simulacral dreamscape of late capitalism, a 'Surrealism without the unconscious' in the critic Fredric Jameson's terms.[33] Perhaps more to the point is Grimonprez's own pithy observation: 'Soon we will mistake reality for a commercial break.'[34]

In one sense, Grimonprez's film has a moral message: it reveals to us how the mass media participates in the construction of reality, such that our collective historical memory may be falsely accelerated and distorted by broadcast imagery. But this in no way accounts for the sense of sheer exhilaration and fascination that the piece exerts. Memory here translates into a kind of nostalgia for the 'culture of catastrophe' that we have become inured to. The sad irony is that, as we shall see at the start of the chapter 9, the piece spoke to the future as much as to the past.

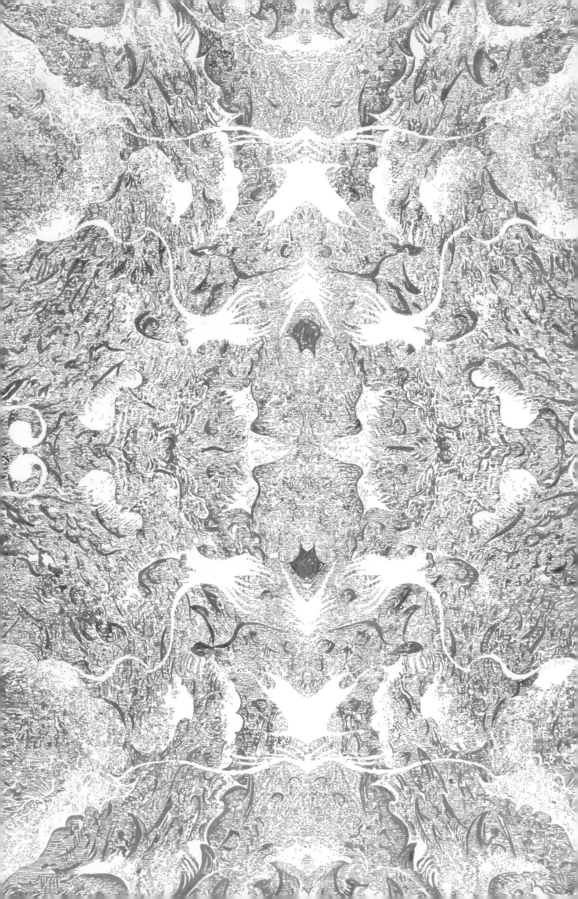

Art and the New Millennium

On 11 September 2001 the Twin Towers of the World Trade Center, New York, a symbolic centre of Western finance, were engulfed in flames, having been hit by two aircraft piloted by terrorists representing the radical Islamic group al-Qaeda. Johan Grimonprez's examination of the fascination of terror, discussed at the end of Chapter 8, seemed prescient. The event provoked ill-considered comments by artists: Damien Hirst opined that 'it's kind of an artwork in its own right. It was wicked, but it was devised in this kind of a way for this kind of impact. It was devised visually'.[1] On a deeper level, Walter Benjamin had noted in the mid-1930s that mankind's self-alienation had reached a point where it could experience its own annihilation in aesthetic terms.[2] It would be utterly wrong to confuse 9/11 with aesthetics, but it was undoubtedly epoch-defining, not only politically but, as Hirst grasped, visually: millions saw it on their TV screens. Bringing what US leaders saw as war to the very heart of the USA, the event marked the beginning of a distinct post-Second World War phase in the history of the West in which fears of internal enemies crept back into the Western imagination.

Three years later an event occurred in art publishing that some humorously compared to the landing of the monolith in Stanley Kubrick's film, *2001: A Space Odyssey*. This huge tome, *Art Since 1900*, co-authored by the American critics associated with the journal *October*, could be seen as signalling an ending. As I have argued, Western post-war art might be understood as dominated by America, with the pre-1960 dissemination of Modernism skirting close to cultural imperialism. European art frequently operated in critical counterpoint to this. The appearance of Art Since 1900 saw the entire history of modernism placed in the hands of a powerful group of New York-based critics, confirming for some a long-standing sense of US cultural hegemony. Much as the formal emphasis of Greenberg's Modernism had been disparaged in late twentieth-century art, a logic of stylistic innovation largely underpinned the narrative of the book, aside from its theoretical claims. Even more worrying for some was the absence of any sense of the global expansion that was reorientating the art world at the very moment of the book's appearance, with the emphasis largely placed on North America and Europe.[3] Such a US-centric viewpoint seemed out of touch with the times, and the critics seemed weary in any case of what they considered a downturn in the quality of contemporary art.

This final chapter begins, then, with a sense of historical completion. Just as 9/11 marked a watershed in terms of the global dominance of the US, so New York could no longer claim pre-eminence in art, with its critics

Detail of 145

bookending a historical phase. Arguably, British art saw a pronounced resurgence between the early 1990s and early 2000s, but it would be fatuous to talk of 'leading art nations'; globalization had led to a more complex international art game in which the West *in toto* was virtually a regional player. Eventually, Europe would face its own political crises. In June 2016 the British people voted to leave the European Union, presaging the unravelling of a long-standing political formation. At the same time, in the wake of the Twin Towers attack, Western ideology was galvanized by the threat of Islamic extremism. A spate of terrorist atrocities in key European cities stimulated an intense preoccupation with territorial borders. Religious fundamentalism and a return to national self-consciousness set the terms for what many perceived to be the return of atavistic forces as part of an overall crisis in the Western neo-liberal project. The sense was that new forces were shaping the West's destiny.

The idea that the trajectory of American–European art that this book has followed could, or should, be perceived as 'completed' will be returned to. So too will the idea, stated at the book's outset, that the Duchampian paradigm established its direction. One of the features of cultural discourse around globalization since the 1990s has been an exacerbation of the postmodern perception that artistic production is inseparable from other social processes. According to Michael Hardt and Antonio Negri, authors of the epoch-defining *Empire* (2000), 'the economic, the political, and the cultural increasingly overlap and invest one another'.[4] At the same time, the sense that we inhabit a postcolonial, global art world has made it problematic to talk of consolidated 'centres' and 'peripheries'. In this final chapter, for the sake of both overall coherence and continuity, I look mainly at the US–European constellation, but it is important to see artists increasingly moving to Western cities from what were once patronizingly referred to as the 'peripheries', whilst westerners have increasingly established their practices elsewhere on the globe. The West's cultural borders have become highly permeable at the very point when diasporic processes affecting huge populations (such as the Syria conflict), along with fears of terrorism, have caused politicians to reaffirm the importance of physical borders. It is this dynamic that has brought forth some of the characteristic art of the last decade and a half. In terms of its operational underpinnings, however, the Western art world has not experienced any ruptures post-2000 comparable to the political events that have impinged on it. In Britain and the US, the financial crash of 2007–8 led to substantial economic downturn, with public galleries in particular suffering debilitating cuts, but the art world generally pursued 'business as usual' (with business very much to the fore, as will be discussed). A number of structural shifts, though, have given it a distinctively new appearance. Art has both absorbed and reacted against these shifts.

The spectacle of capital: art and the Internet

Andreas Gursky's photograph of the thirty-three-storey atrium of the Grand Hyatt hotel, Shanghai, one of the highest structures of its kind in the world, conveys a powerful sense of both vertigo and anonymity. The photograph itself is huge, measuring some 9 by 6 feet (2.7 by 1.8 metres) [**136**]. Dazzled initially by the blaze of its yellow colouration and its satisfying symmetry,

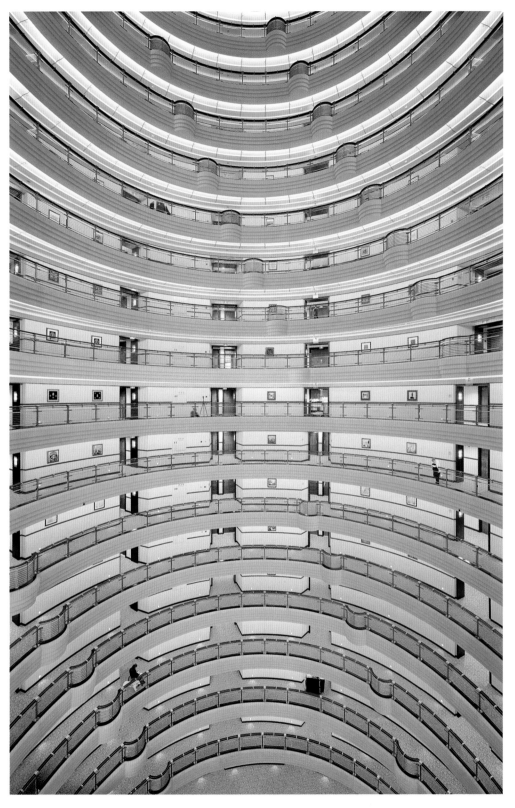

the spectator gradually takes in the fact that two figures are dwarfed within the depicted interior, which apparently has neither top nor bottom. Aesthetic impersonality is played off against actual impersonality. When one realizes that Gursky, a major German artist of the millennial decades, was initially trained at the Düsseldorf Kunstakademie—alongside other important photographers of the period such as Thomas Ruff and Thomas Struth—by Bernd and Hilla Becher [**93**], one appreciates that this impersonality is part of a distinct tradition of conceptualist German photography in which systematicity and objectivity are emphasized.

However, considerable contrivance often informs this work. Thomas Demand, a slightly younger photographer in this tradition, goes so far as to physically fabricate the apparently soulless interiors that he photographs on the basis of press photographs. This process can be extremely loaded when, as in *Corridor* (1995), the source image is fraught with significance, in this case a corridor outside the apartment of the serial killer Jeffrey Dahmer. Gursky's images are similarly 'constructed' in some cases (for example, in his famous image of a horizontally stretched display case of shoes, *Prada 1* (1996), in which he fabricated the unit himself) and are often digitally enhanced so that we appear to see huge tracts of land or enormous buildings far more comprehensively than would be possible in reality. Gursky's photographs frequently function as metaphors for human powerlessness in the face of ungraspable forces or structures. At the turn of the millennium, international capital presented itself as such a force, and Gursky's subjects included the bustle of activity on the floors of stock exchanges or ranks of multicoloured products in supermarkets. The Shanghai photograph, alongside others that Gursky took of Far Eastern locations, could even be seen as a symbolic foreshadowing of shifts in global power such that, at the turn of the twenty-first century, China stood poised to eclipse the US as the world's leading economy.

In a rather different visualization of capital, between 2001 and 2004 London-based artists Lise Autogena and Joshua Portway produced two variations, at Tate Britain and at a Copenhagen Art Centre, of an installation titled *Black Shoals Stock Market*. As in a planetarium, spectators were positioned beneath a constellation of glittering pinpricks of light projected onto the inner, inky black surface of a dome. As T. J. Demos notes, 'The heavenly bodies corresponded not to real suns or planets, but rather to publicly traded companies, as a computer programme transl[ated] the real time financial activity of the world's stock markets into glimmering stars.' He goes on to write, 'The points of light flashed brightly whenever their stocks (were) traded…only to be preyed on by digital creatures', finally adding, 'The famine of a market downturn [led] them to die out.'[5] Financial systems were figured as things beyond our imagining, like the immensity of the solar system. The piece presaged the way millions would perceive the financial crash of 2007–8, an event brought about by irresponsible banking practices, which led to 'austerity' programmes being pursued by governments.

It is interesting that, unlike the relatively traditional photographic practice of Gursky, this installation used computational systems. To what extent, then, did new technologies affect turn-of-the-millennium art? It was often asserted that the Internet in particular would produce a moral counterweight to the increasingly market-driven art world of the period. (In 2002 a work by Gursky fetched over £400,000, an indication that photography had achieved a commercial status akin to painting.) Julian Stallabrass asserted that the Internet 'cuts through the regular systems of media dissemination', creating a new participatory arena in which 'anyone who has access to a networked computer can put work on the Web without the say-so of an art institution'.[6] The sense of a newly democratized Internet avant-garde had briefly emerged in the late 1990s, its key exponents being a close-knit network comprising Heath Bunting from Britain, Vuk Cosic from Slovenia, and Olia Lialina and Alexei Shulgin from Russia. However, by 1998 the group had fragmented, with London's artspace, an important early meeting point, closing in 2000. The best Internet art often exploited the medium's collaborative possibilities: Douglas Davis's *The World's First Collaborative Sentence* (1994), a project in which thousands of people added to an ongoing sentence, would mutate wildly as the technology of the Web improved, with accretions of colour, sound, or video supplementing the basic text (along with numerous rogue full stops). In 1999 Heath Bunting and Olia Lialina instituted a project titled *IDENTITISWAPDATABASE* in which people could shrug off the official state-sanctioned markers of their identities (such as nationality) and use other Internet flotsam, such as details from supermarket loyalty cards, to forge new identities.

137 etoy
The Twelve Days of
Christmas, 1999

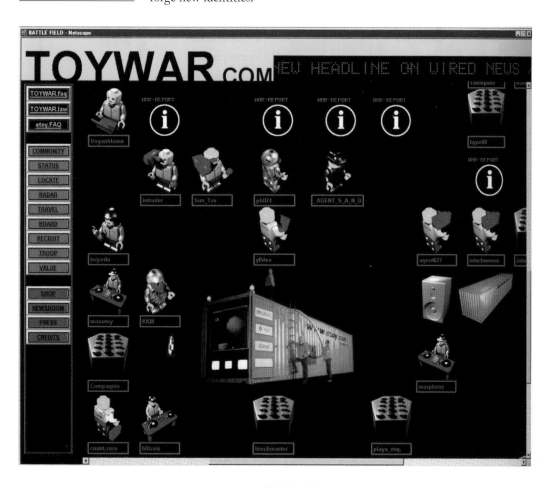

Bunting and Lialina's project underlines Internet Art's potential for societal intervention. The most remarkable instance of this came with a turn-of-the-millennium project involving *etoy*, a largely Swiss grouping which, since 1995, had specialized in parodying dot-com advertising. In 1999 their domain name was contested by the newly formed and almost identically named commercial company *eToys*, which, aiming to corner the Christmas toy market, asserted that *etoy*'s site contained socially subversive content that was upsetting their customers. A legal battle ensued. The indomitable *etoy*, with the aid of other activist websites, mounted a veritable 'TOYWAR', using an Internet campaign called *The Twelve Days of Christmas* to interfere with *eToys'* online advertising during the crucial December period [137]. On the back of a wave of customer complaints, the price of *eToys* stock fell dramatically. Their lawsuit against *etoy* fizzled out, and they agreed to pay their adversary's costs. With the Internet market simultaneously in crisis, they ended up bankrupt.[7]

The art system post-2000

The case of *etoy* demonstrated how effectively Internet Art could infiltrate and affect the world of finance. It also indicated that, to function effectively as sociopolitical critique, it might be necessary for art to immerse itself in the workings of capitalism. The structural imbrication of art with capitalist forms had, as noted earlier, been a major worry for theorists of postmodernism. On this line of reasoning, Internet Art's reliance on technological systems would potentially limit its ability to achieve the distance required for critique. Further objections follow from this. Despite being participatory at one level, the solipsistic nature of Internet activity arguably offers a depleted sense of the social. The computer screen similarly offers a bleak sensory horizon compared with the aesthetic plenitude offered by other visual art forms. Such considerations aside, the rise of Internet Art was an expression of the widespread marketization that fundamentally transformed art-world structures after the year 2000. These important shifts now require some consideration.

As suggested by the *etoy* episode, finance was fundamental to the art world's changed identity post-2000. New patterns of art-buying were key. The 1990s had seen increasing corporate involvement in the buying of art as US and UK governments withdrew public funding and companies such as BP or the cigarette firm, Philip Morris, involved themselves in sponsoring, commissioning, and collecting art.[8] After 2000 the traditional model of art dealership was put under pressure in various ways. Previously prestigious dealers had been located in major urban centres. The rise of the art fair after 2000 changed this. The first of such fairs, in Cologne, had emerged in 1967, but they proliferated from the end of the 1990s with Art Basel and its many satellites (such as Art Basel Miami Beach) being pre-eminent, whilst venues sprang up internationally with the stepping-up of global trade. (Important fairs included *Frieze* in London, *ARCO* in Mexico City, *Art Dubai*, and *Shanghai Contemporary*.) Now, instead of travelling extensively to view work in dealers' galleries, wealthy international buyers could see art from far-flung locations amassed under one roof.

Biennials were also a major feature of the post-millennium years, fuelled by the dynamic of globalization. Venice, of course, had long been an important location for showcasing new art (as had the five-yearly *Documenta* in Kassel), whilst the São Paulo Biennale dated back to 1951. But numerous international biennials had sprung up in the 1990s and continued to flourish, for instance Johannesburg (founded 1995); Gwangju, South Korea (1995); Shanghai (1996); Berlin (1998); and Prague (2003). Opening events at both biennials and art fairs became increasingly glitzy affairs. Critics were shipped in as VIPs and a tourist ethos developed around them. In 2007, for instance, a group of major art events—*Documenta*, *Skulptur Projekte Münster*, the *Venice Biennale*, and *Art Basel*—were jointly promoted as a 'grand tour', reviving the elite cultural tourism indulged in by nineteenth-century aesthetes. By the same token, the locales of certain biennials functioned as scenic backdrops: for the 2008 *Prospect* in New Orleans, the organizers capitalized on the city's partial decimation by Hurricane Katrina to create a setting for art.[12] If biennials had, in the past, functioned as summations of trends, they now tended to underline difference within an overarching global framework. This in turn called for a new phenomenon, the star curator, a figure who, nomadically travelling from venue to venue, was uniquely able to comprehend the diversity of art production and curate shows accordingly. Major curators such as Okwui Enwezor, Carolyn Christov-Bakargiev, and Hans-Ulrich Obrist became art's legislators. Satirizing the tendency, David Balzer recalled that in 2012 the artist Bill Burns had an aircraft hover over Miami, the location of a key art fair, towing a banner bearing the half-humorous plea 'HANS ULRICH OBRIST HEAR US'.[13]

This increasingly modish and money-driven international art scene was far from universally admired, but whatever criticisms might be levelled at it, the resilience of the Western economies, at least prior to the crash of 2007–8, also led to major national and regional museum projects being set up. The Guggenheim Museum, Bilbao, designed by the Canadian-American architect Frank Gehry and opened in 1997, was the trailblazer for a spate of innovative, architecturally significant projects. Seen as a sculptural masterpiece in its own right, the titanium-clad Bilbao structure 'sits lightly on its site', according to one commentator, 'suggesting flow across the river's edge site, a ship-like movement, like hulls lurching at sea...or...a reptile, stirring within its scaled skin.'[14] Envisaged by its first director, Thomas Krens, as capable of accommodating everything from a Picasso drawing to the heaviest of modern sculptures, and therefore functioning as both a modern art museum and contemporary display space, the interior boasts an unusual spatial diversity, covering some 118,000 square feet (11,000 square metres) of exhibition space.

Three years later the Bilbao museum was rivalled by Tate Modern, designed by Swiss architects Herzog & de Meuron. A £134-million, lottery-funded adaptation of an existing building—the massive Bankside Power Station in Southwark, London—the design retained certain features of the original structure, such as the enormous turbine hall measuring 115 feet (35 metres) high and 499 feet (152 metres) long. (Huge installations would subsequently be housed here, such as the Danish-Icelandic artist Olafur Eliasson's *The Weather Project* of 2003, which saw spectators languidly basking in the cavernous, mist-filled space under the glow of an artificial sun.) Assuming the role of international modern art museum formerly held by what now became Tate Britain, as well as something of the remit of London's Institute of Contemporary Arts, it was an instant success. Its attendance figures in 2004 stood at 4.1 million (compared with MoMA New York's 2.67 million).[15] Its director Nicholas Serota also oversaw shifts in curatorial policy reflecting a populist ethos: a thematic hang replaced a chronological one (this would also be implemented by MoMA a little later). The size of Tate Modern—with some 35,520 square feet (3,300 square metres) of exhibition space occupying the floors *above* the turbine hall—would before long be surpassed by the Dia: Beacon museum, which opened in Beacon, New York, in 2003, its 162,000 square feet (15,000 square metres) dedicated to the Dia Art Foundation's major collection of space-consuming Land Art and minimalist works by the likes of Walter De Maria and Richard Serra. Other new museum projects included Renzo Piano's celebrated rebuilding of New York's Whitney Museum of American Art (2015) and an extension to Tate Modern in 2016. As more and more money was pumped into it, contemporary art was bursting the museum's seams.

Public projects such as these did much to raise the profile of modern/contemporary art, attracting an increasingly diverse audience that identified art-going with leisure, but critics warned that the growing commercialization of art institutions infected art itself. Just as the top galleries became obsessed with branding themselves (the 'Tate' logo appeared on objects far removed from art), so celebrity artists followed suit. As Julian Stallabrass gloomily asserted, 'Artists as brands are allegorical figures that, like robots, deliver particular and predictable behaviour along with other outputs.'[16] Stallabrass argued that a certain kind of corporate 'museum art'—with a generic 'yBa' look to it—flooded contemporary art. More generally, a melancholia descended on the criticism of the early 2000s, with major critics of post-war art registering bewilderment at this market-driven art world. In a round table in *October* magazine, lamenting the loss of the avant-garde and its support structures, Benjamin Buchloh talked of 'social and institutional formations for which we not only do not have any concepts and terms yet, but whose modus operandi remains profoundly opaque and incomprehensible to most of us'.[17] Arguably, though, much of the vital art of the early 2000s skirted warily around these institutional formations and came not from the complacently well-off urban centres of the West, but from the so-called peripheries, although it frequently became snagged in the net of global biennials and art fairs thrown up by economic globalization. This opening-up of Western art to a multitude of other voices and cultural viewpoints, along with the ways in which artists expressed the pressing realities of cultural displacement and migration, demands a new discussion.

Global aesthetics: displacement, migration, borders, identity

It is generally agreed that *Documenta 11* of 2002, in taking globalization and postcolonial critique as its overriding themes, represented a turning point in recent Western art. Its curator, the Nigerian-born Okwui Enwezor, was well aware of previous multicultural exhibitions such as *Magiciens de la terre* (1989). The *Magiciens* exhibition could, however, be seen as effectively levelling issues of cultural difference. By contrast, on the model of the *Manifesta* biennial, which had migrated between European centres since its beginning in Rotterdam in 1996, Enwezor made global dispersal a structural rationale for his event. Although the final, consolidated showing of the exhibition was in Kassel, it was preceded by a series of five 'platforms', each presided over by a co-curator, in distant locations: Berlin, St Lucia, Vienna, New Delhi, and Lagos. Through a cumulative process of preparatory dialogue Enwezor therefore hoped to reconsider contemporary art as formed 'through processes of translation, interpretation, subversion, hybridization, creolization, displacement, and reassemblage'.[18]

What Enwezor meant by displacement, translation, and hybridization is exemplified by the work of one of the artists exhibited in *Documenta 11*, Shirin Neshat. Born in Iran, Neshat was moved by her father to the USA when aged 17, just before the Iranian Revolution of 1978–9. During the years of the Iran–Iraq war, Neshat remained in America, returning home after the death of Ayatollah Khomeini in 1989. Deeply affected by Iran's turn to Islamic fundamentalism, she settled back in America, her sense of displacement, as someone positioned between two radically opposed ideologies, providing the subject of her major *Women of Allah* photographs of 1993–7 [**138**]. Looking at these images, which are all self-portraits of a kind, translation is clearly at issue, although highly ironically. Addressed to a Western audience, the images contain elements that *resist* easy translation, namely the Farsi calligraphy, imparting Persian love poetry, which frequently overlays Neshat's hand or face or appears as a backdrop. However, Neshat does, to some extent, meet the expectations of her audience. She creates a mysterious image of herself whilst simultaneously undercutting orientalist cliches of passive sensuality by meeting the (male) spectator's gaze and by gripping a gun. The overriding assertion is a feminist one: that she in fact *possesses* the phallus, which references women bearing arms in the Iranian Revolution and the continuing global reverberations of the latter. Hybridization thus becomes the ruling trope of the images. Questioning the role of women in both Islamic and Western societies, Neshat allows opposite viewpoints to play out across her body. She is simultaneously secretive and available, threatening and sensual.

Around the turn of the millennium, Neshat produced a sequence of videos and films which explored gender dichotomies in a more specifically Iranian

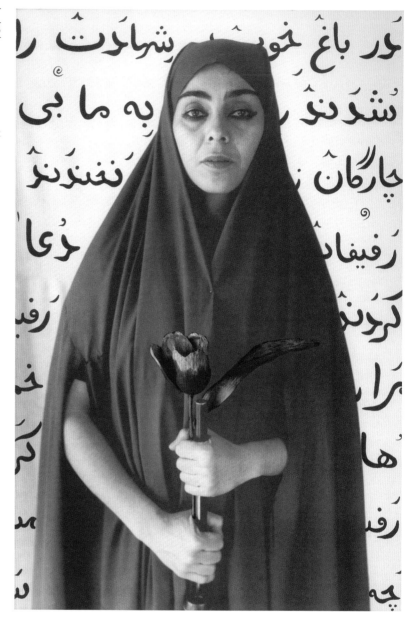

138 Shirin Neshat

Seeking Martyrdom #2, 1995

Neshat's critique of orientalist assumptions, in respect to the way they affect the reading of images of Middle Eastern women, can be seen in parallel with the work of other artists of the late 1990s to the present such as Mona Hatoum, Gülsün Karamustafa, and Emily Jacir.

context: *Turbulent* (1998), *Rapture* (1999), *Fervour* (2000), *Possessed* (2001), and *Passage* (2001). All of them alluded to archetypal structures, but the last in particular, its action set against timeless landscape features, approached the mystical. The film builds up through a series of montage sequences accompanied by music by the American composer Philip Glass. A group of women dig what seems to be a burial site in a desert landscape. A group of black-suited men carry a shrouded object (corpse) from the edge of the ocean to the burial site. A solitary girl plays near the women at the site, building a campfire from stones. Only at the end do the narrative threads converge: the men's journey comes to an end, the burial site and the furnace are completed. Suddenly, as the men's burden is laid down, the earth bursts into flames and a raging fire spreads along a V-shaped stone wall, witnessed by the child. Here Neshat makes her personal odyssey, involving an atavistic journey back to an archaic, religiously driven culture, resonate poignantly for the agnostic Western culture to which she belongs. She speaks in a symbolic language that most avant-gardists fight shy of (Gary Hill or Bill Viola, as mentioned in Chapter 8, being possible exceptions).

Neshat's practice turns displacement into an aesthetic advantage, but it is worth returning to another of Enwezor's categories—creolization—to consider another, very different artist who participated in *Documenta 11*, the British film-maker and installation artist Isaac Julien. Although the term creolization, which was initially taken up by the Martiniquan theorist Édouard Glissant, largely refers to social processes in Latin America, it more broadly designates the interracial/cultural mixing that characterizes postcolonial societies. Born in London in the 1970s, of West Indian parentage, Julien grew up at a time of mass immigration from the West Indies and Asia. By the early 1980s, in the context of Margaret Thatcher's Conservative administration, riots, stimulated by racial tensions as well as inner-city deprivation, broke out throughout Britain, notably in Brixton (London) and Toxteth (Liverpool). It was in this fractious climate that Julien began to examine his creole identity. London had, for him, been a melting pot of subcultural influences. The sociologist Stuart Hall has talked of subcultural groups developing their own modes of behaviour: 'They cluster around particular locations. They develop specific rhythms of interchange, structured relations between members...the world is marked out, linguistically by names or an *argot*.' In certain respects this supplants the traditional model of an oppositional artistic avant-garde, suggesting that innovative cultural forms often emerge when orthodoxies are contested from specific class or ethnic positions.[19] In his early work as a film-maker, influenced by art-house experimentalists such as Chris Marker and alternative mainstream figures such as Derek Jarman, Julien explored such subcultural issues, recalling the 1980s London of punk and soul music in *Young Soul Rebels* (1991), his own gay sexuality in *Looking for Langston* (1989, a film about the Harlem Renaissance poet Langston Hughes), and the wider issue of colonial diaspora in *Frantz Fanon: Black Skin, White Mask* (1996), a part-fictional biopic of Frantz Fanon, the Martiniquan-born theorist of negritude.

There are links here with another British-born artist with West Indian roots, Steve McQueen, who also explored black experience. During the late 1990s McQueen produced a sequence of short video works, such as his four-minute *Deadpan* (1997), a cool re-enactment of a scene from Buster Keaton's *Steamboat Bill Jr*. By the mid-2000s he had, like Julien, turned to film, becoming hugely successful as an Oscar-winner with the mainstream feature *12 Years a Slave* (2013) dealing with the harrowing, formative historical stages of the black diaspora, the slave trade. Stereotypes of black identity, particularly images of slavery, had incidentally been treated very tellingly by the African-American Kara Walker at the turn of the millennium. Resurrecting the nineteenth-century genre of the silhouette or paper-cut, Walker created a series of large-scale installations for American galleries (for instance, *Virginia's Lynch Mob* at the Forum for Contemporary Art,

St Louis, 1998). Her fantastical scenes, alluding to the place of black Africans in American history and popular culture, played on spectators' desire to read into what were highly ambiguous black cut-out shapes. Borrowing the jaunty style of popular illustration, they in fact harboured tales of abuse.

If McQueen moved from video to film in the post-2000 decade, Julien transferred his film-making concerns to the gallery, creating innovative multiscreen installations in line with wider trends towards digitization and narrativity (other key figures included Rodney Graham, Stan Douglas, Doug Aitken, Douglas Gordon, and Christian Marclay, the latter's *The Clock* of 2010, a twenty-four-hour long video-montage, being a particularly innovatory work). Creolization was still at stake in Julien's trilogy *True North* (2004), *Fantôme Africa*, and *Fantôme Créole* (2005) but he now responded, poetically, to pressing global issues. In the later installation work, *Ten Thousand Waves*, first shown at the 2010 Biennale of Sydney, he dealt with migration; the work was inspired by the story of twenty-three Chinese asylum seekers who, having undertaken a perilous sea journey to Britain, drowned whilst working as cockle-pickers on Britain's west coast. The experience of these people was partly underlined by the structure of the installation: nine variously positioned screens encouraged spectators to become migratory themselves in moving from one to another. The opening images, an immersive array of crashing ocean waves, set up an association, not only with the ordeal of the Chinese asylum seekers, but with the larger forces that had helped determine their fate. The latter was made clear via images of contemporary Shanghai, or more particularly its wealthy financial district (filmed incidentally from the iconic Grand Hyatt hotel, which Gursky had photographed [136]), which alluded to the economic rise of China. But a redemptive corollary to the fate of the cockle-pickers was provided by a section of the film based on an ancient Chinese myth dealing with the wanderings of a group of fishermen in an idyllic landscape, watched over by their protectress, the goddess Mazu [139].

This description is inevitably partial, but it should be clear that the work has multiple layers, folding together different temporal and thematic strands. It also juxtaposes different filmic idioms in line with Julien's call for an aesthetic creolization, a 'broken mixture of different languages'.[20] Combining an echo of Allen Sekula's analysis of the human outcomes of globalization (see Chapter 8) with the spirituality noted earlier in Neshat, the work fuses high and low cultural allusions to produce effects that are unashamedly 'beautiful' (a term welcomed by Julien).

As something often considered inimical to avant-garde aesthetics, beauty has had a new place in post-2000 art. It is exemplified, for instance, in the work of the South Korean sculptor and installation artist Haegue Yang, where migration and nomadism are not so much themes as preconditions for a new sculptural language utilizing glitzy mass-cultural materials and readymade, shop-bought items. (A similar sculptural mode was developed in the early 2000s by the German artist Isa Genzken, who moved from a previous architecturally derived, post-minimalist style to the use of deliberately tacky materials, connotative of commodity-culture, in striking works such as her *Empire/Vampire, Who Kills Death* series (2002–3).[21]) Born in Seoul, Yang has shuttled between South Korea and Germany since the late 1990s.

139 Isaac Julien

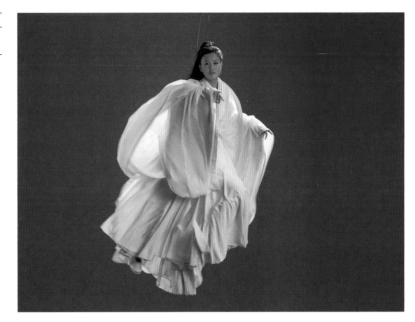

139 Isaac Julien

Green Screen Goddess (Ten Thousand Waves), 2010

The image of the goddess Mazu (played by Chinese actress Maggie Cheung), hovering against an abstract field of green with the wires suspending her billowing garment made plainly visible, reminded the film historian Laura Mulvey not just of avant-garde aesthetics but also of the musical film *Singin' in the Rain* (1952) with its 'effects and rain machines'.[22]

Described by one critic as a 'professional global artist...."parachuting" into a location, making or installing work swiftly and then moving on',[23] Yang's installations regularly feature her signature sculptures. Echoing her fragmented lifestyle, these marry together unlikely partners. Tinned goods are wrapped in woollen comforters, an idiosyncratic take on the idea of 'preservation', which alludes to personal memories of her grandmother stockpiling tinned foods but also unavoidably harks back art-historically to Manzoni's 1950s cans [**41**]. Drying racks are sheathed in rugs and fabrics, as though their potential for erratic movement is being constrained. Most typically, tangled light bulbs and diaphanous shawls hang from clothing-store display stands, evoking other-worldly personages [**140**]. A disconnection between people and things is ever-present, with the latter taking on their own peculiar life. The concept of 'no place', developed by the French theorist Marc Augé, speaks to Yang's work in general.[24] Augé sees airports—points between locations which are virtually identical the world over—as exemplifying 'non-places'. A 2012 installation by Yang bore the title *Multi Faith Room*. Alluding to the prayer rooms in airports designated to accommodate all faiths, the installation contained a massive photographic wallpaper print by Manuel Raeder of an inverted Asian landscape. Around this stood Yang's sculptures, with Shinto grave markers close by. The world of the global artist seemed to offer both melancholic displacement and a fragile, hybridized beauty.

Works by Neshat, Julien, and Yang gain poignancy, in very different ways, against the backdrop of recent geopolitics— the so-called 'War on Terror', the movement of asylum seekers. Borders have become highly potent symbols of the current age, and several key works of the immediate post-2000 years took them as a theme. For instance, the Spanish performance/installation artist Santiago Sierra's contribution to the Venice Biennale of 2003 involved sealing off the entrance to that year's Spanish pavilion with

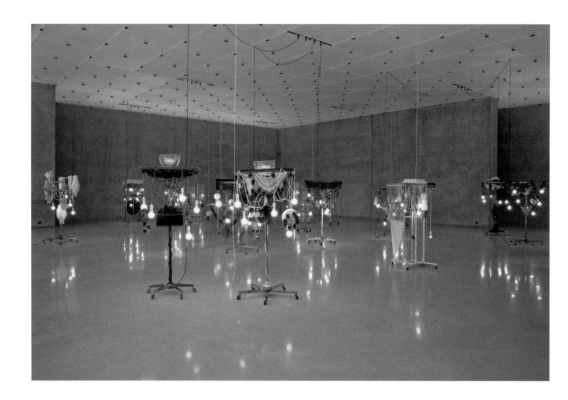

140 Haegue Yang

Warrior Believer Lover, 2011, installation

In certain Yang installations, her assemblages stand like exotic figures in environments in which coloured lighting, smells from scent-emitters, and reflections produced via light bulbs and her ever-present Venetian blinds, produce seductive effects.

concrete blocks. On entering the building, spectators came up against a wall, preventing their entrance to the galleries. Spanish passport-holders were subsequently allowed in by an alternative entrance after inspection of their documents by immigration officers, while all non-Spanish nationals were denied access. The Venice Biennale had originally been conceived as a platform for European nations to demonstrate a cultural coming-together after World War II. Sierra set this history against the growing rise of nationalist sentiment in the West, which happened in spite of the European Union's overriding principle of free movement between countries. (In late 2016 the idea of walls, or barriers, between territories, once symbolized by the Berlin Wall, would be revisited when American president-to-be Donald Trump controversially called for the erection of a wall to extend existing barriers between the US and Mexico.) Since 2000, opportunities to take part in such summative exhibitions, with their connotations of inclusiveness, have occasionally been used by artists to demonstrate the opposite principle of exclusivity. For instance, the Swiss installation artist Thomas Hirschhorn's contribution to *Documenta 11* was the creation of his *Bataille Monument*, a communal area in which people could drink, relax, and make use of a library of Georges Bataille's writings (the French twentieth-century 'excremental philosopher', as we have already seen, being a highly influential theorist of the overturning of idealist modes of thought). This was situated some miles from the main *Documenta* site in a working-class district of Kassel. Art lovers at the main event were obliged to take taxis to see Hirschhorn's work and to feel like intruders in the domain of the locals who were implicitly viewed as Bataille's true audience.

*Looking for a Husband with
EU Passport,* 2000–5

Powerfully responding to the
objectification of the female
body in Western advertising,
Ostojić's pubescent-looking
body is ambiguously coded
as both 'unfeminine' (shaved
head) and highly sexualized
(nudity, shaved pubis). Her
feminist concern with the
politics underpinning
representations of female
sexuality is manifested in
another work of the *Crossing
Borders* series, *Untitled/
After Courbet (L'origine du
monde, 1886, 46 x 55 cm)*
of 2004. Taking as its
reference point Courbet's
notorious close-up painting
of a female crotch, Ostojić's
colour photograph presented
her own similarly positioned
genital region, although
covered with panties
emblazoned with the
European Union motif of
a circle of twelve yellow
stars set against a blue
background. She therefore
allegorized the way in which
a young woman from East
Europe sought entry into the
capitalist club of the West by
ironically employing Western
sexualized advertising
conventions.

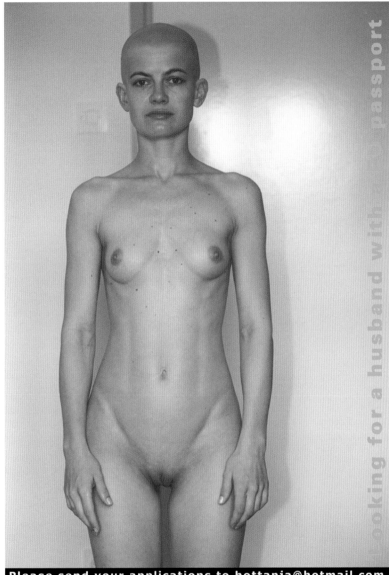

Please send your applications to hottanja@hotmail.com
Do not hesitate to contact me with any further questions or details

The issue of borders was further explored by Tanja Ostojić, an artist born
in 1972 in the former Yugoslavia, in a participatory Web project and mixed-
media installation, *Looking for a Husband with EU Passport* (2000–5), a further
example of the way the Internet has been used to bring art and politics
together [**141**]. Part of the *Crossing Borders* series, which featured her crossing the Slovenian-Austrian border illegally for a three-day period, the work
saw Ostojić effectively offering to sell her body for the much-desired EU
passport as part of an arranged marriage. Stripped and vulnerable in the
Web image, with her head shaved in an uncanny echo of the appearance of
women collaborators during World War II (women who had 'slept with the

enemy'), Ostojić exemplifies what the art historian Angela Dimitrakaki has seen as a primary topic of post-2000 art—the 'economic subject'.[25] It may be reassuring to know that the artist received some 500 offers of marriage, was eventually duly married, acquired her passport, and moved for a period to Germany—all of which, including the eventual divorce, was treated as a 'performance'. The category of performance is nevertheless of limited use here. Ostojić's entire being is at stake in what can be characterized as 'biopolitical' art, with the human subject reduced, via economic and political contingencies, to what the Italian philosopher Giorgio Agamben describes as 'bare life'.[26]

If performance as a term matches up inadequately to such a practice, this key genre from the 1970s should perhaps be understood rather differently in many of its recent incarnations. Significant figures such as the Yugoslavian-born Marina Abramović have, it is true, produced major works that continue to deal with the live confrontation of artist and audience, such as her marathon *The Artist is Present* (2010), performed at MoMA, New York, in which, over 736.5 hours, a succession of visitors attempted to peer into the artist's eyes for as long as they could manage. However, performance has given way to other modes of enacting subjectivity. This passing of performance as a historical genre was perhaps signalled by a wave of 're-performances' at the turn of the millennium, such as those included in the *Short History of Performance* programme at the Whitechapel Art Gallery, London, in April 2002, including Carolee Schneemann's famous *Meat Joy* (1964) and Jannis Kounellis's *Horses* (1969) with its twelve horses [**87**]. (Abramović participated in this tendency when, in 2005, she performed *Seven Easy Pieces* at New York's Guggenheim Museum, which involved her re-performing works by the likes of Acconci and Beuys.) In being re-enacted, events which had once derived their impetus from being live were rendered doubly 'historical'.[27] (It is telling that Jeremy Deller's *The Battle of Orgeave* [**129**] of the previous year had actually used the restaging of history as its raison d'être.) In the hands of artists such as Ostojić, performance was now made identical with lived experience. At the same time, questions of sexual and/or gender identity, which had been at the forefront of art since the 1970s, acquired a renewed intensity.

Gay identity was at the centre of many works of the period. Certain male performers—such as the American Ron Athey and the Italian-born British artist Franko B—ratcheted up the self-inflicted bodily pain that had characterized 1970s Body Art in harrowing performances. For instance, Franko B's *I Miss You*, performed in Tate Modern's turbine hall in 2003, saw him walking naked along a catwalk, surrounded by paparazzi as well as spectators, as blood from vents in his arms flowed over both his flabby, white-painted body and the white sheets spread beneath him. However, it was clear that the masochistic excesses of such actions were rooted not in aesthetic experimentation, as was often the case in 1970s performance, but in the day-to-day emotional sufferings that were inseparable from non-normative gender positionalities: Franko B's performance powerfully underlined this vulnerability. Emphasizing their links to his lifestyle, Athey's gruelling performances, dating back to the early 1990s, which involved the self-insertion of multiple needles, often took place in gay clubs as opposed to galleries.

The mutability of gender identity is especially well exemplified by the work of the Canadian artist Cassils. Transgender embodiment has been an area of political contestation since the turn of the millennium, sex reassignment (often involving surgery) having been legalized in Britain in 2004. Cassils has made the troubling of conventional signifiers of masculinity and femininity—which, for Cassils, has involved the development of a transgender identity without recourse to medical intervention or the adoption of a male Christian name—the crux of powerful statements, in which the body becomes a sculptural object. In the *Becoming an Image* performance of 2012, which took place at the One National Archives, the largest LGBTQI archive in North America, spectators entered a blackout chamber. All they heard was the sound of Cassils pummelling what transpired to be a huge 2,000-pound (907-kilogram) block of clay placed at its centre. The artist's actions were spectrally lit by the occasional flashes of a camera, the only way

142 Cassils

Advertisement (Homage to Benglis), 2011

The title refers to a feminist provocation by the American sculptor Lynda Benglis, published in *Artforum* magazine in 1974, in which Benglis appeared naked in a mock advertising photograph, looking like a defiant porn star and holding a large double-headed latex dildo to her crotch. In Cassils's image, by contrast, the phallic musculature of Cassils's entire body substitutes for Benglis's borrowed phallus.

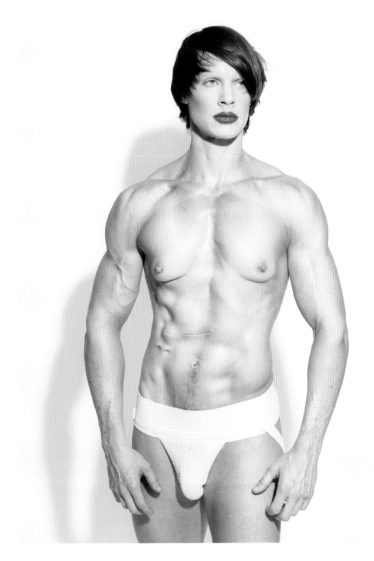

the performance was rendered visible, which in itself spoke of the absence of representations of transgender experience. The sheer effort involved in forcing a physical form to conform to an image was starkly conveyed, although whether Cassils was allegorizing bodily transformation or the social expectation of normativity—given that the piece partly responded to episodes of violence against transgendered people—was left open.

Cassils's strenuous fashioning of bodily identity took a further turn in *Cuts: A Traditional Sculpture* (2011), a durational performance project involving bodybuilding techniques and nutritional discipline, which partly responded to an earlier work by Eleanor Antin. In the piece Cassils virtually sculpted their body to produce a beefcake transmasculine form. Carried out over six months, partly at the legendary Gold's Gym in Santa Monica, it involved the artist building up some 23 pounds (10.4 kilograms) of muscle in a twenty-three-week period. A remarkable photograph, titled *Advertisement (Homage to Benglis)*, was taken on the 160th day of this durational project when the artist was at peak mass gain [**142**]. Cassils's image, in which the artist appropriated masculinity by donning a white, well-stuffed jockstrap, was redolent of the porn consumed by gay men, a connotation which Cassils deliberately undercut when, along with fashion photographer and collaborator Robin Black, the artist published the photograph in the webzine *LadyFace/ManBody*. The lipstick on Cassils's 'lady face' now became a subtle signal for men to reread the image and discover a woman's body within it. In challenging the assumptions of even a non-normatively defined (gay) audience, Cassils implicitly argued for the artist's sovereign right to gender self-determination.

Aesthetic trends: relational art

As we have seen, the globalized and identity-based practices of the post-2000 years elude stylistic categorization. The notion of performance, for instance, falls short of conveying the deep biopolitical or identitarian investments of Tanja Ostojić or Cassils. Is it possible, though, to discern any overarching aesthetic tendencies in the period? One significant strand emerged from the ideas developed by the French curator Nicolas Bourriaud in his *Traffic* exhibition (Musée d'Art Contemporain, Bordeaux, 1996) and then in his book *Relational Aesthetics* of 1998. He argued that the most distinctive art of the late 1990s—in line with the work of artists he supported such as Pierre Huyghe, Liam Gillick, and Rirkrit Tiravanija—was committed to forging a new relationship with its audience. In a world in which 'the social bond has turned into a standardised artefact', he argued for an art that took as its theoretical horizon 'the realm of human interaction and its social context'.[28] Paradigmatic examples of art that 'tightens the space of relations' would be works by the Argentinian-born Rirkrit Tiravanija. In an early piece of 1992, at 303 Gallery, New York, he moved everybody, director included, out of the main gallery spaces, set up a temporary kitchen in the storeroom, and dedicated himself to cooking curries for visitors, displaying the remnants of meals when he was not in residence. Three years later, in *Tomorrow is Another Day* at the Kölnischer Kunstverein in Cologne, he reconstructed his entire apartment as an independent, self-sufficient building within the gallery space and invited the public to inhabit it, cooking food, using the bathroom, and so forth.

Arguably nothing particularly new was involved here. As already noted, Gordon Matta-Clark had made the cooking of food for friends an artistic activity in the early 1970s. However, given that much turn-of-the-millennium art projected political despair, Bourriaud struck a reassuringly humanist note: 'It seems more pressing to invent possible relations with our neighbours...than to bet on happier tomorrows.'[29] Dialogue became a medium in itself. The British artist, writer, and curator Liam Gillick, for instance, set up spaces that, in terms of their decor, mimicked anodyne conference rooms, his Plexiglas screens shrewdly referencing the minimalism of Don Judd. Rather than being locations where managerial decisions were reached, his environments invited permanently open-ended negotiation around questions of aesthetics, politics, and related issues. Gillick saw himself as an enabler; his work functioned, he said, like the light in a fridge—'It only works when there is someone there to open the fridge door.'[30]

Gillick's work might be seen as a return to conceptualist or Fluxus strategies. However, in a 2002 publication, Bourriaud extended his ideas to suggest that significant new technical trends accompanied the rise of relationality. Using a model of 'post-production', he linked the figure of the relational artist to the DJ and the computer programmer, people who 'remix available forms and make use of *data*'. Rather than 'producing', artists now recycled, processes which were also given a moral inflection: 'Art challenges passive culture, composed of merchandise and consumers. It makes the form and cultural objects of our daily lives *function*.'[31] Such rhetoric heralded a wide range of art practices which reclaimed and repurposed socio-cultural forms. On the one hand, there were socially engaged/activist projects such as Jeanne van Heeswijk's transformation of a disused shopping mall in Rotterdam into a cultural centre for local residents (*De Strip*, 2001–4) or the activities of the Danish artists' group Superflex, one of whose projects was *Superkilen* (Copenhagen), an urban park project, opened in 2012, which involved the multinational population living in the vicinity of the park nominating features for it (park benches, trees, etc.) from their countries of origin. On the other hand, there were conceptually dense projects such as those of the French artist Pierre Huyghe. In *Streamside Day* (2003) he conceived of a fictitious rural community based in a newly created US village, 'Streamside Knolls', located next to the Hudson River. The artist envisaged the community celebrating its inauguration (along with its myth of origins) in an event which would take place on the same day annually (photographs of the inaugural ceremony, including printed schedules announcing the consumption of 'Stream Day Cake', were included as part of an associated exhibition). Projected into the future, the ceremony would actualize the fiction of the community whilst failure to repeat the celebration would bring about its cessation. The artwork therefore set up an auto-generative system, analogous to the way a social organism evolves.[32]

However esoteric some of its offshoots, relational art was often thought to be synonymous with social activism (as with Superflex). Such activism might be seen as responding to the old avant-garde dream of a *rapprochement* between art and life, but arguably, in seeking Bourriaud's goal of social 'coexistence', it lacked tension. This was certainly the objection raised by the British critic Claire Bishop, who pointed out that whatever dialogue

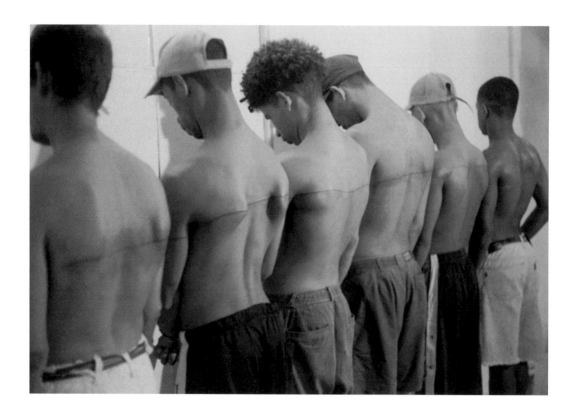

Tiravanija's cooking event managed to facilitate largely took place among art-world insiders. By contrast, she asserted that the best relational art possessed an unresolved, antagonistic dimension.[33] One of her examples was Jeremy Deller's re-enactment of the 'Battle of Orgreave' [129], as discussed in Chapter 8, which, rather than being affirmative, she saw as productively paradoxical: 'both politically legible and utterly pointless: It summoned the experiential potency of political demonstrations but only to expose a wrong seventeen years too late.'[34] Bishop also championed the practice of the earlier-mentioned Santiago Sierra. In a series of notorious works in the late 1990s Sierra had paid workers to carry out tasks for him. A representative example would be *250 cm Line Tattooed on Six Paid People* (1999), an event staged in Havana, in which the artist tattooed a line across the backs of six men who, largely resistant to the idea but in need of money, were paid $30 for their compliance [143]. Critics argued that such work brazenly reinforced the exploitative conditions of labour under capitalism: the men were paid low wages whilst Sierra accrued both real and cultural capital within the art world. Furthermore, he had located the project outside Europe as though underlining its abusive dimension. Alternatively, it might be argued that Sierra simply trained a spotlight on the inequalities intrinsic to the way both global art and labour operate.

Sierra's practice sits interestingly alongside that of Francis Alÿs, a Belgian-born artist who chose to live in Mexico from 1986, producing work that often reflected on European values from within a different culture. In 2002, with the help of assistants, Alÿs realized one of the most poetic artworks of the new

250 cm Line Tattooed on Six Paid People, 1999

This piece demonstrates how a supposedly neutral aesthetic entity (a line) can be implicated in the social power relations of the everyday world. In 1998 Sierra produced another key work focusing ironically on the utilization of (low-paid) human labour in the realization of an aesthetic gesture. In *Eight People Paid to Be in Cardboard Boxes*, carried out in Guatemala City, Sierra presented eight huge Minimalist-style cubes, in each of which sat a worker who was paid 9 dollars for four hours of sitting. In 2000 the artist produced a work in Berlin titled *Six People Who Are Not Allowed to be Paid for Sitting in Cardboard Boxes*. On this occasion the hidden human components of the work were asylum seekers who, under German law, could not be paid for their participation. Such pieces assert that aesthetics can no longer be pursued in a social vacuum.

millennium when, in Ventanilla, a new town north of Lima, Peru, some 500 manual labourers were asked to form a line and, with the aid of shovels, displace a 1,640-foot (500-metre) sand dune a matter of inches (centimetres) from its original position, the poignant title of the piece being *When Faith Moves Mountains*. Alÿs himself noted that the motto underlying the piece was 'maximum effort, minimum result', suggesting that the piece allegorized a social situation in Latin America, where 'minimal reforms are achieved through massive collective action'.[35] The workers in this piece had given their labour voluntarily, joining together to realize a vision: their recompense was spiritual or communitarian. Sierra's work cynically rebuts this kind of mysticism, underlining the fact that relations of production are never innocent, even when visionary sensibility is involved. His very use of the line as a motif in the tattooing piece is telling. The line, of course, was isolated for attention in numerous post-war art gestures: as noted earlier, Manzoni had put lines of various lengths in canisters in the early 1960s and the Land Artist Richard Long had produced a line 'by walking' in 1967.[36] Sierra, however, turns the line into something that no longer functions within an economy of artistic form but has become an indelible mark on socialized bodies. Just as Alÿs had ironically invoked the massive American Land Art projects of the 1970s with his piece in Peru, Sierra looks back to the Performance Art of the same period, especially that of Chris Burden, where self-inflicted harm was involved [99]. Sierra, though, reveals that art, like business or torture, can harm others. He represents the antithesis of relational art's utopianism.

Post-medium/return to medium

Although relational art represented a distinct trend in postmillennial art, the artistic exploration of 'relations' hardly represented a new medium to work in. What can be said then about artists' attentiveness to the notion of 'medium' during this period? As noted towards the end of Chapter 7, traditional categorizations of art forms according to medium-specificity (painting, sculpture, installation, and so on) had broken down with the rejection of Modernism. Disciplinary promiscuity was the order of the day: since the 1980s art-college departments such as painting, sculpture, film, and photography had often merged. But to what extent could or should art focus on its own technical means?

With the millennium approaching, the *October* critic Rosalind Krauss had observed that art was now being created in a 'post-medium condition'—a situation largely ushered in by conceptualism—but she also made a valiant attempt to rescue the idea of medium. Acknowledging that medium-specificity had largely been debased by the reduction of painterly problems in the post-Greenberg tradition to catchphrases such as 'flatness', she redefined medium as 'a set of conventions derived from (but not identical to) the material conditions of a given support'.[37] Using this idea, Krauss asserted that the artists she favoured had virtually invented their own 'technical supports': for example, Ed Ruscha had used the automobile as his support: in his *Every Building on Sunset Strip* (1966) each image of the titular location in the photographic strips at the top and bottom of the associated fold-out book had been shot from a moving van. The aesthetic structure of the work thus followed from its technical means.[38] According to this view, rather than being part of an ongoing aesthetic direction, medium-specificity is something that is continually rediscovered. However, Krauss was still searching for a self-reflexive, or 'recursive', basis for art—a means to make secure judgements of value—and her criticism primarily served to bookend Modernism. A return to medium-specificity was indeed one of the characteristics of post-millennium art, but it took place aside from the formal strictures of modernist aesthetics.

The example of painting is fascinating in this respect. By the end of the 1990s, painting, having long been relegated in importance, regained its status within advanced art, as was reflected in its increased value at auction. Possibly its renewed status paralleled shifts in social processes. One historian has argued that painting's prioritization of the personal touch of the artist had a renewed prestige as Western economies became increasingly geared towards our 'cognitive and affective capacities', with 'lifestyle' becoming more central to new social-media forms such as Twitter, Instagram, and Facebook. According to this view, paintings have again become desirable as objects which enshrine personal modes of interaction; they allow for levels of bodily and cognitive intimacy and immediacy which is lacking from, say, video or installation art.[39] This might chime with the nostalgic *fin-de-siècle* mood discussed in Chapter 8, suggesting that authorial presence—the *bête noir* of advanced post-1960s art—has some new, almost consolatory, role.

However, painting has actually renewed itself simply by *absorbing* the lessons of the readymade, institutional critique, conceptualism, and so forth. In a survey of the enormous variety of modes of painting that existed at the millennial moment—many of which incorporated conceptualist idioms—the American critic Barry Schwabsky argued that painting has become 'knowingly gratuitous', no longer concerned with modernist or even post-modernist protocols and more preoccupied with issues of style. In this situation, which at one point he characterizes as 'mannerist', painting becomes highly eclectic: 'A painting is not only a painting but also the representation of an idea about painting.' Released from the obligation to respond to any zeitgeist, it is concerned, Schwabsky says, 'with how to use the materials, methods, concepts or traditions of painting to make a work that should not necessarily be called a painting. *What* it is will then merge from *how* it is.'[40]

The countless ways in which painting has been rejuvenated is a massive topic, but the centrality of two figures, whose work dates back to the late 1980s, should initially be mentioned. The first of these, the Belgian-born Luc Tuymans, appropriately registers ambivalence about painting's raison d'être. Accepting that the practice of painting is out of date, his paintings are entirely predicated on a principle of belatedness. He continues to work with traditional materials but his signature style—washed-out muddy colour, rigid and apparently amateurish drawing, fragmentary form—encodes an irresolution both towards the effectiveness of painting as such and its capacity to express meanings.

Based on second-hand visual sources (photographs, films, or TV) and ranging widely in subject matter from portraits to banal objects such as Christmas decorations, Tuymans's work alights disconcertingly on highly charged themes. In *Recherches ('Investigations')* (1989), for instance, he offered a series of three small, notational images of a lampshade, a blurred image of a tooth, and a window onto a laboratory—each derived from objects at museums at former Nazi concentration camps. The partiality of the imagery seemed to metaphorize the discontinuities and failures of memory as well as the inability of the painterly medium to adequately negotiate such imagery. In this respect his work stands in counterpoint to Richter's large Baader-Meinhof-related paintings [111] which, although irresolute in terms of fusing painting and photography, had represented an ironic form of contemporary history painting. By contrast, Tuymans had no faith in painting's public function. In exhibitions such as *Heimat* (Zeno X gallery, Antwerp, 1996) and *Mwana Kitoko—Beautiful White Man* (Venice Biennale, 2001) he showed himself capable of a highly elliptical commentary on the politics of his native Belgium, dealing with Flemish nationalism and Belgian imperial rule in the Congo respectively. It is telling, though, that when he was featured in *Documenta 11*, rather than produce the kind of mordant response to the previous year's terrorist attack in New York expected of him by critics, he produced an enormous traditional still-life painting, saying, 'The attacks [of 9/11] were also an assault on aesthetics. That gave me the idea of reacting with a sort of anti-picture, with an idyll, albeit an inherently twisted one.'[41]

If Tuymans projects a distanced, self-effacing relationship to painting, Marlene Dumas, a South African-born artist who has lived in Holland since the mid-1970s, has a more engaged and traditionally expressive relationship with the métier. Like Tuymans, though, her work reflects, ambivalently, on second-hand photographic source materials, focusing characteristically on pornographic images, naked children, and black women (the latter evoking memories of apartheid). Her use of thinned-down and smudged paint allows her to express a frequently sensual relationship with her subjects. In *Models* (1994), for instance, she presented a series of 100 identically sized drawings of faces of diverse women, some of whom were indeed *models*—Brigitte Bardot and Claudia Schiffer—whilst others had been featured in a book titled *Portraits of the Insane*. As 'models' for both Dumas personally and for the process of drawing/painting, these women's faces became luminous repetitive ovals, variously inflected by the artist's touch, the ink spreading into the wet ground of each drawing as though registering the artist's empathy, adoration, or desire. A relationship with Richter's practice is again discernible: in a powerful painting titled *Stern* (2004), Dumas made use of precisely the same photograph of the lifeless Ulrike Meinhof that Richter had used in his *Dead* of 1998 [111]. Dumas's depiction, however, had a strangely erotic edge; the critic Adrian Searle spoke of the darkness above the bleached, upturned face, 'flowing in, to course down the open throat and flood the body with death.'[42] In a related painting from a year earlier, titled *The Kiss* [144], Dumas made use of the famous image of the dead woman slumped on the floor of her shower in Alfred Hitchcock's film *Psycho*. Whilst the actress Janet Leigh's eye had been wide open in the original still, Dumas gently closed it in her painted version, turning the flicked brushmark into part of a sequence of lines that stood also for the woman's eyebrow and the hairs plastered to her forehead.

Both Tuymans and Dumas use photographic sources. In this respect they follow on from the ironic postmodern photo-painting discussed in

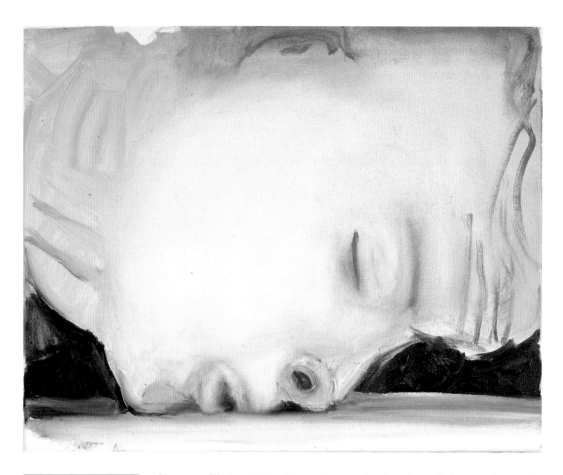

144 Marlene Dumas
The Kiss, 2003

Dumas's sensual painterly touch pervades the entire image. This tactile dimension is further underlined when we appreciate that the depicted woman - rather than being lifeless (as in the film still from which the image is derived) - could be understood as embracing the surface which her lips touch (the title, of course, is 'The Kiss'). The act of 'kissing' might even be equated, at a metaphorical level, with the touch of the artist's brush.

Chapter 7. Their relationship to the grand painterly traditions of the past is, however, more intrinsically respectful. As already noted, other modes of painting since 2000 have evinced an impatience with the associations of the easel-picture metamorphosing into various forms of object and practice. A particularly interesting location for experimentation has been Glasgow. As a city, Glasgow has vied with London since the early 1990s as a centre of art activity, the Environmental Art course at its prestigious School of Art having nurtured a remarkable generation of neo-conceptualists (including Ross Sinclair, Roderick Buchanan, Jacqueline Donachie Christine Borland, Nathan Coley, Douglas Gordon, and Martin Boyce). This conceptual tradition inflected the work of a group of painters who emerged around and after 2000. Louise Hopkins, for instance, painted on readymade supports such as wallpaper fabric, sheets of music, or maps, patiently duplicating or cancelling the pre-given information underneath. In one of a series of song-sheet paintings, *Songsheet (Can't Buy Me Love)* of 1998, for example, she painstakingly painted over the existing musical notations and lyrics on the page in white paint, preserving their exact configurations. All that was left was a seemingly blank sheet of paper covered with a slightly raised, near-invisible set of signs. Both the apparent blankness of the page and the braille-like associations of the overpainted signs argue against the work's visuality; braille, of course, connotes blindness. Similarly, the piece seems to

Richard Wright's wall paintings, and linked works on paper, are enormously varied, but often hark back to the Op and psychedelic art of the 1960s. Formative influences, testifying to his range of sources, include the record-sleeve art of the American West Coast designer Rick Griffin (notably the Grateful Dead's *Aoxomoxoa* of 1969) and the visionary deluge drawings of Leonardo da Vinci. In his wall paintings Wright often reacts intuitively to the atmosphere of a particular location. Sarah Lowndes elaborates: 'This is what Richard described as the "smoke detector" aspect of his work, in which he translates the shadows and stains of everyday use into something captivating. A poignant example of this came in the BQ exhibition in Berlin. The apartment had recently been vacated by a woman tenant who had lived there for over fifty years. It was empty of furniture but full of traces...including a discernible faded rectangle on the floor where the bed had once been situated. This prosaic form was given a memorial quality when Richard framed it with a fine outline of gold leaf, evoking associations of sleep, dreams and death.' (Sarah Lowndes, 'Learned by Heart: The Paintings of Richard Wright', in *Richard Wright*, Gagosian Gallery/Rizzoli, New York, 2009, p. 58.)

cancel out another sensory dimension—sound—as the Beatles melody conjured in the spectator's mind is symbolically rendered mute by the operations carried out in the picture. A dense cluster of conceptual possibilities are thus reconciled with the elegant nullity of the painted object.

This kind of conceptual painting is exemplified in a different way by Richard Wright. Building on the kind of wall-drawing practice developed by Sol LeWitt in the 1960s [70], Wright's interventions in architectural spaces (usually galleries) saw him carefully enhancing the atmosphere or character of the spaces by incorporating discrete painted areas in completely unexpected locations, such as ceiling wells or corners. From 2005, Wright started to use gold leaf or silver leaf as materials, introducing a sensual, immaterial shimmer to patterns which were already complex. His gold-leaf wall-painting for the 2009 Turner Prize exhibition in London, measuring some 13 by 23 feet (4 by 7 metres), was prepared for via processes of fresco technique such as pouncing (transferring a design to the wall via pouncing dust through a pricked drawing) which harked back to the Renaissance. This sense of a return to historical models was reinforced by the often kaleidoscopic repeat patterns used in this and other paintings of the period whose associations lurched from baroque ornamentation to the apocalyptic skies of the English Romantic painter John Martin to the psychedelic graphics of 1960s LP covers [145].

The hallucinatory dimension of certain of Wright's work connects it to that of an apparently dissimilar artist from Glasgow, Jim Lambie, who provides a further spin on the possibilities of painting. Rather than walls, Lambie painted on floors. Coming from a background in which music was as important as visual art (he was, at various times, a member of a post-punk band and a DJ in Glasgow's club scene), Lambie gave his floor-painting installations the generic title 'ZOBOP'. These involved the artist and a group of helpers applying strips of brightly coloured vinyl tape to the floors of spaces in such a way that the perimeter of the space was reiterated towards the middle, thereby producing highly idiosyncratic 'ripples'. The conceptual principles of Frank Stella's seminal 1960s paintings, in which internal structure was deduced from external shape, were updated to produce what one commentator described as a 'vertiginous disco floor laced with hallucinogenics'.[43] Such was its success as decor that by 2015 Lambie's work would be installed in the time-honoured bastion of British fine art, the Royal Academy, his tape flowing around the vestibule and down the stairs at that year's 247th annual Summer Exhibition like multi-coloured lava.

It should be clear from this that painting has cheerfully migrated from easel to environment but has preserved its identity as a medium. This situation has meant that painters of a traditional cast have found revitalized conditions for their practice. In the Glasgow context, Carol Rhodes has extended her conceptual approach to develop a melding of figurative and abstract painterly modes in imaginary aerial views which sometimes double as bodily metaphors. Merlin James has evinced a trenchant regard for traditional painterly problems, readdressing the range of genres in the art-historical canon but choosing to make small-scale and seemingly unprepossessing pictures which allude knowingly to past artists. In the broader

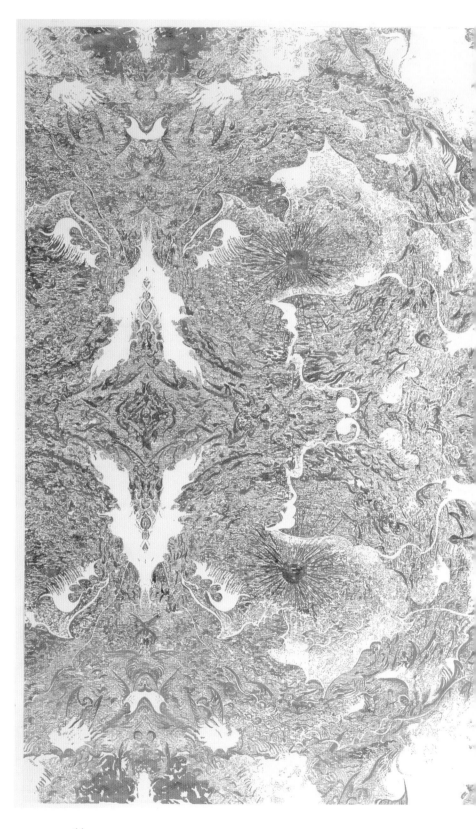

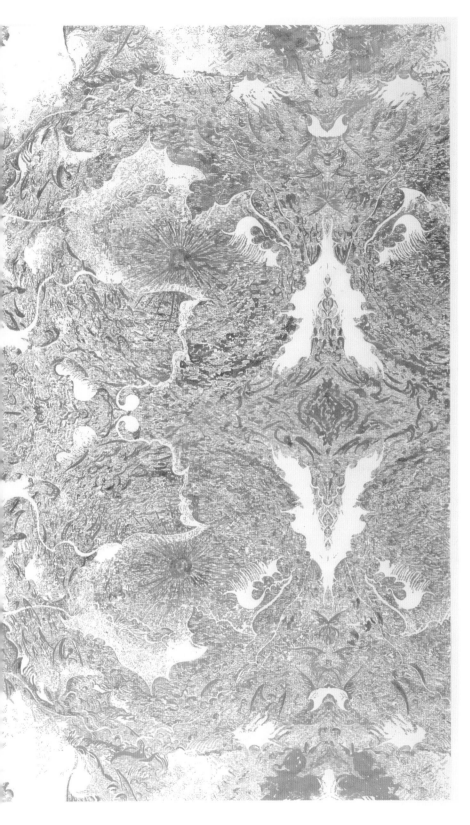

international context, beyond figures such as Tuymans and Dumas, the Trinidad-based Scottish painter Peter Doig and the American John Currin have continued, unapologetically, to deal with painterly issues: the former producing enigmatic landscapes in which abstraction and figuration pull against each other; the latter revelling in a kitsch and politically incorrect revival of the polished realism of the likes of Lucas Cranach or Otto Dix, with ageing women and cheesecake nudes as his subjects. At times such artists seem to have entered into a self-willed amnesia regarding the intractable problems of postmodernist aesthetics. They, along with the numerous other painters re-embracing the notion of 'medium', summon up the almost redemptive idea that it might still be possible to make ambitious *pictures*.

'Contemporary art': the sense of an ending

Having looked at the main tendencies of the period, what can we say about the overall character of art since 2000? Are we still too close to it? A snapshot of two major exhibitions of 2009 and 2012 may be useful here. In the catalogue for the *Tate Triennial* exhibition of 2009, which included some twenty-eight British artists, its curator Nicolas Bourriaud argued that a principle of 'Altmodernity' was in operation. His neologism had its basis in the concept of otherness and amounted to the acknowledgement of 'a multitude of possibilities, of alternatives to a single route'. Interestingly, he did not abandon the idea of modernism, but envisaged a new synthesis of modernism and postcolonialism. Altmodernism, he asserted, 'embodies a cultural exodus, an escape from the confines of nationalism and identity-tagging'.[44] Beyond such brave words, Bourriaud's vision was not far removed from that of Okwui Enwezor's curatorship of *Documenta 11* (2002) in terms of an emphasis on nomadism and displacement. Bourriaud particularly championed the globality encapsulated by the English-born conceptualist Simon Starling who, he enthused, 'relocates a piece of furniture designed by Francis Bacon from one continent to another by radio waves'.[45]

In contrast to the Tate show, Kassel's *Documenta 13*, of 2012, was an enormous, sprawling affair, with some 220 international artists and additional locations in Kabul, Alexandria, Bamiyan (Afghanistan), and Banff. This time the mood of the curator Carolyn Christov-Bakargiev's catalogue introduction was downbeat. Much of the work in the show, she asserted, was intentionally 'uncomfortable, incomplete, nervously lacking'. Locating the exhibition within worrying global conditions—massive inequalities of wealth, 'the subjugation of economy, science and nature to financial systems'— she identified themes of ecological sustainability and human interaction as key artistic preoccupations. *Documenta*, she felt, was pledged to an act of remembering; after all, an attempt to deal with the trauma of World War II had been its initial rationale. 'We are told', she said, thinking of the philosopher Giorgio Agamben, 'that we live in an age of permanent crisis, emergency and exception.'[46] The implication was that *Documenta*, and the art contained therein, could function as an act of conscience, warning against possible historical repetition.

Both of these shows argued against any progressive ethos, let alone grand narrative, in the art of our times. How, though, might the period as a whole be defined? It is widely asserted that we live in an era of 'contemporary art'.

Concurring with the premise contained in the title of this book, Terry Smith argues that modern art was the art of a period that is now 'substantially complete' and that the concept of 'contemporary art' accurately designates the art of our times. Smith is certainly helpful in discerning three interrelated currents of contemporary art: first, the art that has benefited from neoliberalism and globalized capital (which he splits into two categories—'retro-sensationalist', referring to art such as that of the yBas, and 'Remodern' referring to the art of late modern masters such as Richard Serra and Gerhard Richter); second, the art of postcolonialism and global diffusion, in which local and international tendencies are in constant dialogue; and third, more obscurely, the art of younger artists who, linked in 'mediated interactivity', seek to grasp the 'nature of time, place, media and mood today'.[47] Brushing aside the common-sense view that today's contemporaneity will be tomorrow's history, he argues that we have now, effectively, entered into a state of continuous contemporaneity. 'Never before', he argues, 'has art been made with such a sense that currency and contingency is all there is in the world, all that there may ever be.' On his view the most characteristic contemporary art is replete with 'doubt-filled gestures…tentative projections' and is broadly characterized by a 'multiplicity of relationships between being and time'.[48]

One wonders, though, how substantially this model of contemporaneity differs from Baudelaire's 1863 construction of *modernity*, whose artistic agent 'sets up house in the heart of the multitude, amid the ebb and flow of movement, in the midst of the fugitive and the infinite'.[49] Here too there is a collapse of temporalities. It may well be that the global spread of art away from the previous centres of 'modernity' has meant that the modernist sense of temporal instability has had to become reconciled with a new apprehension of *spatiality*. (There are analogies here with David Harvey's thinking on the 'condition of postmodernity'.[50]) Possibly this accounts for a pervasive mood of anxiety or restlessness, but it does not necessarily add up to a new historical phase and 'Contemporary Art' amounts to little more than a tautological pointer to that which is currently being produced.

Much as Smith's attempt to separate the modern from the contemporary seems problematic, the 'after modern art' of this book's argument demarcates an aftermath phase (largely comprising the doctrinal Modernism of Greenberg, the reaction against this ethos, and the rise of postmodernism) that does indeed appear to be reaching a conclusion. The conclusion, though, is to the notion of 'Western art' on which this book has been predicated. A secure concept of the 'West', as applied to art, arguably began breaking down after the fall of the Berlin Wall in 1989, when the idea of what had formerly been the 'East' had suddenly to be rethought (the former separation between East and West may anyway have been more porous than hitherto assumed). The destruction of New York's Twin Towers in 2001 came, if anything, as the decisive blow to the idea of a monolithic West. Just as the modernist/postmodernist debates of Western art seem to have played themselves out concurrent with the global decentring of the West, so the cohesiveness of the West as a political/cultural entity, at least on the model that has existed since 1945, seems to be in transition. At the risk of sounding overly dramatic, there is in the air 'the sense of an ending' or at least a reconfiguration. A new phase of American and European art may well arise from this, but its conceptual parameters will need to be reconsidered.[51]

Looking back on the history tracked in this book, it is worth reprising the notion that the Duchampian paradigm seems most consistently to have been in play. This is not to stake everything on one man's work. It is to argue that the significance of the implications arising from one practice achieved a consensus of agreement; in this sense 'Duchampian' designates a *modus operandi* rather than a concept of 'influence'. Various Duchampian themes have been prominent in the preceding narrative: the readymade; the dematerialized and the conceptual; gender and identity indeterminacy; the offhand and the humorous. More recently, Bourriaud's concept of 'post-production' borrowed heavily from the 'assisted readymades' of Duchamp. The Internet artist Vuk Cosic even asserted that digital artists were 'Duchamp's ideal children'.[52] It comes as no surprise, therefore, that in 2004 a group of 500 art-world professionals, in a poll conducted by Gordon's (then sponsors of the Turner Prize), voted Duchamp's *Fountain* readymade (1917) the most influential art work of the twentieth century.[53]

This book has equally argued, however, for intense social and political contestation in post-1945 art, especially regarding the reception of US Modernism in Europe, which falls outside of the Duchampian model (Duchamp often professed an indifference to hard politics) and leans more towards the traditions of Beuys or the French situationists. Taking stock in 2017, artists seem faced more urgently than ever with issues that call for ethical, social, and political responsiveness. Concerns regarding American cultural hegemony are perhaps reduced, but renewed nationalisms, the oppressive consolidation of power and capital in advanced technological systems, and planetary neglect are pressing realities for artists, as the curator of *Documenta 13* asserted.

The overall director of 2017's *Documenta 14*, Adam Szymczyk, has taken this further recently by talking dramatically of planning the exhibition in the midst of 'catastrophes': 'the disastrous war in Syria and the continuing arrival of refugees, by land and sea, to Greece and southern Europe, and finally the dark rise of authoritarian rule, right wing rule, and fascism across the continent and the world at large.'[54] As the culmination of a trend towards the decentralizing of *Documenta* that had been apparent since the late 1990s, the 2017 iteration of the exhibition actually took place across two locations, Kassel and Athens, a pairing designed to demonstrate creative continuities between a city on the margins of Europe's economic centre and a city that had been brought to its knees as a result of the austerity measures introduced by European governments after the global economic downturn post-2008. With the exhibition starting earlier in Athens than Kassel, Szymczyk was able to assert: 'The classic time-space unity of an exhibition is...profoundly called into question here.'[55]

With such an example in mind, it is appropriate to talk of a reawakened sense of conscience in recent art. Scientists have talked over the last decade of the emergence, with the twentieth century, of the 'Anthropocene', an epoch in which human intervention on the Earth has altered biospheric conditions more substantially than in thousands of years previous. In this respect, the ethical commitments of relational/participatory art projects, such as the Danish group Superflex's development of alternative

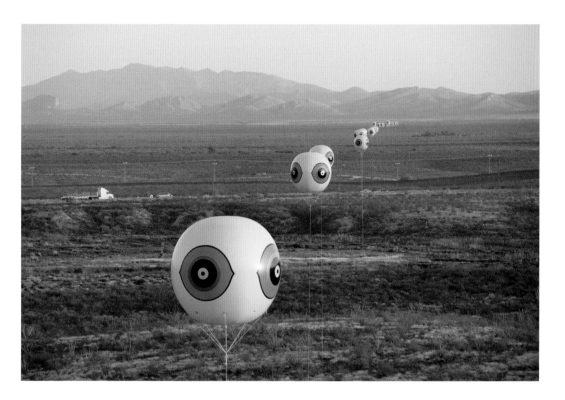

146 Postcommodity

Repellent Fence, 2015

Ironically prefiguring Donald Trump's campaign-trail talk of a US–Mexican wall a year later, Postcommodity's work resonates powerfully with the ongoing discourse around borders that has characterized art since 2000.

energy systems, have particular relevance. One of their innovations, *Supergas,* involved the development of a biogas derived from organic materials such as animal dung, which could be used to provide cheap, sustainable energy in areas of the planet depleted by deforestation; having first been used in 1997 in Tanzania, it has since been introduced in Cambodia (2001), Thailand (2002), Zanzibar (2007), and Mexico (2011).

Another artist collective, the three-man Postcommodity, drew attention, in a fascinating Land Art project of 2015, to the way in which indigenous communities have been forced apart by current political and societal divisions. Pointedly alluding, at least in its title, to Christo's comparatively apolitical *Running Fence* of 1976 (see Chapter 6), their *Repellent Fence* [**146**] consisted of some twenty-six 10-foot (3-metre) diameter balloons flown at about 100 feet (30 metres) above the ground at staggered points along a 2-mile (3.2 kilometre) route bisecting the US town of Douglas, Arizona, and the Mexican town of Agua Prieta, Sonora. The piece metaphorically 'lifted' the barrier that physically existed between the locations, symbolically restoring communitarian links and challenging stereotypical notions of criminality and violence that had affected the borderland's reputation. The eye motifs on the balloons on the one hand connoted surveillance (they were partly appropriated from a product designed to scare away predatory birds from gardens), whilst on the other echoing the ancient 'open eye' motif of the Native Americans (even the colouration of the balloons evoked traditional Indian medicine colours). Possessing something of the character of 1960s hippy art, the project evoked a holistic response to the land and its people at a time when the political rhetoric favoured division and mistrust.

Turning from the land to the city, projects of urban renewal or regeneration also show artists turning outwards rather than inwards. In 2015 Britain's Turner Prize was won by an eighteen-member collective titled Assemble which had been involved with a local community in renovating a cluster of ten tinned-up council-owned houses in the Granby Four Streets, Toxteth, Liverpool, an area that had fallen into severe decline. At a time when a lack of affordable housing was a national problem in Britain, the project—an exemplary fusion of art, architecture, and design practices—aided residents in restoring these properties for their own use at low cost. Assemble's Turner Prize exhibition consisted of a workshop in which prototypes and material tests for house fittings were displayed. An accompanying catalogue listed all of the available products which the Granby Four Streets' residents, in league with craftsmen, could materialize. Combining a do-it-yourself ingenuity worthy of the classic BBC TV children's programme *Blue Peter* with considerable design acumen, the products included benches and stools made from recycled timber, burned and charred to produce stark black/white contrasts, and cabinet handles and light pulls conjured from knobs of clay, smoke-fired to produce a range of mottled patterns [**147**].

Assemble's intervention may seem modest, but as well as exhibiting an exemplary environmentalism, it chimes with a socialist concern with the democratization of design in Britain that goes back to the nineteenth-century design reformer William Morris. In respect of the latter, a more wide-ranging political statement was made in 2013 by British artist Jeremy Deller, instigator of the aforementioned *Battle of Orgreave* (see Chapter 8). As part of his contribution to the Venice Biennale, Deller presented a symbolic blow against the leviathan of global capital in the form of an enormous blown-up photo-collage of William Morris in the process of hurling a yacht, owned by the Russian oligarch Roman Abramovich, into the waters of the city's lagoon. (Moored alongside the Giardini, the enormous yacht had previously been responsible for obscuring the view of the Biennale site.)

Beyond direct social or ethical engagement, current art practice has the symbolic or allegorical functions that art has always possessed. A couple of final examples of work by young artists, utilizing technology to reflect on the existential anxieties of our times, bears this out. First, the British video artist and writer Ed Atkins makes use of high-definition video and pre-existing film stock to produce dreamily alienating digital productions. The 'actors' in Atkins's videos are CGI (computer-generated imagery) avatars—often uncanny surrogates or stand-ins for the artist himself—which are animated using motion capture, producing a derealizing, staccato effect. *Ribbons* (2014), for example, sees a menacing, laddish avatar, mouthing emotionally ambiguous phrases ('Help me communicate without debasement, darling') amid fragments of blurred imagery (such as beer glasses), and the occasional emergence of isolated words on-screen ('REBUTTAL!'). Atkins's use of avatars speaks of the disturbing usurpation of human functions by technology. *Safe Conduct*, a three-channel video work shown as part of an installation at the National Gallery of Denmark in 2016, deals with a common contemporary experience—the airport security check. Mimicking the CGI effects used in security check-in videos, the work features one of Atkins's signature avatars, who peels the skin from his face, layer after layer,

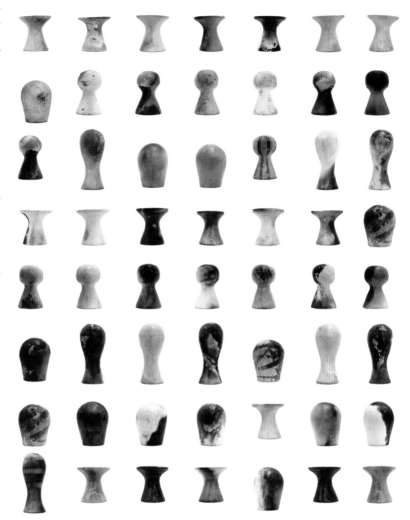

like a series of masks. He then places a series of objects in the various trays on the security conveyor belt: his spleen, his intestines, as well as his laptop. (The animations of the Czech surrealist Jan Svankmajer, in which shockingly graphic visceral images are inserted into patently artificial animated scenarios, are a clear precedent.) This installation, in which the video is accompanied by a looped recording of Ravel's already-repetitive *Bolero*, is described by the artist as 'a computer-generated-slapstick-horror-ballet-security-video'.[56] The overall effect of the burlesque is to lay bare the technological 'violence' (to invoke Atkins's terms) underlying the rituals we have become inured to.

Second, and by contrast to Atkins, the Canadian-born, British-based artist Melanie Gilligan exploits the conventions of a more widely familiar form of entertainment—television—producing Orwellian science-fiction fantasies in the form of soap-opera-style narratives which are played out simultaneously on a series of monitors. Viewers thus have to switch between them to assemble overarching meanings for themselves. In one work, *Popular Unrest* (2010), the story concerns a collective immaterial principle called 'The Spirit' which binds people together rather like religion but which also materializes occasionally as a punitive force in the form of a stabbing knife, eliminating any opposition. As one commentator on the work observes: '[The spirit] exists more as an internalized and normalized relationship within ourselves than an external reality.'[57] It thereby allegorizes global capital, whose values have now become internalized to the extent that revolutionary opposition seems almost unimaginable. Eschewing the protest mentality underlying Deller's earlier-mentioned 2013 Venice intervention, and chiming in with the alienating mood of Atkins, Gilligan offers a bleak vision of political stasis. If conscience has figured as one pole of recent art, melancholy emerges as the other.

Works by the likes of Atkins and Gilligan reveal much about the way art currently functions. The pieces attempt to do what much of the advanced art of the post-1945 period attempted to do: to *say the unsayable*. This, as I intimated in the Introduction, would be art's difficult role, post-Auschwitz. Often the task was conceived as hard, highly specialized, solipsistic. Both artists in different ways, however, deal with one of the most urgent tasks facing contemporary artists: finding a means of undercutting the expectation of 'difficulty' that is so often levelled at current art practice. Their solutions involve hijacking the conventions of two of the most ubiquitous cultural forms of our age, computer videos in the case of Atkins and television in the case of Gilligan. In doing this, however, the artists risk entanglement in the very mechanisms they appear to oppose. Greenberg—the *éminence grise* behind the early stages of this book's narrative—thought that it would be necessary in the post-war period for art to strategically distance itself from mass culture, since art would only end up being compromised via such a process. To diehard critics of postmodernism, some of the art discussed in the last few chapters might bear this out. But how can advanced art retain ethical distance from an increasingly immersive social realm and yet speak to a mass audience that sees its language as remote, if not impenetrable? After modern art, this is the huge challenge confronting the art of the twenty-first century.

Notes

Introduction

1. Adorno, 'On Commitment', as reprinted in Charles Harrison and Paul Wood, *Art in Theory*, Oxford, 1992, p. 761.

Chapter 1. The Politics of Modernism: Abstract Expressionism and the European *Informel*

1. First published in translation in *Partisan Review*, vol. IV, no. 1, New York, Fall 1938, pp. 49–53.
2. Mark Rothko and Adolph Gottlieb, letter to *The New York Times*, 7 June 1943.
3. See Michael Leja, *Reframing Abstract Expressionism*, Yale, 1993, chs 2–4. Links to film noir are made on pp. 109–14.
4. Arthur Schlesinger: *The Vital Center*, Boston, 1962, p. 57. (Originally published Boston, 1949.)
5. See Leja, *Reframing*, p. 198.
6. See Serge Guilbaut, *How New York Stole the Idea of Modern Art*, Chicago, 1983, p. 242, note 50.
7. T. J. Clark, 'Jackson Pollock's Abstraction', in S. Guilbaut (ed.), *Reconstructing Modernism*, Cambridge, Mass., 1990, p. 180.
8. Guilbaut, *Reconstructing Modernism*, pp. 91 and 115.
9. Clement Greenberg, 'The Decline of Cubism', *Partisan Review*, March 1948, p. 369.
10. Guilbaut, 'Postwar Painting Games: The Rough and the Slick', in Guilbaut, *Reconstructing Modernism*, pp. 39–43.
11. Barnett Newman, in 'Frontiers of Space' (interview), in J. P. O'Neill (ed.), *Barnett Newman: Selected Writings and Interviews*, Berkeley, 1992, p. 251.
12. Greenberg, 'The Situation at the Moment', *Partisan Review*, January 1948.
13. Newman, 'The Sublime is Now', in O'Neill, *Barnett Newman*, p. 173.
14. Michel Tapié, *Un Art Autre où il s'agit de nouveaux dévidages du réel*, Paris, 1952.

15. Jean Dubuffet, quoted in Peter Selz, *Jean Dubuffet*, MoMA, New York, 1962, p. 64.
16. Ibid.
17. See, for instance, Melanie Klein, 'A Contribution to the Psychogenesis of Manic-Depressive States' (1935), in J. Mitchell (ed.), *The Selected Melanie Klein*, London, 1986, pp. 115–46.
18. For Guilbaut on Bataille see his 'Postwar Painting Games', *Reconstructing Modernism*, pp. 50–60, whilst for a counterargument see Sarah Wilson, 'Paris Post War: In Search of the Absolute', in *Paris Post War: Art and Existentialism 1945–55* (ex. cat.), Tate Gallery, 1993, pp. 27 and 45.
19. Mark Rothko, 'The Romantics were Prompted…', in R. Motherwell and H. Rosenberg (eds), *Possibilities*, no. 1, 1947/8, p. 84.
20. Robert Motherwell, quoted by Guilbaut, *Reconstructing Modernism*, p. 177.
21. Greenberg, 'Review of Exhibitions of Jean Dubuffet and Jackson Pollock', *The Nation*, 1 February 1947.
22. Published in *Partisan Review*, Fall 1939 and July/August 1940 respectively.
23. Greenberg, 'American-Type Painting', *Partisan Review*, Spring 1955.
24. Ibid.
25. Greenberg, 'The Present Prospects of American Painting and Sculpture', *Horizon*, October 1947.
26. See John O'Brian, *Clement Greenberg: The Collected Essays and Criticism*, vol. 3, Chicago, 1995, pp. xxxvi–xxxviii.
27. See Roszika Parker and Griselda Pollock, *Old Mistresses: Women, Art and Ideology*, London, 1981, pp. 145–51. See also Pollock's discussion of Frankenthaler, 'Killing Men and Dying Women', in F. Orton and G. Pollock, *Avant-Gardes and Partisans Reviewed*, Manchester, 1996, pp. 221–94.
28. Patrick Heron, 'The Ascendancy of London in the Sixties', *Studio International*, December 1966, pp. 280–1.

29. Ibid., p. 218.
30. Greenberg, 'Present Prospects'.
31. Edwin Denby, *The 1930s: Painting in New York*, New York, 1957. Quoted in Dore Ashton, *The Life and Times of the New York School*, London, 1972, p. 4.
32. See T. J. Clark, 'Clement Greenberg's Theory of Art', in F. Frascina (ed.), *Pollock and After*, London, 1985, pp. 47–63.
33. Ibid., p. 59.
34. Harold Rosenberg, 'The American Action Painters', *Art News*, December 1952.
35. Fred Orton, 'Action, Revolution and Painting', in Orton and Pollock, *Avant-Gardes*, p. 195. See also David Craven, *Abstract Expressionism as Cultural Critique* (Cambridge, 1999) for a discussion of continuing left-wing sympathies among the Abstract Expressionists in the 1950s and 1960s.
36. Allan Kaprow, 'The Legacy of Jackson Pollock', *Art News*, 57, no. 6, 1958.

Chapter 2. Duchamp's Legacy: The Rauschenberg–Johns Axis

1. Marcel Duchamp, 'The Creative Act', trans. in M. Sanouillet and E. Peterson, *Salt Seller*, New York, 1973.
2. John Cage, 'Experimental Music', in *Silence* (1971), London, 1980, p. 12.
3. See 'The Richard Mutt Case' in *The Blind Man*, no. 2, May 1917.
4. Leo Steinberg, 'Other Criteria', in *Other Criteria: Confrontations with Twentieth Century Art* (1972), Oxford, 1975, p. 88.
5. David Halberstam, *The Fifties*, New York, 1993, p. 501.
6. Brian O'Doherty, 'Rauschenberg and the Vernacular Glance', *Art in America*, September–October 1973.
7. Steinberg, 'Other Criteria', p. 90.
8. Robert Rauschenberg, letter to Betty Parsons, 18 October 1951, reproduced in Walter Hopps, *Robert Rauschenberg: The Early 1950s* (ex. cat.), Menil Collection/Houston, 1991, p. 230.
9. See my 'Questioning Dada's Potency', *Art History*, vol. 15, no. 3, September 1992. See also James Leggio, 'Robert Rauschenberg's "Bed" and the Symbolism of the Body', in *Essays on Assemblage*, MoMA, New York, 1992.
10. See Helen Molesworth, 'Before Bed', *October*, no. 63, Winter 1993, pp. 68–82.
11. Mary Douglas, *Purity and Danger: An Analysis of the Concepts of Pollution and Taboo*, London, 1966.
12. The term first appears to have been used by Robert Rosenblum in a review of an exhibition incorporating Rauschenberg and Johns at Castelli's gallery in May 1957.
13. William Seitz, *The Art of Assemblage* (ex. cat.), MoMA, New York, 1961, p. 87.
14. Allen Ginsberg, 'Howl' (1955), *Selected Poems*, Harmondsworth, 1996, p. 49.
15. See Laurie Monahan, 'Cultural Cartography: American Designs at the 1964 Venice Biennale', in Serge Guilbaut (ed.), *Reconstructing Modernism*, Cambridge, Mass., 1990, pp. 369–407.
16. William de Kooning, 'Content is a Glimpse' (interview with David Sylvester), *Locations*, 1, Spring 1963, pp. 45–8.
17. Clement Greenberg, 'After Abstract Expressionism', *Art International*, October 1962.
18. For close examination of the picture's surface see Fred Orton, *Figuring Jasper Johns*, London, 1994, pp. 125–7.
19. Moira Roth, 'The Aesthetics of Indifference', *Artforum*, November 1977, pp. 46–53.
20. Ibid., p. 51.
21. Orton, *Figuring Jasper Johns*, pp. 145–6.
22. For Duchamp's position on the readymades in the 1960s see William Camfield, *Marcel Duchamp: Fountain*, Menil Collection/Houston, 1989, pp. 81–99.
23. Duchamp, note 18 in P. Matisse (ed.), *Marcel Duchamp, Notes*, Boston, 1983.

Chapter 3. The Artist in Crisis: From Bacon to Beuys

1. John Russell, *Francis Bacon*, London, 1979, p. 10.
2. Georges Bataille, 'La Bouche' (The Mouth), *Documents*, Paris, no. 5, 1930, pp. 299–300.
3. Dawn Ades, 'Web of Images', in *Francis Bacon* (ex. cat.), Tate Gallery, London, 1985, pp. 13–15.
4. David Sylvester, *Interviews with Francis Bacon*, London, 1980, reprinted 1985, p. 17.
5. John Berger, 'Staying Socialist', *New Statesman and Nation*, 31 October 1959.
6. Jean-Paul Sartre, 'The Search for the Absolute', in *Alberto Giacometti: Sculptures, Paintings, Drawings*, Pierre Matisse Gallery, New York, 1948.
7. Jean Genet, 'L'atelier d'Alberto Giacometti', *Derrière Le Miroir*, June 1957, p. 7.
8. Jacques Lacan, *The Four Fundamental Concepts of Psycho-analysis*, London, 1977, pp. 72–3.
9. Antonin Artaud, 'Le Visage Humain' (manuscript version), as quoted by Agnes de la Beaumelle in M. Rowell (ed.), *Antonin*

Artaud: Works on Paper, MoMA, New York, 1996, p. 90.

10. See Rowell, *Antonin Artaud*, p. 13.

11. Peter Selz, *New Images of Man* (ex. cat.), MoMA, New York, 1959, p. 12.

12. Michel Foucault, *Les Mots et les Choses* (Paris, 1966), trans. as *The Order of Things*, London, 1989, p. 387.

13. Daniel Spoerri, *An Anecdoted Topography of Chance*, trans. M. Green, Atlas, London, 1995, p. 87.

14. Yves Klein, 'Le vrai devient réalité', *Zero*, Düsseldorf (1958–61), reprinted Cambridge, Mass., 1973, p. 88.

15. Yves Klein, 'Mon Livre', section published in *Yves Klein*, Musée National d'Art Moderne, Paris, 1983, p. 172.

16. Thierry de Duve, 'Yves Klein or the Dead Dealer', *October*, 49, Summer 1989.

17. Marcel Duchamp, note of 1914, as trans. in M. Sanouillet and E. Peterson (eds), *The Writings of Marcel Duchamp*, Oxford, 1973, p. 24. See also Gerald Silk, 'Myths and Meanings in Manzoni's 'Merda d'Artista'', *Art Journal*, Fall 1993, vol. 52, no. 3, pp. 65–75.

18. Benjamin Buchloh, 'Beuys: The Twilight of the Idol', *Artforum*, vol. 18, January 1980, pp. 39–40.

19. Beuys, quoted in Caroline Tisdall, *Joseph Beuys*, London, 1979, p. 17.

20. Tisdall, *Joseph Beuys*, p. 105.

21. See Caroline Tisdall, 'Beuys: Coyote', *Studio International*, July/August 1976, pp. 36–40.

22. Buchloh, 'Beuys', p. 38 and passim.

23. Georg Baselitz and Eugen Schönebeck, *Pandemonium 1*, Berlin, November 1961, trans. in *Georg Baselitz, Paintings 1960–83*, Whitechapel Gallery, London, 1983, p. 23.

Chapter 4. Blurring Boundaries: Pop Art, Fluxus, and their Effects

1. Thomas Crow, 'Modernism and Mass Culture in the Visual Arts', in his *Modern Art in the Common Culture*, New Haven and London, 1996, pp. 3–37.

2. Lawrence Alloway, 'The Long Front of Culture', *Cambridge Opinion*, no. 17, 1959.

3. Walter Benjamin's essay was first published in *Zeitschrift für Sozialforschung*, vol. V, no. 1, New York, 1936.

4. Richard Hamilton, 'Persuading Image', *Design*, February 1960, pp. 28–32.

5. Hamilton, 'An Exposition of he', *Architectural Design*, October 1962.

6. Hamilton, Letter to the Smithsons, 16 January 1957, in his *Collected Words*, London, 1982, p. 28.

7. Dick Hebdige, 'Towards a Cartography of Taste', *Block*, no. 8, 1983, pp. 54–68, and David Alan Mellor, 'A Glorious Techniculture', in D. Robbins (ed.), *The Independent Group: Postwar Britain and the Aesthetics of Plenty*, Cambridge, Mass., 1990, pp. 229–36.

8. Lawrence Alloway, 'The Development of British Pop', in L. Lippard (ed.), *Pop Art*, London, 1966, reprinted 1974, p. 66.

9. Theodor Adorno, 'On Commitment', trans. in A. Arato and E. Gebhardt (eds), *The Essential Frankfurt School Reader*, New York, 1978, p. 318.

10. See Kristine Stiles, 'Between Water and Stone: A Metaphysics of Acts', in *In the Spirit of Fluxus* (ex. cat.), Walker Art Center, Minneapolis, 1993, pp. 77–9 and passim.

11. Ibid., p. 72.

12. Susan Sontag, 'Notes on Camp', *Partisan Review*, Fall 1964, pp. 515, 526–7.

13. Andreas Huyssen, 'Mass Culture as a Woman', in *After the Great Divide: Modernism, Mass Culture, Postmodernism*, Indiana University Press, 1986.

14. Harold Rosenberg, 'The American Action Painters', *Art News*, 51, December 1952, pp. 21–2.

15. Charles Baudelaire, 'The Painter of Modern Life', in *The Painter of Modern Life and Other Essays*, trans. Jonathan Mayne, New York, 1964, p. 33.

16. Andy Warhol, interview with Gene Swenson, 'What is Pop Art?', *Art News*, 62, November 1963, p. 25.

17. See Crow, 'Saturday Disasters: Trace and Reference in Early Warhol', in his *Modern Art in the Common Culture*, pp. 49–65. For the issue of social conscience in Warhol, see also Anne Wagner: 'Warhol Paints History, or Race in America', *Representations*, 55, 1996, pp. 98–119.

18. Warhol, interview with Gene Swenson, 'What is Pop Art?'.

19. For Warhol's work and the 'pathological public sphere' see Hal Foster, 'Death in America', *October*, Winter 1996, pp. 37–59.

20. See Caroline Jones, *Machine in the Studio: Constructing the Postwar American Artist*, Chicago, 1996, pp. 221–2.

21. See Gene Swenson, 'The F-III: An Interview with James Rosenquist', *Partisan Review*, vol. XXXII, no. 4, Fall 1965, pp. 589–90.

22. S. Polke and G. Richter, joint text for ex. cat., Galerie h, Hanover, 1966. Trans. D. Britt in H.-U. Obrist (ed.), *Gerhard Richter: The Daily Practice of Painting*, London, 1995, p. 42.

Chapter 5. Modernism in Retreat: Minimalist Aesthetics and Beyond

1. See his 'Art-as-Art', *Art International* (Lugano), December 1962.
2. Clement Greenberg, 'After Abstract Expressionism', *Art International*, October 1962.
3. Robert Rosenblum, *Frank Stella*, Harmondsworth, 1971, p. 21.
4. Michael Fried, *Three American Painters: Noland, Olitski, Stella* (ex. cat.), Fogg Art Museum, Cambridge, Mass., 1965, reprinted in his *Art and Objecthood*, Chicago, 1998, p. 256.
5. See Anna Chave, 'Minimalism and the Rhetoric of Power', *Arts Magazine*, vol. 64, no. 5, January 1990, pp. 46–51 and passim. See also Brenda Richardson, *Frank Stella: The Black Paintings* (ex. cat.), Baltimore Museum of Art, 1976.
6. See Caroline Jones, *The Machine in the Studio: Constructing the Post-War Artist*, Chicago, 1996, pp. 156–7.
7. Ibid., p. 167.
8. 'Questions to Stella and Judd', interview by Bruce Glaser, ed. Lucy Lippard, *Art News*, September 1966.
9. See Donald Judd, 'Specific Objects', *Arts Yearbook*, 8, New York, 1965, pp. 74–82.
10. Richard Wollheim, 'Minimal Art', *Arts Magazine*, January 1965.
11. Robert Morris, 'Notes on Sculpture, Part 2', *Artforum*, vol. 5, no. 2, October 1966, pp. 20–3.
12. Ibid., p. 1.
13. See Hal Foster, 'The Crux of Minimalism', in H. Singerman (ed.), *Individuals: A Selected History of Contemporary Art 1945–86*, Museum of Contemporary Art, Los Angeles, 1988, pp. 162–83.
14. Rosalind Krauss, 'LeWitt in Progress', in *The Originality of the Avant Garde and Other Modernist Myths*, Cambridge, Mass., 1985, pp. 245–58.
15. Sol LeWitt, 'Paragraphs on Conceptual Art', *Artforum*, vol. V, June 1967, p. 79.
16. Fried, 'Art and Objecthood', *Artforum*, vol. V, June 1967.
17. Greenberg, 'Recentness of Sculpture', first published in *American Sculpture of the Sixties* (ex. cat.), Los Angeles County Museum of Art, 1967.

18. Carl Andre, quoted in David Bourdon, 'The Razed Sites of Carl Andre', *Artforum*, October 1966.
19. Andre, quoted ibid., p. 107.
20. See the editorial, *Burlington Magazine*, April 1976, pp. 187–8, and Richard Morphet's response in the same journal, November 1976, pp. 762–7.
21. See Agnes Martin, 'Answer to an Inquiry', in Dieter Schwarz, *Agnes Martin: Writings/Schriften*, Winterthur Kunstmuseum, Switzerland, 1992, p. 29.
22. Krauss, 'Afterthoughts on "Op" ', *Art International*, June 1965, pp. 75–6.
23. Krauss, *The Optical Unconscious*, Cambridge, Mass., 1993, ch. 3.
24. Robert Morris, 'Anti Form', *Artforum*, vol. 6, no. 8, April 1968, pp. 33–5.
25. Lucy Lippard, catalogue essay of 1966, cited by Lippard in *Eva Hesse*, New York, 1976, p. 83.
26. For a sophisticated psychoanalytic approach to Hesse see Briony Fer, 'Bordering on Blank: Eva Hesse and Minimalism', *Art History*, vol. 17, no. 3, September 1994.
27. Eva Hesse, *Notebooks*, cited by Anne Wagner, *Three Artists (Three Women)*, California, 1996, p. 238.
28. See Douglas Crimp, 'Serra's Public Sculpture: Redefining Site Specificity', in Laura Rosenstock (ed.), *Richard Serra/Sculpture*, MoMA, New York, 1986, pp. 40–56.

Chapter 6. The Death of the Object: The Move to Conceptualism

1. See Douglas Crimp, 'The End of Painting', *October*, 16, 1981, pp. 69–86.
2. Asger Jorn, 'Detourned Painting', in Elizabeth Sussman (ed.), *On the Passage of a Few People Through a Rather Brief Moment in Time: The Situationist International 1957–72*, ICA, Boston, 1989, p. 140.
3. Daniel Buren, interview with David Batchelor, *Artscribe*, November/December 1987, pp. 51–4.
4. This reading relies heavily on Alexander Alberro's 'The Turn of the Screw…', *October*, 80, 1997, pp. 57–84.
5. See Stefan Germer, 'Haacke, Broodthaers, Beuys', *October*, 45, 1988, pp. 63–75.
6. Quoted by Haacke in *Hans Haacke: Unfinished Business*, ed. Brian Wallis, Cambridge, Mass., 1986, p. 96.
7. See Peter Bürger, *Theory of the Avant Garde*, trans. M. Shaw, Minneapolis, 1984, esp. ch. 4.

8. Gordon Matta Clark, as quoted by Donald Wall, 'Gordon Matta Clark's Building Dissections', *Arts Magazine*, 50, no. 9, 1976, p. 76.

9. Germano Celant, from Celant (ed.), *Arte Povera*, Milan, 1969, trans. as *Arte Povera. Conceptual or Impossible Art*, London, 1969, p. 226.

10. Ibid., p. 230.

11. Robert Smithson, interview with Bruce Kurtz, in Nancy Holt (ed.), *The Writings of Robert Smithson*, New York, 1979, pp. 200–4.

12. Smithson, 'The Spiral Jetty', in Holt, *The Writings*, p. 113.

13. Smithson, 'A Sedimentation of the Mind: Earth Projects', *Artforum*, September 1968.

14. Ian Hamilton Finlay, 'Unconnected Sentences on Gardening', in *Nature Over Again After Poussin: Some Discovered Landscapes* (ex. cat.), University of Strathclyde, Glasgow, 1980, pp. 21–2.

15. Lucy Lippard, *Six Years: The Dematerialization of the Art Object*, New York, 1973.

16. Joseph Kosuth, 'Art After Philosophy' (parts I–III), *Studio International*, vol. 178, nos 915–17, October, November, and December 1969.

17. See Benjamin Buchloh, 'From the Aesthetics of Administration to Institutional Critique…', *October*, 55, 1990, pp. 124–8 and passim.

18. See Lippard's preface to her *Six Years*.

19. See Tony Godfrey, *Conceptual Art*, London, 1998, p. 224.

20. See Buchloh, 'Aesthetics', pp. 128–9 and passim.

21. See Charles Harrison, *Essays on Art & Language*, Oxford, 1991, chs 3 and 4.

22. Roland Barthes, 'Myth Today', in *Mythologies*, trans. A. Lavers, London, 1973, reprinted 1981, p. 116.

23. See Victor Burgin, 'Sex, Text, Politics', interview with Tony Godfrey, *Block*, 7, 1982, pp. 7–8.

24. Robert Hughes, 'An Obsessive Feminist Pantheon…', *Time*, vol. 15, December 1980, p. 85.

25. See Griselda Pollock, 'Screening the Seventies…', in her *Vision and Difference*, London, 1988, pp. 155–99.

26. See Laura Mulvey, 'Visual Pleasure and Narrative Cinema', *Screen*, 16, no. 3, 1975, pp. 6–18.

27. For instance, *Of Grammatology* (1967), published in a 1976 edition (Johns Hopkins University Press), and *Writing and Difference* (1967), published London, 1978.

28. Willoughby Sharp, 'Body Works', *Avalanche 1*, Fall 1970, pp. 14–17.

29. Mary Kelly, 'Re-Viewing Modernist Criticism', *Screen*, 22, no. 23, 1981, pp. 41–62 (section on 'The Crisis of Authorship').

30. Jacques Derrida, 'The Theater of Cruelty and the Closure of Representation', *Writing and Difference*, London, 1978.

31. See Amelia Jones, *Body Art: Performing the Subject*, University of Minnesota Press, 1998, ch. 4. Jones's book has closely informed aspects of my reading of Body Art.

32. See Carolee Schneemann, *More Than Meat Joy: Performance Works and Selected Writings*, New York, 1997, pp. 234–9.

Chapter 7. Postmodernism: Theory and Practice in the 1980s

1. This periodization was developed by Ernest Mandel in his *Late Capitalism* (London, 1978) and taken up by Fredric Jameson in his seminal 'Postmodernism, or the Cultural Logic of Late Capitalism', *New Left Review*, no. 146, July–August 1984, pp. 59–92. For an account of 'post-Fordism' see David Harvey, *The Condition of Postmodernity*, Oxford, 1989, pp. 121–97.

2. See Ihab Hassan, 'The Culture of Postmodernism', *Theory, Culture and Society*, vol. 2, no. 3, 1985, pp. 123–4.

3. Charles Jencks, *The Language of Post-Modern Architecture*, London, 1977, repr. 1987, p. 9.

4. Jean-François Lyotard, *La Condition Postmoderne, Rapport sur le Savoir*, Paris, 1979.

5. Habermas's lecture is published in Hal Foster (ed.), *Postmodern Culture*, London, 1985, pp. 3–15.

6. Jameson, 'Postmodernism'.

7. For Baudrillard on simulation see his 'Simulacra and Simulations', in *Selected Writings*, ed. Mark Poster, Oxford, 1988, pp. 166–84.

8. Jameson, 'Postmodernism'.

9. See Harvey, *The Condition of Postmodernity*, pp. 284–307.

10. Christos Joachimides, 'A New Spirit in Painting', from *A New Spirit in Painting* (ex. cat.), Royal Academy of Arts, London, 1981, p. 14.

11. Pierre Restany, 'Some Opinions on Documenta 7', *Flash Art*, November 1982, p. 42.

12. Achille Bonito Oliva, *La Transavanguardia Italiana*, trans. as *The Italian Transavantgarde*, Milan, 1980.

13. Donald Kuspit, 'Flak from the Radicals: The American Case Against German Painting', in Brian Wallis (ed.), *Art After Modernism: Rethinking Representation*, New York, 1984, p. 141.

14. Andreas Huyssen, 'Anselm Kiefer: The Terror of History, the Temptation of Myth', *October*, 48, Spring 1989, pp. 25–45.

15. Benjamin Buchloh, 'Figures of Authority, Ciphers of Regression…', *October*, 16, Spring 1981, pp. 39–68.

16. Schnabel was then aged 36. For a general account see Irving Sandler, *Art of the Postmodern Era*, New York, 1996, p. 438 and related notes.

17. Rosalind Krauss, 'Notes on the Index Parts I and II', *October*, nos 3 and 4, Spring and Fall 1977.

18. See Richard Bolton, 'Enlightened Self-Interest: The Avant-Garde in the 80s', in G.H. Kester (ed.), *Art, Activism and Oppositionality*, Duke University Press, pp. 41–2.

19. See Foster, *Postmodern Culture*, introduction.

20. Craig Owens, 'The Allegorical Impulse: Towards a Theory of Postmodernism, parts I and II', *October*, 12 and 13, Spring 1980, pp. 67–86, and Summer 1980, pp. 59–80, and Rosalind Krauss, 'The Originality of the Avant Garde…', *October*, 18, Fall 1981, pp. 47–66.

21. Thomas Lawson, 'Last Exit: Painting', *Artforum*, 20, no. 2, October 1981, pp. 40–7.

22. Eric Fischl, interview with Donald Kuspit in *Fischl*, New York, 1987, p. 53.

23. For Richter on *October 18, 1977* see Kai-Uwe Hemken, 'The Sons Die Before Their Fathers', in E. Gillen (ed.), *German Art from Beckmann to Richter*, Cologne, 1997, pp. 374–88. See also Benjamin Buchloh, 'A Note on Gerhard Richter's "October 18, 1977"', *October*, 48, Spring 1989, pp. 88–109.

24. See Jameson, 'Postmodernism', pp. 76–7.

25. See Gerhard Richter, statement in *Documenta 7* (ex. cat.), Kassel, 1982, vol. 1, pp. 84–5.

26. For a study of how racial difference becomes constituted see Homi Bhabha, 'The Other Question: The Stereotype and Colonial Discourse', *Screen*, vol. 24, no. 4, 1983.

27. See Peter Halley, 'Nature and Culture', *Arts Magazine*, September 1983.

28. See Hal Foster, 'The Art of Cynical Reason', in *The Return of the Real*, Cambridge, Mass., 1996, pp. 99–124.

29. See Foster's 'The Return of the Real' in ibid., pp. 127–68.

30. Julia Kristeva, *Powers of Horror: An Essay on Abjection*, Paris, 1980, repr. New York, 1982.

31. See Marina Warner, 'In the Garden of Delights: Helen Chadwick's "Of Mutability"', in Helen Chadwick, *Of Mutability* (ex. cat.), ICA, London, 1986.

32. Hal Foster, 'The Artist as Ethnographer', in *The Return of the Real*, p. 184. Foster's broader points are made on pp. 199–202.

Chapter 8. The 1990s: A New *Fin de Siècle*?

1. This reading owes much to Terry Atkinson, 'Dead Troops Talk', in *Jeff Wall: Dead Troops Talk* (ex. cat.), Kunstmuseum Lucerne and Irish Museum of Modern Art, 1993, pp. 29–45.

2. For accounts of Kulik see Ewa Lajer-Burcharth, 'Old Histories: Zofia Kulik's Ironic Recollections', in *New Histories* (ex. cat.), ICA, Boston, 1996, pp. 120–36, and essays by Simon Herbert and Adam Sobota in *The Human Motif: Zofia Kulik*, Zone Gallery, Newcastle upon Tyne, 1995.

3. See Richard Bolton (ed.), *Culture Wars: Documents from the Recent Controversies in the Arts*, New York, 1992.

4. Grant H. Kester, 'Rhetorical Questions: The Alternative Arts Sector and the Imaginary Public', in G. Kester (ed.), *Art, Activism and Oppositionality: Essays from 'Afterimage'*, Duke University Press, 1998, pp. 103–35.

5. For a critique of the yBas see Simon Ford, 'The Myth of the Young British Artist', *Art Monthly*, no. 194, March 1996, pp. 3–9.

6. See John Roberts, 'Mad For It! Philistinism, the Everyday and the New British Art', *Third Text*, Summer 1996, pp. 29–42.

7. For Gordon's interest in Hogg, and associated links to notions of Scottish identity, see David Hopkins: *Dada's Boys: Masculinity After Duchamp*, Yale, 2007, pp. 147–57.

8. For a full discussion of these issues see David Hopkins, '"Out of It": Drunkenness and Ethics in Martha Rosler and Gillian Wearing', in Gill Perry (ed.), *Difference and Excess in Contemporary Art: The Visibility of Women's Practice*, Blackwell, 2004, pp. 22–45.

9. Sophie Calle and Paul Auster, *Double Game*, Violette Editions, London, 1999.

10. Peter Wollen, 'Into the Future: Tourism, Language and Art', in his *Raiding the Icebox: Reflections on Twentieth-Century Culture*, London, 1993, pp. 190–212.

11. See Claire Bishop, *Artificial Hells: Participatory Art and the Politics of Spectatorship*, London, 2012, p. 34. Bishop's overall account of the work is very illuminating; see pp. 30–7.

12. Jeremy Deller, as cited in Dave Beech, 'The Uses of Authority', *Untitled*, 25, 2000, p. 10.

13. Allan Sekula: *Fish Story*, Witte de With Centre for Contemporary Art, Rotterdam/ Richter Verlag, 1995, p. 48.

14. Ibid., p. 32.

15. Jeremy Deller and Alan Kane, *Folk Archive*, Book Works, London, 2005, p. 2.

16. Hal Foster, 'L'Amour Faux', *Art in America*, January 1986, p. 128.

17. Foster's *The Return of the Real* (1996) is informed throughout by his earlier work on Surrealism (in *Compulsive Identity*, 1993). See also David Hopkins, *Dada and Surrealism: A Very Short Introduction*, Oxford, 2006.

18. Susan Hiller, interview with Stuart Morgan, in *Susan Hiller*, ex. cat., Tate Publishing, 1996, p. 44.

19. See David Hopkins, *Childish Things*, ex. cat., Fruitmarket Gallery, Edinburgh, 2010.

20. This interpretation of *Cremaster 4* is indebted to Norman Bryson, 'Matthew Barney's Gonadotrophic Cavalcade', and Michel Onfray, 'Mannerist Variations on Matthew Barney', in *Parkett*, no. 45, 1995, pp. 29–33 and 50–7 respectively.

21. See round-table discussion, 'The Predicament of Contemporary Art', in Hal Foster et al., *Art Since 1900*, Thames & Hudson, London, 2004, p. 676.

22. See Rosalind Krauss, *Richard Serra/ Sculpture*, ed. Laura Rosenstock, MoMA, New York, 1986.

23. For the full discussion of this, see David Hopkins, *Dada's Boys*, op. cit. at note 7 above, pp. 203–19.

24. See, in this respect, Abigail Solomon-Godeau: *Male Trouble: A Crisis in Representation*, Thames & Hudson, London, 1997, esp. ch. 1.

25. For a full discussion see David Hopkins, *Dada's Boys*, op. cit. at note 7 above, pp. 147–57.

26. See David Hopkins, *Dada's Boys*, pp. 192–201.

27. Tacita Dean, in *Tacita Dean*, ex. cat., Museu d'Art Contemporani, Barcelona, 2001, p. 52.

28. Tacita Dean, interview with Marina Warner in Jean Christoph Royoux et al., *Tacita Dean*, Phaidon, Oxford, 2006, p. 15.

29. Hal Foster, 'Archive' (ch. 2) in his *Bad New Days: Art, Criticism, Emergency*, Verso, London, 2015, pp. 30–60.

30. Adrian Searle, 'Slow Developer' (exhibition review of Gerhard Richter, *Atlas*, Whitechapel Art Gallery, London, 2003), *The Guardian*, 9 December 2003.

31. Johan Grimonprez, interview with Catherine Bernard, 'Supermarket History', in Johan Grimonprez, *It's a Poor Sort of Memory That Only Works Backwards*, Fruitmarket Gallery/Hatje Cantz, 2011, p. 229.

32. Angela Dimitrakaki, 'Sightings: Surrealist Idiolect, Gothic Marxism, Global Perils', in David Hopkins (ed.), *A Companion to Dada and Surrealism*, Blackwell, Chichester, 2016, p. 454.

33. Fredric Jameson: *Postmodernism, or the Cultural Logic of Late Capitalism*, Duke University Press, Durham, 1991, pp. 67 and 174.

34. Johan Grimonprez, op. cit. in note 31 above, p. 230.

Chapter 9. Art and the New Millennium

1. Rebecca Allison, '9/11 wicked but a work of art, says Damien Hirst', *The Guardian*, 11 September 2002.

2. Walter Benjamin, 'The Work of Art in the Age of its Technological Reproducibility', in H. Eiland and M. Jennings (eds), *Walter Benjamin: Selected Writings*, vol. 3, Harvard University Press, Cambridge, Mass., and London, 2002, p. 122.

3. For a range of views on *Art Since 1900*, many of which register the US-centric nature of its position, see *Art Bulletin*, vol. 87, issue 2, June 2006, pp. 376–9.

4. Michael Hardt and Antonio Negri: *Empire*, Harvard University Press, Cambridge, Mass., 2000, pp xiii, xvi.

5. T. J. Demos, *Decolonizing Nature*, Sternberg Press, Berlin, 2016, p. 101.

6. Julian Stallabrass, *Internet Art: The Online Clash of Culture and Commerce*, Tate Publishing, 2003, p. 9.

7. For a full account see Stallabrass, *Internet Art*, pp. 96–101.

8. For a detailed account see Chin-Tao Wu: *Privatising Culture: Corporate Intervention since the 1980s*, Verso, London, 2002.

9. Artprice, 'The Contemporary Art Market 2007/2008', *The Artprice Annual Report*, Lyons, 2008.

10. Olav Velthuis, 'Globalization and Commercialization of the Art Market', in Alexander Dumbadze and Suzanne Hudson (eds), *Contemporary Art: 1989 to the Present*, Blackwell, 2013, p. 371.

11. Sunday Times Rich List: http://features.thesundaytimes.co.uk/richlist/live.

12. See Tim Griffin, 'Worlds Apart: Contemporary Art, Globalization, and the Rise of Biennials', in Dumbadze and Hudson, *Contemporary Art: 1989 to the Present*, pp. 13–14.

13. See David Balzer, *Curationism: How Curating Took Over the Art World and Everything Else*, Pluto, London, 2014, p. 8 .

14. Terry Smith, *What is Contemporary Art?*, University of Chicago Press, p. 78.

15. Ibid., p. 66.

16. Julian Stallabrass, *Contemporary Art: A Very Short Introduction*, Oxford University Press, 2004, p. 97.

17. Benjamin Buchloh, comment in 'The Predicament of Art' (Roundtable), in H. Foster et al., *Art Since 1900*, London, 2004, p. 679.

18. Okwui Enwezor, 'The Black Box', introduction to *Documenta 11: Platform 5* (ex. cat.), Ostfildern-Ruit/Hatje Kantz, 2002, p. 55.

19. Stuart Hall, quoted by Thomas Crow in 'Modernism and Mass Culture in the Visual Arts', in F. Frascina, *Pollock and After: The Critical Debate*, London, 1985, p. 247.

20. Isaac Julien, 'Mirror', in his *Riot*, MoMA, New York, 2013, p. 51.

21. See Lisa Lee, 'Make Life Beautiful: The Diabolic in the Work of Isa Genzken (A Tour through Berlin, Paris, and New York)', in Lisa Lee (ed.), *Isa Genzken*, October Files 17, MIT Press, 2015, pp. 136–40 and passim.

22. Laura Mulvey in ibid., p. 207.

23. Julian Stallabrass, 'Frozen Dialectics in the Work of Haegue Yang', in *Haegue Yang: Wild Against Gravity*, Aspen Art Museum/Museum of Modern Art, Oxford, 2011, p. 96.

24. Marc Augé, *Non-Places: Introduction to an Anthropology of Supermodernity*, Verso, London, 2009 (originally Paris, 1995).

25. See Angela Dimitrakaki and Kirsten Lloyd (eds), *Economy: Art, Production and the Economic Subject in the 21st Century*, Liverpool UP, 2015. My account of Ostojić here is indebted to Dimitrakaki's book *Gender, Artwork and the Global Imperative: A Materialist Feminist Critique*, Manchester University Press, 2013, pp. 76–81.

26. Giorgio Agamben: *Homer Sacer: Sovereign Power and Bare Life*, trans. D. Heller-Roazen, Stanford UP, 1998.

27. The phenomenon of the 'reinstallation' of exhibitions is also worth considering here. See, for instance, the account of the reinstallation of Harald Szeemann's classic Kunsthalle Bern exhibition of 1969, *When Attitudes Become Form*, in Venice in 2013: Germano Celant and Chiara Costa (eds), *When Attitudes Become Form*, Fondazione Prada, Milan, 2013.

28. Nicolas Bourriaud, *Relational Aesthetics*, Les Presses du réel, trans. Simon Pleasance and Fronza Woods, 2002 (first published 1998), p. 14.

29. Ibid., p. 45.

30. Liam Gillick, 'Renovation Filter: Recent Past and Near Future', Arnolfini Gallery, Bristol, 2000, p. 16.

31. Nicolas Bourriaud, *Postproduction: Culture as Screenplay: How Art Reprograms the World*, Lukas & Sternberg, New York, 2002, pp. 17–20.

32. See Pierre Huyghe, *Pierre Huyghe* (ex. cat.), Centre national d'art et de la culture/Centre Pompidou, Paris, 2013, pp. 116–29.

33. See Claire Bishop, 'Antagonism and Relational Aesthetics', *October*, Fall 2004, pp. 51–79. See also her later 'The Social Turn: Collaboration and its Discontents', *Artforum*, February 2006, pp. 179–85, and the response to this, on the issue of activism, by Grant Kester, pp. 187–9.

34. Bishop, 'The Social Turn', p. 183.

35. Francis Alÿs, interview with Russell Ferguson, in Cuauhtémoc Medina et al., *Francis Alÿs*, Phaidon, Oxford, 2007, p. 48.

36. For a further discussion of Manzoni's lines see Briony Fer, *The Infinite Line*, Yale UP, New Haven and London, 2004, ch. 2.

37. Rosalind Krauss: 'Re-inventing the Medium', *Critical Inquiry*, vol. 25, no. 2, 1993, p. 296.

38. See Rosalind Krauss, *Under Blue Cup*, MIT Press, Cambridge, Mass., and London, 2011, p. 20.

39. Isabelle Graw, 'The Value of Liveliness: Painting as an Index of Agency in the New Economy', in I. Graw and E. Lajer-Burcharth: *Painting Beyond Itself: The Medium in the Post-Medium Condition*, Sternberg Press, Berlin, 2016, pp. 82–3 and passim.

40. Barry Schwabsky: 'Painting in the Interrogative Mode', in Schwabsky et al., *Vitamin P*, Phaidon, Oxford, 2002, pp. 110–11.

41. Luc Tymans: as cited in *Luc Tymans*, Exhibition Guide, Tate Modern, 2004.

42. Adrian Searle, 'Fatal Attraction', *The Guardian*, 23 November 2004.

43. Douglas Fogle: in Schwabsky op. cit. at note 38, p. 184.

44. Nicolas Bourriaud *Altermodern: Tate Triennial 2009*, Tate Publishing, 2009.

45. Ibid.

46. Carolyn Christov-Bakargiev: 'The dancing was very frenetic', introduction to *Documenta (13): Catalog 1/3: The Book of Books*, Hatje Cantz, Ostfildern, 2012, pp. 31, 36.

47. Terry Smith, *What is Contemporary Art?*, University of Chicago Press, 2009, pp. 7–8.

48. Ibid.; all quotations taken from pp. 1–4.

49. Charles Baudelaire: 'The Painter of Modern Life,' trans. J. Mayne, in Baudelaire, *The Painter of Modern Life and Other Essays*, Da Capo, New York, 1964, p. 9.

50. See Chapter 7, note 9.

51. One recent research project advocates the use of the phrase 'former West' as a means of signalling the new structural position of the West. See Maria Hlavajova and Simon Sheikh, *Former West: Art and the Contemporary After 1989*, MIT Press, 2016, esp. pp. 33–137.

52. Tilman Bäumgartel, interview with Vuk Cosic, *Telepolis*, 26 June 1997, https://www.heise.de/tp/artikel/6/6158/1.html.

53. *The Guardian*, 2 December 2004.

54. Adam Szymczyk, 'Iterabilty and Otherness—Learning and Working from Athens', in Quinn Latimer and Adam Szymczyk (eds), *The Documenta 14 Reader*, Documenta und Museum Fridericianum, Kassel/Prestel Verlag, Munich, 2017, p. 23.

55. Ibid., p. 27.

56. Ed Atkins, interview, http://smk.dk/en/visit-the-museum/exhibitions/ed-atkins-safe-conduct, accessed 16 July 2017.

57. Angela Dimitrakaki, 'Sightings: Surrealist Idiolect, Gothic Marxism, Global Perils', in David Hopkins (ed.), *A Companion to Dada and Surrealism*, Wiley Blackwell, Chichester, 2016, p. 456.

Further Reading

Significant magazine articles and essays or chapters from books are normally referred to in the notes to the text. This section largely concentrates on introductory books and exhibition catalogues. A few useful monographs on artists are included.

Abbreviations:
MoMA: Museum of Modern Art
MoCA: Museum of Contemporary Art

General

For the entire period see the second half of *Hal Foster, Rosalind Krauss, Yve-Alain Bois, and Benjamin Buchloh, Art Since 1900* (London, 2004, and subsequent editions); note, however, my comments on this at the start of Chapter 9. *Modernism in Dispute: Art Since the Forties* (Open University and Yale, 1993) by **Paul Wood, Francis Frascina, Jonathan Harris, and Charles Harrison** offers a series of challenging politicized readings of various moments within modernism and postmodernism, although it concentrates mainly on America. A notable attempt to get away from a formalist Americanist model is **Benjamin Buchloh**'s essay, 'Formalism and Historicity...', in Art Institute of Chicago, *Europe in the Seventies*, 1977. See also **Buchloh**'s *Neo-Avantgarde and Culture Industry* (Cambridge, Mass., and London, 2000). For a wide-ranging series of essays on the period see **Amelia Jones** (ed.), *A Companion to Art since 1945* (Blackwell, Oxford, 2006). Four well-written studies have also addressed themselves to various aspects of post-war art: **Michael Archer**'s *Art Since 1960* (London, 1997), **Thomas Crow**'s *The Rise of the Sixties* (London, 1996), **Brandon Taylor**'s *The Art of Today* (London, 1995), and **David Joselit**'s: *American Art since 1945* (London, 2003). By far the most useful anthology of artists' statements and critical theory is **Charles Harrison and Paul Wood** (eds), *Art in Theory: An Anthology of Changing Ideas* (Oxford, 1992). For artists' writings see also **Kristine Stiles and Peter Selz** (eds), *Theories and Documents of Contemporary Art* (University of California, 1996). In terms of exhibitions see **Bruce Altshuler**'s two-volume *Exhibitions that Made History*: vol. 1 (1863–1959) and vol. 2 (1962–2002) (Oxford, 2008 and 2013 respectively). Possibly the best primary sources for an understanding of the period as a whole are the catalogues for Kassel's *Documenta* exhibitions, nos 1–14 (1955–2017).

Chapter 1. The Politics of Modernism: Abstract Expressionism and the European *Informel*

For Abstract Expressionism see **Irving Sandler**, *Abstract Expressionism: The Triumph of American Painting* (London, 1970) and **David Anfam**'s *Abstract Expressionism* (London, 1990). **Michael Leja**'s *Reframing Abstract Expressionism* (Yale, 1993) is a major revisionist study, whilst Ann Eden Gibson's *Abstract Expressionism: Other Politics* (New Haven and London, 1997) also offers a rereading of the topic. On individual Abstract Expressionists see **Kirk Varnedoe and Pepe Kermel**, *Jackson Pollock* (MoMA, New York, 1998), **Thomas B. Hess**, *Willem de Kooning* (MoMA, New York, 1968), and **David Anfam**, *Mark Rothko: The Works on Canvas: A Catalogue Raisonné* (National Gallery of Art, Washington, 1998). A major recent catalogue is **David Anfam** (ed.), *Abstract Expressionism* (Royal Academy of Arts, London, 2017).

The social background for Abstract Expressionism is set out in **Erika Doss**, *Benton, Pollock and the Politics of Modernism: From Regionalism to Abstract Expressionism* (Yale, 1991). Cold War issues are dealt with in **Serge Guilbaut**'s ground-breaking *How*

New York Stole the Idea of Modern Art
(Chicago, 1983) and **Francis Frascina** (ed.),
Pollock and After: The Critical Debate (New
York, 1985), which collects together many
key texts. A further addition is **David
Craven**, *Abstract Expression as Cultural
Critique* (Cambridge University Press,
1999). For communist-affiliated realism in
Europe see **Francis Frascina**'s essay in **Paul
Wood et al.**, *Modernism in Dispute* (cited in
General section above).

Useful essays on French post-war art
appear in the **Tate Gallery**'s *Paris Post War*
catalogue (1993) and the **Barbican Art
Gallery**, *Aftermath: France 1945–54: New
Images of Man* (London, 1982). On Wols see
Kunsthaus Zürich (ex. cat.) (1990), and on
Dubuffet see **Mildred Glimcher and Jean
Dubuffet**, *Jean Dubuffet: Towards an
Alternative Reality* (New York, 1987). For
Arshile Gorky see **Diane Waldman**, *Arshile
Gorky 1904–1948: A Retrospective* (Solomon
R. Guggenheim Museum, New York, 1981).

Key texts relating to Greenberg's and
Fried's 'Modernist' aesthetics are collected
in **Francis Frascina** (ed.), *Pollock and After:
The Critical Debate* (New York, 1985), but
see also **Caroline Jones**'s major study
*Eyesight Alone: Clement Greenberg's Modernism
and the Bureaucratization of the Senses*
(University of Chicago, 2008). Texts central
to the foundations of 'modernist' thought
are reprinted in **Francis Frascina** and
Charles Harrison (eds), *Modern Art and
Modernism: A Critical Anthology* (Open
University and London, 1982), whilst the
social origins of modernist sensibility are
explored in **Marshall Berman**'s *All that is
Solid Melts into Air: The Experience of
Modernity* (New York, 1982).

For British abstraction of the 1950s see
Tate Gallery, *St Ives 1939–64* (London,
1985, rev. 1996). On Peter Lanyon see
Whitworth Art Gallery, *Peter Lanyon*
(Manchester, 1978). Patrick Heron's
criticism is collected in **Mel Gooding** (ed.),
*Painter and Critic: Patrick Heron Writings
1945–97* (London, 1998). A good general
study of British post-war art of the Cold
War era is **Margaret Garlake**, *New Art New
World* (Yale, 1998).

Chapter 2. Duchamp's Legacy: The Rauschenberg–Johns Axis

For comprehensive studies of Duchamp
and his impact see **Dawn Ades, Neil Cox,
and David Hopkins**, *Marcel Duchamp*
(London, 1999), and **Martha Buskirk and
Mignon Nixon** (eds), *The Duchamp Effect*
(Cambridge, Mass., 1996).

For **John Cage**'s ideas see his writings
collected in *Silence* (London, 1971). A study
of Black Mountain College is provided by
Mary Emma Harris, *The Arts at Black
Mountain College* (Cambridge, Mass., 1987).

On Rauschenberg see especially the
Solomon R. Guggenheim Museum's
massive catalogue, *Robert Rauschenberg: A
Retrospective* (New York, 1998) and **Walter
Hopps**'s superb *Robert Rauschenberg: The
Early 1950s* (Menil Foundation, Houston,
1991). **William Seitz**'s important catalogue
The Art of Assemblage was published by
MoMA, New York, in 1961. For Joseph
Cornell see **Kynaston McShine** (ed.), *Joseph
Cornell* (MoMA, New York, 1980). Art's
relation to Beat culture is discussed in **Lisa
Phillips**'s *Beat Culture and the New America
1950–1965* (Whitney Museum, New York,
1995).

For Cy Twombly the most comprehensive monograph is **Kirk Varnedoe**, *Cy
Twombly: A Retrospective* (MoMA, New York,
1994). As regards Lucio Fontana, see the
centenary exhibition catalogue edited by
Enrico Crispolti, *Fontana* (Milan, 1999).

Gender has become a major issue in the
literature on Abstract Expressionism and
the 1950s; see **Anne Wagner**'s fascinating
*Three Artists (Three Women): Modernism and
the Art of Hesse, Krasner and O'Keefe*
(Berkeley, 1996). For Jasper Johns, see
Kenneth Silver's important essay in *Hand
Painted Pop: American Art in Transition
1955–1962* (ed. Russell Ferguson, MoCA,
Los Angeles, 1992). **Fred Orton**'s *Figuring
Jasper Johns* (London, 1994) also touches on
issues of masculinity, as does his excellent
catalogue on the artist's sculpture, *Jasper
Johns: The Sculpture* (Henry Moore
Foundation, Leeds, 1996). Duchamp's
attitude to the readymade in the 1960s is
discussed in the latter half of **William
Camfield**'s *Marcel Duchamp: Fountain*
(Menil Foundation, Houston, 1988). For
literature on Sherrie Levine et al. in
relation to replication, see Chapter 7.

Chapter 3. The Artist in Crisis: From Bacon to Beuys

Links between existentialism and art are
established in **Tate Gallery**'s *Paris Post War*
catalogue (1993), which also discusses
Giacometti. For Henry Moore, **John
Russell**'s *Henry Moore* (Harmondsworth,
1973) provides a readable introduction. For

Francis Bacon see **David Sylvester**'s crucial *Interviews with Francis Bacon* (London, 1971, revised 1979) and **John Russell**'s introductory *Francis Bacon* (London, 1975). For Lucian Freud see the monograph edited by **Bruce Bernard and Derek Birdsall** (London, 1996).

For Giacometti see **Reinhold Hohl**'s monograph (London and Lausanne, 1972). See also **Fondation Maeght**, *Germaine Richier* (1996) and **Margit Rowell** (ed.), *Antonin Artaud: Works on Paper* (MoMA, New York, 1996).

Nouveau Réalisme as a movement is discussed in **Musée d'Art Moderne de la Ville de Paris**, *1960 Les Nouveaux Réalistes* (1986). For individual artists see **Museum of Fine Arts**, *Arman* (Houston, 1995), and **Sidra Stich**'s comprehensive *Yves Klein* (Hayward Gallery, London, 1995). A useful introduction to French Structuralism is **John Sturrock** (ed.), *Structuralism and Since* (Oxford, 1979). For Piero Manzoni see the catalogue for the **Musée d'Art Moderne de la Ville de Paris** (Paris, 1991).

The Beuys literature is extensive but good general studies are **Caroline Tisdall**, *Joseph Beuys* (Solomon R. Guggenheim Museum, New York, 1979) and **Gotz Adriani, Winifried Konnertz, and Karin Thomas**, *Joseph Beuys: Life and Works* (New York, 1979).

For Berlin as an artistic centre see **Kynaston McShine** (ed.), *Berlin Art 1961–1987* (MoMA, New York, 1987). For Georg Baselitz see **Solomon R. Guggenheim Museum**, *Georg Baselitz* (New York, 1995).

Chapter 4. Blurring Boundaries: Pop Art, Fluxus, and their Effects

The Independent Group: Postwar Britain and the Aesthetics of Plenty (London and Cambridge, Mass., 1990) contains excellent essays on the Independent Group, whilst **Anne Massey**'s *The Independent Group: Modernism and Mass Culture in Britain, 1945–59* (Manchester, 1995) should be consulted. See also **Robin Spence,** *Eduardo Paolozzi: Writings and Interviews* (Oxford, 2000), **W. Konnertz**, *Eduardo Paolozzi* (Cologne, 1984), and **Tate Gallery**, *Richard Hamilton* (London, 1992). **Ben Highmore**'s *The Art of Brutalism* (Yale, 2017) is an important related study. For British Pop of the 1960s see **David Alan Mellor**, *The Sixties Art Scene in London* (London, 1993). British Pop of the 1960s is usually discussed as part of an overall trend; see **Marco Livingstone**, *Pop Art: A Continuing History* (London, 1990), or **Lucy Lippard** (ed.), *Pop Art* (London, 1966, repr. 1974). For key individuals see **Maurice Tuchman and Stephanie Barron** (eds), *David Hockney: A Retrospective* (Los Angeles County Museum of Art, 1988–9), **South Bank Centre**, *Patrick Caulfield* (London, 1999), and **Tate Gallery** (London), *Peter Blake* (London, 1983).

Michael Kirby (ed.), *Happenings* (New York, 1966) includes descriptions of these events, whilst many important documents are brought together in **Mariellen Sandford**'s *Happenings and Other Acts* (London, 1995). For digestible accounts of Fluxus see **Thomas Kellein**, *Fluxus* (London, 1995) and the superb essays in **Walker Art Center**, *In the Spirit of Fluxus* (ex. cat.) (Minneapolis, 1993). As regards Oldenburg's early Happenings, see the documents collected in **Claes Oldenburg and Emmett Williams** (eds), *Store Days* (New York, 1967).

Most general works on Pop discuss America, but **Lawrence Alloway**'s *American Pop Art* (Whitney Museum, New York, 1974) is an important early study. The criticism is collected in **Steven Madoff**, *Pop Art: A Critical History* (University of California Press, 1997), whilst **Mark Francis** and **Hal Foster** produce a superb survey of the topic in *Pop* (Oxford, 2005). Two absorbing monographs on Pop are **Hal Foster**, *The First Pop Age* (Princeton University Press, 2014) and **Thomas Crow**, *The Long March of Pop: Art, Music and Design 1930–1995* (Yale University Press, 2014). An anecdotal account of the formation of a market and ambience for the style is given in **Calvin Tomkins**, *Off the Wall* (New York, 1980). **Cécile Whiting**'s *A Taste for Pop: Pop Art, Gender and Consumer Culture* (Cambridge, 1997) discusses the topic in relation to taste and consumerism.

For Roy Lichtenstein, see **Diane Waldman**'s catalogue (Solomon R. Guggenheim Museum, New York, 1993). Standard studies of Warhol are **Rainer Crone**, *Andy Warhol* (New York, 1970), and **Kynaston McShine** (ed.), *Andy Warhol: A Retrospective* (MoMA, New York, 1989), whilst an interesting set of essays is collected in **Gary Garrels** (ed.), *The Work of Andy Warhol* (Washington, 1989).

Weegee's career is surveyed in **Miles Barth**, *Weegee's World* (International Center of Photography, New York, 1997).

Sidra Stich's *Made in the USA: An Americanization in Modern Art, the 50s and 60s* (Berkeley, 1987) provides social backgrounds for many American Pop works. For Rosenquist see *James Rosenquist: The Early Pictures 1961–1964* (Gagosian Gallery, New York, 1992). A good general introduction to Ed Kienholz is given in **Walter Hopps** (ed.), *Kienholz: A Retrospective* (Whitney Museum, New York). An excellent overview of Öyvind Fahlström is provided by **Museu d'Art Contemporani de Barcelona**, *Öyvind Fahlström: Another Space for Painting* (ex. cat., 2000). For Polke and Richter see **Sigmar Polke**, *The Three Lies of Painting* (London, 1997), the **Tate Gallery** catalogue, *Gerhard Richter* (London, 1991), and **Terry Neff** (ed.), *Gerhard Richter: Paintings* (London, 1988).

Chapter 5. Modernism in Retreat: Minimalist Aesthetics and Beyond

Ad Reinhardt's writings are collected in **Barbara Rose** (ed.), *Art-as-Art* (New York, 1975, repr. Berkeley, 1991). The standard monographs on Ad Reinhardt and (early) Frank Stella remain those of **Lucy Lippard** (New York, 1985) and **William Rubin** (MoMA, New York, 1970) respectively. **Don Judd**'s own writings, collected as *Complete Writings 1959–1975* (New York, 1975), are indispensable. For David Smith, **Rosalind Krauss**'s *Terminal Iron Works: The Sculpture of David Smith* (Cambridge, Mass., 1971) is a key study, whilst for Anthony Caro, **William Rubin**'s *Anthony Caro* (MoMA, New York, 1975) is a model of Modernist-style criticism.

Gregory Battcock's *Minimal Art: A Critical Anthology* (New York, 1968, repr. 1995) is the main collection of critical texts on Minimalism, whilst **James Meyer**'s *Minimalism* (Oxford, 2000) provides an excellent overview. For a very concise general study see **David Batchelor**'s *Minimalism* (Tate Gallery, London, 1997). **Frances Colpitt**'s *Minimal Art: The Critical Perspective* (Washington, 1993) carefully follows the critical debates. For Robert Morris see **Solomon R. Guggenheim Museum**, *Robert Morris: The Mind/Body Problem* (New York, 1994). **Alicia Legg**'s edited monograph on Sol LeWitt (MoMA, New York, 1978) is useful on his early output.

For Carl Andre see **Diane Waldman** (ed.), *Carl Andre* (Solomon R. Guggenheim Museum, New York, 1970). A good monograph on Agnes Martin is **Barbara Haskell** (ed.), *Agnes Martin* (Whitney Museum, New York, 1992).

For Bridget Riley see the **Serpentine Gallery** catalogue (London, 1999); for James Turrell see **Craig Adcock**'s monograph (Berkeley, 1990).

There have been few in-depth studies on 'process art', but Anti Form's relation to Minimalism has underpinned a recent thematic reading of post-1945 art, **Yves Alain Bois and Rosalind Krauss**'s *Formless: A User's Guide* (New York, 1997, originally a catalogue for an exhibition at the Centre Georges Pompidou, Paris, 1996). For Eva Hesse the outstanding monograph is **Lucy Lippard**, *Eva Hesse* (New York, 1997). **Louise Bourgeois**'s writings and interviews are collected in *Destruction of the Father/Reconstruction of the Father* (London, 1998). Good general monographs are **Robert Storr** et al., *Louise Bourgeois* (Oxford, 2003) and **Marie-Louise Bernadac**, *Louise Bourgeois* (Paris, 1996).

The outstanding study of Richard Serra is *Richard Serra: Sculpture* (MoMA, New York, 1986). Film post-1945 is a topic in its own right, but useful essays are collected in **Russell Ferguson** (ed.), *Art and Film Since 1945: Hall of Mirrors* (MoCA, Los Angeles, 1996). See also **Michael O'Pray** (ed.), *Andy Warhol: Film Factory* (London, 1989). Bruce Nauman had several big exhibitions in the 1990s: see the catalogues for the Walker Art Center (Minneapolis, 1994) and Centre Georges Pompidou and Hayward Gallery (Paris and London, 1997–8).

For post-Minimalist developments in British sculpture see **Charles Harrison**'s essay in **Terry A. Neff** (ed.), *A Quiet Revolution: British Sculpture Since 1965* (New York, 1987). See also **Jon Thompson, Pier Luigi Tazzi, and Peter Schjeldahl**, *Richard Deacon* (London, 1995) and the **Liverpool Tate Gallery**'s useful *Rachel Whiteread: Shedding Life* (Liverpool, 1997).

Chapter 6. The Death of the Object: The Move to Conceptualism

COBRA: 1948–1951 (Paris, 1980) includes reprints of their journal. The literature on Lettrism is sparse but see the relevant sections of **Greil Marcus**'s freewheeling *Lipstick Traces* (London, 1989). For Situationism see **Peter Wollen**'s essay in **Elisabeth Sussman** (ed.), *On the Passage of a Few People Through a Rather Brief Moment in Time* (Cambridge, Mass., 1989); also **Simon**

Sadler's *The Situationist City* (Cambridge, Mass., 1998).

For **Daniel Buren** it is essential to read his own writings; see *Five Texts* (London, 1973) or *Limites Critiques* (Paris, 1970). The catalogue for the Marcel Broodthaers exhibition at the Walker Art Center (Minneapolis, 1989) is particularly recommended, whilst for a general study of Hans Haacke see **Brian Wallis** (ed.), *Unfinished Business* (Cambridge, Mass., 1986).

For Gordon Matta Clark see **MoCA**, *Gordon Matta Clark: A Retrospective* (Chicago, 1985).

Germano Celant's publications on *Arte Povera* are essential introductory texts; see, for instance, his *Arte Povera: Actual or Impossible Art?* (Milan and London, 1969). An excellent overview of the movement and its critical literature is **Carolyn Christov-Bakargiev**, *Arte Povera* (London, 1999).

For Robert Smithson his own writings are crucial: see **Nancy Holt** (ed.), *The Writings of Robert Smithson* (New York, 1979). He is often dealt with best from a quasi-philosophical standpoint. In this respect, see **Gary Shapiro**, *Earthwards: Robert Smithson and Art after Babel* (Berkeley, 1995). For concrete poetry see **Emmett Williams** (ed.), *An Anthology of Concrete Poetry* (New York, 1969). For Ian Hamilton Finlay see **Yves Abrioux**, *Ian Hamilton Finlay: A Visual Primer* (Edinburgh, 1985). Land Art is usefully surveyed in **Jeffrey Kastner and Brian Wallis**, *Land and Environmental Art* (London, 1998) and **Gilles A. Tiberghien**'s *Land Art* (London, 1995).

For Conceptual Art the essays in two catalogues—**Ann Goldstein and Anne Rorimer** (eds), *Reconsidering the Object of Art: 1962–1975* (MoCA, Los Angeles, 1995) and *L'art conceptuel, une perspective* (Musée d'Art Moderne de la Ville de Paris, 1988)—are indispensable, as is the overview presented in **Peter Osborne** (ed.), *Conceptual Art* (Oxford, 2002). **Tony Godfrey**'s *Conceptual Art* (London, 1998) is a very readable general study, and **Michael Newman and Jon Bird** (eds), *Rewriting Conceptual Art* (London, 1999) offers a wide-ranging set of historical studies. **Lucy Lippard**'s *Six Years: The Dematerialization of the Art Object, 1966–1972* (New York, 1973, repr. Berkeley, 1997) remains an indispensable chronicle, whilst **Alexander Alberro and Blake Stimson**'s *Conceptual Art: A Critical*

Anthology (Cambridge, Mass., 1999) collects together key texts. An important reassessment of the global reach of the movement was **Queens Museum of Art**'s *Global Conceptualism: Points of Origin, 1950s–1980s* (New York, 1999). **Joseph Kosuth**'s seminal writings are reprinted in his *Art after Philosophy and After* (ed. Gabriele Guercio, Cambridge, Mass., 1991). For Art & Language see **Charles Harrison**'s *Essays on Art & Language* (Oxford, 1991); for **Victor Burgin**'s 1970s art production see his *Between* (Oxford, 1986).

The classic early texts of feminist art history are **Linda Nochlin**'s essay 'Why Have There Been No Great Women Artists?', *Art News*, vol. 69, January 1971, and **Rozsika Parker and Griselda Pollock**, *Old Mistresses* (London, 1981). **Randy Rosen and Catherine C. Brawer**'s *Making Their Mark: Women Artists Move into the Mainstream 1970–1985* (New York, 1989) is useful on the increasing representation of women in 1970s and early 1980s art. For an excellent overview of Judy Chicago and related 'essentialist' forms of feminist art see **Amelia Jones** (ed.), *Sexual Politics* (Berkeley, 1996); for 'central-core' imagery **Lucy Lippard**'s *From the Center* (New York, 1976) is crucial. Theoretical opposition to 'essentialist' feminism is succinctly expressed in **Mary Kelly and Paul Smith**'s discussion 'No Essential Femininity', in **Mary Kelly**, *Imaging Desire* (Collected Writings, Cambridge, Mass., 1996). Mary Kelly's *Post-Partum Document* was published in book form (London, 1983).

Juliet Mitchell's *Psychoanalysis and Feminism* (London, 1974) is a key text for understanding feminist reinterpretations of Freud, whilst Jacques Lacan's ideas are usefully summed up in **Kaja Silverman**, *The Subject of Semiotics* (Oxford, 1983). For 'scripto-visual' feminist art see **Kate Linker and Jane Weinstock**, *Difference: On Representation and Sexuality* (New Museum of Contemporary Art, New York, 1985).

Derrida's thought, like Lacan's, presents difficulties, but a good introduction is via his interview with Henri Ronse: see **Jacques Derrida**, *Positions* (trans. Alan Bass, London, 1987).

General histories of Performance Art are **Roselee Goldberg**, *Performance Art: From Futurism to the Present* (New York, 1979, substantially revised 1988) and *Performance Art: Live Art Since the 1960s* (London, 1998), whilst **Gregory Battcock and Robert Nickas**, *The Art of Performance: A Critical Anthology*

(New York, 1984), contains essays on 1970s performance. A comprehensive catalogue, with several important essays, is **MoCA**, *Out of Actions: Between Performance and The Object 1949–1979* (Los Angeles, 1998).

Recent studies of Body Art include **Amelia Jones**'s *Body Art/Performing the Subject* (Minneapolis, 1998) and **Kathy O'Dell**, *Contract with the Skin: Masochism, Performance Art and the 1970s* (Minneapolis, 1998), whilst **Tracey Warr**, *The Artist's Body* (Oxford, 2000), provides an excellent overview. Carolee Schneemann's performances are documented in **Bruce McPherson** (ed.), *More Than Meat Joy: Carolee Schneemann: Performance Works and Selected Writings* (New York, 1979, repr. 1997). An introductory account of *écriture féminine* and related French feminist doctrines is given in **Toril Moi**, *Sexual/Textual Politics* (London, 1985). Useful monographs on male performance artists are: **Newport Harbour Art Museum**, *Chris Burden: A Twenty Year Survey* (Newport, 1988), **Kate Linker**, *Vito Acconci* (New York, 1994), and **ICA**, *Stuart Brisley* (London, 1981).

Gilbert and George 1968 to 1980 (Municipal Van Abbemuseum, Eindhoven, 1980) is comprehensive. For **Laurie Anderson** see her *Stories from the Nerve Bible: A Retrospective 1972–1992* (New York, 1994). Issues of performativity and masquerade are broadly discussed in **Jennifer Blessing** (ed.), *Rrose is a Rrose is a Rrose: Gender Performance in Photography* (Solomon R. Guggenheim Museum, New York, 1997).

Chapter 7. Postmodernism: Theory and Practice in the 1980s

Hans Bertens's *The Idea of the Postmodern* (London and New York, 1995) provides a useful history of the concept, and **Perry Anderson**'s *The Origins of Postmodernism* (London, 1998) summarizes the main theoretical ideas. No comprehensive study on the concept's applicability to art exists, although **Henry M. Sayre**'s *The Object of Performance: The American Avant-Garde Since 1970* (Chicago, 1989) and **Irving Sandler**'s *Art of the Postmodern Era* (New York, 1996) are substantial accounts with an American bias. **Sandy Nairne**'s *State of the Art* (London, 1997) is good on the institutional support systems for 1980s art. Two essential anthologies combine theoretical texts and

key critical writings on art: **Hal Foster** (ed.), *Postmodern Culture* (New York, 1995) and **Brian Wallis** (ed.), *Art After Modernism: Rethinking Representation* (New Museum of Contemporary Art, New York, 1984). A very useful survey of the period is **Helen Molesworth** (ed.), *This Will Have Been* (ex. cat.) (MoCA, Yale University Press, 2012).

Cindy Sherman's early work is surveyed in **MoCA**, *Cindy Sherman: A Retrospective* (Los Angeles, 1997), whilst **David Thistlewood** (ed.), *Sigmar Polke: Back to Postmodernity* (Liverpool University Press and Tate Gallery, Liverpool, 1996) specifically addresses a 'postmodern' reading of this artist.

The catalogues for *A New Spirit in Painting* (Royal Academy, London, 1981) and *Zeitgeist* (Martin-Gropius-Bau, Berlin, 1982) are important for the return to painting.

Useful monographs on American painters are **Dore Ashton**, *A Critical Study of Philip Guston* (Berkeley, 1976) and **ICA**, *Leon Golub, Mercenaries and Interrogations* (text by **Jon Bird**, London, 1982). For Italian and German art see **Achille Bonito Oliva**'s polemical *The Italian Transavantgarde* (Milan, 1980) and **Thomas Krens, Michael Govan, and Joseph Thompson** (eds), *Refigured Painting: The German Image 1960–88* (Munich, 1988). Donald Kuspit's writings on German painting, along with other aspects of 1980s art, are collected in **Donald Kuspit**, *The New Subjectivism: Art in the 1980s* (New York, 1988). Monographs on individual German artists include **Philadelphia Museum of Art**, *Anselm Kiefer* (Philadelphia, 1987) and **Museum of Modern Art Oxford**, *Jörg Immendorff* (Oxford, 1984). For Julian Schnabel see **Whitechapel Art Gallery**, *Julian Schnabel: Paintings 1975–1987* (London, 1987).

The criticism identified with *October* can be sampled by looking at two anthologies: **Annette Michelson, Rosalind Krauss, et al.** (eds), *October: The First Decade 1976–1986* (Cambridge, Mass., 1987) and *October: The Second Decade 1986–1996* (Cambridge, Mass., 1997). **Krauss**'s influential critical writings are collected in *The Originality of the Avant Garde and Other Modernist Myths* (Cambridge, Mass., 1985). Writings by *October*-related writers on issues such as photography, authorial removal, and 'situational aesthetics' are assembled in the following collections: **Douglas Crimp**, *On the Museum's Ruins* (Cambridge, Mass., 1993), **Craig Owens**, *Beyond Recognition: Representation, Power and Culture* (Berkeley, 1992), and **Hal Foster**, *Recodings: Art, Spectacle, Cultural Politics* (Washington, 1985). Monographs on individual artists include **Diane Waldman**, *Jenny Holzer* (New York, 1997), **Kate Linker**, *Love For Sale: The Words and Pictures of Barbara Kruger* (New York, 1990), **Hirshhorn Museum**, *Sherrie Levine* (Washington, 1988), and **Lisa Phillips** (ed.), *Richard Prince* (Whitney Museum, New York, 1992).

Photorealism of the 1960s was the subject of **Gregory Battcock**'s anthology, *Super Realism: A Critical Anthology* (New York, 1995), as well as a lavishly illustrated study, *Photo-realism*, by **Louis K. Miesel** (New York, 1980). Little has appeared since. For Malcolm Morley see the catalogue for the **Whitechapel Art Gallery**, London (1983); for Eric Fischl see **University of California Art Museum**, *Eric Fischl: Scenes Before the Eye* (1986). For Vija Celmins see the **ICA**, *Vija Celmins* (London, 1996). There is an extensive literature on **Gerhard Richter**. Along with books cited earlier in this section (end of Chapter 4), see **Richter**'s own writings: *The Daily Practice of Painting: Writings and Interviews 1962–1993* (trans. David Britt, London, 1995).

Art and ethnicity is a massive theme, but the following catalogues offer different approaches: **Centre Georges Pompidou**, *Magiciens de la Terre* (Paris, 1989), **University of California Art Museum**, *Mistaken Identities* (1993, with an essay by **Abigail Solomon-Godeau**), and **ICA**, *New Histories* (ex. cat.) (Boston, 1996). Two stimulating sets of essays are **Jean Fisher** (ed.), *Global Visions: Towards a New Internationalism in the Visual Arts* (London, 1994) and **Russell Ferguson** (ed.), *Out There: Marginalization and Contemporary Cultures* (New Museum of Contemporary Art, New York, 1990).

For **Terry Atkinson** see his *The Indexing, The World War I Moves and the Ruins of Conceptualism* (Circa Publications and Irish Museum of Modern Art, Belfast, 1992); for **Jimmie Durham** see his selected writings, *A Certain Lack of Coherence* (ed. Jean Fisher, London, 1993). On Robert Mapplethorpe see **Germano Celant**'s *Mapplethorpe* (Hayward Gallery, London, 1992). For Lorna Simpson see **Deborah Willis**, *Lorna Simpson* (San Francisco, 1992).

For late 1990s American art **Hal Foster**'s collection of critical essays, *The Return of the Real* (Cambridge, Mass., 1996), is invaluable.

For Simulation see also **ICA Boston**, *Endgame: Reference and Simulation in Recent Painting and Sculpture* (Cambridge, Mass., 1986). For Jeff Koons see the catalogue produced by **MoMA** (San Francisco, 1992). A useful catalogue on Tony Cragg is the one for the **Hayward Gallery**, London (1987). **Sidra Stich**'s edited exhibition catalogue, *Rosemarie Trockel* (University of California Art Museum, 1991), is also recommended.

An interesting set of essays relating theories of abjection to art is the **Whitney Museum**'s *Abject Art: Repulsion and Desire in American Art* (New York, 1993). Monographs include those by **Thomas Kellein**, *Mike Kelley* (Kunsthalle Basel and ICA, London, 1992) and **Museum Boymans-van Beuningen**, *Robert Gober* (Rotterdam, 1990). For **Helen Chadwick** see her *Effluvia* catalogue (Serpentine Gallery, London, 1994).

For installation as a medium of the late 1980s and early 1990s, see the catalogue of *Dislocations* (MoMA, New York, 1992). A useful general account of the topic is provided by **Claire Bishop** in *Installation Art: A Critical History* (Tate Publishing, 2005).

There is no major monograph as yet on Richard Wilson but see the **Serpentine Gallery**'s *Richard Wilson Jamming Gears* (London, 1996). For **Damien Hirst**, his own *I Want to Spend the Rest of my Life Everywhere, With Everyone, One to One, Always, Forever, Now* (London, 1997) provides a catalogue of his output.

Chapter 8. The 1990s: A New *Fin de Siècle*?

The range of European and American practices of the 1990s can be appreciated via *Parkett* magazine (based in New York, Zurich, and Frankfurt), which devoted special issues to artists' works. *Frieze* magazine, based in London, was also very influential. See also the catalogues for Kassel's *Documenta* exhibitions (nos 9 and 10, 1992 and 1997) and the Venice Biennale (1990, 1993, 1995, 1997, 1999).

Few attempts have so far been made to characterize 1990s art. **Bonnie Clearwater**'s catalogue, *Defining The Nineties:*

Consensus-Making in New York, Miami and Los Angeles (MoCA, Miami, 1996), interprets changes in taste formation in American art centres. A useful set of essays on European art is collected in **Gianfranco Maraniello** (ed.), *Art in Europe 1990–2000* (Skira, Milan, 2002). Two significant British exhibitions, seemingly arguing for a newly reflective spirit in art, were the **Hayward Gallery**, *Double Talk: Collective Memory and Current Art* (London, 1992) and the **Tate Gallery**, *Rites of Passage: Art at the End of the Century* (London, 1995). The Tate's *Abracadabra: International Contemporary Art* (London, 1999) attempted to survey the international scene at the end of the decade.

As far as Jeff Wall is concerned, see **Thierry de Duve, Arielle Pelenc, and Boris Groys**, *Jeff Wall* (London, 1996). For Ilya Kabakov see **Boris Groys, David A. Ross, and Iwona Blazwick**, *Ilya Kabakov* (London, 1998).

The yBa phenomenon in Britain has generated a lively, if often insubstantial, literature. The catalogue for *Sensation*, the important Royal Academy, London, exhibition of 1997, has a good essay by **Richard Shone** plotting the origins of the phenomenon. **Patricia Bickers**'s pamphlet *The Brit Pack: Contemporary British Art, the View from Abroad* (Cornerhouse, Manchester, 1995) carefully tracks its international flowering. A set of polemical essays on the yBa phenomenon, *Occupational Hazard*, by **Duncan McCorquodale, Naomi Siderfin, and Julian Stallabrass** (eds), was published in London (1998), whilst Stallabrass's *High Art Lite* (London, 1999) offers a sustained critique of the 1990s British art scene. For individual artists who emerged under the yBa umbrella see **Sarah Lucas** (ex. cat., Tate Liverpool/Tate Publishing, 2005) and **Mandy Merck and Chris Townsend**, *The Art of Tracey Emin* (London, 2002), alongside the brief essays in **Sarah Kent**, *Shark Infested Waters: The Saatchi Collection of British Art in the 90s* (London, 1994). For Sarah Lucas see also *Parkett* magazine, no. 45, 1995. For Mark Wallinger see the exhibition catalogues for the **Serpentine Gallery** (London, 1995) and **Tate Liverpool** (Tate Publishing, 2000).

For the *fin de siècle* morbidity of 1990s art see **Christoph Grunenberg**, *Gothic: Transmutations of Horror in Late Twentieth Century Art* (Cambridge, Mass., 1997), or, in a different register, the exhibition catalogue *Secret Victorians* (South Bank Centre, London, 1998).

For Douglas Gordon see **MoCA (Los Angeles)**, *Douglas Gordon* (2001), and **National Galleries of Scotland**, *Douglas Gordon; superhumanatural* (2007), whilst for Gillian Wearing see **Russell Ferguson, Donna De Salvo, and John Slyce**, *Gillian Wearing* (London, 1999).

A general introduction to video art is provided by **Michael Rush**, *Video Art* (London, 2003), whilst one useful catalogue, with a historical component, is the **Albright-Knox Art Gallery**'s *Being and Time: The Emergence of Video Projection* (1996). For Nam June Paik's pioneering use of the medium see also **Edith Decker-Phillips**, *Paik Video* (New York, 1998). **Bill Viola**'s writings are collected in *Reasons for Knocking at an Empty House: Writings 1973–1994* (London, 1995). A useful catalogue on Gary Hill is **MoMA and Tate Gallery**, *Gary Hill: In Light of the Other* (Oxford and Liverpool, 1993). For Willie Doherty see **Tate Gallery**, *Willie Doherty: Somewhere Else* (Liverpool, 1998).

Sophie Calle's photographs relating to *Suite vénitienne* were published with a text by **Jean Baudrillard**, *Suite vénitienne/please follow me* (Seattle, 1988). See also *Parkett*, no. 36, 1993. Yinka Shonibare features in **Ikon Gallery**, *Yinka Shonibare: Dressing Down* (Birmingham, 1999). For **Jeremy Deller** see his *Joy in People* (Hayward Publishing, London, 2012), along with **Jeremy Deller and Alan Kane**, *Folk Archive* (London, 2005). **Alan Sekula**'s *Fish Story* was published by Witte de With/Richter Verlag, Rotterdam, 1995.

For **Hal Foster**'s essays on 1990s art in relation to Surrealism see the aforementioned *The Return of the Real* (1996). More on Louise Bourgeois's *Red Rooms* appears in the **Tate Gallery**'s *Rites of Passage* catalogue (London, 1995). A general retrospective of Susan Hiller's output is provided in **Ann Gallagher**, *Susan Hiller* (Tate Publishing, London, 2011). Jeff Koons's later output is surveyed in **Hans Holzwarth** (ed), *Jeff Koons* (Taschen, Cologne, 2009), whilst for a discussion of the significance of the toy in late twentieth-century art see **David Hopkins**, *Childish Things* (Fruitmarket Gallery, Edinburgh, 2010). For Matthew Barney see **Nancy Spector**'s exhaustive *The Cremaster Cycle* (Guggenheim Museum, New York, 2002) and **Museum Boymans-van**

Beuningen, *Matthew Barney: Pace Car for the Hubris Pill* (Rotterdam, 1996), whilst *Parkett* no. 45, 1995, contains some interesting essays. A good general monograph on Fischli and Weiss is **Robert Leck et al.**, *David Fischli and Peter Weiss* (Oxford, 2005), whilst the most useful of the many publications on Kippenberger is **Eva Meyer-Hermann and Susanne Neuberger**, *Nach Kippenberger* (Museum Moderner Kunst Stiftung Ludwig, Vienna, 2003). Masculinity as a theme in late twentieth-century art is discussed in **David Hopkins**, *Dada's Boys: Masculinity After Duchamp* (Yale University Press, 2007).

The theme of memory is interestingly surveyed in the anthology *Memory*, edited by **Ian Farr** (Whitechapel Art Gallery, London, 2012). For a good general survey of Tacita Dean's output see **Jean-Christophe Royoux et al.**, *Tacita Dean* (Oxford, 2006). A good selection of writings relating to Richter's *Atlas* is **Adrian Searle and Benjamin Buchloh** (eds), *Gerhard Richter: Atlas: The Reader* (Whitechapel Art Gallery, London, 2012). On Johan Grimonprez see the **Fruitmarket Gallery, Edinburgh et al.**, *'It's a poor sort of memory that only works backwards'—on the work of Johan Grimonprez* (Edinburgh/Hatje Cantz, Ostfildern, 2011).

Chapter 9. Art and the New Millennium

As yet, few attempts have been made to produce an overview of post-2000 art. The sociopolitical (globalizing) shifts underpinning the period are discussed in **Michael Hardt and Antonio Negri**, *Empire* (Harvard University Press, 2000); see also **Antonio Negri**, *Multitude* (Cambridge, 2011). Useful compilations of essays on recent art include **Alexander Dumbadze and Suzanne Hudson** (eds), *Contemporary Art* (Chichester, 2013), whilst two particularly interesting monographs are **Terry Smith**, *What is Contemporary Art?* (University of Chicago Press, 2009) and **Julian Stallabrass**'s polemical *Contempoary Art: A Very Short Introduction* (Oxford, 2004), although it is confined to art prior to 2003. **Hal Foster**'s *Bad New Days: Art, Criticism, Emergency* (London, 2015) collects some of his recent critical writings.

Possibly the best way to review the period so far is via the huge Kassel *Documenta* catalogues for 2002, 2007, 2012 and 2017 (*Documenta* nos 11,12, 13 and 14).

The catalogues for the Venice Biennale (twice-yearly since 2001) are also indispensable. A useful, although disappointingly cursory, account of key exhibitions of the period is **Jens Hoffmann**, *Show Time: The 50 Most Influential Exhibitions of Contemporary Art* (London, 2014).

A general account of Gursky's photography is provided by **Peter Galassi**, *Andres Gursky* (MoMA, New York, 2001), whilst a useful set of critical essays on recent photography is **Diarmuid Costello and Margaret Iversen** (eds), *Photography after Conceptual Art* (Chichester, 2010).

In terms of art and the Internet, and digitization more generally, see **Edward A. Shanken**, *Art and Electronic Media* (Oxford, 2009), **Julian Stallabrass**, *Internet Art* (Tate Publishing, 2003), **Rachel Greene**, *Internet Art* (London, 2004), and **Christiane Paul** (ed.), *A Companion to Digital Art* (Chichester, 2016). **Amelia Jones**'s *Self/Image: Technology, Representation and the Contemporary Subject* (Routledge, 2006) is interesting in this context. For some useful essays on the institutional and support structures of the post-2000 art world see **Alexander Dubadze and Suzanne Hudson** as cited above. A fascinating historical background for the topic is also provided in **Caroline Jones**, *The Global Work of Art: World's Fairs, Biennials and the Aesthetics of Experience* (University of Chicago, 2017). In terms of curatorship see **Hans Ulrich Obrist**, *A Brief History of Curating* (Geneva, 2008). The first section of **Terry Smith**'s *What is Contemporary Art?*, previously cited, is strong on museums, whilst an interesting short discussion on recent museum policy is **Claire Bishop**, *Radical Museology* (London, 2013).

There is a sizeable literature on art in a globalized context but see in particular the essays in **Jonathan Harris** (ed.), *Globalization and Contemporary Art* (Chichester, 2011), whilst **Terry Smith**'s *Contemporary Art: World Currents* (London, 2011) provides an encyclopaedic account of pre-2010 world art. For *Documenta 11* see the large catalogue published by **Hatje Cantz Verlag**, Ostfildern, 2002. In terms of individual artists, see **Castello di Rivoli Museo Contemporanea, Milan**, *Shiran Neshat* (2002); **MoMA New York**, *Isaac Julien: Riot* (2013); **Kara Walker**, *Narratives of a Negress* (Cambridge, Mass., and London, 2003); and **Aspen Art Museum/ Museum of Modern Art, Oxford**, *Haegue Yang, Wild Against Gravity* (2011).

The issue of beauty is interestingly covered in **Dave Beech** (ed.), *Beauty* (Whitechapel Art Gallery, London, 2009). On Tanja Ostojić and 'the economic subject' see **Angela Dimitrakaki**, *Gender, artWork and the Global Imperative* (Manchester University Press, 2013). Recent performance art is discussed in an excellent set of essays in **Adrian Heathfield** (ed.), *Live: Art and Performance* (Tate Publishing, London, 2004), whilst the work of Cassils is the subject of **David J. Getsy**'s *The Image of Becoming: Heather Cassils's Allegories of Transformation* (MU, Eindhoven, 2015).

In terms of relational art see **Nicolas Bourriaud**, *Relational Aesthetics* (Les presses du réel, 2012), **Claire Bishop**'s general study of participatory art, *Artificial Hells: Participatory Art and the Politics of Spectatorship* (London, 2012), and **Grant Kester**'s study of global participatory art, *The One and the Many* (Duke University Press, 2011). **Bourriaud**'s slim *Postproducton* was published in New York, 2002. For individual artists see **Centre Georges Pompidou, Paris**, *Pierre Huyghe* (2014); **Liam Gillick**, *Proxemics: Selected Writings* (London, 2005); **Gridthiya Gaweewong and Maria Lind**, *Rirkrit Tiravanija: A Retrospective (Tomorrow is Another Fine Day)* (Geneva, 2007); **Santiago Sierra and Eckhard Schneider**, *Santiago Sierra: 300 Tons and Previous Works* (Cologne: Walther König, 2004); and **Cuauhtémoc Medina et al.**, *Francis Alÿs* (Oxford, 2007).

The issue of the post-medium condition is discussed in the introduction to **Rosalind Krauss**, *A Voyage on the North Sea; Art in the Age of the Post-Medium Condition* (London, 1999); see also her *Under Blue Cup* (Cambridge, Mass., and London, 2011). An overview of recent painting practices is provided in the three volumes of *Vitamin P: New Perspectives in Painting* (Oxford, 2007, 2016, and 2016) by **Barry Schwabsky**. For Tuymans see **Luc Tuymans et al.**, *Luc Tuymans* (Oxford, 2003), and for a recent catalogue on Marlene Dumas see **Leontine Coelewij et al.** (eds), *Marlene Dumas: The Image as Burden* (Tate Publishing, London, 2014).

On the recent Glasgow art scene see **Sarah Lowndes**, *Social Sculpture* (Stopstop, Glasgow, 2003), whilst for individual artists see the **Fruitmarket Gallery, Edinburgh**, *Louise Hopkins: Freedom of Information* (2005); **Russell Ferguson et al.**, *Richard Wright* (Gagosian Gallery, 2009); and **Daniel Baumann**, *Jim Lambie* (Rizzoli, New York, 2017). For Peter Doig see **Adrian Searle et al.**, *Peter Doig* (Oxford, 2007), and for John Currin see **Lawrence Jones**, *John Currin* (Gagosian Gallery, New York, 2016).

Nicolas Bourriaud's concept of 'Altmodernity' is explored in *Altermodern* (Tate Publishing, London, 2009), whilst the catalogue for *Documenta 13* was published by **Hatje Cantz**, Ostfildern, 2013. For Simon Starling see **Dieter Roelstraete et al.**, *Simon Starling* (Oxford, 2012). **Terry Smith**'s discussion of contemporaneity appears in his *What is Contemporary Art?*, as cited previously. A particularly useful discussion of ecological issues in contemporary art is **T. J. Demos**, *Decolonizing Nature* (Sternberg Press, Berlin, 2016). For **Assemble** see their *Granby Workshop Catalogue 2015* (included in the Turner Prize exhibition, Tramway, Glasgow, 2015). On Ed Atkins see **Beatrix Ruf and Julia Stoschek** (eds), *Ed Atkins* (ex. cat.) (Kunsthalle, Zurich, 2014). There is as yet no monograph devoted to **Melanie Gilligan** but see her *Five Scripts* (Bard College Publications, 2009).

Timeline
Galleries and Websites
Picture Credits
Index

Art	Events
1945	
1945	Jackson Pollock paints *There Were Seven in Eight* (MoMA, New York).	1945	America drops atom bombs on Hiroshima and Nagasaki. End of Second World War.

<table>
<tr><td colspan="2">Art</td><td colspan="2">Events</td></tr>
</table>

1945

1945 Jackson Pollock paints *There Were Seven in Eight* (MoMA, New York).
Jean Fautrier's 'Hostages' exhibition. René Drouin's gallery, Paris.
Special issue of New-York-based Surrealist magazine *View* on Marcel Duchamp.
Howard Putzel's exhibition 'A Problem for Critics' in New York.

1946 Francis Bacon's *Three Studies for Figures at the Base of a Crucifixion* (Tate Gallery, London) exhibited in London.
Arts Council of Great Britain is formed.
Lucio Fontana's *White Manifesto* published in Buenos Aires (leads to Italian artist's concept of 'Spatialism').
Duchamp begins work on *Etant Donnés* in New York.

1947 Jackson Pollock produces first 'drip' paintings.
Alberto Giacometti produces his sculpture *Man Pointing* (MoMA, New York).
International Surrealist exhibition held in Paris.
Antonin Artaud makes dramatic appearance at Vieux Colombes theatre, Paris.

1948 Suicide of Arshile Gorky.
Willem de Kooning produces important 'black paintings' (series begun in 1946) [**16**].
Germaine Richier in France completes *The Storm* [**36**].
The American journal *Possibilities 1* (Winter 1947/48) carries key statements by Pollock and Rothko.

1949 CoBrA group publishes its journal, *Copenhagen*.
Robert Motherwell's *At Five in the Afternoon* [**12**] initiates his series of *Elegies to the Spanish Republic*.
Life magazine runs an article on Pollock: 'Is He the Greatest Living Artist in the US?'
Willem de Kooning paints *Asheville* (Phillips Collection, Washington) and *Attic* (Metropolitan Museum and Newman Collection).

1950

1950 Jean Dubuffet begins *Corps de Dames* series [**9**].
Willem de Kooning starts large-scale series of *Women* [**23**].
Mark Rothko's mature style crystallizes.
American sculptor David Smith produces welded-steel sculptures at Bolton Landing, upstate New York.

1951 Pablo Picasso paints *Massacre in Korea* (Musée Picasso. Paris).
Barnett Newman's *Vir Heroicus Sublimis* [**6**].
Robert Rauschenberg's *White Paintings*.
Publication of the book *The Dada Painters and Poets* edited by Robert Motherwell.

1945 America drops atom bombs on Hiroshima and Nagasaki. End of Second World War.
Maurice Merleau-Ponty's treatise *The Phenomenology of Perception* (English translation, 1962).
George Orwell's book *Animal Farm*.
Roberto Rossellini's film *Rome, Open City*.

1946 Churchill denounces Soviet Union in 'Iron Curtain' speech in Fulton, Missouri, US.
War in French Indochina.
Italy becomes a republic.
Jean-Paul Sartre's booklet 'Existentialism and Humanism' (English translation, 1948).

1947 Cominform established at Warsaw Conference imposing common policies on all Eastern European Communist Parties (President Tito's Yugoslavia expelled in 1948).
Marshall Plan extends US aid to Europe.
Greek Civil War breaks out, leading to Truman Doctrine.
First transistor radios.

1948 Berlin Blockade and Airlift.
Soviet-backed *coup* establishes Communist government in Czechoslovakia.
Alfred Kinsey publishes *Sexual Behavior in the Human Male*.
Alfred Hitchcock's film *Rope*.

1949 Federal German Republic established in West Germany. German Democratic Republic in East Germany.
North Atlantic Treaty (NATO) alliance signed in Washington DC.
USSR explodes its first atomic bomb.
Simone de Beauvoir's book *The Second Sex*.

1950 Senator Joseph McCarthy warns President Truman that the US State Department is 'riddled with Communists'. Alger Hiss convicted of perjury.
Korean War begins.
First colour televisions in US.
Jean Cocteau's film *Orphée*.

1951 Rosenbergs sentenced to death as Soviet spies in US.
Chrysler introduces power steering for cars.
'Festival of Britain' exhibition on London's South Bank.
J.D. Salinger's book *The Catcher in the Rye*.

Art	Events
1952 Harold Rosenberg's essay 'The American Action Painters' appears in *Art News*. Cage–Rauschenberg 'Happening' at Black Mountain College. North Carolina, and first performance of John Cage's *4′33″* in Woodstock, New York. Helen Frankenthaler paints *Mountains and Sea* (National Gallery, Washington). Eduardo Paolozzi epidiascope lecture showing 'Bunk' materials at London's ICA.	1952 Dwight D. Eisenhower becomes US President. Britain conducts first atomic tests. America develops hydrogen bomb. First contraceptive pill developed. Samuel Beckett's play *Waiting for Godot*.
1953 Robert Rauschenberg's *Erased de Kooning* gesture. André Fougeron's *Civilisation Atlantique* [5]. Larry Rivers repaints *Washington Crossing the Delaware* (MoMA, New York). London's Independent Group mount 'Parallel of Life and Art' exhibition [46].	1953 Stalin dies. Khrushchev becomes USSR Party Secretary. Anti-French riots in Morocco (until 1955). Kinsey's *Sexual Behavior in the Human Female*. Henry Miller's play *The Crucible*.
1954 Painter Henri Matisse dies in France. Robert Rauschenberg begins producing 'Combines'. Arensberg Collection of Duchamp's work goes on display at Philadelphia Museum of Art. Jasper Johns begins first *Flag* painting [28] (completed early 1955).	1954 War begins in Algeria (continues until Algeria achieves independence from France, 1962). Censure of Senator Joseph McCarthy by US Senate. William Golding's novel *The Lord of the Flies*. Tennessee Williams's play *Cat on a Hot Tin Roof*.
1955 Alberto Burri's work [21] popular in New York. Included in 'The New Decade: Twenty-two European Painters and Sculptors' at MoMA. First Documenta exhibition, Kassel, West Germany. Robert Rauschenberg produces his 'Combine painting' *Bed* [19]. Richard Hamilton's 'Man, Machine and Motion' exhibition, Newcastle-upon-Tyne and London.	1955 Warsaw act established in Eastern Europe. West Germany joins NATO, African-American Rosa Parks refuses to give up her seat on a bus to a white man in Alabama, US. Successful black boycott of Montgomery bus service. French forces leave Vietnam.
1956 Tate Gallery, London, shows 'Modern Art in the United States' exhibition. Independent Group contributes to 'This is Tomorrow' exhibition, Whitechapel Art Gallery, London. Kurt Schwitters retrospective, Hanover. Jackson Pollock dies in a car crash.	1956 Khrushchev denounces Stalin's crimes in Soviet Union. Hungarian uprising suppressed by Soviet troops. Allen Ginsberg's poem *Howl* published in US. Elvis Presley's US single *Heartbreak Hotel*.
1957 Situationist International founded at Cosio d'Arroscia in Italy. Duchamp delivers 'Creative Act' lecture in US. Leo Castelli's gallery opens in New York. Yves Klein exhibits monochromes at Galleria Apollinaire, Milan.	1957 USSR launches first intercontinental ballistic missiles, followed by Sputniks I and II. Treaty of Rome establishes European Economic ommunity. Roland Barthes's essays published as *Mythologies* in France. Jack Kerouac's *On The Road* published in US.
1958 'The New American Painting' exhibition starts touring in Europe. Jasper Johns has first solo exhibition at Leo Castelli's, New York. Zero Group founded in Düsseldorf. Allan Kaprow's essay 'The Legacy of Jackson Pollock' published in *Art News*.	1958 Return of De Gaulle as French president. US launches first space satellite. Campaign for Nuclear Disarmament (CND) founded, London. First Aldermaston March. Mies Van der Rohe's Seagram Building, New York City.

Art	Events
1959 Lawrence Alloway's essay 'The Long Front of Culture' published in *Cambridge Opinion*. Allan Kaprow's *18 Happenings in 6 Parts* held at Reuben Gallery, New York. Frank Stella works on 'black paintings' (begun previous year) [**65**]. 'New Images of Man', MoMA, New York.	**1959** In Havana Fidel Castro proclaims Cuban revolution. 'Kitchen Debate' between Khrushchev and US Vice-President Nixon on US television. William Burroughs's *The Naked Lunch*. Günter Grass's *The Tin Drum*.
1960 Claes Oldenburg's installation *The Street* at Judson Memorial Church, New York. Followed next year by *The Store* [**53**]. Pierre Restany's manifesto launches 'New Realism' in Paris. Publication of English translation of Duchamp's notes for his *Large Glass*. Yves Klein performs *Leap into the Void* and *Anthropometries of the Blue Age*, Paris [**39**, **40**].	**1960** American U-2 spy plane shot down by USSR. First laser developed in Houston, Texas. Lifting of ban on D.H. Lawrence's *Lady Chatterley's Lover* in Britain after heavily publicized obscenity trial. Alfred Hitchcock's film *Psycho*.
1961 Georg Baselitz and Eugen Schönebeck in West Berlin collaborate on 'Pandemonium Manifesto'. Clement Greenberg's 'Modernist Painting' essay published in *Arts Yearbook*. Piero Manzoni cans his *Merda d'Artista* [**41**]. 'The Art of Assemblage' exhibition, MoMA, New York.	**1961** Berlin Wall is built. Soviet cosmonaut Yuri Gagarin becomes first man in space. John F. Kennedy becomes US president. 'Bay of Pigs' fiasco. Failed invasion by anti-Castro forces supported by the US.
1962 First event under Fluxus banner in Wiesbaden, West Germany, Nam June Paik performs *Zen for Head*. Andy Warhol's *Campbell Soup Cans* shown at Ferus Gallery, Los Angeles. His *Marilyn* series follows. 'The New Realists' exhibition at Sidney Janis Gallery, New York. Daniel Spoerri's *An Anecdoted Topography of Chance* published to coincide with exhibition in Paris.	**1962** Cuban Missile Crisis. After ultimatum by Kennedy, Soviet missiles withdrawn from Cuba. Marilyn Monroe commits suicide in US. Alexander Solzhenitsyn's *One Day in the Life of Ivan Denisovich*. Federico Fellini's film *8½*.
1963 Andy Warhol's *Five Deaths Seventeen Times in Black and White* [**56**]. Duchamp Retrospective at Pasadena Art Museum, California. Robert Morris and Don Judd show proto-Minimalist work at Green Gallery, New York. Richter and Lueg mount 'Life with Pop—A Demonstration of Capitalist Realism'. Düsseldorf.	**1963** President Kennedy assassinated, Dallas, Texas. Martin Luther King leads march on Washington DC. President Ngo Dinh Diem of South Vietnam assassinated in US-supported *coup*. Betty Friedan's book *The Feminine Mystique*.
1964 Carolee Schneemann's *Meat Joy* performed in Paris, London, and New York. Joseph Beuys performs *The Silence of Marcel Duchamp is Over-Rated* live on West German television. Robert Rauschenberg wins the main prize at the Venice Biennale. Susan Sontag's essay 'Notes on Camp' appears in *Partisan Review*.	**1964** Leonid Brezhnev replaces Khrushchev as Soviet leader. Harold Wilson forms Labour government in UK. 'Beatlemania' hits Britain and the US. Antonin Artaud's *The Theatre and its Double* first published in Paris.
1965 James Rosenquist's *F-111* mural shown at Leo Castelli's gallery, New York. Joseph Beuys performs *How to Explain Painting to a Dead Hare*, Schmela Gallery, Düsseldorf. Shigeko Kubota performs her *Vagina Painting* at 'Perpetual Fluxus Festival', New York [**51**]. 'Three American Painters' exhibition at Fogg Art Museum, Harvard.	**1965** Kennedy's successor, President Lyndon Johnson, steps up bombing raids on Vietnam. Race riots in Watts district of Los Angeles. Bob Dylan's LP *Highway 61 Revisited*, including 'Like A Rolling Stone'. Harold Pinter's play *The Homecoming*.

Art	Events
1966 'Primary Structures' exhibition at Jewish Museum, New York. Lucy Lippard's 'Eccentric Abstraction' show at New York's Fischbach Gallery. John Latham and students in London chew up Clement Greenberg's book *Art and Culture*. 'Destruction in Art Symposium' held in London. David Hockney paints bather images in California [**49**].	1966 In China, Mao Zedong launches the Great Proletarian Cultural Revolution to step up his Great Leap Forward begun in 1958. US *Surveyor 1* sends back photographs of the moon's surface. Publication of French intellectual historian Michel Foucault's *Les Mots et les Choses (The Order of Things)*. Publication of Masters and Johnson's *Human Sexual Response*.
1967 Michael Fried's essay 'Art and Objecthood' published in *Artforum*. Roland Barthes's essay 'Death of the Author' published in *Aspen* magazine in US. French publication in 1968 in *Manteia*. Germano Celant launches *Arte Povera* in Italy. Anthony Caro's sculpture *Prairie* [**68**].	1967 British parliament decriminalizes abortion and homosexuality. The Beatles' LP *Sergeant Pepper's Lonely Hearts Club Band* features cover by artist Peter Blake. Jean-Luc Godard's film *Week-end*. Jacques Derrida's post-Structuralist treatises *Of Grammatology* and *Writing and Difference* published in Paris.
1968 Death of Marcel Duchamp. Daniel Buren's 'stripes' borne by sandwich men in Paris [**82**]. Marcel Broodthaers's Musée d'Art Moderne (Section des Aigles) opens in Brussels. Robert Morris publishes 'Anti Form' in *Artforum*.	1968 Martin Luther King and Robert Kennedy assassinated in US. Student unrest throughout Europe. In Paris this leads to a General Strike. Warsaw Pact forces crush liberal reforms of Alexander Dubcek in Czechoslovakia. Electronic composer Karlheinz Stockhausen's choral composition *Stimmung*.
1969 Art Workers' Coalition mounts anti-Vietnam demonstrations at MoMA, New York. 'When Attitude Becomes Form' exhibition at Kunsthalle, Berne. Joseph Kosuth's 'Art After Philosophy' appears in *Studio International*. Gilbert and George's *Singing Sculpture* first performed in London.	1969 De Gaulle resigns as French president. Outbreak of 'Troubles' in Northern Ireland. US astronaut Neil Armstrong becomes first man to set foot on the moon. Woodstock Music Festival in upstate New York.
1970 Robert Smithson's *Spiral Jetty*, Great Salt Lake, Utah [**88**]. Hans Haacke's Visitors' Poll, MoMA, New York. Robert Morris exhibition at Tate Gallery, London, shut down as 'physically dangerous'. Willoughby Sharp inaugurates concept of Body Art.	1970 US President Richard Nixon (elected in 1968) extends American offensive in Vietnam to Cambodia. Four students protesting against Vietnam War are shot by National Guard at Kent State University, US. Alarming increase in international terrorism. Miles Davis's LP *Bitches' Brew*.
1971 'Contemporary Black Artists in America', Whitney Museum, New York. Daniel Buren's contribution removed from Guggenheim International Exhibition, New York.	1971 American losses in Vietnam top 45,000. President Nixon and national security adviser Henry Kissinger pursue *détente* with Soviet Union. Publication of Sylvia Plath's novel *The Bell Jar*.
1971 Linda Nochlin's essay 'Why Have There Been No Great Women Artists?' appears in *Art News*. Vija Cemins's *Untitled (Ocean with Cross, no.1)* [**112**] (theme dates back to the late 1960s).	1971 Stanley Kubrick's film *A Clockwork Orange*.

Art	Events
1972 Vito Acconci's *Seedbed* performance, New York. 'The New Art' exhibition, Hayward Gallery, London. Leo Steinberg's essay 'Other Criteria' describes Rauschenberg's conception of painting as 'post-Modernist'. Art & Language exhibit *Index 01* at Kassel Documenta exhibition.	**1972** Presidents Nixon and Brezhnev sign Strategic Arms Limitation Treaty (SALT 1). 'Bloody Sunday' massacres in Londonderry, Northern Ireland. British troops fire on Republican demonstrators. Pruitt-Igoe housing estate in St Louis, US is demolished. Luis Buñuel's film *The Discreet Charm of the Bourgeoisie*.
1973 Death of Pablo Picasso. Sale of the Robert and Ethel Scull art collection in New York. Robert Smithson dies in plane crash. Mary Kelly begins *Post-Partum Document* [**95**].	**1973** OPEC oil crisis. Prices are quadrupled over next four years. America withdraws troops from Vietnam. Thomas Pynchon's *Gravity's Rainbow*. Bernardo Bertolucci's film *Last Tango in Paris*.
1974 Chris Burden performs *Transfixed*, in Venice, California. (He is 'crucified' against the rear section of a Volkswagen.) Gordon Matta Clark's *Splitting* [**85**]. 'Nice Style' perform *High up on a Baroque Palazzo*, Garage, London. Joseph Beuys performs *Coyote* at René Block Gallery, New York [**42**].	**1974** Miners' Strike in Britain. High inflation begins to affect European economies. President Nixon resigns in US in aftermath of Watergate scandal. Alexander Solzhenitsyn forced into exile.
1975 Anthony Caro exhibition, MoMA, New York. Philip Guston in New York paints *The Magnet* (Saatchi Collection). Carolee Schneemann's *Interior Scroll* performance, Long Island, New York [**98**]. 'Bodyworks' exhibition, MoCA, Chicago.	**1975** North Vietnamese enter Saigon, ending the war. General Franco dies. Democracy, under King Juan Carlos, returns to Spain. US and USSR launch first joint space mission. Video recorders and floppy disks introduced for home use.
1976 *October* journal starts up in New York. Victor Burgin's *Possession* posters appear in Newcastle-upon-Tyne, England [**92**]. Outrage over purchase of part of Carl Andre's *Equivalents I–VIII* by London's Tate Gallery followed by COUM Transmissions 'Prostitution' show at the ICA. Christo's *Running Fence* project, Sonoma and Marin Counties, California.	**1976** Jimmy Carter elected Democrat US president. US space-probe *Viking 1* lands on Mars. Punk rock becomes established in UK. Sex Pistols' single 'Anarchy in the UK' released. Martin Scorsese's film *Taxi Driver*.
1977 Walter De Maria's *Vertical Earth Kilometer* at Kassel Documenta Exhibition. 'Pictures' exhibition, Artists Space, New York. Charles Jencks's *The Language of Post-Modern Architecture* published in London. Cindy Sherman begins *Untitled Film Stills* series [**101**].	**1977** First cases of AIDS diagnosed in New York City. Apple begins boom in home computers. Centre Pompidou opens in Paris, designed by Piano and Rogers. George Lucas's film *Star Wars*.
1978 Death of Giorgio de Chirico. 'Bad Painting' exhibition, New Museum of Contemporary Art, New York. Malcolm Morley's *The Ultimate Anxiety* [**109**]. Jörg Immendorf begins *Café Deutschland* paintings in Düsseldorf.	**1978** Red Brigade terrorism in Italy culminates in murder of a senior Christian Democrat politician, Aldo Moro. First test-tube baby born in UK. Astronauts discover a moon orbiting Pluto. Edward Said's *Orientalism* published.
1979 Judy Chicago's *The Dinner Party* [**94**] exhibited in San Francisco. Joseph Beuys's retrospective exhibition at Guggenheim Museum, New York. Julian Schnabel's first solo exhibition at Mary Boone's Gallery, New York, sells out. Georg Baselitz in Germany begins producing expressionist wood carvings as well as paintings.	**1979** Russia invades Afghanistan. Margaret Thatcher becomes Conservative prime minister of Britain. Publication of Jean-François Lyotard's treatise *The Postmodern Condition* in France. Francis Ford Coppola's film *Apocalypse Now*.

	Art	Events

1980

1980 Achille Bonito Oliva's *La Transavanguardia Italiana* published.
Anselm Kiefer and Georg Baselitz critically acclaimed at Venice Biennale.
Art & Language's *Portraits of V. I, Lenin in the Style of Jackson Pollock* [1].
'Women's Images of Men', ICA, London.

1981 Tony Cragg's *Britain Seen from the North* [118].
'A New Spirit in Painting' exhibition at London's Royal Academy. Publication of Rozsika Parker and Griselda Pollock's feminist art-historical study *Old Mistresses: Women, Art and Ideology*, 'Objects and Sculptures' exhibition, Bristol and London.

1982 'Zeitgeist' exhibition held in Berlin.
Joseph Beuys begins *7,000 Oaks* project at Documenta 7 in Kassel.
Documenta 7 registers return to painting.
Sigmar Polke's *This Is How You Sit Correctly (after Goya)* [102].

1983 Publication of Mary Kelly's book *Post-Partum Document*.
Laurie Anderson's performance *United States I–IV* in New York.
'The New Art' exhibition at Tate Gallery, London.
Gerhard Richter's *July* [113].

1984 Fredric Jameson's essay 'Postmodernism, or the Cultural Logic of Late Capitalism' published in *New Left Review*.
Turner Prize established in Britain. First winner Malcolm Morley.
'Primitivism and 20th Century Art' exhibition, MoMA, New York.
The exhibition 'Difference: On Representation and Sexuality', New Museum of Contemporary Art, New York.

1985

1985 Jenny Holzer's 'Truisms' on electronic billboards in Times Square, New York.
Jimmie Durham's *Bedia's Stirring Wheel* [115].
Saatchi Gallery opens in London.
Jeff Koons's 'Equilibrium' show in New York.

1980 Green Party established in West Germany, devoted primarily to ecological issues.
John Lennon shot dead in New York.
Strikes in Poland's Gdansk shipyards lead to emergence of 'Solidarity' movement demanding reforms.
Martin Scorsese's film *Raging Bull*.

1981 Ronald Reagan inaugurated as Republican US president.
François Mitterand elected Socialist president in France. Chinese scientists successfully clone a golden carp fish.
Facsimile (fax) machines become widespread.

1982 Falklands War between Britain and Argentina.
Helmut Kohl elected chancellor, West Germany.
Launch of insulin manufactured from bacteria marks first commercial use of genetic engineering.
Ridley Scott's film *Blade Runner*.

1983 President Reagan denounces USSR as 'Evil Empire' and announces Strategic Defence Initiative (SDI), or 'Star Wars' programme, for space-based missile systems.
Compact discs first marketed. They quickly replace records and tapes.
First artificially created chromosome produced at Harvard University, US.
Jean Baudrillard's *Simulations* published.

1984 Prolonged miners' strike in Britain. Its defeat heralds measures by Margaret Thatcher's government to reduce power of trades unions.
Ronald Reagan wins second term as US president.
Britain and Hong Kong agree on procedures to return Hong Kong to China in 1997, symbolizing an end to British colonialism.
Angela Carter's *Nights at the Circus* published.

1985 President Gorbachev comes to power in USSR. Inaugurates economic restructuring and greater cultural liberalism.
British scientists discover hole in ozone layer over Antarctica.
Following Greenpeace campaign against nuclear testing, French secret agents sink *Rainbow Warrior* in Auckland Harbour, New Zealand.
Primo Levi's book *The Periodic Table*.

Art	Events
1986 Death of Joseph Beuys. Museum Ludwig opens in Cologne and Museum of Contemporary Art in Los Angeles. Helen Chadwick's *Of Mutability* installation, ICA, London. 'Endgame' exhibition at Boston ICA.	**1986** Privatization of companies begins in UK. Chernobyl nuclear accident in USSR. Reactor explodes in Ukraine. 25,000 cases of AIDS diagnosed in US. David Lynch's film *Blue Velvet*.
1987 Death of Andy Warhol. Mike Kelley's *More Love Hours Than Can Ever Be Repaid* [120]. 'New York Art Now' at Saatchi Gallery, London. Richard Wilson's *20/50* first installed at Matt's Gallery, London [122].	**1987** Stock market crashes on 'Black Monday'. US and USSR sign treaty eliminating intermediate-range missiles. Bill Gates, founder of Microsoft, becomes microcomputer billionaire. Toni Morrison's book *Beloved*.
1988 Gerhard Richter's *October 18, 1977* cycle [111]. 'Freeze' exhibition in London's Docklands. Jeff Koons's 'Banality' works go on show in New York. Jasper Johns's *False Start* (1959) fetches $17.1 million at auction.	**1988** Widespread strikes in Poland. Internet computer virus affects over 6,000 US military computers. Salman Rushdie's *The Satanic Verses* arouses worldwide controversy. Physicist Stephen Hawking's book *A Brief History of Time*.
1989 Reproduction of Andres Serrano's *Piss Christ* (1987) torn up by Republican congressman in US Senate. Richard Serra's *Tilted Arc* (1981) destroyed at order of US authorities. Robert Mapplethorpe's retrospective 'The Perfect Moment' begins to tour in America. 'Magiciens de la terre' exhibition, La Villette and Pompidou Centre, Paris.	**1989** Soviet Army withdraws from Afghanistan. Communist rule ends in East Germany, Poland, Romania, Hungary, and Czechoslovakia. Berlin Wall comes down. Protesters massacred in Tiananmen Square, China. American *Voyager 2* space-probe reaches Neptune. *Galileo* probe launched for Jupiter.
1990 Controversial installation by Gran Fury collective at Venice Biennale, on the subject of AIDS. 'High and Low: Modern Art and Popular Culture' exhibition, MoMA, New York. Rachel Whiteread produces cast sculptures *Ghost* and *Untitled* (bath) (Saatchi Collection).	**1990** After release from prison black South African leader Nelson Mandela negotiates end of apartheid with President De Klerk. Margaret Thatcher resigns as British prime minister. Succeeded by John Major. Union of currencies of East and West Germany as a prelude to reunification.
1991 Christian Boltanski's *The Missing House* installation, East Berlin. 'Dislocations' (installation) exhibition, MoMA, New York. 'Metropolis' exhibition in Berlin. Sherrie Levine's polished bronze urinals, *After Marcel Duchamp* [30]. Damien Hirsts's *In and Out of Love* installation [123] and *The Impossibility of Death in the Mind of Someone Living*.	**1991** Threat of global warming recognized. Gulf War breaks out. UN forces expel Iraqi forces from Kuwait. Boris Yeltsin becomes Russian president. USSR is dissolved. Quentin Tarantino's film *Reservoir Dogs*. Jonathan Demme's film *Silence of the Lambs*.
1992 Ilya Kabakov's *The Toilet* installed at Documenta 9 in Kassel. 'Post Human' exhibition, Lausanne and elsewhere, curated by Jeffrey Deitch. Gary Hill's *Tall Ships* video work. Bill Viola's *Nantes Tryptich* video work.	**1992** Ethnic violence breaks out between Muslims and Serbs in former Yugoslavia. Bill Clinton elected Democrat president in US. 'Euro-Disney' opens in Paris. Digital video is launched.
1993 Hans Haacke's *Germania* installation in German Pavilion at Venice Biennale. Louise Bourgeois represents America at Venice Biennale with five *Cell* installations. 'Abject Art' exhibition, Whitney Museum, New York. Douglas Gordon's *24 Hour Psycho* video.	**1993** Maastricht Treaty comes into effect. Members of European Community agree to introduce a common currency. The Internet or 'Information Super-highway' starts to be promoted widely. Jane Campion's film *The Piano*. Steven Spielberg's film *Schindler's List*.

Art		Events	
1994	Demolition of Rachel Whiteread's *House* [81] in London after press controversy. Death of American critic Clement Greenberg. 'Bad Girls/Bad Girls West' exhibition, New York. Matthew Barney's *Cremaster 4* video [130].	1994	Russian forces invade breakaway republic of Chechnya. Official end of white rule in South Africa. Robert Altman's film *Short Cuts*. Quentin Tarantino's film *Pulp Fiction*.
1995 1995	Damien Hirst wins Turner Prize, London. 'Rites of Passage' exhibition, Tate Gallery, London. 'Brilliant: New Art from London' exhibition at Walker Art Center, Minneapolis. 'Reconsidering the Object of Art', exhibition on Conceptualism at MoCA, Los Angeles.	1995	Serb atrocities in Srebrenica spark NATO air raids on Bosnia-Herzegovina. Dayton Accords lead to peace settlement in the region. On 50th anniversary of Nagasaki, President Clinton announces a halt to nuclear testing. Gaullist Jacques Chirac elected French president. Irish poet Seamus Heaney wins Nobel Prize for Literature.
1996	'L'informe' exhibition, Pompidou Centre, Paris. 'life/live' exhibition in Paris. Publication of American critic Hal Foster's book *The Return of the Real*. Douglas Gordon wins Turner Prize, London.	1996	IRA resumes campaign of violence in Northern Ireland. Controversy over claims to property, confiscated from Jews by Nazis, still being held by Swiss banks 50 years after Second World War. Daniel Liebeskind's Jewish Museum, Berlin.
1997	Death of Willem de Kooning. Documenta 10 at Kassel emphasizes globalization and politics. 'Sensation' exhibition at Royal Academy, London. 'Rrose is a Rrose is a Rrose: Gender Performance in Photography' exhibition, Guggenheim Museum, New York.	1997	Tony Blair becomes Labour prime minister of Britain, ending 18 years of Conservative rule. Evidence of global warming increases in Antarctica. Frank Gehry's Guggenheim Museum, Bilbao, Spain. Cloning of a sheep at Roslin, near Edinburgh, UK, highlights concerns about genetic engineering.
1998	Major retrospective of Jackson Pollock at MoMA, New York (travels to London, 1999). Exhibition 'Out of Actions: Between Performance and the Object 1949–1979' at MoCA, Los Angeles. Painter Chris Ofili wins Turner Prize in London. Exhibition 'Wounds: Between Democracy and Redemption in Contemporary Art' at Moderna Museet, Stockholm.	1998	Peace Deal set up in Northern Ireland. US President Clinton accused of perjury after alleged sexual impropriety. Gerhard Schröder becomes German chancellor. The Coen brothers' film *The Big Lebowski*.
1999	Publication of art historian T. J. Clark's *Farewell to an Idea: Episodes from a History of Modernism*. Opening of Portugal's major contemporary art museum, Museu de Serralves, Oporto. Painter Gary Hume represents Britain at the Venice Biennale. Komar and Melamid represent Russia. Louise Bourgeois is awarded Golden Lion achievement award. Exhibition 'Abracadabra: International Contemporary Art' at Tate Gallery, London.	1999	Controversy over genetically modified foods. President Clinton acquitted of charges of perjury and obstruction of justice by US Senate. Prolonged NATO bombing leads to Serb surrender after Serbian massacres of ethnic Albanians in Kosovo. Massive exodus of refugees from Kosovo.

Art	Events
2000		

2000 Opening of Tate Modern (Bankside) gallery on London's South Bank.
Wolfgang Tillmans wins Turner Prize in London.
Manifesta 3 held in Ljubljana, Slovenia.
Protest and Survive exhibition held at Whitechapel Art Gallery, London (includes *The Bridge* installation by Thomas Hirschhorn, which links the gallery to an anarchist bookshop).

2000 Vladimir Putin elected president of Russia.
George Bush wins US presidential election.
Yugoslavia is readmitted as a new state to the United Nations.
Denmark votes to reject the euro.

2001 Jeremy Deller's *The Battle of Orgreave* performed in UK (**129**).
At the Venice Biennale, Golden Lions for Lifetime Achievement go to Richard Serra and Cy Twombly.
The Short Story: Independence and Liberation Movements in Africa exhibition held in Munich (curated by Okwui Enwezor).
Gregor Schneider (Germany) wins Golden Lion for Best Pavilion at the Venice Biennale.

2001 General election in UK returns Labour government, under Tony Blair, to power.
September 11: two hijacked aircraft destroy the Twin Towers of the World Trade Center, New York; a third hits the Pentagon, and a fourth crashes in Pennsylvania. Death toll estimated at 2,500.
US and British planes attack Taliban positions in Afghanistan. US ground troops in combat in Afghanistan.
First democratic elections held in Kosovo won by Albanian nationalists.

2002 Francis Alÿs's *When Faith Moves Mountains* action performed near Ventanilla, Peru.
Documenta 11, curated by Okwui Enwezor, deals with issues of globalization and migration.
Pierre Huyghe wins Hugo Boss Prize, New York.
Andreas Gursky photograph sells for over £400,000 at auction.

2002 Euro becomes official currency of 12 EU member states.
'Axis of evil' speech by President Bush identifies Iran, Iraq, and North Korea.
Yasser Arafat imprisoned. Israeli army completes reoccupation of West Bank.
A 12,000-page Iraq dossier on arms denies it has any banned arms or weapons of mass destruction.

2003 Frieze Art Fair is established in London.
Opening of Dia:Beacon Museum in Beacon, New York.
Founding of Prague Biennale.
Olafur Eliasson's *The Weather Project* is shown in the turbine hall at Tate Modern, London.

2003 The Human Genome Project (a worldwide scientific collaboration which identified and mapped all the genes of the human genome) is declared complete.
Massive protests against British involvement in the imminent Iraq War see London's biggest ever demonstration on 15 February.
The invasion of Iraq begins with air strikes against Baghdad on 20 March.
Saddam Hussein captured by US troops in December.

2004 Publication of Hal Foster, Rosalind Krauss, Benjamin Buchloh, and Yves-Alain Bois's book *Art After 1900*.
Jeremy Deller wins the Turner Prize in London.
Manifesta 5 is held in Donostia-San Sebastian, Spain.
Rirkrit Tiravanija wins Hugo Boss Prize, New York.

2004 On 10 March bomb blasts on Madrid commuter trains kill 191 people.
Israeli parliament approves plan for withdrawal of soldiers and settlers from Gaza Strip and parts of West Bank.
Palestinian president Yasser Arafat dies in hospital in Paris.
Tsunami kills over 225,000 along the Asian and East African coasts.

2005 Istanbul stages its 9th International Biennial.
At the Venice Biennale Thomas Schütte wins Golden Lion for best artist exhibited in the International Exhibition.
Barbara Kruger wins Golden Lion for Lifetime Achievement at the Venice Biennale.
Simon Starling wins the Turner Prize in London.

2005 On 6 July suicide bombers explode three bombs on the London Underground and one on a bus.
Israeli troops begin removing settlers from Gaza Strip and West Bank.
Angela Merkel elected by the Bundestag as first woman chancellor of Germany.
In Britain, Civil Partnership Act providing for registered unions between same-sex couples comes into force.

2006 *Manifesta 6* is held in Nicosia, Cyprus.
Tomma Abts wins the Turner Prize.
4th Berlin Biennial is held, with the title 'Of Mice and Men'.

2006 UN Security Council calls on Iran to halt uranium enrichment by end of August.
North Korea claims to have tested its first nuclear weapon.

Art	Events
Tacita Dean wins Hugo Boss Prize in New York.	A 700-page report by Sir Nicholas Stern warns of the economic consequences of global warming.

2007 Ten-yearly *Skulptur Projekte Münster* is held in Münster, Germany.
WACK!: Art and the Feminist Revolution exhibition at MoCA, Los Angeles.
Critic Benjamin Buchloh receives Golden Lion for his contribution to contemporary art criticism at the Venice Biennale.
Mark Wallinger wins Turner Prize in London.

2008 Massachusetts Museum of Contemporary Art mounts a retrospective of Sol LeWitt's wall drawings following his death in 2007.
Second phase of renovation at Los Angeles County Museum of Art, with architectural additions conceived by Renzo Piano.
Staging of *Prospect 1*, the first New Orleans international biennial.
Damien Hirst auction at Sotheby's, London. The artist sells work direct from his studio for £111 m.

2009 Golden Lions awarded to Yoko Ono and John Baldessari for Lifetime Achievement at the Venice Biennale.
Golden Lion for best pavilion at the Venice Biennale goes to Bruce Nauman (USA).
Nicolas Bourriaud's *Altermodern* exhibition is held at Tate Modern, London.
Richard Wright wins the Turner Prize in London.

2010 Death of Louise Bourgeois.
Manifesta 8 is held in Murcia, Spain.
Maria Abramović performs *The Artist is Present* over 736.5 hours at MoMA, New York.
First showing of Isaac Julien's installation *Ten Thousand Waves* at the Sydney Biennale (**139**).

2011 Chinese artist Ai Weiwei is imprisoned for 81 days in China.
Christian Marclay wins Golden Lion for Best Artist in the International Exhibition, Venice Biennale; Lifetime Achievement awards go to Elaine Sturtevant and Franz West.
Andreas Gursky's photograph *Rhein II* (1999) sells for £2.7 m at auction.
Martin Boyce wins the Turner Prize in London.

2012 *Documenta 13* takes place in Kassel, Germany.
Opening of Superflex's *Superkilen* (urban park project) in Copenhagen, Denmark.

Saddam Hussein is hanged in Baghdad.

2007 Romania and Bulgaria join the European Union.
Arctic sea ice levels hit a record low.
Lisbon Treaty is signed by EU members, strengthening the European Parliament and signalling greater European centralization.
Sub-prime mortgage crisis in US heralds what experts describe as the biggest financial crisis since the Great Depression.

2008 The oldest example of figurative sculpture, shaped from a mammoth tusk—the *Venus of Hohle Fels* (*c*.35,000 BC)—is discovered in Germany.
The Summer Olympics take place in Beijing, China.
Global banking crisis; in September US investment bank Lehman Brothers files for bankruptcy, the largest such event in US history.
In December Israel launches air strikes against Hamas in the Gaza Strip in response to rocket attacks on Israeli settlements.

2009 Israeli ground forces cross into the Gaza Strip in January.
Barack Obama is inaugurated as 44th and first African-American president of the USA.
British forces in Basra hand over control to US army.
Climate change conference in Copenhagen in December; delegates reach agreement on new measures to be introduced.

2010 Spanish surgeons perform the first full transplant of a human face.
The EU and the International Monetary Fund agree austerity measures with the Greek government, preparing the way for a bailout package for Greece.
After the resignation of Labour leader Gordon Brown, the new British coalition government embarks on austerity cuts in public services.
In July the WikiLeaks website, founded by Australian Internet activist Julian Assange, releases some 90,000 classified intelligence documents relating to the war in Afghanistan.

2011 President Obama announces that al-Qaeda leader Osama bin Laden has been killed by US forces near Islamabad.
Egyptian president Hosni Mubarak resigns in February. The army pledges to oversee a transition to democracy.
President Zine al-Abidine Ben Ali flees Tunisia, sparking protests that become the Arab Spring.
UK military operations in Iraq officially cease.

2012 UK economy in recession after shrinking decisively in first three months of the year.
The Shard, Europe's highest habitable structure, opens in London.

Art	Events
Cassils first performs *Becoming an Image*, in Los Angeles. Elizabeth Price wins the Turner Prize in London.	Major breakthrough in particle physics occurs with the discovery of the Higgs boson, originally hypothesized by Edinburgh physicist Peter Higgs in the 1960s. The International Red Cross declares that Syria is in a state of civil war; 200,000 people flee fighting in Aleppo, northern Syria.
2013 *Art Basel* (international art fair) opens its inaugural show in Hong Kong. Steve McQueen's feature film *12 Years a Slave* is released. Laure Prouvost wins the Turner Prize in London. Roni Horn wins Prix Joan Miró in Spain.	**2013** In June security leaks reveal widespread Internet surveillance by the US National Security Agency (NSA). Edward Snowden admits leaking details and flees to Russia. Deaths of Margaret Thatcher and Nelson Mandela. In October 350 die as a migrant ship from Libya sinks off Lampedusa, an island off southern Italy. By the end of 2013, the number of displaced people in the world reached its highest level since World War II.
2014 Polish artist Monika Sosnowska's *Tower* (twisted steel sculpture, 110 feet [33.5 metres] in length) is unveiled at Hauser & Wirth gallery New York. *Manifesta 10* is held in St Petersburg, Russia. Duncan Campbell wins the Turner Prize in London. Paul Chan wins the Hugo Boss Prize in New York.	**2014** Russia deploys troops in Crimea, where a referendum supports joining Russia. Putin signs Crimea annexation decree. UN General Assembly declares the annexation illegal. New terrorist group ISIS (Islamic State in Iraq and Syria) gains power in parts of Syria and notoriety in the West after beheadings of Western journalists and aid workers. ISIS takes Mosul, Syria, and a new refugee crisis begins; 500,000 flee Mosul. Anti-EU UKIP party comes into prominence in UK. Rise of the populist right in Europe.
2015 *Art Basel* in Basel, Switzerland attracts 98,000 visitors over 6 days; 284 galleries from over 33 countries are represented, and over 4,000 artists take part. The Whitney Museum, redesigned by Renzo Piano, reopens in New York. Willem de Kooning's painting *Interchange* (1955) is sold privately in the USA for $300 m. Jackson Pollock's *Number 17A* (1948) sells privately for $200 m. Hans Haacke's politically incendiary *Gift Horse* sculpture is installed on the fourth plinth in Trafalgar Square, London, for an 18-month period.	**2015** Increase in Islamist terrorist attacks (in Paris, 17 die in attack on the offices of the satirical magazine *Charlie Hebdo*, whilst more than 130 die in a coordinated attack on the Bataclan theatre and other sites in the city). Greece's prime minister Alexis Tsipras accepts the austerity demands from the European Central Bank and the IMF in August in exchange for bailout. In the UK, the Conservative Party wins the general election. Refugee crisis caused by conflict in Syria. By December over 4 million refugees are registered across Turkey, the Middle East, and North Africa.
2016 Bruce Connor and Agnes Martin retrospectives held in New York. Opening of extension to Tate Modern, London, designed by Herzog & de Meuron. Spain is awarded Golden Lion for Best Pavilion at the Venice Biennale of Architecture. Helen Marten wins the Turner Prize in London.	**2016** Terrorist attacks in Belgium, France, and Germany. British people vote to leave the European Union in referendum in June. The Nobel Prize for Literature is awarded to Bob Dylan. Death of David Bowie. Donald Trump defeats Hillary Clinton in US election.
2017 Deaths of Gustav Metzger and Howard Hodgkin in UK. Death of American artist Vito Acconci. A painting by the US artist Jean-Michel Basquiat (1960–88), *Untitled* of 1982, sells for $110.5 m at auction in New York.	**2017** Donald Trump inaugurated as 45th president of the USA. Turkish President Erdogan is granted sweeping new powers as a result of a national referendum, amid widespread criticism of the conduct of the poll.

Art	Events
Documenta 14 takes place in two locations, Kassel and Athens. Lubaina Himid wins the Turner Prize in London.	The US Trump administration withdraws from Paris Climate Agreement talks. In September North Korea tests a hydrogen bomb (its sixth nuclear weapon test since 2006). Addressing the United Nations, President Trump announces that the US is prepared, if necessary, to 'totally destroy' North Korea.

This list represents a selection of the most significant collections and temporary display spaces of artworks relevant to the text of this book.

	Gallery/Museum	Website
Australia	Museum of Contemporary Art Sydney	*http://www.mca.com.au/*
Belgium	Musées royaux des Beaux-Arts de Belgique Brussels	*http://www.fine-arts-museum.be/*
Canada	National Gallery of Canada Ottawa	*http://www.nationalgallery.ca/*
Czech Republic	Galerie Rudolfinum Prague	*http://www.galerierudolfinum.cz/*
Finland	Kiasma Museum of Art	*http://kiasma.fi*
France	Carré d'Art–Musee d'Art Contemporain Nîmes	*http://www.carreartmusee.com/*
	Centre Pompidou Paris	*http://www.centrepompidou.fr/*
	Fondation Cartier Paris	*http://www.fondationcartier.com/*
	Lille Métropole Musée d'art moderne, d'art contemporain et d'art brut Villeneuve d'Ascq	*http://www.musee-lam.fr/*
	Musee des Beaux-Arts de Lyon Lyons	*http://www.mba-lyon.fr/*
Germany	Museum für Moderne Kunst Frankfurt am Main	*http://www.mmk-frankfurt.de/*
	Museum Ludwig Cologne	*http://www.museenkoeln.de/*
	Neue Nationgalerie Berlin	*http://www.smb.museum/museen-und- einrichtungen-neue-nationalgalerie/ home.html*
Hungary	Ludwig Museum of Contmporary Art Budapest	*http://www.ludwigmuseum.hu*
Ireland	Irish Museum of Modern Art Dublin	*http://www.imma.ie/*
Italy	Guggenheim Museum Venice	*http://www.guggenheim-venice.it/museum/*
	Palazzo Grassi Venice	*http://www.palazzograssi.it/*
Japan	National Museum of Western Art Tokyo	*http://www.nmwa.go.jp/*
Mexico	Museo de Arte Moderno Mexico City	*http://www.museoartemoderno.com/*
Netherlands	Museum Boijmans Van Beuningen Rotterdam	*http://www.boijmans.nl/*
	Stedelijk Museum Amsterdam	*http://www.stedelijk.nl/*
	Witt de With Center for Contemporary Art Rotterdam	*http://wdw.nl*
Norway	Astrup Fearnley Museet Oslo	*http://www.afmuseet.no/*
Portugal	Serralves museum of Contemporary Art Porto	*http://www.serralves.pt*

	Gallery/Museum	Website
Spain	**Fundació Antoni Tàpies** Barcelona	*http://www.fundaciotapies.org/*
	Museo Guggenheim Bilbao	*http://www.guggenheim-bilbao.eus/*
	Museo Nacional Centro de Arte Reina Sofia Madrid	*http://www.museoreinasofia.es/*
Sweden	**Moderna Museet** Stockholm	*http://www.modernamuseet.se/*
Switzerland	**Museo d'Arte della Svizzera Italiana** Lugano	*http://www.masilugano.ch/*
UK	**Hayward Gallery** London	*http://www.southbankcentre.co.uk/venues/* *hayward-gallery/*
	Institute of Contemporary Arts London	*http://www.ica.org.uk/*
	Modern Art Oxford Oxford	*http://www.modernartoxford.org.uk/*
	Scottish National Gallery Edinburgh	*http://www.nationalgalleries.org/*
	Tate Modern London	*http://www.tate.org.uk/* (includes links to Tate Britain, Tate Liverpool, and Tate St Ives)
	Whitechapel Gallery London	*http://www.whitechapel.org/*
USA	**Dia:Beacon** Beacon, NY	*http://www.diaart.org/* (includes link to Dia:Chelsea, New York)
	Museum of Contemporary Art Los Angeles	*http://www.moca.org/*
	Museum of Modern Art (MoMA) New York	*http://www.moma.org/*
	National Gallery of Art Washington DC	*http://www.nga.gov/*
	San Francisco Museum of Modern Art San Francisco	*http://www.sfmoma.org/*
	Solomon R. Guggenheim Museum New York	*http://www.guggenheim.org/*
	Walker Art Center Minneapolis	*http://www.walkerart.org/*
	Whitney Museum of American Art New York	*http://www.whitney.org/*

Picture Credits

The publisher would like to thank the
following individuals and institutions who
have kindly given permission to reproduce
the illustrations listed below.

1. Art & Language, *V.I. Lenin by
V. Charangovich (1970) in the Style of Jackson
Pollock II*, 1980. Enamel and cellulose paint
on canvas, 293 × 210 cm. © Art & Language;
courtesy of the Artists and Lisson Gallery.
2. Jackson Pollock, *The Guardians of the
Secret*, 1943. Oil on canvas, 121.9 × 191.8 cm.
San Francisco Museum of Modern Art,
Albert M. Bender Collection, Albert M.
Bender Bequest Fund purchase. © The
Pollock-Krasner Foundation/ARS, New
York and DACS, London 2018. Photo:
Katherine Du Tiel.
3. Jackson Pollock, *Full Fathom Five*, 1947.
Oil on canvas with nails, tacks, buttons,
key, coins, cigarettes, matches, etc., 129.2 ×
76.5 cm. © The Pollock-Krasner
Foundation ARS, New York and DACS,
London 2018. Photo: Museum of Modern
Art, New York, USA/Bridgeman Images.
4. Renato Guttuso, *The Discussion*,
1959–60. © DACS 2018. Photo: © Tate,
London 2017.
5. André Fougeron, *Civilisation Atlantique*,
1953. © ADAGP, Paris and DACS, London
2018. Photo: © Tate, London 2017.
6. Barnett Newman, *Vir Heroicus Sublimis*,
1950, 1951. Oil on canvas, 242.2 × 513.6 cm.
© The Barnett Newman Foundation,
New York/DACS, London 2018. Photo:
The Museum of Modern Art, New York/
Scala, Florence.
7. Jean Fautrier, *La Toute Jeune Fille (Very
Young Girl)*, 1942. Reproduced courtesy of
Lauros-Giraudon, © ADAGP, Paris and
DACS, London 2018. Photo: © Jean
Fautrier/Musée de l'Ile de France, Sceaux,
France/Bridgeman Images.
8. Wols (Alfred Otto Wolfgang Schulze),
Manhattan, 1948–9. Oil on canvas,

146 × 97 cm. The Menil Collection,
Houston. © ADAGP, Paris and DACS,
London 2018. Photo: Hickey-Robertson,
Houston.
9. Jean Dubuffet, *Le Métafisyx*, 1950.
Centre Georges Pompidou, Paris.
© ADAGP, Paris and DACS, London 2018.
© Jean Dubuffet/Musée National d'Art
Moderne, Centre Pompidou, Paris/
Bridgeman Images.
10. Brassaï, *La Mort (Death)*. Musée
National d'art Moderne, Centre Pompidou,
Centre de Creation Industrielle. © Brassaï
Estate - RMN-Grand Palais. Photo: Centre
Pompidou, MNAM-CCI, Dist. RMN-
Grand Palais/Adam Rzepka.
11. Mark Rothko, *Green & Maroon*, 1953. Oil
on canvas, 231.8 × 139.1 cm. © 1998 Kate
Rothko Prizel & Christopher Rothko/ARS,
New York and DACS, London 2018. Photo:
The Phillips Collection, Washington, D.C.,
USA/Acquired 1957/Bridgeman Images.
12. Robert Motherwell, *At Five in the
Afternoon*, 1949. Casein on canvas, 38.1 ×
50.8 cm. © Dedalus Foundation, Inc./
VAGA, New York/DACS, London 2018.
13. Morris Louis, *Blue Veil*, 1958–9. Acrylic
resin painted on canvas, 233.05 × 396.24 cm.
Harvard Art Museums/Fogg Museum, Gift
of Lois Orswell and Gifts for Special Uses
Fund, 1965.28. © Maryland College
Institute of Art (MICA), All Rights
Reserved/ARS, New York and DACS,
London 2018. Photo: Imaging Department/
© President and Fellows of Harvard College.
14. Peter Lanyon, *Bojewyan Farms*, 1951–2.
Oil on masonite. © Sheila Lanyon, All
Rights Reserved/DACS, London 2018.
Photo: Courtesy of the British Council
Collection.
15. Henri Michaux, *Untitled*, 1960. Indian
ink on paper, 74.9 × 109.9 cm. © ADAGP,
Paris and DACS, London 2018. Photo:
The Museum of Modern Art, New York/
Scala, Florence.

16. Willem de Kooning, *Untitled*, 1948–9. Enamel and oil on paper on composition board, 94.8 × 127 cm. The Willem de Kooning Foundation/ARS, New York and DACS, London 2018. Photo: The Art Institute of Chicago/Art Resource, NY/ Scala, Florence.

17. Marcel Duchamp, *Boîte-en-valise*, 1935–41. Leather valise containing miniature replicas, photographs, colour reproductions of works by Duchamp, and one 'original' drawing (*Large Glass*, collotype on celluloid, 19 × 23.5 cm). 40.7 × 38.1 × 10.2 cm. Luxe edition no. IX/XX. James Thrall Soby Fund. Acc. no. 67.1943.a-rrr. © Succession Marcel Duchamp/ADAGP, Paris and DACS, London 2018. Digital image: The Museum of Modern Art, New York/Scala, Florence.

18. Marcel Duchamp, *The Bride Stripped Bare by her Bachelors, Even (The Large Glass)*, 1915–23. Oil, varnish, lead foil, lead wire, and dust on two glass panels (cracked), each mounted between glass panels, with five glass strips, aluminium foil, and a wood and steel frame, 277.5 × 175.9 cm. Philadelphia Museum of Art. © Succession Marcel Duchamp/ADAGP, Paris and DACS, London 2018. Photo: TopFoto.co.uk.

19. Robert Rauschenberg, *Bed*, 1955. Combine painting: oil and pencil on pillow, quilt, and sheet on wood supports, 191.1 × 80 × 20.3 cm. © Robert Rauschenberg Foundation/DACS, London/VAGA, New York 2018. Digital image, The Museum of Modern Art, New York/Scala, Florence.

20. Joseph Cornell, *Untitled (Medici Princess)*, *c*.1948. Wood box with mixed media, 44.5 × 11.4 cm. © The Joseph and Robert Cornell Memorial Foundation/ VAGA, New York and DACS, London 2018. Photo: Private collection/Bridgeman Images.

21. Alberto Burri, *Saccho H8*, 1953. Burlap, oil, and Vinavil on canvas, 86 × 100 cm. Private collection, Italy. © Fondazione Palazzo Albizzini Collezione Burri, Città di Castello (Perugia)/DACS 2018.

22. Cy Twombly, *School of Athens*, 1961. Oil, house paint, crayon, and pencil on canvas, 190.3 × 200.5 cm. Private collection. © Cy Twombly Foundation. Photo: courtesy of the Gagosian Gallery, London.

23. Willem de Kooning, *Woman and Bicycle*, 1952–3. Oil on canvas. 194.3 × 124.5 cm. Whitney Museum of American Art, New York; purchase 55.35. © The Willem de Kooning Foundation/ARS NY and DACS, London 2018.

24. Lee Krasner, *Bald Eagle*, 1955. Oil, paper, and canvas on linen, 195.6 × 130.8 cm. Private collection, Los Angeles. © ARS, New York and DACS, London 2018.

25. Marcel Duchamp and Man Ray, *Belle Haleine, Eau de Voilette*, 1921. © Succession Marcel Duchamp/ADAGP, Paris and DACS, London 2018 and © Man Ray Trust/ADAGP, Paris and DACS, London 2018. Photo: Private collection/Christie's Images/Bridgeman Images.

26. Jasper Johns, *Target with Plaster Casts*, 1955. Encaustic and collage on canvas with plaster casts, 130 × 111.8 × 8.9 cm. © Jasper Johns/VAGA, New York/DACS, London 2018. Photo: Private collection/ Bridgeman Images.

27. Robert Morris, *I-Box*, 1962. Painted plywood cabinet covered with sculptmetal, containing photograph, 48.3 × 32.4 × 3.5 cm. © Robert Morris/ARS, New York and DACS, London 2018. Photo: courtesy Castelli Gallery.

28. Jasper Johns, *Flag*, 1954–5. Encaustic, oil, and collage on fabric mounted on plywood, 107.3 × 153.8 cm. © Jasper Johns/ VAGA, New York/DACS, London 2018. Photo: The Museum of Modern Art, New York/Scala, Florence.

29. Jasper Johns, *Numbers*, 1966. Metallic powder and graphite wash on polyester fabric. © Jasper Johns/VAGA, New York/ DACS, London 2018. Gift of Leo Castelli in memory of Toiny Castelli,1989.82.1. Photo: courtesy of the National Gallery of Art, Washington.

30. Sherrie Levine, *Fountain (After Marcel Duchamp)*, 1991. Bronze, wood base. 66.1 × 36.8 × 35.6 cm. © Sherrie Levine. Photo: Private collection/Christie's Images/ Bridgeman Images.

31. Robert Gober, *Two Urinals*, 1986. Plaster, wire lath, wood, and enamel paints in two parts. Each: 19 × 16 × 14 inches; 48 × 41 × 36 cm. Overall: 19 × 47 × 14 inches; 48 × 119 × 36 cm. © Robert Gober, courtesy of the artist & Matthew Marks Gallery.

32. Henry Moore, *Working Model for Reclining Figure: Internal/External Form*, 1951. Bronze, 53.3 cm (length). © The Henry Moore Foundation. All rights reserved, www.henry-moore.org/DACS, London 2018. Photo: reproduced by permission of the Henry Moore Foundation.

33. Francis Bacon, *Study of a Baboon*, 1953. Oil on canvas, 198.3 × 137.3 cm. © The Estate of Francis Bacon. All rights

reserved, DACS, London 2018. Digital image: The Museum of Modern Art, New York/Scala, Florence.

34. Lucian Freud, *Interior at Paddington*, 1951. Walker Art Gallery, National Museums Liverpool/© The Lucian Freud Archive/Bridgeman Images.

35. Alberto Giacometti, *Standing Figure*, 1946. Pencil, 63.8 × 48.3 cm. Sainsbury Centre for Visual Arts, University of East Anglia. © The Estate of Alberto Giacometti (Fondation Annette et Alberto Giacometti, Paris and ADAGP, Paris), licensed in the UK by ACS and DACS, London 2018. Photo: Robert and Lisa Sainsbury Collection. Photographer: Pete Huggins.

36. Germaine Richier, *L'Orage (The Storm)*, 1947. © ADAGP, Paris and DACS, London 2018. Photo: © Centre Pompidou, Musée National d'Art Moderne-Centre de Création Industrielle, Dist. RMN-Grand Palais/Jean-Claude Planchet.

37. Antonin Artaud, *Self-Portrait*, 1947. Pencil on paper, 55 × 54 cm. Private collection. © ADAGP, Paris and DACS, London 2018.

38. Arman, *In Limbo*, 1961. Broken dolls in wood and glass box, 101.6 × 30.5 cm. © ADAGP, Paris and DACS, London 2018. Photo: courtesy of Marianne and Pierre Nahon, Galerie Beaubourg, Paris.

39. Yves Klein, *Single Day Newspaper (November 27th 1960)*, incorporating a photograph captioned *The Painter of Space Hurls Himself into The Void*. Fontenay-aux-Roses, France, October 23 1960. (Photo) Artistic action by Yves Klein. Museum of Fine Arts, Houston, Texas, USA/Museum purchase funded by Joan Morgenstern, The Manfred Heiting Collection. © The Estate of Yves Klein c/o ADAGP, Paris and DACS, London 2018. Photo: Shunk-Kender/© J. Paul Getty Trust/Bridgeman Images; (newspaper) Metropolitan Museum of Art, New York. © The Estate of Yves Klein c/o ADAGP, Paris and DACS, London 2018. Photo: Shunk-Kender/© J. Paul Getty Trust/akg-images/Mondadori Portfolio/Electa/Fabrizio Carraro.

40. Yves Klein, *Anthropometries of the Blue Age*, performance, 9 March 1960. © The Estate of Yves Klein c/o ADAGP, Paris and DACS, London 2018. Photo: Shunk-Kender/© J. Paul Getty Trust/ Getty Research Institute, Los Angeles (2014.R.20).

41. Piero Manzoni, *The Artist with 'Merda d'artista'*, at Angli Shirt Factory, Herning, Denmark, 1961. © DACS, London 2018. Photo: Ole Bagger. Courtesy of HEART - Herning Museum of Contemporary Art.

42. Joseph Beuys, *Coyote*, 1974. Performance. © DACS, London 2018. Photo: Caroline Tisdall.

43. Joseph Beuys, *Filter Fat Corner*, 1963. © DACS, London 2018. Photo taken in the artist's studio in Dusseldorf by Eva BeuysWurmbach (not preserved).

44. Georg Baselitz, *Die grosse Nacht im Eimer (The Big Night Down the Drain)*, 1962–3. Museum Ludwig, Cologne. © Georg Baselitz 2018. Photo: Jochen Littkemann, Berlin.

45. Eduardo Paolozzi, *Evadne in Green Dimension*, 1952. Collage on paper. Victoria and Albert Museum, London. © Trustees of the Paolozzi Foundation/DACS, London 2018. Photo: akg-images.

46. Independent Group, *Parallel of Life and Art*, photograph of exhibition installation, ICA, London, September–October 1953. © Nigel Henderson Estate. Photo: © Tate, London 2017.

47. Richard Hamilton, *$he*, 1958–61. Oil, cellulose paint, and collage on wood. © R. Hamilton. All Rights Reserved, DACS 2018. Photo: © Tate, London 2017.

48. Nigel Henderson, *Head of a Man*, 1956. Photo collage on paper, 168 × 131 cm. © Nigel Henderson Estate. Photo: © Tate, London 2017.

49. David Hockney, *Sunbather*, 1966. Acrylic on canvas, 72 × 72 in, Collection Museum Ludwig, Cologne. © David Hockney.

50. Jim Dine, *The Car Crash*, 1960, 'Happening'. © Jim Dine/ARS, New York and DACS, London 2018. Photo: Getty Research Institute, Los Angeles (2014.M.7)/© J. Paul Getty Trust.

51. Shigeko Kubota, *Vagina Painting*, 4 July 1965. The Gilbert and Lila Silverman Fluxus Collection Gift. Acc. No. 2308.2008. © Shigeko Kubota/VAGA, New York and DACS, London 2018. Photo: George Maciunas/© ARS, New York and DACS, London 2018. © 2017. Digital image, The Museum of Modern Art, New York, Scala, Florence.

52. Willem de Ridder, *European Mail-Order Warehouse/Fluxshop*, 1964–5. Originally arranged for photograph and reassembled 1984 by Jon Hendricks as installation, Contemporary Arts Museum, Houston, Texas. Photo Rick Gardner. Reproduced courtesy of Gilbert & Lila Silverman Fluxus Collection Foundation, New York.

53. Claes Oldenburg, *The Store*, 1961.
© Claes Oldenburg, 1961. Photo: Robert
McElroy/Getty Research Institute, Los
Angeles (2014 M.7)/© J. Paul Getty Trust.
54. Roy Lichtenstein, *Big Painting VI*, 1965.
Oil and magna on canvas, 233 × 328 cm.
North Rhine-Westphalia Art Collection,
Dusseldorf. © Estate of Roy Lichtenstein/
DACS 2018. Photo: akg-images.
55. Andy Warhol, *Cow Wallpaper*, 1966.
Silkscreen ink on paper, 111.8 × 78.2 cm.
© The Andy Warhol Foundation for the
Visual Arts, Inc./ARS, New York and
DACS, London 2018. Photo: Collection of
The Andy Warhol Museum, Pittsburgh.
56. Andy Warhol, *Five Deaths Seventeen
Times in Black and White*, from *Disasters*
series, 1963. Silkscreen print on canvas,
217 × 418 cm. Kunstmuseum, Basel. © The
Andy Warhol Foundation for the Visual
Arts, Inc./ARS, New York and DACS,
London 2018. Photo: akg-images.
57. Ed Ruscha, *Standard, Amarillo, Texas*,
from *Twentysix Gasoline Stations* (artist's
book), 1963. © Ed Ruscha.
58. Weegee, *'Sudden Death for One…
Sudden Shock for the Other…' Mrs Dorothy
Reportella, Accused of Hitting Bread Truck
with Her Car, September 7, 1944*. Photo:
Weegee (Arthur Fellig)/International
Center of Photography/Getty Images.
59. James Rosenquist, *Painting for the
American Negro*, 1962–3. Oil on canvas,
203 × 533 cm. National Gallery of Canada,
Ottawa (15292). Purchased 1967. © James
Rosenquist/VAGA, New York and DACS,
London 2018. Photo: NGC.
60. Robert Rauschenberg, *Retroactive 1*, 1964.
Oil, silkscreen, ink on canvas. 213.4 × 152.4
cm. © Robert Rauschenberg Foundation/
VAGA, New York and DACS, London 2018.
Photo: Allen Phillips/Wadsworth Atheneum.
61. Ed Kienholz, *Five Car Stud*, 1969–72.
Tableau: cars, plaster casts, guns, rope,
masks, chainsaw, clothing, oil pan with
water and plastic letters, paint, polyester
resin, styrofoam rocks, and dirt. Dimensions
variable. Courtesy of Fondazione Prada,
Milan, and Kienholz/L.A. Louver, Venice,
CA. Photo: Attilio Maranzano.
62. Öyvind Fahlström, *CIA Monopoly
(Small)*, 1971. Variable painting. Acrylic and
India ink on vinyl with magnets and metal
panel, 63.5 × 88.9 cm/25 × 35 inches.
Private collection. © Sharon Avery-
Fahlström/DACS, London 2018.
63. Sigmar Polke, *Bunnies*, 1966. Acrylic
on linen, 149.2 × 99.1 cm. Hirshhorn

Museum, Washington. Joseph H.
Hirshhorn Bequest and Purchase Fund,
1992. © The Estate of Sigmar Polke,
Cologne/DACS, London 2018. Photo:
akg-images.
64. Ellsworth Kelly, *Blue on White*, 1961.
Oil on canvas, 85 5/8 × 67 3/4 inches
(217.5 × 172.1 cm). Smithsonian American
Art Museum, Washington, DC. Gift of S. C.
Johnson & Son, Inc., 1969. © Ellsworth
Kelly Foundation (EK 272).
65. Frank Stella, *Die Fahne hoch!*, 1959.
Enamel on canvas, 308.6 × 185.4 cm.
Whitney Museum of American Art,
New York; gift of Mr. and Mrs. Eugene M.
Schwartz and purchase with funds from the
John I. H. Baur Purchase Fund, the Charles
and Anita Blatt Fund, Peter M. Brant, B. H.
Friedman, the Gilman Foundation, Inc.,
Susan Morse Hilles, The Lauder
Foundation, Frances and Sydney Lewis,
the Albert A. List Fund, Philip Morris
Incorporated, Sandra Payson, Mr. and Mrs.
Albrecht Saalfield, Mrs. Percy Uris, Warner
Communications Inc., and the National
Endowment for the Arts 75.22. © Frank
Stella/ARS, New York and DACS, London
2018.
66. Donald Judd, *Untitled*, 1969.
Galvanized iron and plexiglass, overall:
304.8 × 68.8 × 60.96 cm; 10 boxes, each
box: 15.24 × 68.8 × 60.96 cm. Albright
Knox Art Gallery, Edmund Hayes Fund,
1972. © Judd Foundation/ARS, New York
and DACS, London 2018. Photo: Art
Resource, NY/Scala, Florence.
67. David Smith, *Lectern Sentinel*, 1961.
Stainless steel, 44.8 × 84 × 52 cm. Whitney
Museum of American Art, New York;
purchase with funds from the Friends of
the Whitney Museum of American Art
62.15. © Estate of David Smith/VAGA,
New York and DACS, London 2018.
68. Anthony Caro, *Prairie*, 1967. Steel
painted matt yellow, 96.5 × 582 × 320 cm.
Collection of Lois & Georges De Meril,
USA, c/o National Gallery of Art,
Washington, DC. Courtesy of © Barford
Sculptures Limited.
69. Robert Morris, Installation at the
Green Gallery, New York 1964–5. © Robert
Morris/ARS, New York and DACS, London
2018. Photo: courtesy Castelli Gallery.
70. Sol LeWitt, *Circles, Grids, Arcs from
Four Corners and Sides*, 1973. Detail of wall
drawing in pencil. Draughtsmen: Climbo,
Piccari, Battista, Pranovi. L'Attico, via
Beccaria, Rome. © ARS, New York and

DACS, London 2018. Courtesy Fabio Sargentini, L'Attico Archive.

71. Carl Andre, *144 Magnesium Square*, 1969. 1 × 366 × 366 cm. © Carl Andre/VAGA, New York/DACS, London 2018. Photo: © Tate, London 2017.

72. Agnes Martin, *Flower in the Wind*, 1963. Oil and pencil on canvas, 190.5 × 190.5 cm. © Agnes Martin/DACS 2018 Daros Collection, Switzerland.

73. Bridget Riley, *Blaze 1*, 1962. Emulsion on board, 109 × 109 cm. Private collection. © Bridget Riley 2017. All rights reserved.

74. Eva Hesse, *Accession II*, 1968 (1969). Galvanized steel, vinyl, 78 × 78 × 78 cm. © The Estate of Eva Hesse. Courtesy Hauser & Wirth. Photo: Detroit Institute of Arts, USA/Bridgeman Images.

75. Eva Hesse, *Hang Up*, 1966. Acrylic, cloth, wood, cord, steel, 182.9 × 213.4 × 198.1 cm. © The Estate of Eva Hesse. Courtesy Hauser & Wirth. Photo: The Art Institute of Chicago, IL, USA/Through prior gifts of Arthur Keating and Mr. and Mrs. Edward Morris/Bridgeman Images.

76. Louise Bourgeois, *Double Negative*, 1963. Plaster, latex, textile, dried grass, 49.2 × 95.2 × 79.6 cm. © The Easton Foundation/VAGA, New York and DACS, London 2018. Photo courtesy of Kröller-Müller Museum Collection, Otterlo, The Netherlands.

77. Richard Serra, *Hand Catching Lead*, 1968. Film still. © ARS, New York and DACS, London 2018. Photo: The Art Institute of Chicago, IL, USA/Gift of Society for Contemporary Art/Bridgeman Images.

78. Bruce Nauman, *Dance or Exercise on the Perimeter of a Square*, 1967–8. Film still. © Bruce Nauman/ARS, New York and DACS, London 2018. Photo: courtesy Sperone Westwater, New York.

79. Bruce Nauman, *My Last Name Exaggerated Fourteen Times Vertically*, 1967. Neon tubing with clear glass tubing suspension frame, 160 × 83.8 × 5.1 cm. © Bruce Nauman/ARS, New York and DACS, London 2018. Photo: courtesy Sperone Westwater, New York.

80. Richard Deacon, *Untitled*, 1980. Galvanised steel and concrete, 138 × 374 × 138 cm. Private collection, London. Photo: Edward Woodman. Reproduced courtesy of the artist.

81. Rachel Whiteread, *House*, 1993. 193 Grove Road, London E3. Destroyed 1993. © Rachel Whiteread. Photo: Sue Omerod. Courtesy of the artist and Gagosian.

82. Daniel Buren, *Photo-souvenir: Hommes/Sandwichs*, 1968. Work in situ, April 1968, Paris (detail). © DB-ADAGP Paris and DACS, London 2018. Photo: Bernard Boyer.

83. Asger Jorn, *Le Canard Inquiétant*, 1959. Oil on old canvas, 53 × 54.5 cm. Museum Jorn, Silkeborg, Denmark. © DACS, London 2018. Photo: © Donation Jorn.

84. Marcel Broodthaers, *Musée d'Arte Moderne, Département des Aigles, Section des Figures*, 1972. © DACS, London 2018. Photo: © Maria Gilissen 1972.

85. Gordon Matta-Clark, *Splitting*, 1974. Gelatin-silver print collage mounted on board, 101.6 × 76.2 cm. Purchased with funds provided by Walter J. Brownstone and the Family of Man Fund. 326.1991. © Estate of Gordon Matta-Clark/ARS, New York and DACS, London 2018. Digital image, The Museum of Modern Art, New York/Scala, Florence.

86. Luciano Fabro, *Italia d'Oro (Golden Italy)*, 1971. © Silvia Fabro (Archivio Luciano e Carla Fabro, Milan). Photo: © Archivio Fotografico Annalisa Guidetti e Giovanni Ricci, Milan.

87. Jannis Kounellis, *Horses*, 1969. Mixed media, black and white photo. © DACS, London 2018. Photo: Private collection/Bridgeman Images.

88. Robert Smithson, *Stills from the Spiral Jetty Film (Panel A)*, 1970. Black and white silver gelatin prints. Three panels: each with 12 photographs, size: each panel 26 × 44 inches, overall 26 × 136 inches. © Holt-Smithson Foundation/VAGA, New York and DACS, London 2018. Photo: courtesy of James Cohan Gallery, New York.

89. Ian Hamilton Finlay, *Wave Rock*, 1966. Private Collection. Courtesy of the Estate of Ian Hamilton Finlay.

90. Walter de Maria, *The Lightning Field*, 1977. Long-term installation, western New Mexico. © The Estate of Walter De Maria. Photo: John Cliett. Courtesy Dia Art Foundation, New York.

91. On Kawara, *9 AGO 68*, 1968. Acrylic (Liquitex) on canvas, 20.4 × 25.2 × 4.4 cm. Museum für Moderne Kunst, Frankfurt. © Estate of On Kawara. Photo: Axel Schneider.

92. Victor Burgin, *Possession*, 1976. Photolithographic print, 109.2 × 109.2 cm. Original in colour; 500 copies posted in the streets in centre of Newcastle-upon-Tyne, summer 1976. 'Shocks to the System' exhibition, South Bank Centre Foyer Galleries, 12 March–24 April 1991.

© Victor Burgin. Photo: courtesy of
Richard Saltoun Gallery.
93. Bernd and Hilla Becher, *Typology of
Water Towers* (groups A, B, C, and D),
1972. Six suites of nine photographs, each
40 × 29.8 cm. © The Estate of Bernd &
Hilla Becher. The Eli and Edythe L. Broad
Collection. Photo: Douglas M. Parker
Studio, Los Angeles.
94. Judy Chicago, *The Dinner Party*. Wing
Three, featuring the Virginia Woolf and
Georgia O'Keefe place-settings, 1979. Mixed
media, 121.9 × 106.7 × 7.6 cm. © Judy
Chicago. Photo: © Donald Woodman/ARS,
New York and DACS, London 2018.
95. Mary Kelly, *Post-Partum Document:
Documentation I: Analysed Faecal Stains and
Feeding Charts*, 1974. Perspex, white card,
diaper linings, plastic sheeting, paper, ink,
31 units, 35.5 × 28 cm, 14 × 11 in (each).
Art Gallery of Ontario. Gift from the Junior
Committee Fund, 1987, 87/46. © Mary
Kelly/DACS, London 2018. Photo:
courtesy the artist and Pippy Houldsworth
Gallery, London.
96. Rebecca Horn, *Touching the walls with
both hands simultaneously*, from *Berlin
Exercises* film, 1974. © Rebecca Horn/
DACS, London 2018. Photo: Helmut Wietz.
97. Adrian Piper, *Self-Portrait Exaggerating
My Negroid Features*, 1981. Pencil drawing,
25.4 × 20.3 cm. Collection of Eileen Harris
Norton. © Adrian Piper Research Archive
Foundation Berlin.
98. Carolee Schneemann, *Interior Scroll*,
1975. Performance. © Carolee Schneemann.
Photo: Anthony McCall.
99. Chris Burden, Shoot, 1971. Performance.
© Chris Burden/licensed by The Chris
Burden Estate and DACS 2018.
100. Gilbert and George, *The Alcoholic*,
1978.16 gelatin silver prints, 60.3 × 50.2 cm
each; 242 × 202 cm installed. Twentieth-
Century Purchase Fund, 1978.57a-p. The
Art Institute of Chicago. © Gilbert and
George. Photo: Art Resource, NY/Scala,
Florence.
101. Cindy Sherman, *Untitled Film Still #6*,
1977. Gelatin silver print, 25.4 × 20.3 cm.
Courtesy of the artist and Metro Pictures,
New York. © 2017 Cindy Sherman.
102. Sigmar Polke, *This is How You Sit
Correctly (after Goya)*, 1982. Acrylic,
200 × 180 cm. © The Estate of Sigmar
Polke, Cologne/DACS 2018. Photo:
Private collection/Bridgeman Images.
103. Philip Guston, *Talking*, 1979. Oil on
canvas, 174 × 198 cm. © The Estate of

Philip Guston, courtesy Hauser & Wirth.
Photo: The Museum of Modern Art,
New York/Scala, Florence
104. Leon Golub, *Mercenaries II*, 1979.
Acrylic on canvas, 305 × 366 cm. The
Montreal Museum of Fine Arts, purchase,
Horsley and Annie Townsend Bequest.
© The Nancy Spero and Leon Golub
Foundation for the Arts/DACS, London/
VAGA, New York 2018. Photo: The Montreal
Museum of Fine Arts, Brian Merrett.
105. Anselm Kiefer, *Sulamith (Shulamite)*,
1983. Oil, acrylic, woodcut, emulsion and
straw on canvas, 290 × 370 cm. © Anselm
Kiefer. Courtesy of San Francisco Museum
of Modern Art.
106. Hans Haacke, *Taking Stock (Unfinished)*,
1983–4. Oil on canvas, 241.3 × 205.7 ×
17.8 cm. © DACS, London 2018. Courtesy
of the artist and Paula Cooper Gallery,
New York.
107. Jenny Holzer, from *Survival*, 1983–85
(installation view selection from *The Survival
Series*, Times Square, New York, 1985).
Electronic sign, 6.1 × 12.2 m. © Jenny
Holzer/ARS, New York and DACS/Artimage,
London 2018. Photo: John Marchael.
108. Richard Prince, *Untitled (Cowboy)*,
1991–2. Chromogenic print, 49 1/4 in. ×
70 5/8 in. (125.1 cm × 179.39 cm). San
Francisco Museum of Modern Art,
Accessions Committee Fund purchase: gift
of Jean Douglas, Doris and Donald Fisher,
Elaine McKeon, Byron R. Meyer, and
Helen and Charles Schwab. © Richard
Prince. Photo: Ben Blackwell.
109. Malcolm Morley, *The Ultimate Anxiety*,
1978. Oil on canvas, 184.2 × 248.9 cm.
© Malcolm Morley. Courtesy of Sperone
Westwater, New York.
110. Eric Fischl, *The Old Man's Boat and the
Old Man's Dog*, 1982. Oil on canvas,
213.4 × 213.4 cm. Private collection. © Eric
Fischl. Courtesy of the Artist.
111. Gerhard Richter, *Dead (Tote)* from
October 18, 1977 series,1988. Oil on canvas,
62 × 62 cm. The Museum of Modern Art,
New York. Purchase. © Gerhard Richter
2017 (0246).
112. Vija Celmins, *Untitled (Ocean with
Cross #1)*, 1971. Graphite on acrylic ground
on paper. © Vija Celmins, courtesy of
Matthew Marks Gallery. Photo: The
Museum of Modern Art, New York/Scala,
Florence.
113. Gerhard Richter, *July, 1983*. Oil on
canvas, 250 × 250 cm. Private collection.
© Gerhard Richter 2017 (25072017).

114. Terry Atkinson, *The Stone Touchers 1, Ruby and Amber In The Gardens of their old Empire history-dressed Men*, 1984–5. Acrylic on canvas. 213 × 152 cm. Private collection, Vancouver. © Terry Atkinson. Image courtesy of the Artist and Gimpel Fils.

115. Jimmie Durham, *Bedia's Stirring Wheel*, 1985. Various materials, 121.9 × 48.3 cm. Car steering wheel with shifter, metal car wheel, cotton American flag, cow leather, fur, sheepskin, pigeon feather, dog skull, beads, plastic doll, acrylic paint. 107.3 × 45.7 cm diam. Collection of Karen and Andy Stillpass. © Jimmie Durham. Image courtesy of Andy Stillpass. Photo: Tony Walsh.

116. Lorna Simpson, *Guarded Conditions*, 1989. 18 dye diffusion color Polaroid prints, six frames total (three prints in each), 21 engraved plastic plaques, 17 plastic letters. Overall: 214 × 376.6 × 4.1 cm. Museum of Contemporary Art, San Diego, Museum purchase. Contemporary Collectors Fund, 1990. (12.1–28). © 1989 Lorna Simpson, courtesy of the Artist and Hauser & Wirth.

117. Jeff Koons, *Made in Heaven*, 1989. Lithograph billboard, 152.4 × 228.6 cm. © Jeff Koons.

118. Tony Cragg, *Britain Seen from the North*, 1981, Purchased 1982. © DACS, London 2018. Photo: © Tate, London 2017.

119. Rosemarie Trockel, *Balaclavas*, 1986. Series of five woollen hoods. © Rosemarie Trockel/VG Bild Kunst and DACS, London 2018. Courtesy of Sprüeth Magers.

120. Mike Kelley, *More Love Hours Than Can Ever Be Repaid*, 1987. Handmade stuffed animals and afghans sewn on canvas backing. Whitney Museum of American Art, New York. © Mike Kelley Foundation for the Arts. All rights reserved/ licensed by DACS, London 2018. Photo: Peter Horree/Alamy Stock Photo.

121. Helen Chadwick, *Loop My Loop*, 1991. Cibachrome transparency, glass, aluminium, electrical apparatus. 127 × 76 × 15cm. Edition of 3 (HEC102). © The Estate of Helen Chadwick. Courtesy of Richard Saltoun Gallery.

122. Richard Wilson, *20/50*, 1987. Installation: used sump oil, steel. Dimensions variable. © Richard Wilson. Saatchi Gallery London, 1991–2000.

123a. Damien Hirst, *In and Out of Love (White Paintings & Live Butterflies)*, 1991. Installation. Primer on canvas with pupae, steel, potted flowers, live butterflies, Formica, MDF, bowls, sugar-water solution, fruit, radiators, heaters, cool misters, air vents, lights, thermometers, and humidistats. Dimensions variable. © Damien Hirst and Science Ltd. All rights reserved, DACS/ Artimage 2018. Photo: Prudence Cuming Associates Ltd.

123b. Damien Hirst, *I Love You*, 1994–5. Gloss household paint and butterflies on canvas, 2.13 × 2.13 m. © Damien Hirst and Science Ltd. All rights reserved, DACS/Artimage 2018. Photo: Stephen White.

124. Jeff Wall, *Dead Troops Talk (A Vision After an Ambush of a Red Army Patrol near Moqor, Afghanistan, Winter 1986)*, 1992. Transparency in lightbox, 229 × 417 cm. © Jeff Wall, courtesy of the artist.

125. Zofia Kulik, *All the Missiles Are One Missile*, 1993. 300 × 850 cm. Zak Branicka Gallery, Berlin. © Zofia Kulik. Reproduced courtesy of the artist.

126. Sarah Lucas, *Au Naturel*, 1994. Mattress, water-bucket, melons, oranges, and cucumber, 84 × 167.6 × 144.8 cm. © Sarah Lucas. Courtesy of Sadie Coles HQ, London.

127. Gillian Wearing, *Dancing in Peckham*, 1994. Colour video with sound, 25 minutes. © Gillian Wearing. Courtesy of Maureen Paley, London.

128. Yinka Shonibare, *How Does a Girl Like You Get to be a Girl Like You?*, 1995. Installation of three costumes of wax-print cotton textiles tailored by Sian Lewis, approx. height, 168 cm. © Yinka Shonibare MBE. All rights reserved, DACS, London 2018. Photo: courtesy of Stephen Friedman Gallery.

129. Jeremy Deller, *The Battle of Orgreave*, 2001. © Jeremy Deller. Directed by Mike Figgis. Commissioned by Artangel in association with Channel 4. Photos: © Martin Jenkinson Image Library. All rights reserved, DACS, London/Artimage 2018.

130. Allan Sekula, *Waterfront vendors living in containers*, Veracruz, March 1994 (right half of a diptych), from Allan Sekula's book *Fish Story*, 1989–1995. © The Estate of Allan Sekula. Courtesy of Allan Sekula Studio.

131. Louise Bourgeois, *Red Room (Child)*, 1994. Installation: mixed media, 210.8 × 353 × 274.3 cm. Collection Musée d'Art Contemporain de Montréal. Collection Musée d'Art Contemporain de Montréal. © The Easton Foundation/ VAGA, New York/DACS, London 2018. Photo: Marcus Schneider.

132. Susan Hiller, *An Entertainment*, 1990. Four-channel video installation with sound. Collection Tate, London. © Susan Hiller. All rights reserved, DACS 2018.

133. Matthew Barney, *Cremaster 4*, 1994. Production still. © Matthew Barney. Photo: Michael James O'Brien. Courtesy of the artist and Gladstone Gallery, New York and Brussels.

134. Martin Kippenberger, *Untitled*, 1992. Lantern for documenta IX. Iron, lacquer, glass, light bulb, plexiglass, 250 × 165 × 38 cm. Galerie Gisela Capitain, Cologne. © Estate of Martin Kippenberger.

135. Johan Grimonprez, *dial H-I-S-T-O-R-Y*, 1997. Three hijacked planes on desert airstrip near Amman, Jordan, 12 September 1970. Still from *dial H-I-S-T-O-R-Y*, 1997, 68 minute loop, edition of 35. © Johan Grimonprez. Courtesy of Sean Kelly, New York.

136. Andreas Gursky, *Grand Hyatt Hotel*, 2000. © Andreas Gursky/DACS, London 2018. Courtesy of Sprüeth Magers.

137. etoy, *The Twelve Days of Christmas*, 1999. Internet page. © 1999: the TOYWAR.soldiers represented by the etoy.VC group.

138. Shirin Neshat, *Seeking Martyrdom #2*, 1995. RC print & ink (photo by Cynthia Preston), 27.9 × 35.6 cm. Edition of 10 + 1AP. © Shirin Neshat. Courtesy of the artist and Gladstone Gallery, New York and Brussels.

139. Isaac Julien, *Green Screen Goddess (Ten Thousand Waves)*, 2010. Endura Ultra photograph, 180 × 239.8 × 7.5 cm. © Isaac Julien. Courtesy of the artist and Victoria Miro, London.

140. Haegue Yang, *Warrior Believer Lover*, 2011. Installation view, Kunsthaus Bregenz, 2011. © Haegue Yang and Kunsthaus Bregenz. Photo: Markus Tretter.

141. Tanja Ostojić, *Looking for a Husband with EU Passport*, 2000–5. The "ad" from the participatory web project/combined media installation. © Tanja Ostojić. Photo: Borut Krajnc.

142. Cassils, *Advertisement: Homage to Benglis*, 2011. C-print, 40 × 30 inches, edition of 3. Photo: Cassils with Robin Black. Courtesy of the artist and Ronald Feldman Gallery, New York.

143. Santiago Sierra, *250 cm Line Tattooed on Six Paid People*, 1999. Espacio Aglutinador, Havana, Cuba, December 1999. © Santiago Sierra. Courtesy of Studio Santiago Sierra.

144. Marlene Dumas, *The Kiss*, 2003. Oil on canvas. © Marlene Dumas. Courtesy of the artist and Frith Street Gallery, London.

145. Richard Wright, *Untitled (06.01.08)*, 2008. © Richard Wright. Photo: courtesy of the Gagosian Gallery, London.

146. Postcommodity, *Repellent Fence*, 2015. Land art, installation, and community engagement (earth, cinder block, para-cord, PVC spheres, helium). Installation view, US/Mexico Border, Douglas, Arizona/Agua Prieta, Sonora. Photo: courtesy of Postcommodity and Bockley Gallery.

147. Assemble, Granby Workshop Catalogue, 2015. © Granby Workshop/Assemble.

The publisher and the author apologize for any errors or omissions in the above list. If contacted they will be pleased to rectify these at the earliest opportunity.

Index

Note: References to illustrations and captions are in *italics*; there may also be textual references on the same page.

abjection 206, 208 *see also* Kubota *and*
    Manzoni
Abramović, Maria 256, 305
  The Artist is Present 256
  Seven Easy Pieces 256
Abramovich, Roman 272
Abrioux, Yves 289
Abstract Expressionism 5–10, 19, 22, 26,
    28–32, 36, 40, 47, 49, 50, 56, 59, 69, 102,
    105, 110, 125, 150, 162, 189, 202 *see also*
    post-Abstract Expressionism
  opposition to/critique of 36–7, 39, 47,
    55, 59, 95, 103, 105, 121–2
  and politics 11, 13, 15–16, 28–9, 50
Abts, Tomma 304
Accession II see under Hesse
Acconci, Vito 175, 256, 300, 306
  Seedbed 175
  Step Piece 175
Adcock, Craig 288
Adenauer, Konrad 118
Ades, Dawn 65, 286
Adorno, Theodor 1, 23, 96
Adriani, Gotz 287
Afghanistan 217, *220*, 302, 304
Agamben, Giorgio 256, 268
AIDS 209, 211, 300, 302
Aitken, Doug 252
al-Abidine, Zine 305
Albero, Alexander 289
Albers, Josef 40
Alcoholic, The see under Gilbert and George
Alger Hiss trial, the 43
alienation 241
Alloway, Lawrence 90, 92, 95, 103,
    287, 298
  Six Painters and the Object 103
All the Missiles Are One Missile see under
    Kulik
Althusser, Louis 155
Altman, Robert 303

Altmodernism 268–9
Altshuler, Bruce 285
Alÿs, Francis 260–1, 304
  When Faith Moves Mountains 261
America 5–7, 11–12, 15, 71, 74–5, *81*, 82,
    84–5, 92, 95, 99, 103, 107, 111–13, *115*,
    118, 125, 127–8, 131, 137, *143*, 150, 152,
    154, 156, 162, 177–8, 189, 192, 196,
    208, 211, 217–18, 220, 225, 237, 241–2,
    246, 249, 254, 270–1
  art education in *see under* art education
  Pop Art of *see under* Pop Art
American Artists' Congress 7
American Committee of Cultural
    Freedom (ACCF) 26
American Indian Movement 205
Anderson, Laurie 178, 290, 301
  United States Parts I–IV 178
Anderson, Perry 290
Andre, Carl 128, *133*, 134–5, 137, 141, 144,
    154, 300
  Equivalents I–VIII 134
  Floor Pieces 133
  Lever 133
  Magnesium Square 133
Anfam, David 285
Anselmo, Giovanni 157
Anthropometries of the Blue Age see under
    Klein
anti-art 99–100
Anti-Form 137, 141, 144, 159
anti-idealism 128, 135, 254
Antin, Eleanor 258
anti-rationalism 128
Appel, Karel 149
Arafat, Yasser 304
Aragon, Louis 13
Archer, Michael 285
Arensberg, Walter 52
Arman (Armand Fernandez) 71–2, *73*, 78
  Accumulations 71–2

Arman (Armand Fernandez) (*cont.*)
  In Limbo 73
  Le Plein 72
  Poubelles 72
    Household Rubbish 72
    Small Bourgeois Trash 72
Armstrong, Neil *115*, 299
Artaud, Antonin 68, *71*, 85, 173, 296, 298
  Self-Portrait 70–1
  The Theatre and its Double 173
art market 192–3, 214, 218, 220, 222, 246–9
Art Brut 19
Art & Language 5, 11, 164–5, 178, 179, 201,
    203, 300
  Index 01 165
  *Portrait of V. I. Lenin by V. Charangovich
    (1970) in the Style of Jackson Pollock II*
    5, *6*, 201
art education
  in America 40
  in Britain 66, 94, 97, 100, 179, 181, *206*,
    220, 264
  in Germany 244
Arte Povera (Poor Art) 143, 149, 156–9, 221–2
art fairs 246–7
  ARCO (Mexico City) 246
  Art Basel 246–7, 306
  Art Basel Miami Beach 246
  Art Dubai (Dubai) 246
  Cologne 246
  Frieze (London) 246, 304
  Shanghai Contemporary (Shanghai) 246
Artform (magazine) *257*
Artists' Union 6
Artist with 'Merda d'artista', The see under
    Manzoni
Art-Language (journal) 165
ARTnews (magazine) 195
Arts (magazine) 164, *178*
Arts Council of Great Britain 64, 296
Art Since 1900 241
artspace (London) 245
Art Strike, the 154
Art Workers' Coalition 135, 154, 299
Ashton, Dore 290
Aspen (magazine) 77
assemblage 38, 40, 43, 46, 108, 121, 122, 155
Assemble (collective) 272, *273*, 294
  Granby Workshop Catalogue 273
At Five in the Afternoon see under
    Motherwell
Athey, Ron 256
Atkins, Ed 272–4
  Ribbons 272
  Safe Conduct 272–3

Atkinson, Terry 163, 165, 203, *204–5*, 206,
    280n. 1, 291
  First World War 203
  The Stone Touchers 1 203, *204–5*
auction houses 247
audio-art 236
Auerbach, Frank 65
Augé, Marc 253
Au Naturel see under Sarah Lucas
Auster, Paul 226
  Leviathan 225–6
Australia 164
Austria 188
Autogena, Lise 244
Autogena, Lise and Joshua Portway
  Black Shoals Stock Market 244
automatism 10, 149
Ay-O
  Finger Box Set 100

Baader-Meinhof gang 118, 263
Bacon, Francis 50, 64–5, *66*, 68, 91, *189*,
    268, 296
  Study of a Baboon 66
  *Study for a Portrait of Lucian Freud
    (Sideways)* 65
  *Three Studies for Figures at the Base of a
    Crucifixion* 64
Bainbridge, David 165
Balaclavas see under Trockel
Bald Eagle see under Krasner
Baldessari, John 164, 166, 305
  Cremation Piece 164
Baldwin, Michael 163
Balzer, David 247
Banham, Rayner 94
Bardot, Brigitte 263
Barney, Matthew 179, *232*, 234, 303
  Cremaster 3 232, 234
  Cremaster 4 232–3, 234, 281n. 20
Barr, Alfred J. 11
Barron, Stephanie 287
Barry, Robert 164
Barthes, Roland 71, *73*, 77, 130, 166, 193,
    203, 297, 299
  The Death of the Author 77
  Elements of Semiology 165
  Mythologies 71, *73*
Barth, Miles 287
Baselitz, Georg 85, *86*, 191–2, 298, 300–1
  Grosse Nacht im Eimer, Die (*The Big
    Night Down the Drain*) 85, *86*
  Pandemonium Manifesto 85
Basquiat, Jean-Michel 306
Bataille, Georges 20, 64–5, 160, *210*, 254

Sacrificial Mutilation and the Severed Ear of Vincent Van Gogh 160
Batchelor, David 288
Bates, Harry *193*
Battcock, Gregory 288–9, 291
Baudelaire, Charles 22, 27, 106, 269
   The Painter of Modern Life 106
Baudrillard, Jean 185, 207, 292, 301
Bauhaus 40, 64, 81, *92*
Baumann, Daniel 294
Beat culture 43, 45, 51, 103, 107
Beatles, the 96, 298–9
Beauvoir, Simone de 296
Becher, Bernd and Hilla 107, *168–9*, 244
   Typology of Water Towers 168–9
Beckett, Samuel 142, 297
   Waiting for Godot *139*, 177
Beckmann, Max 85
Bed see under Rauschenberg
Bedia, José 205
Beech, Dave 294
Belgium 165
Bellamy, Richard 102
Belle Haleine, Eau de Voilette see under Duchamp
Benglis, Lynda 257
Benjamin, Walter 90–2, 100, 107, 241
   The Work of Art in the Age of Mechanical Reproduction 90
Berger, John 65
Berman, Marshall 286
Bernadac, Marie-Louise 288
Bernard, Bruce 287
Bertens, Hans 290
Beuys, Joseph 79, *81*, 82, *83*, 84–5, *130*, 139, 155, 157, 177, 188, 191, *205*, 232, 256, 270, 298, 300–2
  'Actions' 84
  The Chief 84
  Coyote 79, *81*, 84–5
  Fat Chair 83
  Filter Fat Corner 82, *83*
  How to Explain Paintings to a Dead Hare 84
  Infiltration Homogen for Grand Piano 84
Beveridge Report, the 64
Bickers, Patricia 292
Bickerton, Ashley 206
Biennials *see under* exhibitions
Big Brother (television programme) 225
Big Painting VI see under Lichtenstein
Bilbo, Jack *91*
Bird, Jon 289–90
Birdsall, Derek 287
Bishop, Claire 259–60, 291, 293–4

The Black Book 206
Black Mountain College 39–40, 43, 97
Black, Robin 258
Blair, Tony 303–4
Blake, Peter 94, 96
Blaze 1 see under Riley
Blazwick, Iwona 292
Blessing, Jennifer 290
Blue Peter (television programme) 272
Blue Veil see under Louis
Bode, Arnold 81
Body Art 36, 55, 64, *71*, *76*, 98, 172–5, 177, 179, 185, 211, 225, 256
body, the 16, *19*, 20, 22, 30, 41, 50, *127*, 129, 137, *140*, *143*, 144, 170, 172, 174–5, *177*, 209–11, 258, 265
Bois, Yves Alain 285, 288, 304
Boite-en-valise see under Duchamp
Bojewyan Farms see under Lanyon
Böll, Heinrich 84
Boltanski, Sergei 302
Boone, Mary *58*, 192, 197
borders 253–4, *255*, 256, *271*
Borland, Christine 223, 264
Boshier, Derek 94
Botticelli, Sandro
  Birth of Venus 40
Boty, Pauline
  It's a Man's World II 96
Bourdelle, Antoine *69*
Bourgeois, Louise 137, *140*, 141–2, 144, 229, 230–1, 288, 302–3, 305
  Destruction of the Father 140, 170
  Double Negative 140
  Red Room (Child) 230–1
Bourriaud, Nicolas 258–9, 268, 270, 294, 305
  Relational Aesthetics 258
  Tomorrow is Another Day 258
Boyce, Martin 264, 305
Brakhage, Stan 141
Brancusi, Constantin 59, 133
  Endless Column 133
Brassaï (Gyula Halasz) *19*, 150
  Mort, La (Death) *19*
Brawer, Catherine C. 289
Brecht, Bertolt 172
Brecht, George 97–9
  Three Aqueous Events 98
  Water Yam 100
Breton, André 7, 23, 38
  Towards a Free Revolutionary Art 7
Brezhnev, Leonid 298, 300
Bride Stripped Bare by her Bachelors, Even, The see under Duchamp

Brisley, Stuart 163, 177
  10 Days 177
Britain 28, 63–6, 68, 75, 89, 92, 94–6,
    99–100, 134, 144, 152, 162, 165, 177,
    193, *198*, *205*, 208, 220–3, 225–9, 231,
    237, 242, 246, 251–2, 264, 272
  art education in *see under* art
    education
  Pop Art of *see under* Pop Art
  sculpture of 30, 63, *64*, 66, 125, 135, 144,
    147, *193*, 208
Britain Seen from the North see under Cragg
Broodthaers, Marcel 152, *153*, 154–5, 299
  *Musée d'Arte Moderne, Department of
    the Eagles 153*, 154
Brown, Gordon 305
Brown, Trisha 129
Brus, Günter 173
Brutalism 94
Bryson, Norman 28n. 20
Buchanan, Roderick 264
Buchloh, Benjamin 83, 165, 192, 248, 285,
    293, 304–5
Bunnies see under Polke
Bunting, Heath 245–6
Buñuel, Luis 300
Burden, Chris 174–5, 177, *178*, 261, 300
  Shoot 174, *178*
Buren, Daniel 149, *150*, 152, 154–6, 158, 166,
    193, 289, 299
  *Photo-souvenir: Hommes/Sandwichs
    149, 150*
Bürger, Peter 155
Burgin, Victor 165–6, *167*, 168, 172, 206,
    289, 300
  Possession 166, *167*
Burns, Bill 247
Burri, Alberto *45, 46*, 297
  Saccho H8 45
Burroughs, William 298
Bush, George 304
Butler, Reg 68
Butterfield, Jan *178*

Cage, John 38–40, 43, 51, 55, 74, 76–7, 82,
    97–8, 183, 297
  4'33˝ 39, 84
Calle, Sophie 225
  Double Game 225
  Suite vénitienne 225
Camfield, William 286
Campbell, Duncan 306
Campion, Jane 302
Camus, Albert
  The Rebel 65
Canard Inquiétant, Le see under Jorn

Cantz Verlag, Hatje 293–4
capitalism 11, 16, 25, 28, 34, 71, 77, 90, 102–3,
    124, 128, 153, 155, 158, 183, 185, 192,
    208, *209*, 226, 228, 238, 241–2, 244,
    246–7, 260, 268–70, 274, 302, 305 *see
    also* consumerism/consumption
Capital Realism (later Capitalist
  Realism) 115, 119, 187
Capp, Al 189
Car Crash, The see under Dine
Caro, Anthony 100, 125, *128*, 131, 143, 146,
    299–300
  Prairie 128
Carter, Angela 301
Carter, Jimmy 300
Cassils 257, 258, 306
  Advertisement (Homage to Benglis) 257,
    258
  Becoming an Image 257
  Cuts: A Traditional Sculpture 258
Castelli, Leo 15, 53, 103, 125, 141, 297
Castro, Fidel 298
Catholicism 38, 74, 79, 86, 106, 217
Cattelan, Maurizio 222
  Twentieth Century 222
Caulfield, Patrick 94–5
Celan, Paul 191
Celant, Germano 157–8, 289, 291, 299
Celmins, Vija 199, *201*, 299
  Burning Man 201
  Untitled (Cross #1) 201
censorship 218
Chadwick, Helen 210, 211–12, 291, 302
  Loop My Loop 210, 211
  Of Mutability 211
  Nostalgie de la Boue 210
Chadwick, Lynn 68
Chan, Paul 306
Chapman, Jake and Dinos 223
Charlton Comics
  Strange Suspense Stories 104
Chave, Anna 135
Cheung, Maggie *253*
Chia, Sandro 193
Chicago, Judy 168, *170*, 300
  The Dinner Party 168, *170*
childhood/children 229–30, *231*, 232, 251
China 155, 244, 247, 252, 299, 302
Chirac, Jacques 303
Chirico, Giorgio de 190, 300
Chopin, Henri 161
Christo 162, 300
  Running Fence 162, 271
Christov-Bakargiev, Carolyn 247,
    268, 289
Churchill, Winston 296

Circles, Grids, Arcs from the Four Corners and Sides see under LeWitt
Civilisation Atlantique see under Fougeron
Civil Rights issues 106, 119
Cixous, Hélène 174
Clark, T.J. 11, 30–1, 303
Clearwater, Bonnie 291
Clemente, Francesco 190
Clinton, Bill 302–3
Clinton, Hillary 306
Close, Chuck 197
Coates, Robert 7
Cobbing, Bob 161
CoBrA 149, *151*, 152, 296
Cocteau, Jean 296
Coelewij, Leontine 294
Coen brothers, the 303
Cohen, Bernard 135
Cold War 10–12, 15, 24, 28, 43, 55, 112, 149, 152, 217, 238
Coley, Nathan 264
collaboration 245–6
collage 47, *48*, 53, 61, 90, *91*, 94, 104 *see also under* photography
Collishaw, Mat 220
Colpitt, Frances 288
communism 6–7, 11–15, 43, 45, 49, 52–3, 65, 72, 112, 118, 150, 152, 155, 201, 217, 296, 302
computers/computing 228, 244, 246, 272, 300, 302 *see also* internet, the
Conceptual Art 72, 78, 131, 144, 149, 163
Conceptualism 106, 149, 152, 161, 163–6, 168, 185, 188, 192–3, 201, *205*, 238, 244, 259, 261–2 *see also* Neo-Conceptualism
concrete poetry 161
Conner, Bruce 43, 141, 306
conscience 270, 274
Constant (Constant Anton Nieuwenhuys) 149
Constructivism 63, 83, 93, 97, 125
consumerism/consumption 76, 77, 86, 90, 92–4, 104–7, 110, 124, 143, 150, 158, 188, 208, 212, 228
Coppola, Francis Ford 300
Cornell, Joseph 43, 49, *73*
Untitled (Medici Princess) 44–5
Cosic, Vuk 245, 270
Costello, Diarmuid 293
counterculture 149–50, 152, 166, 299
Courbet, Gustav 255
Cow Wallpaper see under Warhol
Cox, Neil 286
Coyote see under Beuys
Cragg, Tony 144, *208*, 301
Britain Seen from the North 208

Cranach, Lucas 268
Craven, David 286
Cremaster 4 see under Barney
creolization 251–2
Crimp, Douglas 147, 193, 196, 291
Crone, Rainer 287
Crowhurst, Donald 236
Crow, Thomas 89, 94, 107, 119, 285, 287
Crumb, Robert 189
Cubism 8, 26, 30, *31*, 40, *135*
Cunningham, Merce 39, 98, 129
Currin, John 268

Dada 27, 35, 39–40, 43, *45*, 49, 71–2, 81, 97, 99, 106, 150, 161, 221 *see also* Neo-Dada
Dahmer, Jeffrey 244
Daley, Richard 154
Dalí, Salvador 72, 202
dance events 137, 139
Dance or Exercise on the Perimeter of a Square see under Nauman
Dancing in Peckham see under Wearing
David, Catherine 237
Davie, Alan 28
Davis, Douglas
The World's First Collaborative Sentence 245
Davis, Miles 299
da Vinci, Leonardo *143*, *265*
Mona Lisa 151
Deacon, Richard 144, *145*
For Those Who Have Ears 145
Untitled 145
Dead see under Gerhard Richter
Dead Troops Talk see under Wall
Dean, Tacita 236–7, 305
'Bubble House' 236
Teignmouth Electron 236
Trying to Find the Spiral Jetty 236
Debord, Guy 151–2
The Society of the Spectacle 151
Decker-Phillips, Edith 292
deconstruction 197
décollage 150
de Kooning, Willem 7–8, 20, 29–30, *31*, 41, 46–7, 49, 54–6, 93, 296, 303, 306
Untitled 31
Woman and Bicycle 48–9
Women 33, 41
Deller, Jeremy 227, 228–9, 272, 274, 292, 304
Acid Brass 227
The Battle of Orgreave 227, 229, 236, 256, 260, 272
'Folk Archive' project 228–9

Demand, Thomas 244
   Corridor 244
De Maria, Walter *162*, 163, 234, 248, 300
   Lightning Field *162*, 163
   Vertical Earth Kilometer 163, 234, *235*
dematerialization 163, 173, 180
Demme, Jonathan 302
Demos, T.J. 244, 294
Demuth, Charles 49
Denby, Edwin 30
Denmark 162, 304–5
Denny, Robyn 29, 135
Derrida, Jacques 77, *172*–3, 203, 289, 299
   Grammatology 279n. 27
   Writing and Difference 279n. 27
De Salvo, Donna 292
De Stijl 6
Dibbets, Jan 164
Diebenkorn, Richard 29
Die Brücke 85
Diem, Ngo Dinh 298
Dimitrakaki, Angela 256, 294
Dine, Jim *98*, 106
   The Car Crash *97*, *98*
Dinner Party, The see under Chicago
Discussion, The see under Guttoso
Dix, Otto 268
Documents (journal) 65
Doherty, Willie 225
Doig, Peter 268
Dondero, George 11
Dotremont, Christian 149
Double Negative see under Bourgeois
Douglas, Mary 41
Douglas, Stan 252
Doyle, Tom *139*
Dubadze, Alexander 293
Dubuffet, Jean 17, *19*, 20, 22–3, 46–7, 90,
     93, 95, 286, 296
   Corps de Dames 19–20
   Métafisyx, Le *18–19*
Duchamp, Marcel 27, 35–8, 41, 43, 47, 49, *51*,
     52–5, 57, *58*, 59–60, 63, 74, 77, 79, *83*,
     92, *93*, 105, 130, 136–7, 142, *151*, 153, 163,
     183, 188, 193, 196, 206, 242, 270, 296–9
   Allégorie de genre 57
   Belle Haleine/Eau de Voilette 54
   Bicycle Wheel 41, 83
   Boîte-en-valise 35, *36*, 39, 43, 49, 99, *100*
   Bride Stripped Bare by her Bachelors,
     Even, The 36, *37 see also* Duchamp,
     Marcel, *Large Glass*
   Etant Donnés (Given…) 38, 51, 53, 59,
     79, 212
   Female Fig Leaf 51
   Fountain 35, *36*, 39, 270

Green Box 36
Large Glass 35, *36*–7, 38, 53, 55, *58*, 60, *83*,
     93, *171*
Paris Air 36
readymades 35, *36*, 39, 41, 57–8, 62–4,
     71–2, 83, 153, 163, 196, 262, 270
   Traveller's Folding Item 36
   Wayward Landscape 36–7
Rotorelief 136
Dumas, Marlene 263, *264*, 268
   The Kiss 263, *264*
   Models 263
   Portraits of the Insane 263
   Stern 263
Durham, Jimmie *205*, 206, 291, 301
   Bedia's Stirring Wheel 205
Duve, Thierry de 76, 292
Dylan, Bob 152, 298, 306
   Subterranean Homesick Blues 152

Earth Art *see* Land Art
Ehrenzweig, Anton *136*
Eisenhower, Dwight 45, 107, 297
Eisenstein, Sergei
   Battleship Potemkin 65
Eliasson Olafur 304
   The Weather Project 248
Elizabeth II (Queen) 107
Emin, Tracey 221, *222*
   Everyone I Have Ever Slept With 221
   My Bed 221
Enlightenment, the 184
environment, the 84–5, 155, 158–61, 170,
     184, 259, 268, 270, 272, 301, 305, 307
Environmental Art 264
Enwezor, Okwui 247, 249, 251, 268, 304
erasure 50, 52
Ergodan, Recep Tayyip 306
Ernst, Max 7, 81, 84, *203*
Estes, Richard 197
etoy *245*, 246
   The Twelve Days of Christmas *245*, 246
European Mail-Order Warehouse/Flux-Shop
     see under Ridder
Evadne in Green Dimension see under
     Paolozzi
Evans, Walker *110*, 196
exhibitions 247, 268, 282n. 27
   Art of Assemblage, The (New York) 43,
     50, 71, 298
   Banality 223–4
   Berlin Biennale 247, 304
   Bodyworks (Chicago) 300
   BQ (Berlin) 265
   Brilliant: New Art from London
     (Minneapolis) 221, 303

Contemporary Black Artists in
America (New York) 299
COUM Transmissions–Prostitution
(London) 177
Cybernetic Serendipity (London) 165
Difference: On Representation and
Sexuality (New York) 172, 301
Documenta (Kassel) 247, 268, 270, 297
Documenta 5 (Kassel) 11, 81, 91, 113
Documenta 6 (Kassel) 163, 165
Documenta 7 (Kassel) 190, 301
Documenta 9 (Kassel) 217, 234, 235
Documenta 10 (Kassel) 237, 303
Documenta 11 (Kassel) 249, 251, 254,
263, 268, 304
Documenta 13 (Kassel) 268, 270, 305
Documenta 14 (Kassel) 270, 307
Eccentric Abstraction (New York) 138,
140, 299
Equilibrium 223–4
Freeze (London) 220, 302
Gwangju Biennale 247
Heimat (Antwerp) 263
Information (New York) 154–5, 164
January 5–21, 1969 (New York) 164
Johannesburg Biennale 247
life/live (Paris) 221
Luxury and Degradation 223–4
Magiciens de la terre (Paris) 205,
249, 302
Manifesta (various cities) 249, 304–6
Mirobolus, Macadam et Cie 17
Modern Art in the United States
(London) 28, 297
Monochrome (Milan) 78
New American Painting, The 11, 28,
85, 297
The New Art (London) 164, 300–1
New Generation (London) 135
New Images of Man (New York) 68
New Realists, The (New York) 76
A New Spirit in Painting
(London) 188, 301
9 at Castelli's (New York) 141
Objects and Sculptures 144
Otages (Hostages) 15
Parallel of Life and Art (London) 90, 92
Pictures (New York) 193, 196, 300
Place (ICA) 29
Prague Biennale 247, 304
Primary Structures (New York) 128, 299
Primitivism and 20th Century Art
(New York) 205, 301
Problem for Critics, A 7
Prospect (New Orleans) 247, 305
Responsive Eye (New York) 136

Royal Academy Summer exhibition
(London) 265
São Paulo Biennale 247
Sensation (London) 220–1, 303
Shanghai Biennale 247
Short History of Performance
(London) 256
Situation (London) 29, 135
Skulptur Projekte Münster 247, 305
Sydney Biennale 252, 305
Systemic Abstraction (New York) 135
Tate Triennial (London) 268
This is Tomorrow 93–4, 97
Traffic (Bordeaux) 258
Venice Biennale 47, 68, 103, 136, 247,
253–4, 263, 272, 274, 302–6
When Attitude Becomes Form
(Berne) 164, 299
Young Contemporaries 94
Zeitgeist (Berlin) 188, 301
existentialism 66–8, 75, *139, 143*
Expressionism 65, 74, 85, 115, 190–1, 201

Fabro, Luciano 157, *158*
Golden Italy (Italia d'oro) 157, *158*, 208
Fahlström, Öyvind 113, 115, *118*
CIA Monopoly (Small), 1971 113, *116–18*
Fahne hoch!, Die see under Stella
The Little General (Pinball Machine) 118
Fanon, Frantz 251
Farr, Ian 293
fascism 6, 10, 12, 22, 85, 135, 206, 207
Fautrier, Jean 15, 17, 20, 68, 296
Very Young Girl 16
Federal Art Project 5–6, 13, *50*
Fellig, Arthur *see* Weegee
Fellini, Federico 298
feminism 95–6, 168, 170, 172, 174, 184, 221,
222, 255, *257*
Feminist Art Program, University of
California 184
Ferguson, Russell 288, 291–2, 294
Fernandez, Armand *see* Arman
Figgis, Mike *227*
film 43, 141–2, *143*, 144–5, 185, *186*, 226, 238,
251–2, 262 *see also* video art
film noir 11, 33, 110
Filter Fat Corner see under Beuys
Finlay, Ian Hamilton *161*
Wave Rock 161
Fischer, Konrad *see* Konrad Lueg
Fischl, Eric 197–8, *199*, 234
*Old Man's Boat and the Old Man's Dog,
The* 198, *199*
Fischl, Eric and David Weiss
Carpet Shop 234

Fischl, Eric and David Weiss (*cont.*)
   Fashion Show 234
   Sausage Series 234
Fisher, Jean 291
Five Car Stud see under Kienholz
Five Deaths Seventeen Times in Black and
   White see under Warhol
Flag see under Johns
Flanagan, Barry 144
Flanagan and Allen
   Underneath the Arches 177
Flavin, Dan 128, 135, 143
   Diagonal of May 25th 1963 135
Flower in the Wind see under Martin
Fluxkits 100
Fluxshop 100
   events 88, 97–8 *see also* 'Happenings'
Fluxus Internationale Festspiele Neuester
   Musik 98
Fluxus movement 72, 99–100, 103, 129,
   141, 163–4, 173, 221, 223, 259, 298
Fluxus Policy Newsletter 99
Fluxus Year Boxes 100
Flynt, Henry 99, 163
Fondation Maeght 287
Fontana, Lucio 45, 78, 157, 296
Food (restaurant) 155
Forbidden Planet (film) 94
Ford, Henry 93
formalism 84
Forti, Simone 129
Foster, Hal 193, 208, 213, 229, 236, 285, 287,
   290–3, 303–4
   The Return of the Real 281n. 17
Foucault, Michel 71, 77, 155, 184, 299
Fougeron, André: *Civilisation*
   Atlantique 12–13, *14*, 15, 16, 297
Fountain (After Marcel Duchamp) see under
   Levine
Frampton, Hollis 141
France 13, 14–15, 16–18, 32, 64, 66, 68, 71,
   75, 77, 81, 140, 149–50, 152, 155, 161,
   166, 192
Francis, Mark 287
Franco B 256
   I Miss You 256
Franco, Francisco 300
Frankenthaler, Helen 27, 297
   Mountains and Sea 27
Franks, Robert 107
Frascina, Francis 285–6
Free International University 84
Freud, Lucian 65, *66*
   Interior at Paddington 65, 66–7
Freud, Sigmund 77, 79, 170–1

Fried, Michael 27–9, 122, 125, 131, 133,
   135–7, 158, 183, 232, 299
   Art and Objecthood 131, 133
Friedan, Betty 95–6, 298
   The Feminine Mystique 96
Friedman, Ken
   Flux Clippings 100
Fuchs, Rudi 190
Full Fathom Five see under Pollock
Furness, Betty *93*
Futurism 45, 65

Gabo, Naum 28
Gagarin, Yuri 74, 298
Galassi, Peter 293
Gallaccio, Anya 220
Gallagher, Ann 292
galleries 71, 134, 137, 158, 242, 246, 265
   AG (New York) 98
   Albright-Knox 292
   Apollinaire (Milan) 75
   Art of This Century 7
   Artists Space (New York) 193
   Barbican (London) 286
   Charles Egan's (New York) 43
   Drouin's 15–16, 19
   Dwan (New York) 159
   F-Space (Santa Ana) 174, *178*
   Ferus (Los Angeles) 75, 105, 112
   Fischbach (New York) 138
   Fondation Cartier (Paris) 309
   Forum for Contemporary Art
      (St Louis) 251–2
   Fruitmarket (Edinburgh) 293–4
   Galleria L'Attico (Rome) 157, *159*
   Green (New York) 102, *107*,
      129, *130*
   Guggenheim 35, 85
   Hanover (London) 68
   Hayward (London) 164, 291–2, 310
   ICA (London) 29, 165, 177, 248, 290–1,
      301, 310
   Ikon (Birmingham) 292
   Internationale d'Art Contemporain
      (Paris) 76
   Iris Clert's (Paris) 72
   Kunsthalle (Berne) 164, 282n. 27
   Kunsthalle (Düsseldorf) *153*
   Kunsthaus (Zürich) 286
   Lefevre (London) 64
   Leo Castelli's (New York) *105*, 112, 152,
      276n. 12, 297
   Mary Boone's (New York) *62*,
      192, 197
   Matt's (London) *211*

National Gallery of Denmark
(Copenhagen) 272
Peter Blum's (New York) 230
RBA (London) 29, 146
René Block's (New York) 84, 300
Reuben 97, 100
Rudolfinum (Prague) 309
Saatchi 211, 212, 220, 222, 301–2
Schmela (Düsseldorf) 84
Schwartz (Milan) 58
Serpentine (London) 288, 291–2
Sidney Janis's (New York) 71, 298
South Bank Centre (London) 287,
296, 304
Stable (New York) 107
Stefanotty (New York) 155
Tate (Liverpool) 288
Tate (London) 28, 134, 177, 193, 198, 244,
248, 286–8, 292, 297, 299
303 (New York) 258
Walker Art Center (Minneapolis) 221
Whitechapel (London) 93, 135, 256,
290–1, 304, 310
Whitworth (London) 286
Woodstock Road (London) 212
Zeno X (Antwerp) 263
Garlake, Margaret 286
Garrels, Gary 287
Gates, Bill 302
de Gaulle, Charles 152, 297, 299
Gaweewong, Gridthiya 294
Gehry, Frank 247, 303
gender issues 23, 27, 38, 41, 49, 53–4, 60,
106, 129, 139, 166, 168, 170–2, 174–5,
194, 206, 222, 256–8, 270
femininity 93, 96, 99, 106, 118, 137, 168,
172, 174, 177, 186, 208, 255, 257
homosexuality 49–51, 64, 95, 97, 104,
251, 256–8, 299
male sexuality 93, 129, 144
masculinity 43, 47, 49, 55, 59, 68, 76, 95,
106, 135, 141, 167–8, 175, 177, 210,
229–30, 232, 234, 257
Genzken, Isa 252
Empire/Vampire, Who Kills Death 252
geometric abstraction 242
Géricault, Théodore 199
Raft of the Medusa 198
Germany 65, 79, 81, 84–6, 89, 152, 168,
191–2, 217, 234, 244, 296, 302
art education in see under art
education
East 18–19, 85, 217, 296, 302
Pop Art of see under Pop Art
sculpture of 82, 84, 139, 150, 234, 235

West 79, 81–2, 84–5, 86, 98, 106, 115, 118,
191, 199, 208, 217, 296–7, 301–2
Gestalt psychology 129, 131, 142
Getsy, David J. 294
Giacometti, Alberto 66–7, 68, 75, 296
Standing Figure 68
Giedion, Siegfried
Mechanization Takes Command 90
Gilbert and George 177, 179, 217, 299
Alcoholic, The 179
Paki 179
Singing Sculpture 177
Gillick, Liam 258–9, 294
Gilligan, Melanie 273, 294
Popular Unrest 273–4
Ginsberg, Allen 43, 297
Glasgow School of Art 264
Glass, Philip 141, 250
Glimcher, Mildred 286
Glissant, Édouard 251
globalization 192, 225, 228–9, 241–2, 249,
258, 268–9, 304
Gober, Robert 59, 209–10, 212, 222
Two Urinals 59
Goddard, Jean-Luc 299
Godfrey, Tony 289
Goldberg, Roselee 289
Golden Italy (Italia d'oro) see under Fabro
Golding, William 297
Goldsmith's College (London) 220
Goldstein, Ann 289
Golub, Leon 189, 190
Interrogation 189
Mercenaries II 189, 190
Gomringer, Eugen 161
Gonzales-Torres, Felix 210
Gooding, Mel 286
Gorbachev, Mikhail 301
Gordon, Douglas 223, 234–5, 252, 264, 302–3
A Divided Self 223
Self-portrait as Kurt Cobain, as Andy
Warhol, as Myra Hindley, as
Marilyn Monroe 234–5
24 Hour Psycho 223
Gorky, Arshile 5, 7, 22, 296
Gothicism 29–30
Gottlieb, Adolph 7
Govan, Michael 290
Goya, Francisco 22
graffiti 19, 21, 33, 50, 163
Graham, Dan 164
Homes for America 164, 166
Graham, Rodney 252
Grass, Günter 298
The Tin Drum 86

Grateful Dead
   Aoxomoxoa 265
Greenberg, Clement 7, 11, 14, 23, 26–31, 35,
       40, 46, 54–5, 63, 97, 118, 121–2, 125,
       128, 136, 143, 261, 274, 298–9, 303
   Art and Culture 100
   Avant-Garde and Kitsch 23, 89, 100
   critiques of 30–4, 121
   Modernism of 29, 31, 35, 89, 96, 106,
       119, 121, 131, 183–4, 241, 269
   Towards a New Laocoon 23
Greene, Rachel 293
Greer, Germaine
   The Female Eunuch 96
Griffin, Rick 265
Grimonprez, Johan 237, 238, 241
   dial H-I-S-T-O-R-Y 237, 238
Grosse Nacht im Eimer, Die (*The Big Night
   Down the Drain*) *see under* Baselitz
Grosz, George 192
Groys, Boris 292
Grunenberg, Christoph 292
Guarded Conditions see under Simpson
Guardi, Francesco 197
The Guardians of the Secret see under
   Jackson Pollock
Guggenheim, Peggy 7, 35, 92, *210*
Guilbaut, Serge 10–11, 285
Gursky, Andreas *242–3*, 244, 304–5
   Grand Hyatt Hotel 242–3, 244, 252
   Prada I 244
Guston, Philip *189*, 190, 300
   Talking 189
Guttuso, Renato 12
   Crucifixion 12
   The Discussion 13, 14

Haacke, Hans 152, 154–6, 158, 193, 299,
      302, 306
   Information 154–5
   Taking Stock (Unfinished) 193–4
Habermas, Jürgen 184
Hains, Raymond 150
Halasz, Gyula *see* Brassaï
Hall, Stuart 251
Halley, Peter 207
Hamilton, Richard 92, *93*, 94, *95*, 97, 297
   Hers is a Lush Situation 93
   *Just What Is It That Makes Today's Homes
      So Different, So Appealing?* 94
   $he 93
Hand Catching Lead see under Serra
Hanson, Duane 197
'Happenings' 32, 42, 94, 97–100,
      102, 106
Hardt, Michael 242, 293

Hardt, Michael and Antonio Negri
   Empire 242
Harper's Bazaar (magazine)
Harris, Jonathan 285, 293
Harris, Mary Emma 286
Harrison, Charles 285–6, 288–9
Hartley, Marsden 49
Harvey, David 185, 269
Haskell, Barbara 288
Hassan, Ihab 183
Hawking, Stephen 302
Haworth, Jann 96
Head of a Man see under Henderson
Heaney, Seamus 303
Heartfield, John 195
Heathfield, Adrian 294
Hebdige, Dick 94
Heeswijk, Jeanne van 259
   De Strip 259
Heindel, Max 74
   The Rosicrucian Cosmo-conception 72
Heizer, Michael 162
   Double Negative 162
Helms, Jesse 218
Henderson, Nigel 90, 92, 94, *95*
   Head of a Man 95
Hendricks, John *100*
Hepworth, Barbara 28, 63
Heron, Patrick 28–9
Herzog & de Meuron 248, 306
Hess, Thomas B. 285
Hesse, Eva 135, 137, *138–9*, 140–2, 144
   Accession II 138
   Hang Up 138, *139*
   Rope Pieces 140
Higgins, Dick 97
Higgs, Peter 306
Highmore, Ben 287
Hiller, Susan *231*
   An Entertainment 231
   Psi Girls 231
Hill, Gary 225, 251, 302
   The Only Good One is a Dead One 225
   Tall Ships 225
Hilton, Roger 28
Himid, Lubaina 307
Hirschhorn, Thomas 254, 304
   Bataille 254
Hirst, Damien *198*, 212, 214, 220–1, 223,
      241, 247, 291, 302–3, 305
   Away from the Flock 223
   In and Out of Love 212–13, 220
   I Love You 212
   *The Physical Impossibility of Death in the
      Mind of Someone Living* 221
   A Thousand Years 212

Hitchcock, Alfred 296, 298
  Psycho 223, 263
Hockney, David 94–5, 97, *205*, 299
  A Bigger Splash 95
  Sunbather 96–7
Hoffmann, Hans *50*, 173
  Struwwelpeter 173
Hoffmann, Jens 293
Hoggart, Richard 92
  The Uses of Literacy 92
Hogg, James
  The Private Memoirs and Confessions of
    a Justified Sinner 223
Hohl, Reinhold 287
Holland 7, 18, 32–3, 178
Holman Hunt, William
  The Hireling Shepherd 223
Holt, Nancy 289
Holzer, Jenny 194, *195*, 196, 301
  Survival 195
  Truisms 194
Holzwarth, Hans 292
Hopkins, David 286, 292–3
Hopkins, Louise 264
  Songsheet (Can't Buy Me Love) 264–5
Hopper, Edward 198
Hopps, Walter 112, 286, 288
Horn, Rebecca 173
  Touching the walls with both hands
    simultaneously 173
Horn, Roni 306
House see under Whiteread
How Does a Girl Like You Get to be a Girl
  Like You? see under Shonibare
Hudson, Suzanne 293
Hudson, Tom 97
Huebler, Douglas 164
Hughes, Langston 251
Hughes, Robert 168
Hume, Gary 220, 303
Hurrell, Harold 165
Hussein, Saddam 304–5
Huyghe, Pierre 258–9, 304
  Streamside Day 259
Huyssen, Andreas 104, 191
hybridization 249, 251–3, 272 *see also*
  creolization

I-Box (Morris) 55, *57*
ICA (Institute of Contemporary Arts) 31,
  89–91, *92*, 97, 98, 179, 194, 211
IDENTITISWAPDATABASE 245–6
IG (Independent Group) 89–90, *92*,
  93–4, *95*, 97, 297
Immendorf, Jörg 192, 300
  Café Deutschland 192

In and Out of Love see under Hirst
information technology *see* computers/
  computing *and also* internet, the
informel 16–17, *19*, 20, 22, 45–7, 64, 81
In Limbo see under Arman
Installation at the Green Gallery
  (Morris) *140*
installations 78, *97*, *140*, *173*, 209, 211–14,
  225, *231*, 244, 248, 252, 254, 262,
  272–3, 282n. 27
Interior at Paddington see under Freud
Interior Scroll see under Schneemann
International Klein Blue (*I.K.B.*) 75
internet, the 242, 244–6, 255, 262,
  270, 302
Iran 249
Iraq 304–5
Irwin, Robert 137
Isou, Isidore 150
Italy 12–14, 49–50, 78–9, 89, 152, 156–8, *159*,
  190, 238–9, 296
Iverson, Margaret 293

James, Merlin 265
Jameson, Fredric 185–6, 188, 195, 200–1,
  203, 238, 301
  Postmodernism, of the Cultural Logic of
    Late Capitalism 185, 279n. 1
Jandl, Ernst 161
Japan 164, 296, 303
Jarman, Derek 251
Jencks, Charles 184, 300
  The Language of Post-Modern
    Architecture 184
John XXIII (Pope) 79
Johns, Jasper 41, 43, 49, 51, *52*, 53, *54*, 55–9,
  71, 78–9, 89, 95, 103, 111, 114, 122–3,
  276n. 12, 297, 302
  Alphabets 78
  False Start 192
  Flag 49, *54*, 55, 57, 78, 206
  Numbers 56–7, 78
  Painted Bronze (Ale Cans) 57, *59*
  Painting with Two Balls 55
  Target with Plaster Casts 49, *52*, 53
Johnson, Lyndon B. 112–13, 298
Jones, Allen
  Girl Table 96
Jones, Amelia 285, 289–90, 293
Jones, Caroline 286, 293
Jones, Lawrence 294
Jopling, Jay 220
Jorn, Asger 149, *151*, 152
  Modifications 151
  Le Canard Inquiétant 151
Joselit, David 285

Judd, Don 122, 125, *126*, 127–9, 137, *138*, 144,
 150, 157, 259, 288, 298
 Untitled 126
Judson Memorial Church 104
Judson Memorial Theatre 129
Julien, Isaac 251–2, *253*, 305
 Fantôme Africa 252
 Fantôme Créole 252
 *Frantz Fanon: Black Skin, White
  Mask 251*
 *Green Screen Goddess (Ten Thousand
  Waves) 252, 253*
 Looking for Langston 251
 True North 252
 Young Soul Rebels 251
July see under Gerhard Richter

Kabakov, Ilia 217, 302
 The Toilet 217
Kandinsky, Wassily 82
Kane, Alan 292
Kant, Immanuel 184, 200
Kapoor, Anish 144
Kaprow, Allan 32, 97, 99, 297–8
 18 Happenings in 6 Parts 97
Karp, Ivan 103
Kastner, Jeffrey 289
Kawara, On 164, *165*
 9 AGO. 68 165
Keaton, Buster
 Steamboat Bill Jr. 251
Kienholz, Ed 47, 112, *115*
 Five Car Stud 115
Kellein, Thomas 287, 291
Kelley, Mike 209, 212, 222, 232, 302
 *More Love Hours Than Can Ever Be
  Repaid 209*
Kelly, Ellsworth 110, 122, *123*
 Blue on White, 1961 *123*
Kelly, Mary 168, 170, *171*, 172–4, 179, 203,
 289, 300–1
 Post-Partum Document 170, 171
Kennedy, John F. 106–7, 111–12, *115*, 118,
 154, 298
Kent, Sarah 292
Kermel, Pepe 285
Kerouac, Jack 43, 107, 297
Kester, Grant 294
Khrushchev, Nikita 107, 297–8
Kidner, Michael 135–6
Kiefer, Anselm *191*, 192, 301
 Interior 191
 Sulamith (Shulamite) 191
 The Unknown Painter 191
Kienholz, Ed 43, 112–13
Kinetic Art 137

King, Martin Luther 99, 154, 298–9
King, Phillip 135
Kinsey, Alfred 296–7
Kippenberger, Martin 234, *235*, 236
 Untitled 235
 *With the Best Will in the World I Can't
  See a Swastika 234*
Kirby, Michael 287
Kitaj, R.B. 94
kitsch 89, 104, 115, 118–19, 151, 184,
 207, 268
Klee, Paul 16, *19*, 90
Klein, Melanie 20
Klein, Yves 59, 71–2, *74*, 75, *76*, 77–9, 82,
 84, 105–6, 157, 173, 184, 297–8
 Anthropometries of the Blue Age 76
 Monochrome paintings 75, 78
 Monochrome symphony 76
 *Painter of Space Hurls Himself into the
  Void, The 74, 77*
 *Rituals for the Relinquishment of the
  Immaterial Pictorial*
 Sensibility Zones 79
 *Single Day Newspaper (November 27th,
  1960) 74, 83*
 Theatre of the Void 74
 Le Vide 72, 74–5
 Yves Peintures 75
Knorr, Karen 206
Kohl, Helmut 301
Konnertz, Winifried 287
Koons, Jeff 206, *207*, 208, 234, 236, 301–2
 Balloon Dogs 232
 Banality 207
 Equilibrium 207
 Luxury and Degradation 207
 Made in Heaven 207
 Michael Jackson and Bubbles 207
Kossoff, Leon 65
Kosuth, Joseph 143, 163, *165*, 289, 299
 Art After Philosophy 163
 Art as Idea as Idea 163
 Five Words in Blue Neon 143
Kounellis, Jannis 157, *159*, 188, 222
 Horses 157, 159, 256
Krasner, Lee 10, 47, *50*
 Bald Eagle 50
 Little Images 47
Krauss, Rosalind 130, 136–7, 193, 196,
 261–2, 285, 288, 290, 294
Krens, Thomas 248, 290
Kristeva, Julia 77, 208
Kruger, Barbara 195–6, 203, 207, 304
 Untitled 195
Kubota, Shigeko 98, *99*, 174, 298
 Vagina Painting 98, 99

Kubrick, Stanley 299
  2001: A Space Odyssey 241
Kulik, Zofia 217, *220–1*
  All the Missiles Are One Missile 220–1
Kuspit, Donald 191, 290
Kwick, Przenyslaw *221*

Lacan, Jacques 68, 77, 171
LadyFace/ManBody (webzine) 258
Lambie, Jim 265
  ZOBOP 265
Land Art (Earth Art) 149, 158–9, *160*, 161,
    162, 163, 173–4, 236, 248, 261, 271
Lanyon, Peter *28*, 29
  Bojewyan Farms 28
Large Glass see under Duchamp
Latham, John 99–100, 299
  Still and Chew 100
Latin America 164
Lawrence, D.H. 298
Lawson, Thomas 197
Lebel, Robert 52
Leck, Robert 293
Lectern Sentinel see under David Smith
Lefebvre, Henri 77
Legg, Alicia 288
Leigh, Janet 263
Leja, Michael 10–11, 285
Lennon, John 301
Lennon, John and Yoko Ono
  Bed-In for Peace 221–2
Lettrism (*Lettrisme*) 150, 161
Leutze, Emanuel 57
Levine, Sherrie *58*, 59, 193, 196–7, 302
  Fountain (After Marcel Duchamp) 58
Levi, Primo 301
LeWitt, Sol 122, 130–1, 138, *139*, 163, 265, 305
  *Circles, Grids, Arcs from Four Corners
    and Sides 132–3*
  Variations of Incomplete Open Cubes 130
Lialina, Olia 245–6
Lichtenstein, Roy 103, *104*, 118
  Big Painting VI 104
  Brushstrokes 104, 202
Liebeskind, Daniel 303
Life (magazine) 103, 296
Light and Space Movement 137
Lightning Field see under De Maria
Lind, Maria 294
Linker, Kate 289–91
Lippard, Lucy 138, 140, 150, 152, 163–4,
    170, 287–9, 299
Literalism 128, 131
Livingstone, Marco 287
Living Theatre (New York) 129
localism 225, 228–9

London Docklands Development
    Corporation 220
Longo, Robert 193
Long, Richard 144, 160, 261
  A Line Made for Walking 144, 261
Loop My Loop see under Helen Chadwick
Lorca, Federico García 22
Lorrain, Claude 161
Louis, Morris 27–30, 122, 136
  Blue Veil 24–6, 27
Lowndes, Sarah *265*, 294
Lucas, George 300
Lucas, Sarah 220–1, *222*, 292
  Au Naturel 221, *222*
Lueg, Konrad (also known as Konrad
    Fischer) 115, 118
Lüpertz, Marcus 85, 191–2
Lynch, David 302
  Blue Velvet 198
Lyotard, Jean-François 184, 300
  The Postmodern Condition 184

Maciunas, George 97–100
MacLeish, Archibald 10
Made in Heaven (Koons) *224*
Madoff, Steven 287
Magnesium Square see under Andre
Magritte, René 153
Major, John 302
Malevich, Kasimir 42, 75
Mallarmé, Stéphane 22
Mandela, Nelson 302, 306
Mandel, Ernest
  Late Capitalism 279n. 1
Manet, Édouard
  Dead Toreador 199
Manhattan see under Wols
Man Ray 25, 49, 141
Manzoni, Piero 78, *79*, 105–6, 157, 176, 253,
    261, 298
  Achrome paintings 78
  Artist's Breath works 78
  Line of Infinite Length 163
  Living Sculptures 78
  Merda d'artista 78, *79–80*
Mapplethorpe, Robert 206, 210–11, 302
Maraniello, Gianfranco 292
Marclay, Christian 252, 305
  The Clock 252
Marcuse, Herbert 152
Marcus, Greil 288
Marker, Chris 251
Marshall Plan 11–12, 71, 296
Marten, Helen 306
Martin, Agnes *135*, 306
  Flower in the Wind 134–5

Martin, John 265

Martins, Maria 36

Marxism 5, 23, 31, 76, 100, 134, 149, 151, 155, 158, 165, 172, 184 *see also* communism

Masters, William and Virginia Johnson 299

Mathieu, Georges 29, 77

Matisse, Henri 47, *123*, 236, 297

Matta-Clark, Gordon 155, 259, 300
  Splitting 156–7

Matta, Roberto 155

McCarthyism 26, 43, 45, 47, 49, 56, 296–7

McCarthy, Paul 209

McCorquodale, Duncan 292

McCray, Porter 11

McHale, John 94

McLean, Bruce 177

McPherson, Bruce 290

McQueen, Steve 251–2, 306
  Deadpan 251
  12 Years a Slave 251

McShine, Kynaston 286–7

Medina, Cuauhtémoc 294

Meijer, Dorothy *100*

Meinhof, Ulrike 263

Mekas, Jonas 141

Mellor, David Alan 94, 287

memory/nostalgia 235–8

Mendieta, Ana 174
  Siluetas 174

Mercenaries II see under Golub

Merck, Mandy 292

Merkel, Angela 304

Merleau-Ponty, Maurice 15, 129, 296
  Phenomenology of Perception 68, 129

Merz, Mario 143, 157–8

Messer, Thomas 155

Metafisyx, Le see under Dubuffet

Metzger, Gustav 100, 306
  Destruction in Art Symposium 100, 299

Meyer-Hermann, Eva 293

Meyer, James 288

Michaux, Henri 29
  Untitled 30

Michelson, Annette 193, 290

Miesel, Louis K. 291

migration/displacement 249, 252–3, 255–6, 268–9, 303–4, 306

Minimalism 83, *107*, 110, *123*, 125, 128–31, 133, *135*, 137–8, 141, 143–5, 147, 157–9, 163–4, 168, 212, *242*, 248, 259 *see also* post-Minimalism

Miró, Joan 149

Mitchell, Juliet 289
  Psychoanalysis and Feminism 171

Mitterand, François 301

modernism 25–30, 64, 87, 90, 106, 172, 183–5, 200, *205*, 212, 226, 268–9

Modernism 12, 15, 23–32, 54, *57*, 79, 84, 89, 95–6, 100, 104–6, 110, 115, 118–19, 122, 124–5, 127, 130–1, 133, 136–7, 141, 155, 161, 163–5, 183–5, 188, *196*, 207, 241, 261–2, 269–70 *see also* Altmodernism *and under* Greenberg *and* modernism
  definition of 27, 29, 183
  opposition to/critiques of 38, 54–5, 106, 122, 124, 127, 135, 168, 183–5, 188, *196*, 261

'Modern Man' theme 11, 30

Moholy-Nagy, László *92*

Moi, Toril 290

Molesworth, Helen 290

Mondrian, Piet 16, 63, *135*

Monroe, Marilyn 94, 106, 298

Moore, Henry 63, *64*, 65–6, 125, 147
  King and Queen 64
  Working Model for Reclining Figure 63, *64*

More Love Hours Than Can Ever Be Repaid see under Kelley

Morley, Malcolm 197, *198*, 199, 203, 300
  The Day of the Locust 197
  SS Amsterdam in Front of Rotterdam 197
  The Ultimate Anxiety 197, *198*

Moro, Aldo 300

Morrison, Toni 302

Morris, Robert *53*, 83, 92, *107*, 128–9, *130*, 131, 135, 137, 139–42, 144, 154, 212, 298–9
  Anti-Form 83, 137–8, 140
  Column 129, 135
  I-Box *53*, 129
  Installation at the Green Gallery *130*
  Notes on Sculpture 129
  Site 129
  Untitled (Three L-Beams) 129
  Waterman Switch 129

Morris, William 272

Mort, La (Death) see under Brassaï

Motherwell, Robert 7–8, 22, 23, 39, 55, 115, 296
  At Five in the Afternoon 22
  Elegies to the Spanish Republic 22, 105
  The Dada Painters and Poets 39

Mubarak, Hosni 305

Muehl, Otto 174

Mulvey, Laura *253*

Mumford, Lewis 10

Musée d'Arte Moderne, Département des Aigles *see under* Broodthaers

museums 153–4, *226*, 248
Aspen Art Museum 293
Astrup Fearnley Museet (Oslo) 309
Castello di Rivoli Museo
    Contemporanea Milan 293
Copenhagen Art Centre 244
Dia: Beacon (New York) 248, 304, 310
Fogg (Harvard) 29, 298
Fundació Antoni Tàpies 309
Guggenheim Bilbao 247–8, 309
Guggenheim Venice 309
Hirschhorn Museum 291
Irish Museum of Modern Art
    (Dublin) 309
Jewish (New York) 128, *192*
Kölnischer Kunstverein (Cologne) 258
Lille Métropole (Villeneuve
    d'Ascq) 309
Metropolitan Museum of Art 167
Moderna Museet (Stockholm) 309
Musée d'Art Moderne de la Ville de
    Paris 287
Musées des Beaux-Arts de Lyon 309
Musées royaux des Beaux-Arts de
    Belgique (Brussels) 309
Museo de Arte Moderno Mexico
    City 309
Museo de Arte della Svizzera Italiana
    (Lugano) 309
Museo Nacional Centro de Arte Reina
    Sofia (Madrid) 309
Museu d'Art Contemporani de
    Barcelona 288
Museu de Serralves (Oporto) 303
Museum Boymans-van
    Beuningen 291–3, 309
Museum of Contemporary Art
    (Sydney) 309
Museum of Fine Arts (Houston) 287
Museum Ludwig (Cologne) 302, 309
Museum of Modern Art
    (Oxford) 290, 293, 310
Museum für Moderne Kunst
    (Frankfurt) 309
MoCA (Los Angeles) 289–90, 305, 310
MoMA (Museum of Modern Art,
    New York) 11, 64, 68, 100, 102, 128,
    248, 256, 291–3, 303, 310
    exhibitions at 43, 68, 71, 85, 110, 136,
    154, 164, 205
National Gallery of Art (Washington
    DC) 310
National Gallery of Canada
    (Ottawa) 309
National Museum of Western Art
    (Tokyo) 309

New Museum of Contemporary Art
    (New York) 172, 207
Newport Harbour Museum 290
Palais de Beaux-Arts (Brussels) 153
Palazzo Grassi (Venice) 309
Philadelphia Museum of Art 38, 52, 290
Queen's Museum of Art (New York) 289
San Francisco Museum of Modern
    Art 168, 310
Scottish National Gallery
    (Edinburgh) 310
Solomon R. Guggenheim (New
    York) 103, 135, 154–5, *195*, 256,
    286–8, 303, 310
Stedelijk Museum (Amsterdam) 309
Tate Modern (London) 248, 256, 304,
    306, 310
University of California Art
    Museum 291
Walker Art Center (Minneapolis) 287,
    310
Whitney (New York) 207, 248, 291,
    306, 310
Muybridge, Eadweard 65
*My Last Name Exaggerated Fourteen
    Times Vertically see under* Nauman
mythology *8*, 10, 19, 21, 90
9/11 241–2, 269

Nairne, Sandy 290
Namuth, Hans 63, 77
Nation, The (journal) 23, 28
Nauman, Bruce 141–2, *143*, 144–5,
    173, 223
    A Cast of the Space Under My Chair 145
    *Dance or Exercise on the Perimeter of a
        Square* 143
    Hanged Man 144
    *My Last Name Exaggerated Fourteen
        Times Vertically* 142, *143*
Nay, Ernst Wilhelm 81–2
NEA (National Endowment for the
    Arts) 211, 218
Neff, Terry 288
Negri, Antonio 242, 293
Neoclassicism 161
Neo-Conceptualism 223, 264
Neo-Dada 47, 62, 76, 155
Neo-Expressionism 191–2, 197, 201
Neo-Geo 207
neon works 143
Neo-Romanticism 28, 43, 63, 89, 157
Neshat, Shirin 249, *250*, 251–3
    Fervour 250
    Passage 250
    Possessed 250

Neshat, Shirin (*cont.*)
  Rapture 250
  Turbulent 250
  Seeking Martyrdom #2 249, *250*
Neuberger, Susanne 293
Neue Sachlichkeit (New Objectivity) 65, 192
'New Image Painting' 189
Newman, Barnett 7, 14, *15*, 20, 26–7, 40,
    54–5, 110, 296
  Vir Heroicus Sublimis 14, *15*, 16
Newman, Michael 289
New Realism (Nouveau Réalisme) 71, 100,
    150, 162, 298 *see also* Klein, Yves
New School for Social Research
    (New York) 97
Nice Style (band) 177, 300
Nicholson, Ben 28
Nickas, Robert 289
Nieuwenhuys, Constant Anton *see* Constant
9 AGO. 68 see under Kawara
Nitsch, Herman 173
Nixon, Mignon 286
Nixon, Richard 107, 113, 154, 298–300
Nochlin, Linda 168, 289, 299
Noland, Kenneth 27, 29
Northern Ireland 205, 225, 300, 303
Nouveau Réalisme see New Realism
Numbers see under Johns

Obama, Barack 305
'objective chance' 237
O'Brian, John 26
Obrist, Hans-Ulrich 247, 293
October (magazine) 193, 196–7, 232, 241,
    248, 261, 300
October 18, 1977 see under Gerhard
    Richter
O'Dell, Kathy 290
O'Doherty, Brian 41
Ofili, Chris 303
Oldenburg, Claes 100, *102*, 137, 147,
    287, 298
  Clothespin 147
  Ray Gun Theater 102
  Soft Drainpipes 102
  Snapshots from the City 102
  The Store 102
  The Street 100
Old Man's Boat and the Old Man's Dog, The
    see under Fischl
Olitski, Jules 29
Oliva, Achille Bonito 190, 290, 301
Olson, Charles 40, 43
One National Archives (Los Angeles) 257
Ono, Yoko 99, 222, 305
  Cut Piece 99

Op Art *136*, *265*
Oppenheim, Meret
  Fur Cup and Saucer 138
O'Pray, Michael 288
opticality 29, 131, 136–7, 140
Orage, L'The Storm see under Richier
Orozco, José Clement 13
Orton, Fred 31, 57, 286
Orwell, George 296
Osborne, Peter 289
Ostojić, Tanja *255*, 256, *258*
  Crossing Borders series 255
  Looking for a Husband with EU
    passport 255
  Untitled/After Courbet 255
Owens, Craig 193, 196, 291
Ozenfant, Amédée
  Foundations of Modern Art 90

Paik, Nam June 98–9, 223, 298
  One for Violin Solo 99
  Zen for Head 98
painting 262–5, 268
Painting for the American Negro see under
    Rosenquist
Palach, Jan 177
Pane, Gina 174
Paolozzi, Eduardo 68, 90, *91*, 92–4, *95*, 297
  Bunk 90
  Evadne in Green Dimension 91
Paracelsus 82
Paris Match (magazine) 166
Parker, Rozsika 289, 301
Parks, Rosa 297
Participatory art 227
Partisan Review (journal) 23
Pasmore, Victor 97
Paul, Christiane 293
Paulhan, Jean 20
Pearlstein, Philip 197
Pelenc, Arielle 292
Penrose, Roland 89
Performance Art 76, 98, 129, *143*, 144, 161,
    163, 172–4, *177*, 178, *179*, 209, 225,
    227, 256, 258, 261
  'Happenings' 34, 42, 100, 104–10
performance events 84, 126
performance poetry 174
'peripheries' 242, 249, 251–2, 260–1, 263,
    268, 270–1
Perry, Frank
  The Swimmer 97
Phillips, Lisa 286, 291
photography 30, *57*, 65, 90–1, *92*, 107,
    110–11, 118, 126–8, 149, *150*, 166,
    168, 173, 178–9, *185*, 186, 193, 196–7,

206, 210–11, 214, 234, 237, 242, 244, 249, 252, 262–3
photo-collage 100, *101, 168, 169,* 195, *221*
photo-installations 225
photo-painting 197, 263
photorealism 197–202
'Photo League', the *111*
Piano, Renzo 248, 305
Picabia, Francis 41, 187–8, 190
   Sainte Vierge 41
   Transparencies 187
Picasso, Pablo 8, 12, *13, 19, 22,* 30, 43, 63, 125, 190, 248, 296, 300
   Baboon and Young 43
   Guernica 105, 111
   Massacre in Korea 13
Pinot-Gallizio, Giuseppe 151
Pinter, Harold 298
Piper, Adrian 174, *175*
   Mythic Being 174
   Self Portrait Exaggerating My Negroid Features 175
Piper, John 28
Pistoletto, Michelangelo 157
   Venus of the Rags 157
   Vietnam 157
Plath, Sylvia 299
Polke, Sigmar 85, 115, 118–19, *187–8,* 208, 288
   Playboy Bunnies 118, *119,* 209
   Rasterbilder 118
   This Is How You Sit Correctly (after Goya) 187–8
Pollock, Griselda 168, 289, 301
Pollock, Jackson 5–7, *8,* 10, 13, 20, 23, 26–30, 32, *33,* 37, 41, 46–7, 63, 77, 81, 85, 90, 98, 139, 296–7, 303, 306
   Autumn Rhythm 10
   drip paintings 8, *9, 10,* 16, *18,* 32, 37, *84,* 140
   Full Fathom Five 9, 10
   The Guardians of the Secret 7, 8, 10
   One (Number 31) 10
Pompidou Centre (Paris) 205, 291, 294, 300, 309
Ponge, Francis 20
Poor. Old. Tired. Horse. (magazine) *161*
Pop Art 71, 75, 115, 119, 147, 151
   American 76, 102–3, *104,* 106–7, *110,* 111–12, 115, *118,* 153, 185
   British 89–90, 94–7
   West German *111,* 115, 118–19, 208
Pop culture 95–8
P-Orridge, Genesis 177
Portrait of V. I. Lenin by V. Charangovich (1970) in the style of Jackson Pollock II see under Art & Language

Portway, Joshua 244
Possession see under Burgin
Possibilities 1 (journal) *296*
post-Abstract Expressionism 74
Postcommodity *271*
   Repellent Fence 271
Post-Impressionism 26
post-medium art 261–4, 268
post-Minimalism 147, 252
postmodernism 77, 91, 110, 161, 179, 183–6, 188, 193, 195–7, 200, 203, *205,* 206, 208, 214, 222, 226, 228–9, 262–3, 268–9, 274
'postmodern sublime', the 188, 197, 200–1, 203, 207
Post-Painterly Abstraction 26, 28–9, 125
Post-Partum Document see under Mary Kelly
post-Pop 207
post-Structuralism 71, 172, 193
post-Surrealism 229, 232
Poussin, Nicolas 65, 161
Prague Spring, the 155
Prairie see under Caro
Pre-Raphaelites, the 223
Presley, Elvis 297
Price, Elizabeth 306
primitivism 8, 19, 21, 141, 205
Prince, Richard *196*
   Untitled (Cowboy) *196*
Prouvost, Laure 306
Provos 152
psychic life 229–32
psychoanalysis 8, 10, 19, 28, 72, 77, 79, 82, 138, 150, 152, 170–1
public art *133,* 141, 147, 188, 194, *195,* 197–8, 207, 258, 263
Putin, Vladimir 304
Putzel, Howard 7, 296
Pynchon, Thomas 183, 300

Raeder, Manuel 253
Rainer, Yvonne 129
Ramos, Mel *111*
Raphael
   School of Athens 46, 50
Rauschenberg, Robert 38–41, *42,* 43, *45–6,* 47, 49, 51, 54–7, 71, 74, 77, 79, 89–91, 95, 97, 103, 111, 129, 160, 184, 196, 276n. 12, 296–8
   Asheville Citizen 40
   Bed 41, *42,* 45, *46,* 49, 50, 188, 221
   Birth of Venus 40
   Dirt Paintings 41
   Erased de Kooning 49
   Gold Paintings 41

Rauschenberg, Robert (*cont.*)
  Rebus 40
  Retroactive I 111, *114–15*
  and Twombly 48–9, 53
  White Paintings 39–41, 49, 75
Ravel, Maurice
  Bolero 273
Ray Gun *see* Oldenburg, Claes
Read, Herbert 68, 89, 91
Reagan, Ronald 184, 192, 301
rebirth 90, 92
Rechy, John
  City of Night 97
Red Room (Child) see under Bourgeois
Reinhardt, Ad 121–2, *139*
  'black paintings' 121
  relationality 258–61
Rembrandt 65
Restany, Pierre 71, 190, 298
'retinal art' 36
Retroactive I see under Rauschenberg
Reubens, Peter Paul 105
Rhodes, Carol 265
Richier, Germaine 68, *69*, 296
  Orage, L' (The Storm) 69
Richon, Olivier *206*
Richter, Gerhard 85, 115, 118–19, 127–8,
    197–9, 200, 201, *202, 203*, 237–8,
    263, 269, 291, 298, 301–2
  Atlas 237
  Eight Student Nurses 118
  July 201, *202*
  October 18, 1977 199, *200*
  Dead 200, 263
Richter, Gerhard and Sigmar Polke
  *Life with Pop – A Demonstration of
    Capital Realism* 115 *see
    also* 'Capital Realism'
Richter, Hans 58, 141
Ridder, Willem de 99, *100*
  *European Mail-Order Warehouse/
    Fluxshop* *100–1*
Riley, Bridget 135, *136*, 137
  Blaze 1 *136*
Ringgold, Faith 170
Rivera, Diego 7, 14
Rivers, Larry 57, 297
  Washington Crossing the Delaware 57
Roberts, John 222
Rodchenko, Alexander 195
Rodin, Auguste 68, *69*
Roelstraete, Dieter 294
romanticism 79 *see also* Neo-Romanticism
Rorimer, Anne 289
Rose, Barbara 288
Rosenberg, Harold 31, 105, 297

Rosenbergs, the 296
Rosenblum, Robert 122, 276n. 12
Rosenquist, James 103, 111, *112*, 119, 298
  F-III 103, 111–12
  Painting for the American Negro 111,
    112–13
  President Elect 111
Rosen, Randy 289
Rosicrucianism 72
Rosier, Martha 181
Rosler, Martha 166, 225
  *The Bowery in Two Inadequate
    Descriptive Systems* 225
Ross, David, A. 292
Rosselini, Roberto 296
  Rome, Open City 12
Rosso, Medardo 83
Rothko, Mark 5–8, 10, 15–16, *20–1*, 26, 29,
    40, 54, 110, 296
  Multiforms 20
  Green & Maroon *20–1*
Roth, Moira 55–6
Rousseau, Jean-Jacques 184
Rowell, Margit 287
Royal Academy (London) 188, 220, 265
Royal College of Art (London) 94
Royoux, Jean-Christophe 293
Rrose Sélavy 49, *51*
Rubin, William 122, 288
Ruf, Beatrix 294
Ruff, Thomas 168, 244
Ruscha, Ed 107, 110, 261
  Every Building on Sunset Strip 110, 261
  Some Los Angeles Apartments 110
  Twentysix Gasoline Stations 107, 110
Rushdie, Salman 302
Rush, Michael 292
Russell, John 64, 286–7
Russia/Soviet Union 5, 42, 68, 89, 107, 125,
    155, 199, 217, 220, 296, 300, 306

Saatchi, Charles and Maurice 192–3, 220
Saccho H8 see under Burri
Sadler, Simon 288–9
Said, Edward 300
Saint Martin's School of Art
    (London) 100, 177
Salinger, J.D. 296
Salle, David 188, 197
Sander, August 168
Sandler, Irving 285, 290
Sartre, Jean-Paul 15, 20, 67–8, 296
  Existentialism and Humanism 68
Saussure, Ferdinand de 165
Sayre, Henry M. 290
Schapiro, Miriam 168

Schiffer, Claudia 263
Schjeldahl, Peter 288
Schlesinger, Arthur
   The Vital Center 10
Schmela, Alfred 118
Schnabel, Julian 190, 192–3, 197,
   280n. 16, 300
Schneemann, Carolee 129, 174, *176–7*,
   298, 300
   Interior Scroll 174, *176–7*
   Meat Joy 174, *177*, 256
Schneider, Eckhard 294
Schneider, Gregor 304
Schönebeck, Eugen 85
School of Athens see under Twombly
School of London 66
Schröder, Gerhard 303
Schubert, Karsten 220
Schulze, Alfred Otto Wolfgang *see* Wols
Schütte, Thomas 304
Schwabsky, Barry 262, 294
Schwarz, Arturo 79
Schwarzkogler, Rudolf 173–4
Schwitters, Kurt 38, 40, 43, *45*, 81, 297
   Hanover Merzbau 38, 40, 81
Scorsese, Martin 300–1
Scotland 64, 97, *161*, 223, 231, 264–5, 292
Scott, Ridley 301
   Touching the walls with both hands
      simultaneously see under Horn
Screen (journal) 172
Scull, Ethel and Robert 103, 300
Searle, Adrian 237–8, 263, 293–4
Segal, George 59
Seitz, William 43, 46, 50, 136, 286
Sekula, Allan 166, 228, *229*, 252, 292
   Fish Story 228, *229*
Self-Portrait see under Artaud
Self-Portrait Exaggerating My Negroid
   Features see under Piper
Selz, Peter 68, 71, 285
semiotics 165
'Serious Culture' 99
Serota, Nicholas 248
Serrano, Andres 218, 302
   Piss Christ 218
Serra, Richard 141, *142*, 144–5, 147, 232,
   248, 269, 302
   Casting 141
   Corner Prop 141
   Hand Catching Lead 141, *142*
   Tilted Arc 145, 147
Seven Up (television programme) *225*
Sex Pistols, the 300
Shapiro, Gary 289
Shapolsky family, the 155

Sharp, Willoughby 172
$he (Hamilton) 99, 100
Sherman, Cindy 179, 185, *185*, 209, 300
   Untitled Film Still #6 185, *185*
Shone, Richard 292
Shonibare, Yinka 226
   How Does a Girl Like You Get to be a
      Girl Like You? 226
Shulgin, Alexei 245
Shunk, Harry 78
Siderfin, Naomi 292
Siegelaub, Seth 164
Sierra, Santiago 253, *260–1*, 294
   250 cm Line Tattooed on Six Paid
      People 260–1
Silver, Kenneth 286
Silverman, Kaja 289
Simpson, Lorna 206
   Guarded Conditions 206
simulation 206–7
Sinclair, Ross 264
Singing in the Rain (film) 253
Single Day Newspaper (November 27th
   1960) see under Klein
Siqueros, David 13
Situationism 151–2, 166, 188, 193, 270, 297
Situationist International 151, 297
Sky Window see under Turrell
Slyce, John 292
Smith, David 125, *127*, 296
   Lectern Sentinel 127
Smith, Kiki 209
Smith, Paul 289
Smith, Richard 29, 94
Smithson, Alison and Peter 90, 94
Smithson, Robert 158–9, *160*, 161–3, 236,
   299–300
   Spiral Jetty 159, *160*, 236
Smith, Terry 269, 293–4
Smith, Tony 133
Snowden, Edward 306
Snow, Michael 141
   Wavelength 141
S.O. 36 (Berlin club) 234
social function of art 13–16, 147, 151, 153,
   155, 165–7, 177, 180, 183–4, 198, 200,
   214, 228, 242, 246, 248–9, 259–61,
   263, 274
Socialist Realism 5, 12–13, 85, 115, 118–19, 201
Solanas, Valerie 115
Solomon-Godeau, Abigail 291
Solzhenitsyn, Alexander 298, 300
Sonnabend, Ileana 103
Sontag, Susan 104, 298
Sosnowska, Monika 306
sound poetry 175

Spain 22, 253–4, 306
spatiality 269
Spector, Nancy 292
Speer, Albert 191
Spencer, Robin 287
Spero, Nancy 174
Spielberg, Steven 302
Spiral Jetty see under Smithson
spirituality/mysticism 72, 75, 78, 82, 84, 98,
        121, 261, 274
Splitting see under Matta-Clark
Spoerri, Daniel 71–2, 78, 298
    An Anecdoted Topography of Chance 72
    Tableaux-pièges 72
Staël, Nicolas de 29
Stalin, Joseph 7, 118, 150, 199, 297
Stallabrass, Julian 245, 248, 292–3
Staller, Ilona 207
Standing Figure see under Giacometti
Starling, Simon 223, 268, 304
Steinbach, Haim 206
Steinberg, Leo 40, 91, 184, 300
    Other Criteria 40
Steiner, Rudolf 82, 84
    About Bees 82
Stella, Frank 29, 121–2, 123–4, 125, 127–8,
        131, 133, 265, 298
    'black paintings' 122–3
    Fahne hoch!, Die 122–3, 124
    Protractor paintings 122
Step Piece (Acconci) 191, 192
Stern, Nicholas 305
Stevenson, Robert Louis
    The Strange Case of Dr Jekyll and
        Mr Hyde 223
Stich, Sidra 287–8, 291
Stiles, Kristine 285
Still, Clyfford 7–8
Stimson, Blake 289
Stockhausen, Karlheinz 99, 299
Stone Touchers 1, The see under Atkinson
Store, The see under Oldenburg
Storr, Robert 288
Stoschek, Julia 294
Structuralism 77 see also post-Structuralism
Struth, Thomas 244
student protest 164, 165, 166, 170
Study of a Baboon see under Bacon
Sturrock, John 287
'Sudden Death for One … Sudden Shock for
    the Other' see under Weegee
Sunbather see under Hockney
Superflex 259, 270, 305
    Supergas 271
    Superkilen 259
Suprematism 75

Surrealism 6–8, 10, 19, 20, 29, 35, 38, 43, 55,
        64, 73, 81, 89, 121, 141, 151, 155, 202,
        229–30, 237–8, 281n. 17, 296 see also
        post-Surrealism
Survival see under Holzer
Sussman, Elisabeth 288
Sutherland, Graham 28
Svankmajer, Jan 273
Sweden 109, 123
Sweeney, James Johnson 7
Swenson, Gene 103
Switzerland 19, 72, 174, 179–80
Sylvester, David 68, 287
Symbolist poetry 43
Syria 242, 270, 306
Szeeman, Harold 164
    When Attitude Becomes Form 164, 282n. 27
Szymczyk, Adam 270

20/50 (Wilson) 228, 229
Tabrizian, Mitra 206
tachisme 32, 81, 85
Taking Stock (Unfinished) see under Haacke
Talking see under Guston
Tapié, Michel 16, 19
Tarantino, Quentin 302–3
Target with Plaster Casts see under Johns
Taslitzsky, Boris 12
'Tate Bricks' scandal 134, 177
Tatlin, Vladimir 83
Taylor, Brandon 285
Taylor, Elizabeth 106
Tazzi, Pier Luigi 288
technocracy 77, 232
terrorism 128, 170, 237, 241–2, 253, 263, 300,
        304, 306
Thatcherism 198–9, 208, 222
Thatcher, Margaret 184, 193–4, 198, 227,
        229, 251, 300–2, 306
Théâtre Sarah-Bernhardt 77
theatricality 133, 158, 211
This is How You Sit Correctly (after Goya)
    see under Polke
Thistlewood, David 290
Thomas, Karin 287
Thompson, John 288
Thompson, Joseph 290
Three American Painters 29
Throbbing Gristle (band) 177–8
    Zyklon B Zombie (single) 177
Thubron, Harry 97
Tiberghien, Gilles A. 289
Tilmans, Wolfgang 304
Time (magazine) 103
Tinguely, Jean 71, 100
    Homage to New York 100

Tiravanija, Rirkrit 258, 260, 304
Tisdall, Caroline 287
Tobey, Mark 26
Tomkins, Calvin 287
Townsend, Chris 292
Transavanguardia 190, 193
transcendence 21–5
translation 249
Trockel, Rosemarie 208, *209*
  Balaclavas 209
Trotsky, Leon 7, 15
Truman, Harry S. 11, 43
Tsipras, Alexis 306
Trump, Donald 254, *271*, 306–7
Tuchman, Maurice 287
Turk, Gavin 222
Turner Prize *159*, *198*, 223, 234, 265, 270,
  272, 301, 304–6
Turrell, James 137
Tutti, Cosey Fanni 177
Tuymans, Luc 262–3, 268, 294
  Heimat 263
  Mwana Kitoko—Beautiful White
    Man 263
  Recherches 262
Twentysix Gasoline Stations see under
  Ruscha
Twombly, Cy 45, *46*, 47, 49
  School of Athens 46
Two Urinals see under Gober
Typology of Water Towers see under Becher

Ultimate Anxiety, The see under Morley
Untitled (Cowboy) *see under* Prince
Untitled Film Still #6 see under Sherman
Untitled (Medici Princess) see under
  Cornell
Untitled (Ocean with Cross #1) see under
  Celmins

Vagina Painting see under Kubota
Van der Rohe, Mies 297
Van Gogh, Vincent 68
  Sunflowers 94
Varnedoe, Kirk 285–6
Vasarely, Victor 135
Vautier, Ben 99
Velasquez, Diego *22*, 65
Very Young Girl see under Fautrier
'Victorianism' 223, *226*
video art 223, 225–6, 231, 238, 251–2, 262,
  272–4
Viennese Actionists 173
Vietnam 103, 112–13, 135, 152, 154, 189, 217,
  296–300
  demonstrations 123, 166, 167, 169

View (art journal) 38, 52, 296
Villeglé, Jacques de 150
Viola, Bill 225, 251, 292, 302
Vir Heroicus Sublimis see under Newman
Voelcker, John 94
Vogel, Herbert and Dorothy 164
Vogue (magazine) 57
Vostell, Wolf 99
VVV (magazine) 57

Wagner, Anne 47, 286
Waldman, Diane 286–8, 291
Walker, Kara 251, 293
  Virginia's Lynch Mob 251
Wallinger, Mark 222, 305
Wallis, Brian 289–90
Wall, Jeff 168, 217
  Dead Troops Talk 217, *218–20*
Wall Street Journal (newspaper) *81*
Warhol, Andy 71, 75, 103–4, *105*, 106, *107*,
  110–11, 115, 118, 125, 141, 161, 177, 185,
  208, 298, 302
  Before and After 106
  Brillo Boxes 107
  Campbell's Soup Cans 75
  Cow Wallpaper 105
  Disasters 106–7, 110, 123
    Car Crashes 106
    Electric Chairs 106
    Five Deaths Seventeen Times in
      Black and White 107–8
    Lavender Disaster 107
    Suicide Jump 106
    Tunafish Disasters 106
  Gold Marilyn 106
  Marilyn Dyptich 106
  Marilyns 106
  Silver Clouds 105
Warr, Tracey 290
Washington, George 57
Watts, Robert
  Flux-stamps 100
Wave Rock see under Finlay
Wearing, Gillian *198*, 223, *224–5*
  Dancing in Peckham 223, *224–5*
  Drunk 225
  Sacha and Mum 223
Weegee (Arthur Fellig) 30, 107, 110, *111*
  Naked City 110
  'Sudden Death for One... Sudden Shock
    for the Other ...' *111*
Weil, Sue 77
Weiner, Lawrence 164
Weinstock, Jane 289
Weiss, David 234
Weiwei, Ai 305

Werner, Michael 192
Wesselmann, Tom 111
Western World, the 242, 249, 251, 254, *255*, 260, 262, 268–9, 283n. 51
Weston, Edward 206
Whiteread, Rachel 145, *147*, 302–3
  House 145, *146–7*
Whiting, Cécile 287
Wild Hawthorn Press *161*
Wilke, Hannah 174
Williams, Emmett 287, 289
  Counting Song 98
Williams, Tennessee 297
Willis, Deborah 291
Wilson, Harold 298
Wilson, Richard *211*, 212, 302
  20/50 211
Wilson, Robert 178
Wittgenstein, Ludwig 142–3
Wollen, Peter 226, 288
Wollheim, Richard 128
Wols (Alfred Otto Wolfgang Schulze) 16, *17*, 68
  Manhattan 17
Wolverton, Basil 189
Woman and Bicycle see under de Kooning

Womanhouse 170
women 47, 139, 168, 170–2, 174–5, *177*, 230, 249–51, 255, 263 *see also* gender issues
Wood, Paul 285–6
Woodrow, Bill 144, 208
  Twin Tub with Guitar 144
Working Model for Reclining Figure see under Moore
World Trade Center, the *see* 9/11
Wright, Richard *265–7*
  Untitled (06.01.08) 265–7

Yang, Haegue 252–3, *254*
  Multi Faith Room 253
  Warrior Believer Lover 254
yBas (young British artists) 220–2, 229, 234, 248, 269, 280n. 5
Yeltsin, Boris 302
Yippies 152
Young, La Monte 98

Zedong, Mao 299
Zen Buddhism 39, 74
Zero Group 82, 297
Zhdanov, Andrei 12
Zorio, Gilberto 157